SPURGEON COMMENTARY

HEBREWS

SPURGEON
COMMENTARY

HEBREWS

Charles Spurgeon

Elliot Ritzema and Jessi Strong

Editors

LEXHAM PRESS

Spurgeon Commentary: Hebrews

Copyright 2015 Lexham Press

Lexham Press, 1313 Commercial St., Bellingham, WA 98225
LexhamPress.com

Print ISBN 9781577996408
Digital ISBN 9781577996156

Lexham Editorial Team: Lynnea Fraser
Cover Design: Jim LePage
Typesetting: ProjectLuz.com

According to this book, God estimates men by their faith, and "without faith it is impossible to please him" (Heb 11:6). Faith is well pleasing to the Most High, but it is in proportion to its strength, for there are cases in which weakness of faith has evidently been followed by chastisement, and other cases in which strength of faith has been abundantly honored.

The more you believe, the more God blesses you. If you believe with faith as small as a grain of mustard seed you will be saved, for where there is faith there is salvation; but if your faith is weak you will miss many comforts, and only as your faith shall grow and become strong through divine grace will you be a receiver of the greater, deeper, and higher things of the covenant of grace. More faith is what we want, and the Lord is willing to give it, grace upon grace. He delights, especially, to strengthen the faith that we already possess by trying it, by sustaining it under the trial, and thus rooting and grounding it, and causing it to become firm and vigorous.

—Charles Spurgeon,
"The Hiding of Moses by Faith"

Contents

Foreword...ix

Introduction 1

Hebrews 1..5

   Hebrews 1:1–4 6

   Hebrews 1:5–14..15

Hebrews 2..23

   Hebrews 2:1–9...24

   Hebrews 2:10–18 34

Hebrews 3..57

   Hebrews 3:1–11..58

   Hebrews 3:12–19...67

Hebrews 4 83

   Hebrews 4:1–10..84

   Hebrews 4:11–16...99

Hebrews 5...115

   Hebrews 5:1–10 116

   Hebrews 5:11–14 134

Hebrews 6 141

   Hebrews 6:1–12 142

   Hebrews 6:13–20..155

Hebrews 7...171

   Hebrews 7:1–10 172

   Hebrews 7:11–28.. 184

Hebrews 8 201

   Hebrews 8:1–13..202

Hebrews 9 .... **219**

Hebrews 9:1–14 220

Hebrews 9:15–22 238

Hebrews 9:23–28...250

Hebrews 10 .... **265**

Hebrews 10:1–18...266

Hebrews 10:19–25.. 288

Hebrews 10:26–39 298

Hebrews 11 .... **315**

Hebrews 11:1–7 316

Hebrews 11:8–22...336

Hebrews 11:23–31 358

Hebrews 11:32–40 371

Hebrews 12 .... **383**

Hebrews 12:1–4.. 384

Hebrews 12:5–11 396

Hebrews 12:12–17...409

Hebrews 12:18–24...420

Hebrews 12:25–29...432

Hebrews 13 .... **443**

Hebrews 13:1–6.. 444

Hebrews 13:7–19.. 454

Hebrews 13:20–25...471

Sources **479**

Scripture Index **497**

Index of Illustrations by Theme **502**

Foreword

When 19-year-old Charles Spurgeon was called to the New Park Street pulpit in 1854, London newspapers derided him as a brash upstart. Critics complained that his plainspoken, direct speaking style was too edgy—and dangerously innovative. A secular magazine referred to his colloquial speech as "slang." A newspaper editorial categorized his preaching as "ginger-pop sermonizing." One particularly harsh critic wrote:

> He is nothing unless he is an actor—unless exhibiting that matchless impudence which is his great characteristic, indulging in coarse familiarity with holy things, declaiming in a ranting and colloquial style, strutting up and down the platform as though he were at the Surrey Theatre, and boasting of his own intimacy with Heaven with nauseating frequency. His fluency, self-possession, oratorical tricks, and daring utterances, seem to fascinate his less-thoughtful hearers, who love excitement more than devotion.[1]

During that first year, pundits regularly predicted an early end to Spurgeon's ministry in London: "He is a nine days' wonder—a comet that has suddenly shot across the religious atmosphere. He has gone up like a rocket, and ere long will come down like a stick."[2]

Secular newspapers were not the only ones to voice their disapproval of the young preacher. One distinguished older minister published a vitriolic critique of Spurgeon in an evangelical periodical.

---

1. From an article in the *Sheffield and Rotherham Independent*, April 28, 1855, cited in *C. H. Spurgeon's Autobiography, Compiled from His Diary, Letters, and Records, by His Wife and His Private Secretary: Volume 2, 1854–1860* (Chicago: Fleming H. Revell Company, 1899), 55.
2. Ibid.

Among other things, he wrote, "I have—most solemnly have—my doubts as to the Divine reality of his conversion."[3]

Of course Spurgeon was in no way callow or reckless. On the contrary, for someone so young he was uncommonly well-read, discerning, sober-minded, articulate, and profound. (The record of his published sermons easily substantiates that assessment.) Years later, Spurgeon himself would reflect on his earliest years of ministry, saying, "I might have been a young man at twelve, but at sixteen I was a sober, respectable Baptist parson, sitting in the chair and ruling and governing the church. ... I spent my time at my books, studying and working hard, sticking to it."[4] He was no brash upstart.

Soon Spurgeon outgrew his youthful looks, and the initial wave of criticism eventually subsided. Indeed, he enjoyed several years of unprecedented popularity. His ministry—and his reputation—reached around the world through his published sermons. For a couple of decades he was without rival as the most beloved and most influential preacher in the world.

But by the end of Spurgeon's third decade in London, hordes of critics were again fulminating against him. This time they complained that he was hopelessly behind the times, outmoded—a theological and ecclesiastical fossil. Modernism was in vogue at the time, and Spurgeon was emphatically and outspokenly opposed to the trend, saying, among other things, that "the inventions of 'modern thought' shall be burned up with fire unquenchable."[5]

This time Spurgeon's theological opponents ridiculed him as obsolete, irrelevant, and cluelessly attached to an archaic belief system. The harshest critics openly questioned his mental health. Kinder critics gave him dismissive verbal pats on the head while commenting condescendingly about his age and physical infirmity. Ultimately, for his refusal to compromise with modernism, the

---

3. From an article in *The Earthen Vessel*, December 1854; cited in *Spurgeon's Autobiography*, 2:38.

4. Spurgeon, "Young Men," *South London Press*, 28 November 1874; cited in W. Y. Fullerton, *Charles Haddon Spurgeon: A Biography* (London: Williams and Norgate, 1920), 14.

5. Spurgeon, "Another Word Concerning the Down-Grade," *The Sword and the Trowel* (August 1887), 400.

greatest Baptist preacher in British history was unceremoniously ushered out of the Baptist Union.

Although the critics' complaints about Spurgeon over the years had veered from one extreme to the other, anyone reading Spurgeon's published works can easily see that he did not change substantially from the start of his ministry until the day he died. His theological position, his ministry philosophy, and his style of preaching remained essentially the same throughout the years. Meanwhile, the prevailing climate in English evangelicalism shifted gradually from early Victorian religiosity to full-on modernist rationalism. But Spurgeon never altered his stance. He just kept preaching the truth of Scripture as clearly and as persuasively as possible—with settled conviction and unwavering devotion.

History has vindicated Spurgeon. Modernism was a disaster, as he predicted. Churches that stayed true to the Word of God flourished while whole denominations that imbibed modernism soon died. Today, millions still read Spurgeon's sermons with great profit, and almost no one remembers those who wrote him off as hopelessly out of step with the times. Much less does anyone remember those supposedly venerable voices who raised a chorus of complaint at the start of Spurgeon's London ministry—the ones who warned that he was a dangerous novelty.

Both waves of criticism have been decisively proved wrong. Spurgeon was neither too edgy nor too old-fashioned. What made Spurgeon's preaching exceptional (and what made him a target for such fierce opposition) was the firmness with which he held biblical convictions and the clarity with which he heralded the truth of Scripture. Spurgeon was unashamed and unapologetic about proclaiming and explaining God's Word in the plainest possible language.

The strategy itself is soundly biblical. It is precisely the ministry philosophy the Apostle Paul instructed Timothy to follow: "Preach the word ... in season and out of season; reprove, rebuke, and exhort, with complete patience and teaching" (2 Tim 4:2 ESV).

Spurgeon's description of John Bunyan could just as easily describe Spurgeon himself: "Prick him anywhere; his blood is Bibline, the very essence of the Bible flows from him. He cannot speak without quoting a text, for his very soul is full of the Word of God."[6] Spurgeon frequently used that word, "Bibline," not as an adjective but as a proper noun. He told his students, "Saturate your sermons with Bibline, the essence of Bible truth."[7] As gasoline fuels an internal-combustion engine, Spurgeon described "Bibline" as the necessary fuel for godly living. "A man fed on Bibline is a man indeed," he said. "In the history of heroes, there are none who show so much moral muscle and spiritual sinew as those who make the word of God their necessary food."[8]

In his advice to others, Spurgeon was revealing the secret behind the power of his own preaching. He had saturated his soul and mind with the Word of God. Prick him anywhere, and he bled Bibline.

Spurgeon would not be classified by most seminarians today as an "expository preacher." He didn't necessarily draw his sermon outline and main points directly from the biblical text. In fact, sometimes he treated the text as a jumping-off point for a topical sermon that had little to do with the context of the passage he began with. Nevertheless, his sermons are filled with biblical content—*Bibline*. He could hardly say three sentences without including a phrase, a reference, or an allusion to Scripture. Whenever he spoke, no matter the topic or the venue (even when he was delivering a "lecture" to an academic audience), there was an abundance of Scripture in the message. His daily conversation was saturated with Bibline. Nearly any talk he ever gave would likely exceed some of today's "expository" sermons for sheer biblical content.

Spurgeon also devoted a portion of each Sunday service to formal biblical exposition. He would read and comment on a passage of Scripture, handling the text a phrase at a time. This was distinct from the sermon, usually separated from the sermon by the singing of a psalm or hymn. But hundreds of Spurgeon's formal

---

6. Spurgeon, "The Last Words of Christ on the Cross," in *The Metropolitan Tabernacle Pulpit Sermons, Vol. XLV* (London: Passmore & Alabaster, 1899), 495.
7. C. H. Spurgeon, "A Memorable Milestone," in *The Metropolitan Tabernacle Pulpit Sermons, Vol. LI* (London: Passmore & Alabaster, 1905), 7.
8. C. H. Spurgeon, "Letter to the Bible-classes at Mansfield-street, Southwark," in *The Sword and Trowel: 1883* (London: Passmore & Alabaster, 1883), 33.

expositions were recorded by stenographers and published alongside the sermons.

Elliot Ritzema has created a remarkable and eminently useful resource by culling Spurgeon's expository comments, combining them with key explanatory sections drawn from Spurgeon's sermons, cataloging and organizing them by chapter and verse, and giving us this wonderful commentary from the Prince of Preachers.

Why didn't someone do this long ago? This is an invaluable reference work. I can't imagine preparing a sermon without checking to see what Spurgeon might have said about my passage. The Spurgeon Commentary Series has simplified that step.

—Phil Johnson

Executive Director of Grace to You
Curator of The Spurgeon Archive

Spurgeon_Philippians. inddIntroduction

The great 19th-century Baptist preacher Charles Spurgeon crammed a remarkable amount of writing and speaking into his 57 years. His words fill more than 100 volumes. Although his sermons and writings touch on every book of the Bible at some point, he wrote commentaries only on Psalms (the six-volume *Treasury of David*) and Matthew (*The Gospel of the Kingdom*). It can be difficult to find his teachings on other biblical books within his extensive corpus.

That's why we created the Spurgeon Commentary Series. The idea behind this series is simple: Take material from Spurgeon's sermons and writings and organize it into commentary format. This format includes several features I believe will be particularly helpful for both the devotional reader and the preacher preparing for a sermon.

Each section of the commentary includes three kinds of comments from Spurgeon: exposition, illustration, and application. The exposition sections do not simply deal with a block of biblical text as a whole; they are organized by *verse* as well as the *words within that verse*. This means that you can easily find what Spurgeon says about a particular verse or phrase. The individual phrases Spurgeon comments on within a verse are set in bold text. Some verses have long paragraphs of exposition, while others have a little or none at all. This reflects how much Spurgeon wrote on each verse. I have tried to include as much content as possible in places where Spurgeon wrote a lot, but unfortunately I have had to be selective at times.

When preachers are studying a text in preparation for a sermon, they often watch for good illustrations they can use to drive their point into the hearts of their listeners. To aid in this task, whenever

Spurgeon used a story or a comparison to illustrate a truth found in a verse, I have set that illustration apart for easy reference. Some sections of the commentary will have more illustrations than others, depending on how many Spurgeon used.

The application content at the end of each section contains Spurgeon's exhortations to his hearers to act on the truths he was drawing out from the text. I've often drawn the application content from a few different sermons on a passage. Each section of the commentary includes between one and four applications, depending on how much Spurgeon wrote and preached on that passage.

How much of this commentary is truly Spurgeon, and how much is the editor? Hopefully, there is as much Spurgeon as possible, and the editor fades into the background. Section titles, including those for illustrations and applications, come from the editor. All other words are Spurgeon's, although I have updated his language in some places for greater readability. For example, I have changed "thee" and "thou" to "you." Additionally, I have supplied modern equivalents to archaic words that may be unfamiliar to today's reader. Bible quotations are taken from a recent translation, the Lexham English Bible, rather than the King James Version (KJV), which Spurgeon used. On occasions where Spurgeon calls attention to a particular word in the KJV, however, I have retained his original phrasing.

In an effort to highlight Spurgeon's relevance to a present-day audience, I have left out discussions that were only applicable to the issues and controversies Spurgeon was speaking to in his own day. Instead, I've focused on the content that a present-day audience can relate to. Thankfully, much of what Spurgeon said and wrote is truly timeless. Although I have often gathered content from multiple sources in the same paragraph, I have not used ellipses, which would be more of a distraction than a help. Instead, I have included sources in a list at the end of the volume.

Finally, I would like to thank Jessi Strong and Carrie Sinclair Wolcott for doing much of the editing work on Hebrews and 1–2 Peter. This series is better for their hard work and input.

It is my hope that this commentary series will make Spurgeon's writings more accessible to today's readers, and perhaps even to introduce him to people who have not had the pleasure of reading him before now. Through this series may it be, as it is written on the last page of his *Autobiography*, that Spurgeon "continues to preach the gospel he loved to proclaim while here—the gospel of salvation by grace, through faith in the precious blood of Jesus."[1]

—Elliot Ritzema

Bellingham, Washington

---

1. C. H. Spurgeon, *C. H. Spurgeon's Autobiography, Compiled from His Diary, Letters, and Records, by His Wife and His Private Secretary: Volume 4, 1878–1892* (Chicago; New York; Toronto: Fleming H. Revell Company, 1900), 378.

HEBREWS 1

HEBREWS
1:1–4

¹ While in many parts and many ways God spoke long ago to our ancestors through the prophets, ² in these last days he has spoken to us through the Son, whom he appointed heir of all things, through whom also he made the world. ³ He is the radiance of his glory and the representation of his essence, sustaining all things by the word of power—through him purification of sins was made. He sat down at the right hand of the Majesty on high, ⁴ having become so much better than the angels, as he has inherited a more excellent name than theirs.

EXPOSITION

In this chapter our Savior's glorious person is very plainly set before us, and it is made the ground of our faith, and a reason why we should give the more earnest heed to His words, lest at any time we should let them slip.

1   **God spoke long ago** Saving the best for last is always God's rule. "You have kept the good wine until now" (John 2:10). Prophets are a very blessed means of communication, but how much more sure, how much more condescending is it for God to speak to us by His Son!

2   **he has spoken to us by a Son** *Jesus is God's own Son.* What do I know about that wondrous truth? If I were to try to explain it, and to talk about the eternal filiation, I would only conduct you where I would soon be entirely out of my depth, and very likely I would drown all that I could tell you in floods of words. Deity is not to be explained, but to be adored. The sonship of Christ is to be accepted as a truth of revelation, to be

apprehended by faith, though it cannot be comprehended by the understanding. There have been many attempts made by the fathers of the Church to explain the relationship between the two divine persons, the Father and the Son. But the explanations had better never have been given, for the figures used are liable to lead into mistake. Suffice to say that, in the most appropriate language of the Nicene Creed, Christ is "God of God, Light of Light, very God of very God." He is co-equal with the Father, though how that is, we do not know. He stands in the nearest possible relationship to the Father—a relationship of intense love and delight, so that the Father says of Him, "This is my beloved Son" (Matt 3:17; 17:5; Mark 9:7). Indeed, He is one with the Father, so that there is no separating them, as He Himself said, in reply to Philip's request, "Show us the Father"; "Believe me that I am in the Father and the Father is in me" (John 14:8, 11).

heir of all things Of which nature of Christ does the apostle speak in this sentence, "whom he appointed heir of all things"? I do not think that Paul here separates the two natures, so as to speak with absolute reference to either one or the other; but he speaks of the person of Christ, and in that person there is God, and in that same person there is most surely and most truly man. But we must take this description of Jesus Christ as appointed "Heir of all things" in his person as man, and as God and man combined; for, as God alone, Christ is necessarily "Heir of all things" without any appointment; but in his complex person as God and man conjoined, the Father has appointed him to be "Heir of all things."

Now, what does this mean but that Christ possesses all things as an heir possesses his inheritance, that Christ is Lord of all things, as an heir becomes lord and ruler among his brethren. This appointment is to be fully carried into effect by-and-by; for, "now we do not yet see all things subjected to him" (Heb 2:8). Christ is Lord of all the angels; no seraph spreads his wing except at the bidding of the "heir of all things." There are no bright spirits, unknown to us, that are beyond the control of the God-man, Christ Jesus; and the fallen angels, too, are obliged to bow before His omnipotence. As for all things here below, material substances, people regenerate or unregenerate, God has given Him power over all flesh that he should give eternal life to as many as His Father has given Him. He has put all things under His feet, "and the government shall be upon his shoulder." He is Heir, or Master, and Possessor of all things;—let me say, of all sorts of blessings, and all forms of grace, "because he was well pleased for all the fullness to dwell in him" (Col 1:19); and as surely as time revolves, and you mark the fleeting minutes upon the dial's face, the hour is coming when Christ shall be universally acknowledged as King of kings and Lord of lords. Already I seem to hear the shouts go up from every part of the habitable globe, and from all heaven and all space, "Hallelujah! For the Lord God, the All-Powerful, reigns!" (Rev 19:6). All must willingly, or else unwillingly, submit to His sway, for His Father has appointed Him "Heir of all things."

ILLUSTRATION

Christ Never Lacks Power to Heal

Sometimes, when a physician has a sick man before him—suppose it is on board ship—he may have to say to him, "I think I could cure your disease if I could get such-and-such a medicine. But, unfortunately, I do not have the drug within my reach." Or the doctor might have to say to the sufferer, "I believe an operation would effect a cure, but I have not the instrument that is necessary for it."

Never will the great Physician of souls have to talk like that, for the Father has committed all things into His hand. Have we not beheld Him as the glory of the Father, full of grace and truth? You great sinner, Christ is not lacking in power to save you. If you come, and trust yourself in His hands, He will never have to look about to find the balm for your wounds, or the ointments or liniments with which to bind up those putrefying sores of yours!

---

through whom he also made the world I love to think that He who created all things is also our Savior, for then He can create in me a clean heart and renew a right spirit within me. If I need a complete new creation—as I certainly do—He is equal to the task.

3   **who is the radiance of his glory** Shade your eyes, for you cannot look upon this wondrous sight without being dazzled by it. Some commentators say—and it is not an inappropriate analogy, though we must not push any analogy too far—that, as light is to the sun, so is Jesus to the glory of God. He is the brightness of that glory. That is to say, there is not any glory in God but what is also in Christ: and when that glory reaches its climax, when God the Ever-Glorious is most glorious, that greatest glory is in Christ. Oh, this wondrous Word of God— the very climax of the Godhead—the gathering up of every blessed attribute in all its infinity of glory! You shall find all this in the person of the God-man, Christ Jesus.

representation of his essence Whatever God is, Christ is. The very likeness of God, the very Godhead of Godhead, the very Deity of Deity, is in Christ Jesus.

Dr. John Owen, who loves to explain the spiritual meaning in the Letter to the Hebrews by the types in the Old Testament, explains the brightness of the Father's glory by a reference to the Shekinah over the mercy seat, which was the only visible token of the presence of God there. An extraordinary brightness is said to have shone forth from between the cherubim. Now, Christ is God manifesting Himself in His brightness. But, on his forehead, the high priest wore a golden plate, upon which was deeply engraved, in Hebrew letters, the inscription, "Holiness to [or of] Yahweh." Dr. Owen thinks there is a reference, in this "representation of his essence"—this cut-out inscription of God, as it were—to that which was on the forehead of the high priest, and which represented the glorious wholeness or holiness of Yahweh, which is His great glory.

You see how glorious was His original—the "representation" of His Father's person. How lowly did He become to purge away our sins, and that by Himself, too, using His own body to be the means, by His sufferings, of taking away our guilt. Not by proxy did He serve us, but by Himself. Oh, this is wondrous love!

sustaining all things by the word of power Just think of it. This great world of ours is upheld by Christ's word. If He did not speak it into continued existence, it would go back into the nothingness from which it sprang. There exists not a being who is independent of the Mediator, save only the ever-blessed Father and the Spirit. "In him all things are held together" (Col 1:17), that is, continue to hold together. Just as the foundations uphold a house, so does Jesus Christ "sustain all things by the word of his power."

Only think of it; those innumerable worlds of light that make unbounded space to look as though it were sprinkled over with golden dust, would all die out, like so many expiring sparks, and cease to be, if the Christ who died on Calvary did not will that they should continue to exist. Surely, if Christ upholds all things He can uphold me. If the word of His power upholds earth and heaven, surely, that same word can uphold you, poor trembling heart, if you will trust him.

he had made purification for sins There was never such a task as that since time began. The old fable speaks of the Augean stables, foul enough to have poisoned a nation, which Hercules cleansed—but our sins were fouler than that. Dunghills are sweet compared with these abominations; what a degrading task it seems for Christ to undertake—the purging of our sins! The sweepers of the streets, the scullions of the kitchen, the cleansers of the sewers, have honorable work compared with this task of purging sin. Yet the holy Christ, incapable of sin, stooped to purge our sins. I want you to meditate upon that wondrous work, and to remember that He did it before He went back to heaven. Is it not a wonderful thing that Christ purged our sins even before we had committed them? There they stood, before the sight of God, as already existent in all their hideousness. But Christ came and purged them. This, surely, ought to make us sing the song of songs. Before I sinned, He purged my sins away; singular and strange as it is, yet it is so.

he sat down There is an allusion here, no doubt, to the high priest who, on the great day of atonement, when the sacrifice had been offered, presented himself before God. Now Christ, our great High Priest, having, once for all, offered Himself as the sacrifice for sin, has now gone into the most holy place, and there He sits on the right hand of the Majesty on high.

Notice that *this implies rest*. When the high priest went within the veil, he did not sit down. He stood, with holy trembling, bearing the sacrificial blood, before the blazing mercy seat. But our Savior now sits at His Father's right hand. The high priest of old had not finished his work; the next year, another atoning sacrifice would be needed. But our Lord has completed His atonement, and now, "there no longer remains a sacrifice for sins" (Heb 10:26), for there no longer remains sin to be purged. "But this one, after he had offered one sacrifice for sins for all time, sat down at the right hand of God, from now on waiting until his enemies are made a footstool for his feet. For by one offering he has perfected for all time those who are made holy" (Heb 10:12–14). There He sits, and I am sure He would not be sitting if He had not finished the salvation of His people.

at the right hand of the Majesty Notice that *Christ sits in the place of honor*. Of course, we are talking figuratively now, and you must not interpret this literally. Jesus sits on the right hand of his Father; He dwells in the highest conceivable honor and dignity. All the angels worship Him, and all the blood-washed host adore Him day without night. The Father delights to honor Him.

Not only does Jesus sit in the place of honor, but *He occupies the place of safety*. None can hurt Him now; none can stay His purposes or defeat His will. He is at the powerful right hand of God. In heaven above, and on the earth beneath, and in the waters under the earth, and on every star, He is supreme Lord and Master. They that will not yield to Him shall be broken with a rod of iron; He shall dash them in pieces like a potter's vessel. So His cause is safe; His kingdom is secure, for He is at the right hand of power.

Christ at the right hand of God signifies *the eternal certainty of His reward*. It is not possible that He should be robbed of the purchase of His blood. Christ will have what He bought with His own blood, especially as He lives again to claim His purchase. He shall never be a defeated and disappointed Savior. He "loved the church, and gave himself for her" (Eph 5:25); He has redeemed His loved ones from among men, and He shall have all those whom He has purchased.

4 **better than the angels** They are servants, but they are not sons; they are created, but they are not begotten. You see what he says to the Son—"I will be to him a Father, and he shall be to me a Son."

APPLICATION

A Call to Believers to Trust in Jesus

Let every believer, if he wants to see his sins, stand on tiptoe, and look up. Will he see them there? No. If he looks down, will he see them there? No. If he looks around, will he see them there? No. If he looks within, will he see them there? No. Where shall he look, then? Where he likes, for he will never see them again, according to that ancient promise, "'In those days and at that time,' declares Yahweh, 'the guilt of Israel will be sought, but there is none, and the sins of Judah, but they will not be found, for I will forgive those I left behind'" (Jer 50:20). Shall I tell you where your sins are? Christ purged them, and God said, "I will cast all their sins behind my back." Where is that? All things are before God. I do not know where behind God's back can be. It is nowhere, for God is everywhere present, seeing everything. So that is where my sins have gone. I speak with the utmost reverence when I say that they have gone where Yahweh himself can never see them. Christ has so purged them that they have ceased to be. The Messiah came to finish transgression and to make an end of sin, and He has done it.

Believer, if He has made an end of it, then there is an end to it, and what more can there be of it? Here is a blessed text for you; I love to meditate on it often when I am alone: "As far as east is from west, so he has removed far from us the guilt of our transgressions" (Psa 103:12). This He did on Calvary's cross; there effectually, finally, totally, completely, eternally, He purged all His people from their sin by taking it upon Himself, bearing all its dreadful consequences, canceling and blotting it out, casting it into the depths of the sea, and putting it away forever. It was indeed amazing love that made Him stoop to this purgation, this expiation, this atonement for sin; but, because He was who and what He was, he did it thoroughly, perfectly. He said, "It is finished," and I believe Him. I do not—I cannot—for a moment admit that there is anything to be done by us to complete that work, or anything required of us to make the annihilation of our sins complete. Those for whom Christ died are cleansed from all their guilt, and they may go their way in peace. He was made a curse for us, and there is nothing but blessing left for us to enjoy.

A Call to Sinners to Trust in Jesus

It does seem to me that there is no proof of people's natural blindness that is so conclusive as this: that they will not go and trust in Jesus. O sinners, if sin had left you sane in heart, you would come at once, and fall down at His feet! There is all power laid up in Jesus, and there is all the Father's love concentrated in Jesus, so come and trust Him. If you will but trust Him, you will prove that He has given Himself for you. That simple trust is the secret mark that distinguishes His people from all others. "My sheep listen to my voice, and I know them, and they follow me" (John 10:27). To those who rejected Him when He was upon the earth, our Lord said, "You do not believe, because you are not of my sheep" (John 10:26). O poor souls, do you mean forever to wear the damning mark of unbelief? If you die with that brand upon your soul, you will be lost forever. May you have, instead, that blessed mark of faith which is the token of the Lord's people! May you even now hang out the scarlet line as Rahab hung it out of her window—the scarlet line of confidence in the crimson blood of Jesus! And while Jericho falls—while all the earth shall crumble in one common ruin—your house, though built upon the wall, shall stand securely, and not one who is within its shelter shall be touched by the devouring sword, for all who are in Christ are in everlasting safety. How can they be otherwise, since He has purged their sins? May God give to every one of you a part and lot among this blessed company, for His dear name's sake!

⁵ For to which of the angels did he ever say,

> "You are my son,
> today I have begotten you,"

and again,

> "I will be his father,
> and he will be my son"?

⁶ And again, when he brings the firstborn into the world, he says,

> "And let all the angels of God worship him."

⁷ And concerning the angels he says,

> "He who makes his angels winds,
> and his servants a flame of fire,"

⁸ but concerning the Son,

> "Your throne, O God, is forever and ever,
> and the scepter of uprightness is the scepter of your kingdom.
> ⁹ You have loved righteousness and hated lawlessness;
> because of this, God, your God, has anointed you
> with the olive oil of joy more than your companions."

¹⁰ And,

> "You, Lord, laid the foundation of the earth in the beginning,
> and the heavens are the works of your hands;
> ¹¹ they will perish, but you continue,
> and they will all become old like a garment,
> ¹² and like a robe you will roll them up,
> like a garment, and they will be exchanged;
> but you are the same,
> and your years will not run out."

> [13] But to which of the angels has he ever said,
>
> > "Sit down at my right hand,
> > until I make your enemies a footstool for your feet"?
>
> [14] Are they not all spirits engaged in special service, sent on assignment for the sake of those who are going to inherit salvation?

EXPOSITION

5 **to which of the angels did he ever say** Christ is no created angel. He is sometimes compared to an angel, He is sometimes called the angel of the covenant, but He is not a created angel. He is higher in nature, higher in rank, higher in intellect, and higher in power than they. He is nothing less than very God of very God. The very man who suffered on Calvary.

You are my son But he does say this to Christ in Psalm 2.

today I have begotten you If this refers to the Godhead of our Lord, let us not attempt to fathom it, for it is a great truth, a truth reverently to be received, but not irreverently to be scanned. It may be added that if this relates to the Begotten One in His human nature, we must here also rejoice in the mystery, but not attempt to violate its sanctity by intrusive prying into the secrets of the Eternal God. The things that are revealed are enough, without venturing into vain speculations. In attempting to define the Trinity, or unveil the essence of Divinity, many have lost themselves: here great ships have foundered. What have we to do in such a sea with our frail skiffs?

and again Speaking to Solomon as the type of Christ in 2 Samuel 7:14.

6 **and again** In Psalm 97.

let all the angels of God worship him Or "worship him all you gods."

Jesus is by nature infinitely superior to the noblest created beings, for He is essentially God, and to be worshiped as Lord of all. All powers are bound to recognize the chief Power. Since they derive their only rightful authority from the Lord, they should be careful to acknowledge His superiority at all times by the most reverent adoration.

7 **and concerning the angels** In Psalm 104:4.

who makes his angels winds Angels are pure spirits, though they are permitted to assume a visible form when God desires us to see them. God is a spirit, and He is waited upon by spirits in His royal courts. Angels are like winds for mystery, force, and invisibility, and no doubt the winds themselves are often the angels or messengers of God. God who makes His angels to be as winds, can also make winds to be His angels, and they are constantly so in the economy of nature.

and his servants a flame of fire God's ministers or servants He makes to be as swift, potent, and terrible as fire, and on the other hand He makes fire, that devouring element, to be His minister flaming forth upon His errands.

8 **but concerning the son** Psalm 45:6–7. Angels are servants and not kings. They fly upon the divine errands like flames of fire, but they do not sway a scepter, and neither do they have a throne existing forever and ever.

Your throne, O God, is forever and ever We never appreciate the tender condescension of our King in becoming one flesh with His church, and placing her at His right hand, until we have fully rejoiced in His essential glory and deity. What a mercy for us that our Savior is God, for who but a God could execute the work of salvation? What a glad thing it is that He reigns on a throne that will never pass away, for we need both sovereign grace and eternal love to secure our happiness.

If Jesus could cease to reign we would cease to be blessed, and if He were not God, and therefore eternal, this must be the case. No throne can endure forever but that on which God Himself sits.

the scepter of your kingdom He is the lawful monarch of all things that exist. His rule is founded in right, its law is right, its result is right. Our King is no usurper and no oppressor. Even when He shall break His enemies with a rod of iron, He will do no one wrong; His vengeance and His grace are both in conformity with justice. Hence we trust Him without suspicion; He cannot err. No affliction is too severe, for He sends it; no judgment too harsh, for He ordains it. O blessed hands of Jesus! The reigning power is safe with you. All the just rejoice in the government of the King who reigns in righteousness.

9   **You have loved righteousness and hated lawlessness** Christ Jesus is not neutral in the great contest between right and wrong; as warmly as He loves the one He abhors the other. What qualifications for a sovereign! What grounds of confidence for a people! The whole of our Lord's life on earth proved the truth of these words. His death to put away sin and bring in the reign of righteousness sealed the fact beyond all question. His providence by which He rules from His mediatorial throne, when rightly understood, reveals the same, and His final judgment will proclaim it before all worlds. We should imitate Him both in His love and hate; they are both needful to complete a righteous character.

God, your God, has anointed you with the olive oil of joy Jesus as Mediator owned God as His God, to whom, being found in fashion as a man, He became obedient. On account of our Lord's perfect life He is now rewarded with superior joy. Others there are to whom grace has given a sacred fellowship with Him, but by their universal consent and His own merit, He is prince among them—the gladdest of all because the cause of all their gladness. At Eastern feasts, oil was poured on the heads of distinguished and very welcome guests; God

Himself anoints the man Christ Jesus, as He sits at the heavenly feasts—anoints Him as a reward for His work, with higher and fuller joy than any else can know. Thus the Son of Man is honored and rewarded for all His pains.

more than your companions As man, Christ claims all men as His companions; but as God, He counts it no robbery to be thought equal to God. As man, He is most truly man and only superior to man by reason of the purity of His birth, the perfection of His nature, and the exaltation of his manhood by God. As God, He is nothing less than God, though He took upon Himself the nature of men.

Jesus is the anointed king, and though we share in the anointing, yet is He far above us. Christ is infinitely greater than Christians. We are right glad to have it so.

10–11 **And** We read in Psalm 102:25–27.

12 **like a garment they will be changed** Time impairs all things; the fashion becomes obsolete and passes away. The visible creation, which is like the garment of the invisible God, is becoming old and wearing out, and our great King is not so poor that He must always wear the same robes. Before long, He will fold up the worlds and put them aside as worn-out vestures, and He will array Himself in new attire, making a new heaven and a new earth wherein righteousness dwells. How readily will all this be done. "You will replace them like clothing, and they will be set aside" (Psa 102:26). As in the creation, so in the restoration, omnipotence shall work its way without hindrance.

you are the same Jesus Christ is the same yesterday, today, and forever (Heb 13:8).

As a man remains the same when he has changed his clothing, so is the Lord evermore the unchanging One, though His works in creation may be changed, and the operations of His providence may vary. When heaven and earth shall flee away from the dread presence of the great Judge, He will be unaltered by the terrible confusion, and the world in conflagration will effect no change in Him.

your years will not run out Since the Messiah is thus described as immutable and eternal, He must be divine, and to deny the Godhead of the Savior is a deadly error. Dr. Owen most comfortingly remarks: "Whatever our changes may be, inward or outward, yet Christ changing not, our eternal condition is secured, and relief provided against all present troubles and miseries. The immutability and eternity of Christ are the spring of our consolation and security in every condition. Such is the frailty of the nature of man, and such the perishing condition of all created things, that none can ever obtain the least stable consolation but what arises from an interest in the omnipotency, sovereignty, and eternity of Jesus Christ."[1]

13   **sit down at my right hand, until I make your enemies a footstool for your feet** The sight of Jesus enthroned in divine glory is the sure guarantee that all things are moving onward toward ultimate victory. Those rebels who now stand high in power shall soon be in the place of contempt; they shall be his footstool. He shall with ease rule them. He shall sit and put His foot on them; not rising to tread them down as when a man puts forth force to subdue powerful foes, but retaining the attitude of rest, and still ruling them as abject vassals who have no longer spirit to rebel, but have become thoroughly tamed and subdued.

14   **spirits engaged in special service** They are servants of God and our willing guardians, but they are not to be worshiped. Jesus is Lord of all, and we are bound to adore Him, and Him only.

---

1. John Owen, *An Exposition of the Epistle to the Hebrews, Volume 2*, ed. W. H. Goold, *Works of John Owen 19* (Edinburgh: T&T Clark, 1862), 464.

APPLICATION

Christ's Companions Share in His Joy

We see that in His work our great High Priest was anointed with the oil of gladness above His fellows (Heb 1:9). But we also note that those who are His fellows do, in their degree, partake in this oil of gladness and are enabled to feel joy in the work which is appointed them of the Lord. While our King is anointed with the oil of gladness, it is also written of the virgin souls who wait upon His church, "They are led with joy and gladness. They enter the palace of the king" (Psa 45:15).

If any professing Christian is engaged in a work which he does not feel glad to do, I question if he is in his right place. There may be occasional fits of depression, but these are not because we do not love the work, but because we cannot do it so well as we would desire. We are tired in the work, but not tired of it. The Lord loves to employ willing workers. His army is not made up of forced labor, but of those whom grace has made volunteers. "Serve the Lord with gladness" (Psa 100:2). Our Lord does not set us task work and treat us like prisoners in jail or slaves under the lash. I sometimes hear our life's work called a task. Well, the expression may be tolerated, but I confess I do not like it to be applied to Christian men. It is no task to me, at any rate, to preach my Master's gospel or to serve Him in any way. I thank God every day that "to me, the least of all the saints, was given this grace: to proclaim the good news of the fathomless riches of Christ to the Gentiles" (Eph 3:8). You teachers in the school, I hope your labor of love is not a bondage to you! An unwilling teacher will soon make unwilling scholars. Indeed, I know that those of you who serve the Lord find a reward in the work itself, and gladly pursue it. I am sure you will not prosper in it if it is not so.

If you follow your work unwillingly, and regret that you ever undertook it, and feel encumbered by it, you will do no good. No one wins a race who has no heart in the running. In this respect the joy of the Lord is your strength, and as your Master was anointed with the oil of gladness in His work, so must you be. Yet, beloved fellow laborer, you will never be so glad in your work as *He* was in His, nor will you ever be able to prove that gladness by such self-denials, by such agonies, and such a death. He has proved how glad He was to save sinners, because "for the joy that was set before him, he endured the cross, disregarding the shame" (Heb 12:2). Blessed Emmanuel, you are justly anointed with the oil of gladness above your fellows.

HEBREWS 2

HEBREWS
2:1–9

¹ Because of this, it is all the more necessary that we pay attention to the things we have heard, lest we drift away. ² For if the word spoken through angels was binding, and every transgression and act of disobedience received a just penalty, ³ how will we escape if we neglect so great a salvation? It had its beginning when it was spoken through the Lord and was confirmed to us by those who heard, ⁴ while God was testifying at the same time by signs and wonders and various miracles and distributions of the Holy Spirit according to his will.

⁵ For he did not subject to angels the world to come, about which we are speaking. ⁶ But someone testified somewhere, saying,

> "What is man, that you remember him,
>   or the son of man, that you care for him?
> ⁷ You made him for a short time lower than the angels;
>   you crowned him with glory and honor;
> ⁸ you subjected all things under his feet."

For in subjecting all things, he left nothing that was not subject to him. But now we do not yet see all things subjected to him, ⁹ but we see Jesus—who for a short time was made lower than the angels—crowned with glory and honor through the suffering of death, so that apart from God he might taste death on behalf of all.

EXPOSITION

1 **pay attention to the things we have heard** We have heard them; do not let us forget them. Do not let them be like the driftwood that goes floating down the stream. Let us make a

desperate effort to retain them in our memories; and, above all, to ponder them in our hearts.

2   **received a just penalty** The punishment for disobeying the word spoken by angels was death; what, then, must be the penalty of neglecting the great salvation wrought by the Divine Redeemer Himself? He who does not give earnest heed to the gospel treats with disdain the Lord Jesus Christ, and he will have to answer for that sin when the King shall sit upon the throne of judgment. Trifle not, therefore, with that salvation which cost Christ so much, and which He Himself brings to you with bleeding hands. If you have until now trifled with it, and let it slip, may you now be brought to a better mind, lest by some chance, despising Christ, the "just penalty" should come upon you. And what will that be? I know of no punishment that can be too severe for the man who treats with contempt the Son of God, and tramples on His blood. Every individual who hears the gospel, and yet does not receive Christ as his Savior, is committing that atrocious crime.

3   **how will we escape if we neglect so great a salvation** They could not trifle with the angels' message without receiving just punishment from God. Much less, then, can we trifle with Christ's gospel. We have not an angelic savior, but God Himself, in the person of His Son, has deigned to be the Mediator of the new covenant. Therefore, let us see to it that we do not trifle with these things.

You see that we do not need to be great, open sinners in order to perish; it is merely a matter of neglect. See how it is put here: "How will we escape if we neglect so great a salvation?" You need not go to the trouble of despising it, or resisting it, or opposing it. You can be lost readily enough simply by neglecting it. In fact, the great mass of those who perish are those who neglect the great salvation.

ILLUSTRATION

Neglect Is as Bad as Open Opposition

If a man is in business, it is not necessary that he should commit forgery in order to fail; he can fail by simply neglecting his business. If a man is sick, he need not commit suicide by taking poison; he can do it just as surely by neglecting to take proper medicines.

So is it in the things of God. Neglect is as ruinous as distinct and open opposition.

was confirmed to us by those who heard The apostles and the other followers of our Lord constantly bore witness to His miracles and His resurrection.

4   **God was testifying at the same time by signs and wonders and various miracles** Those who doubt the truth of the gospel, or who say they do, are often found believing historical statements that are not half as well proved. A man sits down and reads the book of the Gallic wars, and he believes that Julius Caesar wrote it. Yet there is not a half or a tenth as much evidence to prove that he did write it as there is to prove that our Lord Jesus lived, and died, and rose again from the dead. The witness to the truth of these great matters of fact has been borne by God Himself with signs, and wonders, and miracles. Honest and true men, apostles and others, have witnessed to them, and they have also been certified by incarnate Deity, even by the Lord who deigns to speak to us by His Spirit. We cannot, therefore, trifle with this gospel without incurring most serious guilt.

and distributions of the Holy Spirit according to his will This gospel of ours is stamped with the seal of God; He has set His mark upon it, to attest its genuineness and authority. The miraculous gifts of the Holy Spirit were the seal that the gospel was no invention of man, but that it was indeed the message of God. Gifts of healing, gifts of tongues, and gifts of miracles of diverse kinds were God's solemn declaration to man, "This is the gospel. This is my gospel that I send to you; therefore, do not refuse it."

5   **he did not subject to angels the world to come** We are the preachers of it—not the angels. The great Author and Finisher of our faith is the man Christ Jesus—not an angel. We do not now have the ministry of angels, but the ministry of men, by whom the Lord of the angels sends His messages to their fellows.

6   **someone testified somewhere** God speaks to people by people. He has made them to be the choice and chosen instruments of His wondrous works of grace upon earth. Oh, what a solemn thing it is to be a preacher of the everlasting gospel! It is an office so high that an angel might covet it, but one that is so responsible that even an angel might tremble to undertake it. Pray for us who preach, not merely to a few, but to many of our fellow creatures, that we may be the means, in the hand of God, of blessing to our hearers.

7   **You made him for a short time lower than the angels** These verses may set forth man's position among the creatures before he fell, but as they are appropriated to man as represented by the Lord Jesus, it is best to give most weight to that meaning. In order of dignity, man stood next to the angels, and a little lower than they; in the Lord Jesus this was accomplished, for He was made a little lower than the angels by the suffering of death. Man in Eden had the full command of all creatures, and they came before him to receive their names as an act of homage to him as the vicegerent of God to them. Jesus in His glory, is now Lord, not only of all living, but of all created things, and, with the exception of Him who put all things under Him, Jesus is Lord of all, and His elect, in Him, are raised to a dominion wider than that of the first Adam, as shall be more clearly seen at His coming.

you crowned him with glory and honor The dominion that God has bestowed on man is a great glory and honor to him; for all dominion is honor, and the highest is that which wears the crown.

8   **you subjected all things under his feet** It is so, in a measure, in the natural world. People are made to be the master of it. The ox and the horse, with all their strength, must bow their necks to them, and the lion and the tiger, with all their ferocity, must still be cowed in the presence of their master. Yet this is not a perfect kingdom that we see in the natural world. But in the spiritual world, people are still to be supreme for the present, and therefore Christ becomes, not an angel, but a man. He takes upon him that nature which God intends to be dominant in this world and in that which is to come.

we do not yet see all things subjected to him Man does not yet rule the world. Wild beasts defy him. Storms vanquish him. There are a thousand things not at present submissive to his control.

While Christ was here below, he was not a ruling Lord, but a suffering servant. He said to His disciples, "I am in your midst as the one who serves" (Luke 22:27). Yet it is in Him that the dominion once given to man is to be seen most clearly displayed.

ILLUSTRATION
Able to See, but Only on Sunday

Sometimes our faith, like our sight, is not quite clear. You do not always see, I suppose, equally well. There are many things that affect the optic nerve, and we know that in fair weather we can see a longer distance than we can in cloudy weather. I was at Newcastle some time ago, in a friend's house, and when I went up to the top window and looked out, he said, "There is a fine view, sir, if you could but see it; we can see Durham Cathedral from here on a

Sunday." "On a Sunday!" I said. "How is that?" "Well, you see all that smoke down there, all those furnaces, and so on; they are all stopped on a Sunday, and then, when the air is clear, we can see Durham Cathedral."

We can see a great deal on a Sunday, when the smoke of the world is gone for a little time; we can see all the way to heaven then. But sometimes, what with the smoke we make in business, and the smoke the devil makes, and the smoke that sin makes, we can scarcely see anything at all. Well, since the natural sight has to undergo variations, both from itself within and from the smoke without, and from the state of the weather, we must not wonder if our faith undergoes variations too. It ought not to do so, but sometimes it does.

---

9   **but** The text begins with "*but*," because it refers to some things which we do not yet see, which are the objects of strong desire. "We do not yet see all things subjected to him." We do not as yet see Jesus acknowledged as King of kings by all mankind, and this causes us great sorrow, for we would gladly see Him crowned with glory and honor in every corner of the earth by everyone of woman born. He is to many quite unknown, by multitudes rejected and despised, and by comparatively few is He regarded with reverence and love. Sights surround us which might well make us cry with Jeremiah, "Oh that my head were waters, and my eyes a fountain of tears" (Jer 9:1), for blasphemy and rebuke, idolatry, superstition, and unbelief prevail on every side. "But," says the apostle, "we see Jesus."

we see Jesus He is not, indeed, in this text referring to any seeing of the Lord by mortal eyes at all; he is speaking of faith. He means a spiritual sight of the Lord Jesus Christ. Sight is very frequently used in Scripture as a metaphor, an illustration, a symbol—to set forth what faith is. Faith is the eye of the soul. It is the act of looking unto Jesus. In that act, by which we are saved, we look unto Him and are saved from the very ends of the earth. We look to Him, and we find salvation.

It does not say, "We can see Jesus"—that is true enough; the spiritual eye can see the Savior. Nor does it say, "We have seen Him"—that also, glory be to God, is a delightful fact. We have seen the Lord, and we have rejoiced in seeing Him. Nor does the text say, "We shall see him," though this is our pride and our hope, that "whenever he is revealed we will be like him, because we will see him just as he is" (1 John 3:2). But the text says, "We see Jesus." We *do* see Him now and continually. This is the common habit of Christians. It is the element of our spiritual life; it is our most delightful occupation; it is our constant practice. We see Jesus, for we are sure of His presence, we have unquestionable evidence of His existence, we have an intelligent and intimate knowledge of His person. Our soul has eyes far stronger than the dim optics of the body, and with these we actually see Jesus.

ILLUSTRATION

Measuring a Mountain and Maturing in Faith

All our measures of distance by the eye are matters that have to be gained by habit and observation. When I first went to Switzerland, with a friend, from Lucerne we saw a mountain in the distance that we were going to climb. I pointed out a place where we should stop halfway up, and I said, "We shall be there in about four and a half hours." "Four and a half hours!" my friend said, "I'd undertake to walk it in ten minutes." "No, not you." "Well, but half an hour!" He looked again, and said, "Anybody could get there in half an hour!" It seemed no distance at all. And yet when we came to toil up, the four and a half hours turned into five or six before we reached the place.

Our eyes were not accustomed to mountains, and we were not able to measure them. It is only by considerable experience that you get to understand what a mountain is, and how a long distance appears. You are altogether deceived, and do not know the position of things till you become wiser. And it is just so with faith. Faith in the Christian, when he first gets it, is true and saving. But it is not in proportion. The man believes one doctrine, perhaps, and that is so delightful that it swallows up every other. Then he gets hold of another, and he swings that way like a pendulum; no doctrine can be true but that one. Perhaps in a little time he swings back like a pendulum the other way. He is unsteady because, while his faith perceives the truth, it does not perceive the harmonies of truth. His faith, for instance, may perceive the Lord Jesus Christ, but as yet it has not learned the position which Christ occupies in the great economy of grace. He is half blind, and cannot see far. He has sight, but it is not the sight that he will yet receive.

---

he might taste death on behalf of everyone Thus lifting man back into the place where he first stood so far as this matter of dominion is concerned.

Oh, how glorious it is to realize our position in Christ, and to see how He has lifted us up, not merely to the place from which the first Adam fell, but He has made us stand so securely there that we shall not again descend among the ruins of the fall! Glory be to His holy name!

APPLICATION

Seeing Jesus Is a Cause of Exultation

"We see Jesus," and in Him *we see our former unhappy condition forever ended*. We were fallen in Adam, but we see in Jesus our ruin retrieved by the second Adam. The legal covenant frowned upon us as we beheld it broken by our first federal head; the new covenant smiles upon us with a whole heaven of bliss as we see it ordered in all things and sure in Him who is head over all things to the church. We weep as we confess our transgressions, but we see Jesus, and sing for joy of heart, since He has finished transgression, made an end of sin, and brought in everlasting righteousness.

The same is sweetly true of the present, for *we see our present condition to be blessed by virtue of our union with Him.* We do not see as yet our nature made perfect, and cleansed from every tendency to evil; rather we groan, being burdened, because of the sin that dwells in us. We might be sorely cast down and dragged into despair were it not that "we see Jesus," and perceive that in Him we are not what the flesh would argue us to be. We see self, and blush and are ashamed and dismayed; "but we see Jesus," and His joy is in us, and our joy is full. Think of this the next time you are upon the dunghill of self-loathing. See Jesus, and know that as He is so are you also before the Infinite Majesty. You are not condemned, for He is enthroned. You are not despised nor abhorred, for He is beloved and exalted. You are not in jeopardy of perishing, nor in danger of being cast away, for He dwells eternally in the bosom of the Lord God Almighty. What a vision is this for you, when you see Jesus, and see yourself complete in him, perfect in Christ Jesus!

Such a sight effectually *clears our earthly future of all apprehension.* It is true we may yet be sorely tempted, and the battle may go hard with us, but we see Jesus triumphant, and by this sign we grasp the victory. We shall perhaps be subjected to pain, to poverty, to slander, to persecution, and yet none of these things move us because we see Jesus exalted, and therefore know that these are under His power, and cannot touch us except as He grants them His permission to do so. Death is at times terrible in prospect, but its terror ceases when we see Jesus, who has passed safely through the shades of the sepulcher, vanquished the tyrant of the tomb, and left an open passage to immortality to all His own. We see the pains, the groans, and dying strife; see them, indeed, exaggerated by our fears, and the only cure for the consequent alarm is a sight of Him who has said, "The one who believes in me, even if he dies, will live, and everyone who lives and believes in me will never die forever" (John 11:25–26). When we see Jesus, past, present, and to come are summed up in him, and over all shines a glorious life which fills our souls with unspeakable delight.

The Difference Seeing Jesus Makes in Our Actions

Ought not this to be the motto of our life: "We see Jesus"? We should not regard the commands of Jesus Christ as being a law left to us by a departed Master whom we cannot see, and to whom we cannot fly. Is it not better to believe that Christ is a living Christ, that He is in the midst of His church still, observing our order, noting our obedience or our disobedience, a Master absent in one sense, but still in another point of view ever present, according to His promise—"Behold, I am with you all the days until the end of the age" (Matt 28:20)?

Should we be so frequently cold and careless if we could always see Jesus? Would our hearts be so hard toward perishing sinners if we always saw that face which was bedewed with tears for them? Do you think we could sit still, or grow worldly, or spend all our energies upon ourselves, if we could see the Crucified, who though "he saved others; he was not able to save himself" (Matt 27:42; Mark 15:31)? I wish I could always preach Jesus, "seeing" Him by my side, and feeling in my heart that I was preaching in my Master's presence. As disciples we would be more punctual in our obedience, more consistent in our imitation of Jesus, if we had Him always before us.

If we see Jesus being always with us, from morning till evening, in life and in death, *what noble Christians* it will make us! Now we shall not get angry with each other so quickly. We shall see Jesus, and we cannot be angry when that dear loving face is in view. And when we have been affronted, we shall be very ready to forgive when we see Jesus. Who can hate his brother when he sees that face, that tender face, more marred than that of any man? May we each one of us have this, and may it be the expression of our life—"We see Jesus." And then we shall be able to go farther and say, "For me to live is Christ and to die is gain" (Phil 1:21).

[10] For it was fitting for him—for whom are all things and through whom are all things—in bringing many sons to glory, to perfect the originator of their salvation through sufferings. [11] For both the one who sanctifies and the ones who are sanctified are all from one. For this reason he is not ashamed to call them brothers, [12] saying,

> "I will proclaim your name to my brothers;
> in the midst of the assembly I will sing your praise."

[13] And again,

> "I will trust in him."
> And again,
> "Behold, I and the children God has given me."

[14] Therefore, since the children share in blood and flesh, he also likewise shared in these things, in order that through death he could destroy the one who has the power of death, that is, the devil, [15] and could set free those who through fear of death were subject to slavery throughout all their lives. [16] For surely he is not concerned with angels, but he is concerned with the descendants of Abraham. [17] Therefore he was obligated to be made like his brothers in all respects, in order that he could become a merciful and faithful high priest in the things relating to God, in order to make atonement for the sins of the people. [18] For because he himself suffered when he was tempted, he is able to help those who are tempted.

EXPOSITION

10   **it was fitting** It seemed to be but the order of natural fitness and congruity, in accordance with the nature and character

of God, that the plan of salvation should be just what it is. It could not be otherwise so as to be in keeping with the divine character. Therefore, it is imperative upon us that we make no alteration in it, no, not of a word, lest we should hear the Apostle's anathema hissing through the air like a thunderbolt from God—"Even if we or an angel from heaven should proclaim a gospel to you contrary to what we proclaimed to you, let him be accursed!" (Gal 1:8).

for whom are all things and through whom are all things Here you have God set forth as being both the beginning and the end of everything. All things are for Him—to do His bidding, to accomplish His purpose, to set forth His glory. And this because all things are by Him—in their first creation, in their subsequent preservation, and in all that is yet to come of them.

If the Holy Spirit describes either God the Father or the Lord Jesus by any term other than His usual name, the title is always very wisely chosen, and is most appropriate in that place. Now, in the matter of our salvation, we need One, "through whom are all things," for none but the Creator can create us anew in Christ Jesus. No one who has less power than the Divine Preserver of men can keep us from falling. None but the Divine Being, who encompasses all things within the range of His infinite mind, can guard us against the many terrible perils on the way to heaven. If ever we are to be brought to glory, it must be by the God "for whom are all things." And certainly, if we are brought there—as I pray that we all may be—it will be by Him "for whom are all things," and we shall forever adore the mystery of His grace which landed us safely on the heavenly shore.

bringing many sons to glory I think that you will find the historical parallel of this enterprise in the Lord's great work of bringing the tribes of Israel out of Egypt, through the Red Sea, through the wilderness, and into Canaan. The Lord, in His deliverance of His ancient people, gives us a type of what

He is doing and will do for all His chosen. The exodus was not merely the bringing of the people out of Egypt into the wilderness, for then they might truly have said to Moses, "Because there were no graves in Egypt? Is that why you have taken us to die in the desert?" (Exod 14:11). But the whole transaction was not completed, the enterprise was not finished, until all those whom the Lord intended to bless had actually crossed the Jordan, and had taken possession of the promised land. He led not the children of Israel merely out of Egypt, but He led them into Canaan. His leadership of them through the desert is a picture and emblem of Christ's leadership of the many sons whom He is bringing unto glory. I want you to think of the salvation of the redeemed in that light.

The Lord Jesus is bringing many sons to glory, just as God brought His ancient people into Canaan. The ultimate destination of every believer is eternal glory. There is not one of us who will be perfect and complete until we stand at the right hand of God, even the Father. There is no secondary position where some of the redeemed may be satisfied to remain, but the many sons are all to be brought to *"glory."*

ILLUSTRATION

We Little Ships Need Not Be Afraid

Sometimes, in the old days of war, there used to be a number of little ships wanting to cross the sea. But the privateers were on the watch, so the seamen were afraid to hoist the sail, and get away from the shelter of the shore, for they would soon be caught by their enemies, like doves by the hawk. Well, what was done? There they lay, in port, until his Majesty sent down a man-of-war, perhaps two or three, to be a convoy. Then the little ships would all be safe; their crews need not any longer be afraid of the Frenchmen or the Spaniards.

So is it with those who are under the protection of God. We, weak little vessels, could never by ourselves reach our desired haven. But the Lord High Admiral of the seas and the great Emperor of the land has come forth in the majesty of His power to conduct us to glory. And we shall get there safely, even though our enemies should be beyond all count.

---

perfect the originator of their salvation through sufferings Is it not wonderful that Christ, who is head over all things, could not be perfected for this work of ruling, or for the work of saving, except by sufferings? He stooped to conquer. Not because there was any sin in Him, but that He might be a sympathetic ruler over His people, He must experience sufferings like those of His subjects. And that He might be a mighty savior, He must be Himself compassed with infirmity, that He might "deal gently with those who are ignorant and led astray" (Heb 5:2).

11   **the one who sanctifies and the ones who are sanctified** What is meant by the expression, being sanctified? The essential part of sanctification means being set apart for holy uses. That which was meant to be used for God alone was sanctified, set apart, regarded as holy. The vessels of the sanctuary were sanctified when they were used only by the priests in the service of God. Of course; there arose out of this fact, which is the essence of sanctification, the further quality of purity, for that which is dedicated to God must be pure, that which is reserved for his service must not be defiled, it must be clean. We cannot imagine the holy God using unholy vessels in his sanctuary; so that sanctification comes to mean purification, the making of that to be holy which was first of all set apart for holy uses. Holiness of character follows upon holiness of design. First are we set apart for God's use, and then afterward we are made pure that we may be fit for God's use.

No man is truly sanctified unless he is sanctified by Christ. The Holy Spirit is made the agent of our purification, but it is in Christ that we are first of all set apart unto God, and it is by His most precious blood, applied to us by the Spirit of God, that we are made clean and pure so as to be used in the divine service. Believers are the sanctified, and Jesus Christ is the sanctifier.

are all from one Consider the remarkable unity between Christ and His people. They are "all from one." They are, first, "all from one" in the divine design. In the great mind of God, it is not Christ alone, and His people alone, but Christ and His Church who are regarded as "all from one." They are fitted, constituted, designed for each other; they are the complement of each other.

Then, next, they who are sanctified and the Sanctifier Himself are "all from one" *in the eternal covenant.* When the Lord Jesus Christ became the Surety of the covenant, the Head and Representative of His people, He struck hands with His great Father in a solemn league and covenant. He did that, not for Himself alone, but for us also. That covenant was made for us in Christ with Christ, as He is one with us. And now today the provisions of the covenant are as much for me as for Christ, and as much for Christ as for the very least of His people.

But there is something better than this, if there can be anything better, for they are "all from one" *as to nature.* Do not let us ever permit our hearts to lose the sweetness of the fact that the Lord Jesus Christ is really and truly one with us as to nature. In Him dwells all the fullness of the Godhead bodily, and yet, notwithstanding that, He is man of the substance of His mother. "Therefore, since the children share in blood and flesh, he also in like manner shared in these same things" (Heb 2:14). It is easy to say, but it is hard to realize that Jesus Christ is as truly man as any of us can be.

Yet further than that, they who are sanctified and their Sanctifier are "all from one" because of *His representative character.* Whatever Jesus did in the past, He did for us, for we are "all from one." He was circumcised, and we are circumcised in Him with the true circumcision not made by hands. When He kept the law, we kept the law in Him, for He stood as our Representative. If He died, we reckon that we died in Him. And henceforth, we recognize that we live because He lives. Now that He has gone into the heavenlies, it is as our Forerunner, and He has raised us up together with Him, and made us sit together with Him in the heavenlies, and in all the glory that is yet to come we shall be partakers.

Hence follows this further oneness. So are we "all from one" that, henceforth, we are *united in our interests.* His concerns and our concerns are one. We have not to speak of what is Christ's and what is His people's, but all that is Christ's belongs to His people, and all that belongs to His people belongs to Him.

he is not ashamed to call them brothers They are poor, they are despised, they are persecuted; what is worse, they are imperfect and faulty, often sorrowful, cast down, condemning themselves, groaning at the mercy-seat; yet "he is not ashamed to call them brothers." There is such a unity between the believer, be he in what sorrow he may, and the Christ, be He in what glory He may, that he is never ashamed to own the close relationship between them.

12   **saying** As this seemed to be a great thing to say, the apostle felt obliged to quote three Old Testament Scriptures to show the brotherliness of Christ, and His being "all of one" with us. The first passage that he quotes is in Psalm 22, verse 22.

The words in these quotations in our English version may not seem to be exactly the same as in the passages referred to. But we must remember, of course, that we are dealing with translations, and not with the original writings. This is a part of that marvelous psalm which was unquestionably the soliloquy of Christ upon the cross.

I will proclaim your name What a precious subject is the name of our God! It is the only one worthy of the only Begotten, whose meat and drink it was to do the Father's will. We may learn from this resolution of our Lord that one of the most excellent methods of showing our thankfulness for deliverances is to tell to our brothers what the Lord has done for us. We mention our sorrows readily enough; why are we so slow in declaring our deliverances?

to my brothers When He was here on earth, He told his brothers much concerning the Father. It was His mission to reveal the Father so that He could say, "The one who has seen me has seen the Father" (John 14:9). When they worshiped the Father in spirit and in truth, it was because He had taught them to do so. His sermons inspired them with that devotion; He spoke to them as a man speaking to men, and so He revealed God to them. This passage also shows that Jesus was one with His disciples, for He revealed God not as to strangers, but as to "brothers." He declared the will of God to them, not as to outsiders, but as to "brothers." He had one way of preaching to the crowd, and He had quite another way of privately talking to His disciples. He declared the name of God unto His brothers in familiar, loving, tender tones, always putting Himself side by side with them, sometimes speaking of "My Father and your Father, and my God and your God" (John 20:17), and always setting forth the great God as belonging as much to them as to Himself.

in the midst of the assembly I will sing in praise of you Did Jesus sing? Yes, literally. After supper, they sang a hymn (Matt 26:30; Mark 14:26). It must have been most thrilling to hear Christ's voice, quivering with emotion, singing the Psalms which constituted the Great Hallel. Those psalms were usually sung after the paschal supper was ended. The Savior went through them, praising and magnifying Yahweh, joining the little band, I should think, Himself the leader of the psalmody, that it might be seen that he was "all from one" with them.

Not in a little household gathering merely does our Lord resolve to proclaim His Father's love, but in the great assemblies of His saints, and in the general assembly and church of the firstborn. This the Lord Jesus is always doing by His representatives, who are the heralds of salvation, and labor to praise God. In the great universal church Jesus is the One authoritative teacher, and all others, so far as they are worthy to be called teachers, are nothing but echoes of His voice.

13   And again there are some passages which we should never have thought related to the Messiah if the New Testament had not told us that they do. Hence I have no doubt that we much more often err in not seeing Christ in the Old Testament than in seeing Him there, for there may be many other passages besides those which are supposed to speak of Christ which do speak of Him.

I will trust in him The pith of the quotation is that *Jesus Christ put His trust in God.* That is to say, He was a partaker of our faith. It is by faith that we are justified; it is by faith that we overcome the world; it is by faith that we do everything. Had Jesus such a faith as that? Yes, He had. It was by His faith that He vanquished the adversary in that triple duel in the wilderness; it was by faith that He prevailed in prayer on the lone mountainside; it was by faith that He went up to the cross alone, by Himself, for His people. I will go further, and say that Jesus Christ is still to us the greatest exemplar of faith. "What!" you exclaim, "In heaven, is He still our greatest Exemplar of faith?" Yes: "From now on waiting until his enemies are made a footstool for his feet" (Heb 10:13). And what is expectation based upon but upon faith?

Moreover, our blessed Lord is always engaged in intercessory prayer. Remember this text: "Ask from me and I will make the nations your heritage" (Psa 2:8). He is asking, and He is asking in faith. And the life of Christ now, concerning His coming, and His kingdom, and the ultimate triumph of His righteous cause, is still an exhibition of faith; and this makes Him very near of kin to us.

Behold The last passage which the apostle quotes is taken from Isa 8:18. This is yet to be fulfilled. There shall be a day when He shall be manifested. At this hour, He is the hidden Christ, and our life is hid with Him; but He is one day to appear. Then will He say, "Behold, here am I," and all shall see Him. Even they who crucified Him shall behold Him when He comes in His glory.

I and the children Observe that, in that day, He is to appear with His children, with those who have received life out of His life, those to whom He is the Adam, the true Father, the everlasting Father. He shall not appear alone; He would not care to do so. He shall be manifested with His saints. When He shall appear, we shall appear with Him. "Behold," says He, "I and the children." You see, He glories in them. He uses a phrase such as you would use of your children.

God has given me And then He uses such a sweet phrase about them. He says, "The children God has given me." You know that, in John 17, in that wonderful prayer of our Lord to His Father, He always calls His disciples, "those whom you have given me" (John 17:11, 24). He likes to dwell on that fact. They are precious to Him in themselves, but far more precious as the Father's gift to Him. Some things are valued by you as keepsakes given by one you love; and so are we dear to Christ because His Father gave us to Him. "The children God has given me." Sweet, sweet words! Do they not show you what oneness there is between Christ and His people? The father and the mother are marvelously one with their own children when those children have not grieved them, but have made them happy, so that they can speak of them as the children that God has given them. Then you see how they are knit together as one.

14   **the children** I cannot help drawing your attention to those two words: "the children." Hear that sweet expression again,

for it is one of the choicest descriptions of the saints: "the children." "You are all sons of God through faith in Christ Jesus" (Gal 3:26). What a wonderful influence the children have in the house! How many of the arrangements are made especially with a view to them! How much of the wear and tear of life to their parents is for their sakes! And we may truly say concerning our Father in heaven that His plans, His arrangements, His actions, His gifts are very emphatically for the children.

share in blood and flesh As you know to your cost, for perhaps you have aches and pains about you at this very moment. We know what it is to be partakers of flesh and blood; we often wish that we did not. It is the flesh that drags us down; it is the flesh that brings us a thousand sorrows. I have a converted soul, but an unconverted body. Christ has healed my soul, but He has left my body still to a large extent in bondage, and therefore it has still to suffer; but the Lord will redeem even that. The redemption of the body is the adoption, and that is to come at the day of the resurrection.

he also in like manner shared in these same things Think of Christ, who was a partaker of the Eternal Godhead, condescending to make Himself a partaker of flesh and blood—the Godhead linked with materialism; the Infinite, an infant; the Eternal prepared to die, and actually dying!

ILLUSTRATION
A Better Protector Than a Hero or an Angel

If one had to be a soldier on the field of battle, it might be a very great assistance to one's courage to stand side by side with the hero of a thousand fights who had always been victorious. If you had to journey tonight along some dark and lonely road, and an angel came from heaven to walk beside you—and you were quite sure that it was an angel—I should think you would be altogether free from

43

fear. With such a companion, you might even wish that the way were still more dangerous, so that you might have the delightful experience of passing through it unharmed under the care of such a glorious protector.

But you have a better protector than any angel could be, even the Lord of the angels, your Lord and Savior, Jesus Christ, so what cause have you for fear? He will be with you all through life, He will be with you when you are called to die, and the pledge of that is that He is a partaker of that very flesh and blood which will bring you down to death.

---

through death he could destroy ... the devil Those persons who always interpret the word "destroy" as meaning "annihilate" would do me a very great favor if they could really prove to me that Jesus Christ annihilated the devil. I have very mournful proof in my own experience that he is not annihilated, and many of you also know that "your adversary the devil walks around like a roaring lion, looking for someone to devour" (1 Pet 5:8). The devil is still alive, but his power in this world has received its death blow. Jesus Christ has trodden on the old serpent's head, and, to the Christian, in the matter of death, the devil is completely destroyed, for he that believes in Christ shall never die. Death seemed to be all dark and evil, like Satan himself, something into which he had put his most venomous sting. But now, to believers in Jesus, death is a messenger from our Father in heaven calling us home to Him—not a dark angel, striking terror to our hearts, but one who is exceeding bright and fair, coming to bid us fly away to realms of light and love.

Remember, Christian, "the sting of death is sin" (1 Cor 15:56), but that has been destroyed for you, and "the power of sin is the law," but that has been fulfilled for you. Rejoice, therefore, that both are gone so far as you are concerned, and thus your greatest causes for fear are entirely removed.

the power of death The devil's power over death lies in three places, and we must look at it in three aspects. Sometimes the devil has power in death over the Christian *by tempting him to doubt his resurrection*, and leading him to look into the dark future with the dread of annihilation. Christ, by being a witness to the fact of the resurrection, has broken the power of the devil in death. In this respect He has prevented him from tempting us to fear annihilation; because, as Christians, we believe that because Christ rose again from the dead, even so they that sleep in Jesus will the Lord bring with Him.

A more common temptation—another phase of the devil's power in death—is that the devil comes to us in our lifetime, and he tempts us by *telling us that our guilt will certainly prevail against us*, that the sins of our youth and our former transgressions are still in our bones, and that when we sleep in the grave our sins shall rise up against us. The death of Christ has destroyed the power that the devil has over us to tempt us on account of our guilt. "The sting of death is sin" (1 Cor 15:56). Our Jesus took the sting away, and now death is harmless to us, because it is not succeeded by damnation.

The evil one has another temptation: "It may be very true," says he, "that you are to live forever and that your sins have been pardoned; but *you have until now found it very hard work to persevere, and now you are about to die you will be sure to fail.*" We turn to answer the devil, and we say to him, "Fiend, you tempt us to think that you will conquer us. Remember, Satan, that the strength that has preserved us against you has not been our own. The arm that has delivered us has not been this arm of flesh and blood, else we had long since been overcome. Look there, fiend, at Him that is omnipotent. His almightiness is the power that preserves us to the end. Therefore, be we never so weak, when we are weak then we are strong, and in our last hour of peril we shall yet overcome you." Christ's death has taken away from Satan the advantage that he has over the saint in the hour of death. We may joyfully descend the shelving banks of Jordan, or may even, if God calls us to a sudden death, glide from its abrupt cliffs, for Christ is with us, and to die is gain.

ILLUSTRATION
Misty Lakes and the Fear of Death

When traveling among the Alps in a dense mist, we have seemed to see vast lakes without a shore, crags that appeared like the battlements of heaven, and awful depths that thrilled us with horror. Yet much of that mystery was only caused by the mist. When we journeyed the same way on a bright morning, the great lake proved to be only a little pond, the mighty battlement was a crag that a child could climb, and the vast depths that had made us shudder with terror were gentle slopes where we could have descended with ease.

So it is the mysteriousness of death that alarms you. That the soul should be divorced from the body to which it has been so long united is something that startles you. Yes, but as the light dissipates the terrors of the mountains, so the fact that Jesus Christ has brought life and immortality to light will scatter all your gloom.

---

15 **could set free those who through fear of death were subject to slavery** It is a very natural thing that man should fear death, for man was not originally created to die. When Adam and Eve were first placed in the garden of Eden, they were in such a condition that they might have remained there for countless years if they had kept their integrity. There was no reason why unfallen man should die; but now that we have sinned, the seeds of corruption are in this flesh of ours, and it is appointed unto men once to die. Yet, as if the body knew that it was not according to the first decree of heaven that it should go to the earth and to the worm, it has a natural reluctance to return to its last bed. And this fear of death, so far as it is natural, is not wrong.

But it can very readily go beyond the point where it is right into the region wherein it becomes evil; and I do not doubt that many godly persons have a fear of death about them which is very evil, and which produces very evil effects. Let us never try to get rid of it, as some do, by forgetting all about death. That would be to live as the brutes that perish; they live their little day here without any thought beyond the present. The ox and the sheep go to the slaughterhouse without the power to look beyond the present life. I would not like to obtain peace of mind by descending to the level of those "dumb, driven cattle." Yet there are many men whose only peace arises from thoughtlessness; yet that is a sorry peace which cannot endure contemplation and consideration.

He so took upon Himself flesh and blood as to die in our nature, that thus He might slay death, and might set us free from all fear of death. Do you not see that, if the representative Man, Christ Jesus, died, He also rose again, and that so also will all who are in Him rise too? If you are in Him, you shall rise again. Therefore, fear not to lie down in your last sleep, for the trumpet shall awaken you, and your bodies shall be molded afresh like unto His glorious body, and your soul and body together shall dwell in infinite bliss forever. "Therefore comfort one another with these words" (1 Thess 4:18).

ILLUSTRATION
The Bigger Fool

I have heard of a certain king who had a jester or "fool" to make fun for him, as kings used to have. But this "fool" was no fool; he had much sense, and he had thought wisely about eternal matters. One day, when he had greatly pleased the king, his majesty gave him a stick, and said to him, "Tom, there is a stick which you are to keep till you see a bigger fool than yourself, and then you may give it to him."

One day, his majesty was taken ill, and it was thought that he would die, and many went to see him, and Tom also went, and said, "What is the matter, your majesty?" "I am going, Tom, I am going." "Where are you going?" asked Tom. "I fear it is a very long way," said the king. "And are you coming back, your majesty?" "No, Tom." "You are going to stop a long while, then?" "Forever," said the king. "I suppose your majesty has a palace ready over there." "No." "But I suppose you have provided everything that you will need there if you are going such a long way, and never coming back? I suppose you have sent a good deal on, and got everything provided on ahead?" "No, Tom," said the king, "I have done nothing of the kind." "Here, then, your majesty, take my stick, for you are a bigger fool than I am."

And if there is a man who has made no provision for eternity, and who has no mansion, no abiding place, no treasure, no Friend, no Advocate, no Helper there, he is a gigantic fool, be he who he may.

---

16   **he is not concerned with angels** Our Lord and Savior Jesus Christ, when He came from heaven to die, did not take upon Himself the nature of angels. It would have been a stoop more immense than if a seraph should have changed himself into an ant for the Almighty Son of God to have been clothed in the garb of even the archangel Gabriel. But His condescension dictated to Him that if He did stoop, He would descend to the very lowest degree; that if He did become a creature, He would become, not the noblest creature, but one of the most ignoble of rational beings—that is to say, man. Therefore, He did not stoop to the intermediate step of angelship, but He stooped right down and became a man.

he is concerned with the descendants of Abraham
Christ's great mission was not to save angels, but to save men.
Therefore he came not in the nature of angels, but in the nature of men.

Men and devils have both sinned and have both deserved to
be damned for their sins. God, if He shall so resolve, can justly destroy them all, or He may save them all, if He can do it
with justice. Or, He may save one of them if He pleases, and
let the others perish. And if as He has done, He chooses to save
a remnant, and that remnant shall be men, and if He allows
all the fallen angels to sink to hell, all that we can answer is
that God is just, and He has a right to do as He pleases with
His creatures.

17 **he was obligated to be made like his brothers** As a father
feels for his children because they are of the same flesh and
blood as himself, so does the Lord sympathize with His people, for they are members of His body, of His flesh, and of His
bones. No father can be so thoroughly one with his offspring
as Jesus is with us.

a merciful and faithful high priest You see God did not
choose angels to be made high priests. However benevolent
they might be in their wishes, they could not be sympathetic.
They could not understand the peculiar wants and trials of the
men with whom they had to deal. Ministers who of God are
made to be a flame of fire (Heb 1:7) could scarce commune familiarly with those who confess themselves to be as dust and
ashes. But the high priest was one of them. However dignified
his office, he was still a man. He was one of whom we read that
he could lose his wife, that he could lose his sons. He had to
eat and to drink, to be sick and to suffer, just as the rest of the
people did. And all this was necessary that he might be able to
enter into their feelings and represent those feelings before
God, and that he might, when speaking to them for God, not
speak as a superior, looking down upon them, but as one who

sat by their side, "a brother born for adversity" (Prov 17:17), bone of their bone, and flesh of their flesh.

Now this is peculiarly so in the case of our Lord Jesus Christ. He is sympathetic above all. There is none so tender as He. He has learned it by His sufferings, but He proves it by His continual condescension toward His suffering people.

18   **he himself** I must not omit to mention the particular use here made by the Spirit of that word *himself*. It is not only in that He suffered being tempted, but you see that He *Himself* has suffered being tempted. That word is sometimes used to make passages emphatic: "Who himself bore our sins in his body on the tree" (1 Pet 2:24). We read again and again of Jesus Christ *Himself*, as if to show that the matters referred to were really, truly, personally, actually His. He *Himself* has suffered. All that there was in Him, that made up Himself, suffered being tempted.

suffered when he was tempted Many persons are tempted, but do not suffer in being tempted. When ungodly men are tempted, the bait is to their taste, and they swallow it greedily. Temptation is a pleasure to them; indeed, they sometimes tempt the devil to tempt them. They are drawn aside of their own lusts and enticed; so that temptation, instead of being suffering to them, becomes a horrible source of pleasure. But good men suffer when they are tempted, and the better they are the more they suffer.

Our Lord Jesus Christ enters into this trying experience very fully. His suffering through being tempted must have been much greater than any suffering that the purest-hearted believer can know, seeing that He is more pure than any one of us. He could not yield to temptation, but He did suffer from it. He did not suffer from it morally; He was too pure for that. But He did suffer from it mentally because of His purity. His mind was grieved, and vexed, and troubled by the temptation that He had to bear. We especially see this when we find Him in the garden. There He showed His grief when He sweat as it were great drops of blood falling to the ground. In many other ways He endured such contradiction of sinners against Himself, such multiplied temptations, that it is said, and truly said, by the Holy Ghost in this verse, that He "suffered" being tempted.

ILLUSTRATION
Christ the Good Physician

A minister, preaching upon the text, "Is there no balm in Gilead? Is there no healer there?" (Jer 8:22), made the remark that Christ is a good Physician. "Christ is not like those doctors who come and say they are sorry for you, whereas in their hearts they are glad you are ill, for if you and others were not ill, there would be no work for them. Or else they look down upon you, and pity you, but not half as much as if they themselves had your complaint, and felt all the pains that you are feeling. But suppose that the doctor had all your pains himself—suppose you had the headache, and that he looked down on you, and had your headache. Suppose, when you had palpitation of the heart, he had palpitation of the heart, too. Why, he would be very quick to cure you. Certainly, he would not let you lie there a moment longer than was necessary, because he himself would be suffering with you."

Now, there is just one objection that may be made to the argument. That is that the physician might be willing to raise the patient up at once, because he was himself suffering with him; yet he might say, "Here are two of us in the same plight, but my skill fails me here. If I could deliver you, you can well imagine that I would gladly do so, for, in so doing, I should deliver myself as well. But it is beyond my power. I cannot lighten your burden, nor my own. We can only sit down together, and mingle our tears, but we cannot assist one another."

But it is not so with the good Physician, for He has both the will and the power to heal us. Remember that you not only have the love of Christ's heart, but you also have the strength of Christ's arm at your disposal. He rules over all things, in heaven, and earth, and hell. So rest in Him, for still He bears the scars of His wounds to show that He has suffered even as you do.

---

he is able to help those who are tempted He lays Himself out to help those that are tempted, and therefore He does not hide Himself from them, nor pass them by on the other side. What an example is this for us! He devotes Himself to this divine business of comforting all who mourn. He is Lord of all, yet makes Himself the servant of the weakest.

Whatever He may do with the strongest, He helps "those who are tempted." He does not throw up the business in disgust. He does not grow cross or angry with them because they are so foolish as to give way to idle fears. He does not tell them that it is all their nerves, and that they are stupid and silly, and ought to shake themselves out of such nonsense. I have often heard people talk in that fashion, and I have half wished that they had felt a little twinge of depression themselves, just to put them into a more tender humor. The Lord Jesus never overdrives a lame sheep, but He sets the bone, and carries the sheep on His shoulders, so tenderly compassionate is He.

ILLUSTRATION

Desiring to Help the Afflicted When You Are Afflicted Yourself

The man that has seen affliction, when he is blessed of God, has the disposition to cheer those that are afflicted. I have heard speak of a lady who was out in the snow one night, and was so very cold that she cried out, "Oh, those poor people that have such a little money! How little fuel they have, and how pinched they must be! I will send a hundred pounds of coals to twenty families, at the least." But I have heard say that, when she reached her own parlor, there was a fine fire burning, and she sat there with her feet on the fender, and enjoyed an excellent tea, and she said to herself, "Well, it is not very cold, after all. I do not think that I shall send those coals. At any rate, not for the present."

The sufferer thinks of the sufferer, even as the poor help the poor. The divine wonder is that this Lord of ours, "although he was rich, for our sakes he became poor" (2 Cor 8:9), and now takes a delight in helping the poor. Having been tempted, He helps the tempted. His own trials make Him desire to bless those who are tried.

APPLICATION

Be Worthy of the Captain Who Leads You to Glory

Seeing that it is the will of the Lord to lead us to glory by the Captain of our salvation, I want you to be worthy of your Leader. Do you not think that, sometimes, we act as if we had no Captain? We fancy that we have to fight our way to heaven by the might of our own right hand, and by our own skill; but it is not so. If you start before your Captain gives you the order to march, you will have to come back again; and if you try to fight apart from your Captain, you will rue the day. "Oh!" says one, "But I have been thinking today what I shall do if so-and-so happens." My dear brother, it would be a great deal better for you to remember that "the Lord lives," and to leave the thinking and arranging in His hands. There are a great many *ifs* in the world that are like a swarm of wasps; if you let those *ifs* out, they will sting you from head to foot; but there is one glorious *if* that will kill them all, it is this,—*if* the Lord Jesus Christ could fail,—*if* he could desert us, then all would be lost. That kills all the other *ifs*, because it is an impossible *if*. He cannot fail us or leave us; He must live; He must conquer; and while that is the case, the other *ifs* do not signify anything to us. Therefore, cast yourselves on your Captain's care. March onward though you cannot see your way; fly at the enemy though they seem to outnumber you ten to one, for greater is He that is for you than all that can be against you. Be not afraid of anything, for your Captain is equal to all emergencies. When the Lord our God chose him as our Leader and Commander, He laid help upon One who was mighty. He did not take some poor weak mortal to be the captain of such a company as we are; He did not even select an angel for this great task. He exalted One chosen out of the people, who was most suitable for the position, and God's wisdom would be dishonored if Christ were found incapable of bringing the many sons unto glory. But He is blessedly capable of all that is required of Him; and the ancient prophecies concerning Him shall be completely fulfilled: "He will not grow faint, and he will not be broken" (Isa 42:4), and the pleasure of the Lord "will succeed in his hand" (Isa 53:10).

Comfort and Fear in the Face of Death

Death has lost its sting, because the devil's power over it is destroyed. Then cease to fear dying. You know what death is: look him in the face, and tell him you are not afraid of him. Ask grace from God, that by an intimate knowledge and a firm belief of your Master's death you may be strengthened for that dread hour. If you so live, you may be able to think of death with pleasure, and to welcome it when it comes with intense delight. It is sweet to die: to lie upon the breast of Christ, and have one's soul kissed out of one's body by the lips of divine affection.

And you that have lost friends, or that may be bereaved, sorrow not as those that are without hope. Remember the power of the devil is taken away. What a sweet thought the death of Christ brings us concerning those who are departed! They are gone; but do you know how far they have gone? The distance between the glorified spirits in heaven and the militant saints on earth seems great, but it is not so. We are not far from home. Our departed friends are only in the upper room, as it were, of the same house. They have not gone far off; they are upstairs, and we are down below.

You that do not know God, you that do not believe in Christ, death is to you a horrible thing. I need not tell you that, for your own conscience tells it to you. You may laugh sometimes at religion, but in your own solitary moments it is no laughing thing. The greatest brags in the world are always the greatest cowards. If I hear a man saying, "Oh, I am not afraid of dying, I don't care about your religion," he does not deceive me; I know all about that. He says that to cover up his fears, when he is alone at night. You are afraid of dying, I know, and what I shall say to you is this: You have good need to be afraid of dying, and you have good need to be afraid of dying now. Do not mock death, and do not despise eternity. But begin to think whether you are prepared for death, lest death should come and find you wanting. And remember, death will make no delays for you. You have postponed the time of thought; death will not be postponed to suit you. When you die, there will be no hour allowed for you in which then to turn to God. Death comes with its first blow; damnation comes afterward, without the hope of reprieve. "The one who believes and is baptized will be saved, but the one who refuses to believe will be condemned" (Mark 16:16). Thus do we preach the gospel of God unto you as God would have us: "Go and make disciples of all the nations, baptizing them in the name of the Father and of the Son and of the Holy Spirit" (Matt 28:19). Behold, I tell you, faith in Jesus is the soul's only escape. Profession of that in immersion is God's own way of professing faith before men. The Lord help you to obey him in the two great gospel commandments, for Jesus' sake.

The Fruit of Suffering in Being Able to Comfort Others

Although our Lord suffered being tempted, He did not suffer in vain. He was made perfect through His sufferings, and fitted for His solemn office of High Priest to His people. From that fact I want you to gather fruit, because our heavenly Father means to bless you also. We cannot comfort others if we have never been comforted ourselves.

I have heard—and I am sure that it is so—that there is no comforter for a widow like one who has lost her husband. Those who have had no children, and have never lost a child, may talk very kindly, but they cannot enter into a mother's broken heart as she bows over a little coffin. If you have never known what temptations mean, you make poor work when attempting to help the tempted. Our Lord obtained a blessing from suffering temptation, and you may do the same. Brother, the Lord means to make of you a man that shall be used like Barnabas to be a "son of encouragement" (Acts 4:36). He means to make a mother in Israel of you, my dear sister, that when you meet with others who are sorely cast down, you may know how to drop in a sweet word by which they shall be comforted. I think you will one day say, "It was worthwhile to go through that sorrow to be enabled to administer relief to that wounded heart." Will you not comfort others when you are delivered? I am sure you will. You will be ready and expert in the sacred surgery of consolation. For this reason, be content to suffer being tempted, and look for the comfortable fruit which all this shall produce in you.

HEBREWS 3

¹ Therefore, holy brothers, partners in a heavenly calling, consider Jesus, the apostle and high priest of our confession, ² who was faithful to the one who appointed him, as Moses also was in his household. ³ For this one is considered worthy of greater glory than Moses, inasmuch as a builder has greater honor than the house. ⁴ For every house is built by someone, but the one who built all things is God. ⁵ And Moses was faithful in all his house as a servant, as a testimony to the things that would be spoken, ⁶ but Christ [was faithful] as a son over his house. We are his house if we hold fast to our confidence and we boast in our hope.
⁷ Therefore, just as the Holy Spirit says,

"Today, if you hear his voice,
⁸ do not harden your hearts as in the rebellion,
as in the day of testing in the wilderness,
⁹ where your ancestors tested me by trial
and saw my works ¹⁰ for forty years.
Therefore I was angry with this generation,
and I said, 'They always go astray in their heart,
and they do not know my ways.'
¹¹ As I swore in my anger,
'They will never enter into my rest.' "

EXPOSITION

1   **holy brothers, sharers in a heavenly calling** What wonderful titles! "Holy brothers," made brothers in holiness and made holy in our brotherhood—"sharers in a heavenly calling"—called of God from among the worlds. Our occupation and our calling henceforth is to serve the Lord.

Heavenly calling means a call *from* heaven. If people alone call you, you are uncalled. Is your calling of God? Is it a call *to* heaven as well as *from* heaven? Unless you are a stranger here, and heaven is your home, you have not been called with a heavenly calling. For those who have been so called declare that they look for a city which has foundations, whose builder and maker is God, and they themselves are strangers and pilgrims upon the earth.

consider Jesus, the apostle and high priest of our confession He is supremely worthy of our perpetual consideration from all points of view. And the more you consider Him the more you may, for there is a depth and breadth about His wondrous personality, His work, and His offices that is well worthy of our deepest thought and admiring worship. Holy brothers, sharers in a heavenly calling, we may well consider him. If you think little of your Leader you will live poor lives. Consider Him, often think of Him, and try to copy Him. With such a Leader what manner of people ought we to be?

2   **faithful to the one who appointed him** See how our Lord Jesus Christ condescended to be appointed of the Father. In coming as a Mediator, taking upon Himself our humanity, He "emptied himself by taking the form of a slave" (Phil 2:7), and being found in fashion as a servant, we find that he was faithful. To every jot and tittle, He carried out His charge.

3   **greater glory than Moses** See the superiority of Christ to Moses; Moses is honored by being called the servant of God, but Jesus is the Son of God, and as Son, Master over His own house.

greater honor than the house And Moses was but one stone in the house. Although in a certain sense he was a servant in it, yet in another, and, for him, a happier sense, he was only a stone in the house which the Lord Jesus Christ had built. Let us think of our Lord as the Architect and Builder of His own Church, and let our hearts count Him worthy of more glory than Moses; let us give Him glory in the highest.

However highly a Jew may think of Moses—and he ought to think highly of him, and so ought we—yet infinitely higher than Moses must ever rise the incarnate Son of God.

4   **the one who built all things is God** And Christ is God. And He is the Builder of all things in the spiritual realm—yes, and in the natural kingdom too, for "apart from him not one thing came into being that has come into being" (John 1:3). So He is to have eternal honor and glory as the one great master-builder.

5   **Moses was faithful in all his house** Christ built the house; He laid us together like stones upon the great foundation; Moses is but a caretaker in the house.

6   **Christ was faithful as a son** You see, then, that the apostle had first made a distinction between Christ and Moses on the ground of the Builder being greater than the house he builds; now, in the second place, he shows Christ's superiority to Moses on the ground that a son in his own house is greater than a servant in the house of his master. How sweetly he introduces the truth that we are the house of Christ! Do we realize that the Lord Jesus Christ dwells in the midst of us? How clean we ought to be, how holy, how heavenly! How we should seek to rise above earth, and keep ourselves reserved for the Crucified! In this house, no rival should be permitted ever to dwell; but the great Lord should have every chamber of it entirely to himself. Oh, that He may take His rest within our hearts as His holy habitation; and may there be nothing in our church life that shall grieve the Son of God, and cause Him even for a moment to be withdrawn from us.

whose house we are We are the house in which He dwells with delight—in which He finds comfort and rest. We are the household over which He rules, and in which He is the delight and the joy of us all.

May our church ever be such a house, so well ordered, that when the Lord comes into it—no, when He ever dwells in it— He may not be grieved in His own house. Whatever trouble a man has, he hopes to find solace at home. And so let the house of God be the house of Jesus—the place where there is peace, obedience, love, holiness.

if we hold fast None are truly Christ's but those who persevere in grace. Men may be nominally Christ's, but they are not Christ's house unless they hold fast to the confidence and the rejoicing of the hope firm unto the end. Temporary Christians are not really Christians.

Perseverance—final perseverance—is the test of election. He whom God has chosen holds on and holds out even to the end, while temporary professors make only a fair show in the flesh, but, by-and-by, their faith vanishes away.

7   **Therefore** Now comes a long parenthesis.

as the Holy Spirit says The apostle is continually quoting from the Old Testament, but he does not often present his quotations in this peculiar fashion. In the very next chapter, when he is speaking of the same passage, he uses the expression, "speaking by David" (Heb 4:7)—mentioning the human author of the psalm. But in this case, to give full emphasis to the truth, he quotes the divine author alone—"As the Holy Spirit says." These words, it is true, are applicable to every passage of sacred Scripture, for we may say of all the inspired books, "As the Holy Spirit says." But it is designedly used here that the passage may have the greater weight with us. The Holy Ghost, in fact, not only speaks thus in Psalm 95, but it is His unvarying utterance. The Holy Ghost says, or continues still to say, "Hear His voice today."

How does the Holy Ghost thus speak? He says this first *in the Scriptures*. Every command of Scripture calls for immediate obedience. The law of God is not given to us to be laid on the shelf to be obeyed at some future period of life, and the gospel of our Lord and Savior Jesus Christ is not so intended for the 11th hour as to be lightly trifled with during the first 10. Wherever the Holy Ghost exhorts, He speaks in the present tense, and bids us now repent, or now believe, or now seek the Lord.

Further, while the Holy Ghost speaks in Scripture, He speaks in the same manner *in the hearts of His people*. He is a living and active agent; His work is not ended; He speaks and writes still. The pen is still in His hand, not to write with ink upon paper, but upon the fleshy tablets of prepared hearts. The like is also true when the Holy Ghost speaks *in the awakened*. They are not yet numbered with the people of God, but they are under concern of soul. Everywhere a truly awakened sinner pleads in the present tense, and cries mightily for a present salvation, and it is certain that whenever the Holy Ghost strives with men, He urgently cries, "Today! Today!"

Once more, the Holy Ghost speaks thus *by His deeds* as well as by His words. We have a common proverb that actions speak more loudly than words. Now the acts of the Holy Spirit in the leading of many to the Savior are so many practical invitations, encouragements, and commands to others. The gate of mercy stands open every day in the year, and its very openness is an invitation and a command to enter. Is not the bringing of one sinner to Himself intended to allure others?

Today Today is the only time we have. Happily for us, the Holy Ghost says, "Today, if you hear his voice." Never do I find Him saying "tomorrow." His servants have often been repulsed by men like Felix who have said, "Go your way for this time. When I have a more convenient season I will send for you." And never did any apostle say, "Repent tomorrow, or wait for some convenient season to believe." The constant testimony of the Holy Ghost, with regard to the one single part of time, which I have shown indeed to be all time, is, "Today if you hear his voice, do not harden your hearts."

ILLUSTRATION

Serving Today, Not Tomorrow

When we intend to do Christian service tomorrow, and do it faithfully and well, we still sin. There is a contract for certain steamers to carry Her Majesty's mails, and they are bound to leave Liverpool at such a time and arrive at New York so long afterward. Suppose they leave six hours after the time. If they make the best voyage they can, they break the contract. And an action which is done tomorrow, but should have been done today, whatever be its acceptableness in itself, is faulty. It is like an untimely fruit, out of date.

if you hear his voice The text inculcates a special duty. The duty is that we should hear the voice of God. The text bids us hear the voice of the Father saying, "Return, O apostate children" (Jer 3:22). "Come now, and let us argue. ... Even though your sins are like scarlet, they will be white like snow" (Isa 1:18). Or it may be the voice of Jesus Christ, for it is of Him that the apostle is here speaking. It is Jesus who calls, "Come to me, all of you who labor and are burdened, and I will give you rest" (Matt 11:28). In fact, the voice to be heard is that of the Sacred Trinity, for with the Father and the Son, the Spirit also says, "Come."

8   **do not harden your hearts** Do not provoke your God by your quibbling, or your murmuring, or your idolatry; act not as those unbelievers did who died in the wilderness.

You are His house. Give Him rest; do not provoke Him. If you belong to Him, be holy; do not grieve Him. If you are His house, be not defiled; surely He should dwell in a holy place.

A common way of provoking God and hardening the heart is that indicated by the context. "Do not harden your hearts as in the rebellion, in the day of testing in the wilderness." That is to say, by unbelief, by saying, "God cannot save me. He is not able to forgive me; the blood of Christ cannot cleanse me; I am too much of a sinner for God's mercy to deal with." That is a copy of what the Israelites said: "God cannot take us into Canaan; He cannot conquer the sons of Anak." Although you may look upon unbelief as a slight sin, it is the sin of sins.

ILLUSTRATION
Hardening Your Heart Against Preaching

I once preached in a certain city, and I was the guest of a gentleman who treated me with great kindness, but I noticed on the third occasion of my preaching that he suddenly left the room. One of my friends followed him out of the place and said to him, "Why have you left the service?" "Well," said he, "I believe I should have been converted altogether if I had stopped any longer, for I felt such an influence coming over me. But it would not pay. You know what I am; it would not pay."

Many persons are of that kind. They are shaped for a while according to the earnest word they hear, but it is all in vain. The dog returns to his vomit, and the sow that was washed to her wallowing in the mire. This is to harden your heart and provoke the Lord.

---

as in the rebellion All the histories of Scripture are written for our examples, but especially the story of the Israelites in the wilderness. It is given to us at a length far exceeding the value of the narrative, except it be intended for purposes of spiritual instruction, for it occupies four books of the Old Testament, and those by no means short ones. These things were written that we might see ourselves in the Israelites as in a mirror, and so might be warned of dangers common to us and to them, and be guided to a worthier use of the privileges we enjoy.

9 **your fathers tested me by trial** That was a house in which it was hard to dwell. It had been Moses' prayer, "If your presence is not going, do not bring us up from here" (Exod 33:15). The curtains had been spread for God's abode, and there was the holy place. But their provocations made it an uneasy house for the Lord of the house, which ultimately He left, rending its veil from the top to the bottom as He left it, for it was finished, and He was done with it.

10 **they always go astray in their heart** God is very tender to errors of judgment—errors of the head. But to err in the heart—this is the heart of erring, and very provoking to the Most High. For it always to be so after having tasted the bitter fruit of erring—after having known God's angers on account of previous errors—this was sad!

they do not know my ways The foundation of sin often lies in ignorance. Ignorance can never be of any benefit to us: "a life without knowledge is not good" (Prov 19:2). But ignorance of God is the constant course of the errors of the heart. "All your children shall be pupils of Yahweh" (Isa 54:13) is a very gracious promise, and where it is carried out, there the errors are rectified by the grace of God.

11 **They will never enter into my rest** Oh, that none of us, as professors of the faith of Christ, may be like Israel in the wilderness! I fear there is too much likeness; God grant that it may be carried no further! May we hear the voice of God, as they did not hear it, for their ears were dull of hearing! May we never harden our hearts, as they did, for they kicked against the command of God, and rebelled against the thunders of Sinai!

If God has had 40 years' patience with you, take heed, sinner, take heed, lest He swear in His wrath that you shall not enter into His rest. Your entrance into that rest depends upon

His good will and pleasure. He will have mercy on whom He will have mercy, and He will have compassion on whom He will have compassion (Rom 9:15). If, then, you provoke Him to swear that you shall not enter into His rest, into that rest you never can enter, for then the gates of hell are barred upon you, and the gates of heaven fast locked against you. Beware, then, lest you provoke Him.

APPLICATION

The Importance of "Today"

You who love the Lord, or profess to do so—Christian people—the Holy Ghost says "Today." That is to say, it is essential to duty that we attend to it at once. Every command of Christ bears the date today. If a thing is right, it should be done at once; if it is wrong, stop it immediately. Whatever you are bound to do, you are bound to do *now*. There may be some duties of a later date, but for the present that which is the duty, is the duty now. There is an immediateness about the calls of Christ. What He bids you do, you must not delay to do. The Holy Ghost says *"Today."* And I would say this with regard to everything. Do you love the Lord? Have you ever professed His name? Then the Holy Ghost says *"today."* Hesitate not to take up His cross at once and follow Him—the cross of Him who was nailed to the cross for you; who by His precious blood has made you not your own, but His.

To you, unconverted sinners, the Holy Ghost says, "Today." Some of you have lived long enough without God. Some of you have lived 50 years without God and long enough to be condemned. You would not like to be converted, and then be of no service to your Lord at all, or only have given Him a few months of your life. Do you know how soon you are to die? Is there any man who is certain that he will live to see another year? Every hour that passes is hardening you if you are remaining out of Christ: it becomes less probable that God will meet with you. There are so many more opportunities wasted, so many more appeals thrown away. The Holy Ghost says, "Today." Do you say, "Today," too?

HEBREWS
3:12–19

12 Watch out, brothers, lest there be in some of you an evil, unbelieving heart, resulting in you falling away from the living God. 13 But encourage one another day by day, as long as it is called "today," so that none of you become hardened by the deception of sin. 14 For we have become partners of Christ, if indeed we hold fast to our original commitment—steadfast until the end. 15 As it is said,

> "Today, if you hear his voice,
> do not harden your hearts as in the rebellion."

16 For who, when they heard it, were disobedient? Surely, was it not all who went out from Egypt with Moses? 17 And with whom was he angry for forty years? Was it not with those who sinned, whose dead bodies fell in the wilderness? 18 And whom did he swear would not enter into his rest, except those who were disobedient? 19 And we see that they were unable to enter because of unbelief.

EXPOSITION

12 **Watch out, brothers** Here the charge is not to the outside world but to those whom he had called "holy brothers." He drops the word "holy," for there are some brothers so called who would not deserve that name, and to them he speaks very pointedly, "Watch out, watch out, lest there be in some of you an evil, unbelieving heart." And how will that be shown? By wandering off, one way or another, away from the living God.

Paul wrote this to the Hebrews, who were his brothers according to the flesh; it was kind of him to call them by that name. He also writes it to all of us who are believers in Christ, and we ought to receive his word with all the greater intensity of attention because he writes to us as his brothers. If your God is not a living God to you, in whom you live and move and have your being, if He does not come into your daily life, but if your religion is a dead and formal thing, then you will soon depart.

ILLUSTRATION

Not Visiting, but Abiding

I remember a minister calling upon a poor old saint, and before coming away he said he hoped that the Divine Father would constantly visit the sick man. He replied, "I do not want you to ask that the Father should merely visit me, for these many months He has been abiding with me, and I have been abiding in Him."

So may it be with each one of you. And that it may be so, give attention to the message of the text: "Watch out, brothers, lest there be in some of you an evil, unbelieving heart, with the result that you fall away"—in any measure or degree—"from the living God" (Heb 3:12).

lest there be in some of you an evil, unbelieving heart
That is the thing that provokes God—unbelief. Not so much the unbelief of the head as the unbelief of the heart, when the heart will not yield to the plan of salvation, when men want to be saved by their own works, or else are indifferent altogether about whether they are saved. It is heart-unbelief that damns men. It is heart-faith that is the means of salvation. "With the heart one believes, resulting in righteousness" (Rom 10:10), but heart-unbelief leads to, and seals, his ruin.

with the result that you fall away from the living God
Even in God's people there is a measure of unbelief and deafness of ear. Even God's children do not hear their Father's voice so readily as they should. We are sometimes so taken up with other things that God speaks again and again, and we do not regard Him. The still small voice of His love is too apt to be altogether unheeded while the thunders of this world's traffic fill our ears.

ILLUSTRATION

Broken Bones May Heal Stronger, but Who Wants to Break a Bone?

I have heard that a broken leg, when it is mended, is sometimes stronger than it was before. It may be so, but I am not going to break my leg to try the experiment. I know one who says that his arm was broken when he was a boy, and that he believes it is stronger than the other one. So it may be, but I will not break my arm if I can help it. May the Lord rather keep me in His hands lest I dash my foot against a stone!

There is a great deal of experience that I hope you will never have, and that is the kind of experience that comes of an evil heart of unbelief, in departing from the living God. Take heed that you never come to know that sorrow.

---

13   **encourage one another** You are to watch over your brothers, to exhort one another daily, especially you who are officers of the church, or who are elderly and experienced. Be on the watch lest any of your brothers in the church should gradually backslide, or lest any in the congregation should harden into a condition of settled unbelief, and perish in their sin. He who bids you take heed to yourself would not have you settle down into a selfish care for yourself alone, lest you should

become like Cain, who even dared to say to the Lord Himself, "Am I my brother's keeper?" (Gen 4:9). Nothing can be more horrible than the state of mind of a man whose talk is like that of Cain, who killed his brother. "Watch out," therefore, you who are in the church of God, not only for yourselves, but to those who are round about you, especially to such as are of your own family.

so that none of you become hardened Notice very carefully that sin has a hardening power over the heart. How does that come about? Partly through our familiarity with sin. We may look at hateful sin till we love it. Familiarity with sin makes the conscience dull and at length deadens sensibility.

Security in wrongdoing leads also to this kind of hardening. A man has been dishonest; he is found out, and he suffers for it. I could almost thank God, for now he may cease from his evil course. But one of the greatest curses that can happen to a man is for him to do wrong with impunity. He will do it again, and again, and again, and he will proceed from bad to worse.

ILLUSTRATION

Hearing the Hard Truth from a Doctor and a Preacher

I have known persons to take offense because the word has been spoken from the pulpit too pointedly. This is to take offense where we ought to show gratitude. Will you give your ear to one who will please you to your ruin, and flatter you to your destruction? Surely you are not so foolish?

Do you choose that kind of doctor who never tells you the truth about your bodily health? Do you trust one who falsely assured you that there was nothing the matter with you when all the while a terrible disease was folding its cruel arms about you? He will send you just a little pill, and you will be all right. He would not have you think of that painful operation that a certain surgeon has suggested to you. Believe me, I would think it a waste of time, no, a crime like that of murder, to prophesy smooth things to you. We must all learn to hear what we do not like. The question is not, "Is it pleasant?" but, "Is it true?"

---

the deception of sin If sin comes to us as sin, we are swift to hate it, and strong to repel it, by the grace of God. When we are walking with God, we only need to know that an action is forbidden, and we avoid it. We shun the evil thing when it is plainly evil. But sin puts on another dress, and comes to us speaking a language that is not its own. So even those who would avoid sin as sin may, by degrees, be tempted to evil, and deluded into wrong.

The deceitfulness of sin will be seen in several points. Its deceit may be seen *in the manner of its approaches to us*. Sin does not uncover all its hideousness, nor reveal its horrible consequences; but it comes to us in a very subtle way, offering us advantage. Next, sin is deceitful *in its object*, for the object that it puts before us is not its actual result. We are not tempted to provoke our Maker, or willfully cast off the authority of righteousness. We are not invited to do these things for their own sake. No, no; we are moved to do evil under the idea that some good will come of it. Sin is deceitful, next, *in the names it wears*. It is very apt to change its title; it seldom cares for its own true description. Fine words are often used to cover foul deeds, yet names do not alter things. Call garlic perfume, and it remains a rank odor. Style the fiend an angel of light, and he is nonetheless a devil. Sin, call it by what names you may, is still evil, only evil, and that continually. Sin also shows its special deceitfulness *in the arguments that it uses*. Sin has often whispered in the vain minds of men, "This action might be very wrong for other people, but it will not be evil in you." Sin will also flatter a man with the notion that he can go just so far, and no farther, and retreat with ease. This deceivableness is further seen *in the excuses that it frames afterwards*.

To screen the conscience from regret is one of the efforts of deceitful sin. The man says to himself, "I did wrong; but what can you expect of poor flesh and blood?" Sin will also add, "And, after all, though you were wrong, yet you were not so bad as you might have been. Considering the temptation, you may wonder at your own moderation in transgression. On the whole, you have behaved better than others would have done." Self-righteousness is poor stuff when it can be fashioned even out of our faults. Such is the deceivableness of sin that it makes itself out to be praiseworthy.

ILLUSTRATION

"How Near Can You Drive to Danger?"

There once was a lady who wanted to hire a driver. When three applied, she had them in one by one. "Well," said she to the first, "How near can you drive to danger?" "Madam," said he, "I believe I could drive within a foot without fear." "You will not do for me," said she. To the second she said, "How near could you drive to danger?" "Within a hair's breadth, Madam," said he, "and yet, you would be perfectly safe." "You will not suit me," said she. The third came in, and when asked the same question, "How near could you drive to danger?" he said, "Madam, I never tried; I always drive as far off as I can."

Such should the Christian act. Some, through the deceitfulness of sin, are always trying to see how near they can go to the edge, so as not to fall over—how near they can sail to the rock and not dash upon it; how much sin they can indulge in and yet remain respected church members. Shame on us, that any of us should be guilty of tampering with that accursed thing that slew the Lord of glory.

---

14   **we have become partners of Christ** The union of believers
with Himself was among the last of all the revelations that
our blessed Lord made known to His disciples when on earth.
With a parable He showed it, and without a parable He declared it plainly.

Every true child of God is one with Christ. This union is set
forth in Scripture by several images. We are one with Christ
and partakers of Him as the stone is cemented to the foundation. It is built upon it, rests upon it, and, together with the
foundation, goes to make up the structure. So we are built into
Christ by coherence and adhesion, joined to Him, and made
a spiritual house for the habitation of God by the Holy Ghost.
We are made partakers with Christ by a union in which we
lean and depend upon Him.

This union is further set forth by the vine and the branches.
The branches are participators with the stem; the sap of the
stem is for the branches. It treasures it up only to distribute it
to them. It has no sap for itself alone; all its store of sap is for
the branch. Similarly, we are vitally one with Christ, and the
grace that is in Him is for us. It was given to Him that he might
distribute it to all His people.

Furthermore, it is as the union of the husband with the wife;
they are participators the one with the other. All that belongs to the husband the wife enjoys and shares with him.
Meanwhile, she shares himself—no, he is all her own. Thus
it is with Christ. We are married to Him—bethrothed to Him
forever in righteousness and in judgment. All that He has is
ours, and He himself is ours. All His heart belongs to each one
of us.

And then, too, as the members of the body are one with the
head, as they derive their guidance, their happiness, their
existence from the head, so are we made partakers of Christ.
Oh, matchless participation! It is "a great mystery" (Eph 5:32),
says the apostle, and, indeed, such a mystery it is as they only
know who experience it. Even they cannot understand it fully;

far less can they hope to set it forth so that carnal minds shall comprehend its spiritual meaning.

The language of the text reminds us that none of us have any title to this privilege by nature. "We have *become* partners of Christ." We all of woman born became partakers of the ruin of the first Adam, of the corruption of humanity, of the condemnation common to the entire race. To be made partakers is a work of grace, of sovereign omnipotent grace—a work that a man cannot sufficiently admire, and for which he can never be sufficiently grateful.

hold fast the beginning of our commitment It is not true that one act of faith is all that is required, except you consider that one act to be continuous throughout life. If a man were a believer once, and if it were possible to cease to be so, then, of course, he is ruined. But the doctrine of the final perseverance of the saints does not speak in that manner. It says that he who is a believer shall continue so—that he who is right with God shall abide so even to the end, and unless it be so we are not partakers of Christ at all.

steadfast until the end Not otherwise. Again I say they who do not hold on and hold out are not really partakers of Christ, but we are made partakers of Christ if we hold the beginning of our confidence steadfast unto the end. Those that fly to this doctrine and that, unsettled spirits, wandering stars, mere meteors of the night, these are not Christ's, but we must hold the beginning of our faith steadfast unto the end.

You are to hold fast, to hold on, and to hold out to the end; and the grace you need in order to do this is waiting for you if you will but look for it, and daily live under the power of it.

15   **do not harden your hearts** Twice over we are warned of this, to avoid hardness of heart. God save us from ossification of heart, petrifaction of heart, till we get a heart of love or a heart of stone—may God save us from this.

ILLUSTRATION
A Heart Hardens Like a Pond Being Covered with Ice

The hardening of a tender conscience is a gradual process, something like the covering of a pond with ice on a frosty night. At first you can scarcely see that freezing is going on at all. There are certain signs that a thoroughly practiced eye may be able to detect as portents of ice, but most of us would see nothing. By and bye, there is ice, but it would scarcely support a pin. If you should place a needle on it ever so gently, it would fall through. In due time you perceive a thin coating that might sustain a pebble. Soon a child trips merrily over it, and if old winter holds his court long enough, it may be that a loaded wagon may be driven over the frozen lake, or a whole army may march without fear across the stream. There may be no rapid hardening at any one moment, and yet the freezing is complete enough in the end.

Apostates and great backsliders do not reach their worst at one bound. The descent to hell is sometimes a precipice, but far more often a smooth and gentle slope.

16 **who, when they heard it, were disobedient** There are many such, and there are no sinners who provoke God so much as those who hear the gospel. A man who never hears the gospel at all may provoke God, but the man that sins after he has heard it again and again and again, and has the sound of it ringing in his ears, provokes God with a sevenfold degree of provocation.

all who went out from Egypt Not all, for there were two faithful ones; Joshua and Caleb were faithful among the faithless found. See how the Spirit of God gathers up the fragments that remain. If there are but two faithful ones out of two millions, He knows it, and He records it.

There were only a few—a mere handful—in Sodom, but the Lord would not consume them with the wicked. They were brought out of it. And so here, if there be only two, the Holy Spirit takes care to be very accurate in the counting of God's elect ones. If you are one of a family, and two of a city, He will take you and bring you into Zion. You may be in so great a minority that in all your acquaintance there may not be one godly person, yet the Holy Ghost will not take the matter in the lump, but He will choose you out, and mark you out, and distinguish you. Do you not notice how careful He was when he spoke about Judas—the good Judas? He says, "Not Iscariot" (John 14:22). No, no; he will not have him mistaken for that traitor. He guards the names of His people, each one of them, if there be but one—and two, if there be but two.

17 **with whom was he angry for forty years** They were a people with whom God had great patience. Has it ever struck you, the great patience that must have been exercised in 40 years of provocation? One would have thought that, surely, in that time these people would turn and repent.

dead bodies fell in the wilderness God speaks very lovingly of the bodies of His saints, but see how the apostle speaks of the bodies of apostates. He does not say that their bodies were buried, but that their carcasses fell in the wilderness. Unbelief degrades us into beasts whose carcasses fall beneath the poleax of judgment. Remember that in the Old Testament the unredeemed man is comparable to the donkey: "If you will not redeem it, then you will break its neck" (Exod 13:13). But the redeemed man is comparable to the sheep. Valuable property is in him, and God esteems him.

18-19 **not able to enter because of unbelief** The great promise that was given to Israel was Canaan, that choice land that God had of old allotted to them. "When the Most High apportioned the nations, at his dividing up of the sons of humankind, he fixed the boundaries of the peoples, according to the number of the children of Israel" (Deut 32:8). He made Palestine to be the center of worship, the joy of all lands, the seat of His oracle, and the place of His abode. In the wilderness, the tribes were journeying toward this country, and it was a very short distance from Egypt, so that they might almost at once have taken possession of the land, and yet it cost them 40 years' traveling. If you trace their journeys, you will see that they ran a perpetual zigzag, backward and forward, to the right and to the left. Sometimes they were actually journeying away from the promised rest, plunging into the deeps of the howling wilderness—and all, we are told, because of their unbelief. It was not the sons of Anak that kept them out. It was not the waste howling wilderness. It was nothing but their own unbelief.

Canaan is a type to us of the great and goodly things of the covenant of grace that belong to believers. But if we have no faith, we cannot possess a single covenant blessing. Today, in the proclamation of the gospel, the demand is made of faith in God. If there is no faith, no matter how rich the gospel, how full its provisions, and how precious the portion which God has prepared, none of us can ever enter into the enjoyment of them.

APPLICATION

Watch Out, No Matter Who You Are

We are all of us called upon to "watch out." True religion is not a thing that can be acquired by carelessness or neglect; we must take heed, or we shall never be found in the narrow way. You may go to hell heedlessly, but you cannot so go to heaven. Many stumble into the bottomless pit with their eyes shut, but no man ever yet entered into heaven by a leap in the dark.

"Watch out, brothers." If ever there was a matter that needed all your thought, all your prudence, and all your care, it is the matter of your soul's salvation. If you do trifle with anything, let it be with your wealth, or with your health, but certainly not with your eternal interests. I recommend all men to take heed to everything that has to do with this life, as well as with that which is to come, for in the little the great may lie concealed, and the neglect of our estate may end in mischief to our immortal spirit. Certainly, the neglect of the body might lead to great injury to the soul, but if ever neglect deserves condemnation, it is when it concerns our higher nature. If we do not carefully see to it, that which is our greatest glory may become our most tremendous curse.

The watchword for every one of us is "watch out." You are an old Christian, but "watch out." You are a minister of the gospel, and there are many who look up to you with veneration, but "watch out." You have learned the doctrines of grace, and you know them well; there is little that any human being can teach you, for you have been well-instructed in the things of the kingdom. But still, "watch out." Even if you were so near to heaven's gate that you could hear the song within, I would still whisper in your ear, "Watch out." Horses fall most often at the bottom of the hill when we think that we need not hold them up any longer, and there is no condition in life that is more dangerous than that feeling of perfect security that precludes watchfulness and care. He who is quite sure of his strength to resist temptation may be also equally certain of his weakness in the hour of trial. God grant us grace, whatever sort of "brothers" we may be, to listen to the admonition of the apostle: "Watch out."

How to Keep a Soft Heart

Your hearts are every day either softening or hardening. The sun that shines with vehement heat melts the wax, but it, at the same time, hardens the clay. The effect of the gospel is always present in some degree: it is a savor of life unto life, or else a savor of death unto death, to all who hear it.

It is often a long and laborious process by which conscience is completely seared. This dreadful work usually begins thus: the man's first carefulness and tenderness departs. The next distressing sign of growing hardness is increasing neglect or laxity of private devotion, without any corresponding shock of the spiritual sensibilities on account of it. Another symptom is the fact that hidings of the Savior's face do not cause that acute and poignant sorrow that they produced in former times. Still further, when the soul is hardened to this extent, it is probable that sin will no longer cause such grief as it once did. The next step in this ladder, down, down, down to destruction, is that sin thus causing less grief, is indulged in more freely. After this there is still a greater hardening of heart: the man comes to dislike rebukes. He has sinned so long, and yet he has been held in such respect in the Christian church, that if you give half a hint about his sin, he looks at you with a sharp look as if you were insulting him. If this hardening work goes on, the day at last comes to such a man that the Word of God loses all effect upon him.

The way to keep from hardness of heart, and from the deceitfulness of sin, is *to believe*. Believe in the living God, and in his righteousness, and in your obligation to serve him—then sin will appear exceeding sinful. Believe in Christ, who took your sin, and bare it in his own body on the tree—then sin will be seen in its black colors. Believe in the Holy Ghost, by whose power you can be delivered from the deceitfulness of sin; and as you believe, so shall it be unto you, and you will stand fast where the half-believer slides.

The next advice I would give is this: if you would be saved from the deceitfulness of sin, confess it honestly before God. It is necessary to lay bare your heart before the living God. Although sin may call itself by another name, you call it by its right name. Pray that sin may appear sin; it cannot appear in a worse light. Thus you will not so readily be caught in its traps and lures. When you have sinned, then confess the great evil of your wickedness. This humble penitence will be not only your way to pardon, but to future purity.

Again, *cultivate great tenderness of heart*. I would be swayed by the Word of God as the ripe corn is swayed by the summer wind. I would be by God's Spirit as readily moved as the leaves of the aspen by the breeze. I would be sensitive to the gentlest breath of my Lord. A conscience seared as with a hot iron is the sure prelude of destruction.

But now the text itself says, "Encourage one another day by day," from which I gather two lessons. First, hear exhortation from others, and, secondly, practice exhortation to others. We ought to be able to take a loving exhortation from our brothers and sisters. We must do so if we are to be preserved from the deceitfulness of sin. Another eye may see for me what I cannot see for myself. Reproofs should be given with great tenderness, but even if they wound us, we must bear them.

And then let us endeavor, if the Lord is keeping us by His grace, to "encourage one another day by day." We are not to scold one another daily, nor to suspect one another daily, nor to pick holes in one another's coats daily. But when we see a manifest fault in a brother, we are bound to tell him of it in love. And when we do not see any fault of commission, but the brother is evidently growing lax and cold, it is well to stir him up to greater zeal by a loving exhortation. Watch over your own children, your wife, your husband, and then do not forget your neighbors and fellow workers. Cry to God to give us union of spirit with all the Lord's chosen, and may that union of spirit be a living and loving one!

Not Entering because of Unbelief?

The Israelites were a highly favored people, yet they could not enter because of unbelief. To these Israelites great things had been revealed, for, during their sojourn in the wilderness, they had been scholars in a gracious school. To what other people did God ever speak as He spoke to them? To whom did He give the tablets of divine command, written with His own mysterious pen? Where else did He dwell between the cherubim, and shine forth with glorious majesty? Where else did He reveal himself in type and shadow, by priest and sacrifice and altar?

We too have enjoyed a clear revelation. We have heard the gospel more plainly than the Israelites ever did. The Bible has more light in it than Moses could impart. The preaching of the gospel, where it is done affectionately and earnestly, and by the help of the Spirit of God, is a greater means of grace to the soul than all the sacred rites of the tabernacle. Shall it be with us as with them? "They were not able to enter because of unbelief." Shall we labor under the same disability?

To me it is especially appalling that a man should perish through willfully rejecting the divine salvation. A drowning man throwing away the life preserver; a poisoned man pouring the antidote upon the floor; a wounded man tearing open his wounds—any one of these is a sad sight, but what shall we say of a soul putting from it the Redeemer, and choosing its own destruction? Be warned, and forbear from eternal suicide. There is still the way of salvation:

"Believe in the Lord Jesus and you will be saved" (Acts 16:31). To believe is to trust. You have to trust in a living person, in the Lord Jesus Christ, who died as the substitute for those who trust Him, and lives to see that those whom He bought with blood are also redeemed from their sins by power, and brought home to heaven. Trust Jesus Christ. Have done with yourself as your confidence, and commit your soul to the keeping of the faithful Redeemer.

HEBREWS 4

¹ The promise to enter his rest remains; therefore, let us fear, lest any of you might seem to fall short of it. ² For we also have had the good news proclaimed to us, just as those also did, but the message they heard did not benefit them, because they were not united with those who heard it in faith. ³ For we who have believed enter into rest, just as he has said,

> "As I swore in my anger,
> 'They will never enter into my rest.'"

And yet these works have been accomplished from the foundation of the world. ⁴ For he has spoken somewhere about the seventh day in this way: "And God rested on the seventh day from all his works," ⁵ and in this passage again, "They will never enter into my rest." ⁶ Since therefore it remains for some to enter into it, and the ones to whom the good news was proclaimed previously did not enter because of disobedience, ⁷ again he ordains a certain day, today, speaking by David after so long a time, just as had been said before,

> "Today, if you hear his voice,
> do not harden your hearts."

⁸ For if Joshua had caused them to rest, he would not have spoken about another day after these things. ⁹ Consequently a Sabbath rest remains for the people of God. ¹⁰ For the one who has entered into his rest has also himself rested from his works, just as God did from his own works.

EXPOSITION

1   **let us fear** Now, the apostle cannot mean that we are to fear lest we should come short of heaven for want of merit. There

is not a man living, nor has one ever lived, nor shall one ever live, who will not come short of heaven if he tries that road. Human merit is not the way to heaven. Since the hour in which our first parent broke the law for us, the perfect keeping of the law has been impossible; neither is the keeping of the law set before us in the gospel of our Lord Jesus Christ as the way of acceptance with God. "For by the works of the law no person will be declared righteous before him, for through the law comes knowledge of sin" (Rom 3:20). The just shall live by faith, and it is in the matter of faith that we are cautioned against coming short. The apostle would with indignation have spurned the idea that the gospel race is to be run at the foot of Sinai, and that its prize would be a reward for good works. Over and over again he has plainly declared, "It is not from works, so that no one can boast" (Eph 2:9); but by grace, as the pure gift of the good pleasure and mercy of God. We must not, therefore, twist his words into a legal injunction, for they were never intended to bear such a meaning. The great point that we are to be concerned about is lest we come short of the heavenly rest by failing in the faith that will give us the rest.

In a word, we must put our trust in the blood and righteousness of the Lord Jesus Christ; we must give up all other confidences, and cast ourselves entirely upon Him, otherwise we shall certainly never enter into the rest that is reserved for believers.

ILLUSTRATION

Faith Like a Soldier

You know with what heart soldiers have trusted their commanders. They have gone into the fight and been outnumbered, but they have felt that their leader was so skillful in war, and so sure to win, that they have remained undaunted under terrible attacks, and their battalions have stood firm as iron walls amid a sleet of deadly missiles. With unstaggering faith they have rested in the prowess of their leader, and have earned the victory; such must be our confidence in Christ. Whatever may discourage our hope, whatever may contradict the promise, ours it is to repose in Jesus with all our soul and strength, for such faith unites to the Lamb and brings salvation through His name.

---

entering into his rest "Rest" is a blessed golden word. It is the one thing, surely, that the world seeks after. It may be true that every man seeks after happiness; I question if it is not equally true that each man seeks after rest. There are some few fiery spirits who wish not to rest, who seem to be like thunderbolts that must speed on in their predestinated pathway, and only an incessant and morbid activity suits them at all; but for the majority of us the expectation of rest is very sweet, and the enjoyment of it now in the poor measure in which we can get it is one of our greatest refreshments.

that none of you appear to fall short of it Not come short of it but even seem to do so. God keep us from the very shadow of sin, from the very appearance of evil.

If you avoid the very seeming of it, you will avoid the thing itself. Oh, that we were careful about this—that there was nothing that should give any reasonable fear to those who observed us, or to ourselves when we search our hearts, lest we should not enter into this rest.

2 **we also have had the good news proclaimed to us** In the old time that gospel that was preached to them was preached to us—but the word preached did not profit them, not being mixed with faith in those who heard it. God send us this holy mixture of the hearing and the believing, to our soul's salvation, to His glory.

just as those also did The message of Moses and the reports of the faithful spies were both typical of the gospel that was brought to us by our Lord and His apostles. Our gospel is clearer than theirs; yet they had the gospel also, in all the essential truths of it. And had they fully believed it, it would have been a saving gospel to them.

did not benefit them Why was it the gospel that they heard did not benefit them? Assuredly, *it was not the fault of the gospel that they heard.* In itself it is calculated to profit all who receive it. It promised liberty, and this should have made them gratefully obedient. It promised an inheritance, and added to it a high and holy calling, and this should have aroused their loftiest aspiration. It promised every help to the getting of the promised blessings, and what could they have more? *It was not the fault of the preacher;* for Moses spoke God's word with great meekness and gentleness. He set before them the truth with all fidelity. *It was not the fault of a lack of confirming signs from God.* No default of divine working hindered Israel's faith. God wrought with His gospel in those days very mightily. The daily manna and the water leaping from the rock, with other signs and wonders, went to prove the word of the Lord. *Neither was it for lack of the Holy Spirit* that these people made the gospel a failure to them; for we read that the Holy Ghost spoke to them, and they rebelled, and vexed the Holy Spirit. It was the Holy Ghost who spoke to them and said, "Today, if you hear his voice, do not harden your hearts" (Heb 3:15; 4:7).

Well, then, what was the cause? We put our finger on it at once: "*They were not united with those who heard it in faith.*" Where there is no faith in the gospel, no good consequence can possibly come of it.

because they were not united with those who heard it in faith Where there is no faith, men remain slaves to the present. If they did not believe in the milk and honey of Canaan, you see why they hankered for the cucumbers of Egypt. An onion is nothing comparable to an estate beyond Jordan;

yet as they think they cannot get the estate, they pine for the onions. When men do not believe in eternal life, they naturally enough cry, "Give me bread and cheese. Let me have a fortune here." They keep their nose to the grindstone, always thinking about this passing life, because they do not heartily believe in heaven and its glories. They are as "dumb driven cattle," who do not see into another state: this life seems real to them, but the next life they suspect to be a dream. As long as there is no faith, this world is all, and the world to come is nothing at all.

ILLUSTRATION

Taking in the Gospel Like Food

That which is not appropriated can be of no use to you. Look at your food. How is it that it builds up your body? Because you take it into the mouth, and it descends into the stomach, and there it is mixed with certain fluids, and is digested, and ultimately is taken up into the system and becomes a life-sustaining force. Being properly mixed, it is taken up and assimilated.

And so it is with heavenly truth: If it is taken into the heart, and then mixed with faith, it is digested, and becomes food to every part of the spiritual nature. Without faith the gospel passes through the soul undigested, and rather feeds disease than promotes life.

---

3   **For we who have believed enter into rest** It is by believing that we get rest—by no other means, not by scheming and plotting and planning and thinking and criticizing and judging and doubting and questioning, but by believing—the submission of the soul to God's truth, the yielding of the heart to God's salvation. This once done, we lie down in green pastures, and are led beside the still waters.

The text does not say that we who have believed *shall* enter into rest. That is a very great truth, but it is not the truth that is taught here. We "enter into rest," even in this present life; all who are believers in the Lord Jesus Christ are already enjoying rest of the heart. And in proportion as faith possesses their souls, in that proportion they enjoy perfect rest. It is not a future privilege, it is a matter of present enjoyment; and I pray my brothers and sisters in Christ not to impoverish themselves by making the text apply to the future, but to seek for the spiritual enrichment that God has given them by accepting the text just as the apostle wrote it, and so realizing that "we who have believed enter into rest."

The believer rests from the guilt of sin because he has seen his sins laid upon Christ, his scapegoat, and knowing well that nothing can be in two places at one time, he concludes that if sin were laid on Christ, it is not on him; and thus he rejoices in his own deliverance from sin, through its having been imputed to his glorious Substitute. The believer in Christ Jesus sees sin effectually punished in Christ Jesus, and knowing that justice can never demand two penalties for the same crime, or two payments for the same debt, he rests perfectly at peace with regard to his past sins. He has, in the person of his surety, endured the hell that was due on account of transgressions. Christ, by suffering in our stead, has answered all the demands of justice, and the believer's heart is perfectly at rest.

I do not say that the believer's life is all peace, for his condition is peculiar in this way. When the children of Israel entered into Canaan, they were a portrait of a saint entering into rest. First, they had to cross the Jordan: believers have to cross the Jordan of their sin. That is dried up, and they march through by divine grace. Then there stand, inside the promised land, the walls of Jericho, namely, their own corruptions and own sinful nature. It takes time to bring them to the ground, but after that, when the walls are leveled, there are Canaanites still in the land. Canaan was not a good type of heaven, for they were always fighting in Canaan, always having to war against the adversary. That is a good type of the rest to which believers come. They do rest. They know that heaven is theirs; that they are saved; that all their troubles work for their good; that they are God's people. Still they have to fight against sin, and that is no more inconsistent with their being at rest than it was inconsistent with the fact of the holy land belonging to the Israelites, though they had still to go on fighting against the Canaanites.

ILLUSTRATION
Finding Rest in a Person

How happy are we to find rest in a person! This is warm and substantial comfort. You cannot rest in the words of a doctrine as you can in the bosom of a person. Take a poor child that is lost in the street. Talk to it upon cheering themes. These ought to comfort it; but the little one goes on crying. Sing to it, and reason with it. It is all in vain. Run, fetch its mother! See how it smiles! It nestles in her bosom, and is at rest. A person yields the heart comfort.

So it is with our Lord Jesus Christ. In life, in death, it is a delightful thought that our salvation rests in the hands of a living, loving personality; we depend upon a divine and human person, an accessible helper, to whom we may come at all times. Oh, yes, "we who have believed enter into rest" in the person of the Well-beloved!

They will never enter into my rest That is God's rest, the rest of a finished work, and into that rest many never enter. The work by which they might live forever, the finished work by which they might be saved, they refuse, and so they never enter into God's rest.

ILLUSTRATION

The More Faith Grows, the More Rest Grows

Some people are always fretting and fuming; they appear to have been born in stormy weather, and to be perpetually agitated in mind so that they cannot rest. Only the other day, a gardener I knew of was complaining greatly of the heavy rain, which had done some damage to the garden where he was working. A Quaker, who stood by, said to him, "Friend, you ought not to complain of the rain, for if it has not done this garden any good, it has done good to the fields of many of your neighbors. Therefore you ought to be glad on their account, and to thank God"; and then the good man very wisely added, "I do not think that, after all, we should have the weather any better managed by you than it is by God, if it could be put into your hands."

That is the right way to look at all things; they are far better ordered by God than by any man. Christian, you could not order them better if you had the ordering of them, so be perfectly content, and say, "Not my will, Lord; but yours be done." The more faith grows, the more rest grows; but when our faith begins to forget the Lord, and we commence to worry and to fret, then our rest goes at once.

4   **And God rested on the seventh day** Why did God rest on the seventh day? Because He had thought of all that man wanted, and had made all things good for him. Our Lord Jesus never rested till He had finished the work that His Father gave Him to do, which work was all for us: and the great providence of God will never rest till all the chosen of God are brought safely home to heaven. Thus you see how God thinks upon us.

5 **They will never enter into my rest** There are many professing Christians who do not understand what it is to rest because the work of salvation is done; they do not even seem
to know that the work is done. They do not understand that
dying word of the Lord Jesus, "It is finished." They think there
is something still to be added to His work to make it effectual;
but it is not so.

6 **it remains for some to enter into it** While we are taught that
some could not enter in because of unbelief; it is implied in
it that believers would enter in. Those who have faith in the
divine promise shall enter in. If unbelief shuts men out, then
faith is the door of entrance to those who have it. I beg you to
grasp the kernel of promise that lies whole and safe within
the shell of the threatening. God swore of those unbelieving
Jews that they should not enter in, but He had declared that
some should enter in; therefore a promise is left which will
be fulfilled in those who have faith, and so are the true seed of
faithful Abraham. These shall enter in; and certain of them in
the text declare that they have done so: "We who have believed
enter into rest."

ILLUSTRATION
Be Honest if You Lack Rest

I remember hearing of a pious minister who was asked to
speak one day upon the subject of joy in God. He stood
up and said, "I am sorry that I have been requested to
speak upon this topic; for the fact is, I am not walking in
the light, but I am crying, 'Restore to me the joy of your
salvation' (Psa 51:12). I have grieved my heavenly Father,
and I am in the dark." He sat down and sobbed; and so
did all his brothers. This honest confession did far more
good than if he had patched up a tale, and told of some
stale experience years before.

If you have not entered into rest, do not say that you have. Fictitious experience is dangerous to the forger of it. Experience borrowed from other people is like the borrowed axe, sure to fall into the ditch.

---

7   **speaking by David** We read of this in Psalm 95, where David was urging those to whom he was writing to hear God's voice, and not be like the unbelievers in the wilderness, so that the rest still remained to be entered upon by somebody. Joshua had not given them rest, or else David would not have spoken of entering into rest.

8   **if Joshua had caused them to rest** While the children of Israel were in the wilderness, they were constantly moving to and fro, dwelling in tents, and enjoying but little comfort. Notwithstanding all the blessings with which God enriched them in the wilderness, it was a wilderness, and Moses truly called it "a howling, desert wasteland" (Deut 32:10). They had no rest there, and they were always looking forward to the land flowing with milk and honey where they were journeying. Their eager longing was for a land where they could settle down, and build houses, and plant vineyards, and dwell in quiet resting places. Canaan is, therefore, the type of the rest that God intends to give his people here. It is not the type of heaven, except very imperfectly, for in Canaan there were Canaanites to be fought, and to be gradually driven out, and there were some that never were driven out of their fastnesses, but we thank God that there are no Canaanites to trouble the saints in heaven. Canaan is the true pattern and type of the believer's condition upon the earth. We who have believed in Jesus have crossed the Jordan. He has divided it for us, and we have entered into rest. It is true that the Canaanites are still in the land, but the Lord also is in the land; and, by His grace, we shall surely drive them all out.

9   **Consequently a sabbath rest remains** The true rest of God lies higher than times and places. The Lord God rests in the person of Jesus: in Him He is well pleased. The Lord speaks of Him as "my chosen one, in whom my soul delights" (Isa 42:1). In the person of His Son, the heart of the Father finds perpetual joy: "This is my beloved Son, in whom I am well pleased." But we also behold His glory—"Glory as of the one and only from the Father, full of grace and truth" (John 1:14). By faith we see that in Him which gives rest to our heart. Therefore was Jesus given: "This one will be the peace" (Mic 5:5). The Lord Jesus is our true Noah, in whom we find safety and rest. He was both given in birth and given up in death to be the rest of weary souls.

This rest, I believe, is partly enjoyed on earth. "We who have believed enter into rest" (4:3), for we have ceased from our own works, as God did from His. But the full fruition and rich enjoyment of it remains in the future and eternal state of the beatified on the other side of the stream of death.

for the people of God God has provided a Sabbath, and some must enter into it. Those to whom it was first preached did not enter in because of unbelief; therefore, that Sabbath remains for the people of God. David sang of it; but he had to touch the minor key, for Israel refused the rest of God. Joshua could not give it, nor Canaan yield it: it remains for believers.

10   **has also himself rested from his works** He says, "It is finished. I am no longer going to do my own works, I have done with them; I now trust the finished work of Christ, and that gives me rest. But as to all that wearied me before, and made life a continual task and toil, it is ended now." God is not a cruel taskmaster to His people; He gives rest to those who trust in Him, and some of us have entered into that rest.

The labor of love for Christ is only another word for rest. He says, "Take my yoke on you ... and you will find rest for your souls" (Matt 11:29). Carry Christ's burden, and your shoulders shall have rest. We do not mean sleep or idleness when we speak of rest; that is not rest, but rust. Our rest is found in the service of God.

APPLICATION

The Believer at Rest

At this very moment you may have complete rest. But if you refuse this, and go about and try to mend your ways, and to find salvation for yourself by your own doings, you will never have rest. You who wish to climb to heaven by the way of Sinai had better look to the flames that Moses saw, and shrink and tremble and despair. Calvary is an easier mount to climb. When God gives grace to believe, rest is immediately obtained. Oh, that the Lord would make some rambler end his ramblings now at the foot of the cross and find perfect peace!

Remember that the door to this sacred garden is an open one. To believe in Jesus is not a matter that needs a great explanation from me. "If you are willing and you are obedient, you shall eat the good of the land" (Isa 1:19). If you would have it, "listen carefully to me, and eat what is good, and let your soul take pleasure in rich food" (Isa 55:2). "Faith comes by hearing, and hearing through the word about Christ" (Rom 10:17).

You have heard the word of God, for this is the testimony of God, that He has given His Son Jesus to be a propitiation for sin, and everyone who believes in Him, that is, trusts in Him, rests upon Him, leans upon Him, depends upon Him for this faith—everyone who does that is pardoned, is a child of God, is accepted, is saved. He shall never be lost; he shall enter heaven as surely as he lives. It is Christ's business to keep him and to perfect him, and to present him faultless before the presence of the Father with exceeding joy. There is the door of faith. Sinner, will you enter? If you refuse to enter, know this, there is no other name given under heaven among men whereby you can be saved or find rest. Do you say, "I am unfit to enter"? It is for the unfit that Jesus died. He died for the ungodly. Remember that! He "came into the world to save *sinners*" (1 Tim 1:15). Catch at that precious word, and let your unworthiness rather console you than depress you, since your unworthiness is your claim to the promise through God's grace. He came to save sinners—even the very chief.

The Believer at Work

You must not suppose that, when we enter into rest, it means that we are idle. Our Lord Jesus Christ said, "My Father is working until now, and I am working" (John 5:17). God rests, yet He works. Heaven is a place of rest, but it is not a place of idleness: there is holy service still to be done there; so you Christian people, who are perfectly saved, devote all your strength to the winning of others for Christ. Show your love to Jesus by trying to find some of his lost sheep for him. Rouse yourselves, my brothers and sisters who have entered into rest, and prove to mankind that the grand old Calvinistic doctrine of a finished salvation does not breed sluggishness. Rise, I pray you, and show that the children of the freewoman are not slothful, but that the motive of gratitude to God is a higher and more potent one than the selfish motive of seeking to save yourselves. Let those who want to save themselves go and work for themselves; but as for you who are saved, go and work for Jesus; and let your deeds of holy heroism prove that you are constrained by love to him to do all that you can to bring others to trust in him. Now, as some of you are coming to this communion table, may it prove to be a feast of rest to your souls! Sitting, as you will be, in the posture of rest, eating the bread and drinking the wine which are the tokens of the finished work of Christ, may you have real rest in him! And oh, that some poor sinner, who has never believed in Jesus, may do so now, for thus shall he find rest unto his soul!

Do You Belong to the "Some"?

The text speaks of a promise that is left, left to believers, and so left that some must enter in. Do you belong to that some? That is the question. You do if you are a true, real, genuine believer in the Lord Jesus, if the word that you hear is mixed with faith, according to the second verse. But if the word you hear is not mixed with faith, there is no promise made to you that you shall enter into God's rest, and you must come short of that which is promised to faith, because you have no faith. The promise is made to the believer in Christ. I will, therefore, fear to doubt my Lord, fear to distrust Him, fear to suspect His veracity. I will believe that He came into the world to save sinners; I will believe that he is able to save to the uttermost those who come unto God by Him. I will not hesitate to trust Him, for I fear to doubt the God who cannot lie, lest it be said of me, "He could not enter in, because of unbelief."

What the apostle would have us do I gather from the chapter in which my text stands. We are to hold fast our profession. If you have believed in Jesus, cleave to Him. If His cross indeed be your support, hold on to it as for dear life; never let it go.

Next, submit yourselves to the whole word of God, for it is living and powerful. It will search your inmost soul even to the joints and marrow; habitually let it do so. Never be afraid of your Bibles. If there is a text of Scripture you dare not meet, humble yourself till you can. If your creed and Scripture do not agree, cut your creed to pieces, but make it agree with this book. If there be anything in the church to which you belong which is contrary to the inspired word, leave that church. To the law and to the testimony, here is the infallible chart of faith, follow it closely, and if you do, you need have no fear of coming short, for this book cannot lead you astray. Follow it to the letter, and be precise about it, even though men shall laugh at you for being too particular. Keep to every jot and tittle, and to the living spirit of it, and you will not come short.

Then, come boldly to the throne of grace. So the chapter concludes. There you will obtain mercy, and find grace to help in time of need. Cling to the mercy seat as Joab to the horns of the altar. Pray much, pray always. Cry to God for help. Your help comes from the eternal hills, and as you become more and more prevalent in prayer, you will feel that you do not come short, for God hears you, and He would not hear you and answer you from day to day if you were after all short of the faith that brings the soul into rest.

In a word, believe fully. If we have been half-and-half Christians, let us be wholly Christians. If we have given up to God a little of our time, a little of our substance, a little of ourselves, let us be baptized into the Lord Jesus Christ, buried with Him, given up to Him totally; no longer sprinkled with a little grace, which may suffice to bespatter us with enough godliness to make us decent, but forever dead unto the world and alive unto God in newness of life.

What to Do if You Are Not Resting

If you can say as much as this—"By believing I have entered into rest," *be thankful;* for this privilege is a gift of love. It is a wonderful instance of sovereign grace that such unworthy ones as we are should enter into God's rest. *But if you cannot say it, do not despair.* Make it a point to question yourself, "Why can I not speak this way? Why have I not entered into rest? Is it because I have not believed"? Perhaps some fault of character may prevent your enjoying perfect rest. See where that flaw is.

Are you living in any sin? If so the sun may have risen, but if there is a bandage over your eyes, you will still be in the dark. Get rid of that which blinds the eye. Or are you trusting yourself as well as trusting in Christ? Are you relying on your experience? Then I do not wonder if you miss the rest of faith. Get rid of all that spoils the simplicity of your faith. Come to the Lord anew. Possibly you are sickly in body, and this may cause you discomfort, for which you cannot otherwise account. Never mind, you may come just as you are, with all your sickness, weakness, or family trouble, and you may now rest in the Lord. Tell out your grief to Jesus, and He will breathe on you, and say, "Peace to you." We ought to be at rest: We err when we are not. A child of God should not leave his bedroom in the morning without being on good terms with his God. We should not dare to go into the world and feel, "I am out of harmony with my Lord. All is not right between God and my soul." Set all straight today, so that you can say, "We who have believed enter into rest." And when that is done, if anything should again happen to break the golden chain, renew it by faith; for by faith alone we stand. Destroy, by the power of God's Spirit, everything that weakens faith; for this will disturb your rest in God. Oh, that all the way between here and heaven we may journey on with restful hearts, led beside the still waters!

HEBREWS
4:11–16

11 Therefore, let us make every effort to enter into that rest, in order that no one may fall in the same pattern of disobedience. 12 For the word of God is living and active and sharper than any double-edged sword, and piercing as far as the division of soul and spirit, both joints and marrow, and able to judge the reflections and thoughts of the heart. 13 And no creature is hidden in the sight of him, but all things are naked and laid bare to the eyes of him to whom we must give our account.

14 Therefore, because we have a great high priest who has gone through the heavens, Jesus the Son of God, let us hold fast to our confession. 15 For we do not have a high priest who is not able to sympathize with our weaknesses, but who has been tempted in all things in the same way, without sin. 16 Therefore let us approach with confidence the throne of grace, in order that we may receive mercy and find grace to help in time of need.

EXPOSITION

11 **make every effort to enter into that rest** It is an extraordinary injunction, but I think he means, let us labor not to labor. Our tendency is to try to do something in order to save ourselves; but we must beat that tendency down, and look away from self to Christ. Labor to get away from your own labors; labor to be clean rid of all self-reliance; labor in your prayers never to depend upon your prayers; labor in your repentance never to rest upon your repentance; and labor in your faith not to trust to your faith, but to trust alone to Jesus.

ILLUSTRATION
Before the Cross

I remember an old countryman saying to me, long ago, "Depend upon it, my brother, if you or I get one inch above the ground, we get just that inch too high"; and I believe it is so. Flat on our faces before the cross of Christ is the place for us; realizing that we ourselves are nothing, and that Jesus Christ is everything.

pattern of disobedience Let us not repeat the story of unbelieving Israel in our own lives. Let us not live and die in the wilderness, but let us go in and take possession of the promised land, the promised rest, in the power of the Holy Spirit.

12   **For the word of God** By the Word of God, are we here to understand the Incarnate Word, the Divine Logos, who was in the beginning with God; or does the passage relate to this inspired Book, and to the gospel, which is the kernel of it, as it is set forth in the preaching of the truth in the power of the Holy Ghost?

It may be most accurate to interpret this passage as relating both to the Word of God incarnate, and the Word of God inspired. Weave the two into one thought, for God has joined them together, and you will then see fresh lights and new meanings in the text. The Word of God, namely, this revelation of Himself in Holy Scripture, is all it is here described to be, because Jesus, the incarnate Word of God, is in it. He, as it were, incarnates Himself as the divine truth in this visible and manifest revelation; and thus it becomes living and powerful, dividing and discerning. As the Christ reveals God, so this book reveals Christ, and therefore it partakes, as the Word of God, in all the attributes of the Incarnate Word; and we may say many of the same things of the written Word as of the embodied Word; in fact, they are now so linked together that it would be impossible to divide them.

is living The Word of God is alive. This is a living book. This is a mystery that only living men, quickened by the Spirit of God, will fully comprehend. Take up any other book except the Bible, and there may be a measure of power in it, but there is not that indescribable vitality in it that breathes, and speaks, and pleads, and conquers in the case of this sacred volume.

It is only because Jesus is not dead that the Word becomes living and effectual, "and sharper than any double-edged sword"; for, if you leave Christ out of it, you have left out its vitality and power. As I have told you that we will not have Christ without the Word, so neither will we have the Word without Christ. If you leave Christ out of Scripture, you have left out the essential truth that it is written to declare.

ILLUSTRATION

Leaving Jesus Out of the Picture

There is a famous picture that represents our Lord before Pilate. It has deservedly won great attention. A certain excellent newspaper, which brings out for a very cheap price a large number of engravings, has given an engraving of this picture; but, inasmuch as the painting was too large for the paper to give the whole, they have copied a portion of it. It is interesting to note that they have given us Pilate here, and Caiaphas there, but since there was no room for Jesus upon the sheet, they have left out that part of the design.

When I saw the picture, I thought that it was wonderfully characteristic of a great deal of modern preaching. See Pilate here, Caiaphas there, and the Jews yonder—but the Victim, bound and scourged for human sin, is omitted. Possibly, in the case of the publication, the figure of the Christ will appear in the next number;

but even if he should appear in the next sermon of our preachers of the new theology, it will be as a moral example, and not as the Substitute for the guilty, the Sin-bearer by whose death we are redeemed. When we hear a sermon with no Christ in it, we hope that He will come out next Sunday; at the same time, the preaching is, so far, spoiled, and the presentation of the gospel is entirely ruined so long as the principal figure is left out. Oh, it is a sad thing to have to stand in any house of prayer and listen to the preaching, and then have to cry, "They have taken away my Lord, and I do not know where they have put him" (John 20:13)!

---

and active Perhaps "energetic" is the best rendering, or almost as well, "effectual." Holy Scripture is full of power and energy. The Word of God is that by which sin is slain, and grace is born in the heart. It is that which brings life with it. How active and energetic it is, when the soul is convinced of sin, in bringing it forth into gospel liberty!

ILLUSTRATION

The Word Is a Growing Seed

Plants unknown in certain regions have suddenly sprung from the soil: the seeds have been wafted on the winds, carried by birds, or washed ashore by the waves of the sea. So vital are seeds that they live and grow wherever they are borne; and even after lying deep in the soil for centuries, when the upturning spade has brought them to the surface, they have germinated at once.

Thus is it with the Word of God: it lives and abides forever, and in every soil and under all circumstances it is prepared to prove its own life by the energy with which it grows and produces fruit to the glory of God.

---

and sharper than any double-edged sword The revelation of God given us in Holy Scripture is edge all over. It is alive in every part, and in every part keen to cut the conscience, and wound the heart. Depend upon it, there is not a superfluous verse in the Bible, nor a chapter that is useless.

The Word of God is so sharp a thing, so full of cutting power, that you may be bleeding under its wounds before you have seriously suspected the possibility of such a thing. You cannot come near the gospel without its having a measure of influence over you; and, God blessing you, it may cut down and kill your sins when you have no idea that such a work is being done. Yes, when Christ comes, He comes not to send peace on the earth, but a sword; and that sword begins at home, in our own souls, killing, cutting, hacking, breaking in pieces. Blessed is that man who knows the Word of the Lord by its exceeding sharpness, for it kills nothing but that which ought to be killed. It quickens and gives new life to all that is of God; but the old depraved life, which ought to die, it hews in pieces, as Samuel destroyed Agag before the Lord (1 Sam 15:33).

and piercing While it has an edge like a sword, it has also a point like a rapier, "Piercing as far as the division of soul and spirit." The difficulty with some men's hearts is to get at them. In fact, there is no spiritually penetrating the heart of any natural man except by this piercing instrument, the Word of God. But the rapier of revelation will go through anything.

as far as the division of soul and spirit It divides asunder soul and spirit. Nothing else could do that, for the division is difficult. In a great many ways writers have tried to describe the difference between soul and spirit; but I question whether they have succeeded. No doubt it is a very admirable definition to say, "The soul is the life of the natural man, and the spirit the life of the regenerate or spiritual man." But it is one thing to define and quite another thing to divide.

able to judge the reflections and thoughts of the heart The Word not only lets you see what your thoughts are, but it criticizes your thoughts. The Word of God says of this thought, "it is vain," and of that thought, "it is acceptable"; of this thought, "it is selfish," and of that thought, "it is Christlike." It is a judge of the thoughts of men. And the Word of God is such a discerner of the thoughts and intents of the heart that when men twist about, and wind, and wander, yet it tracks them. There is nothing so difficult to get at as a man. You may hunt a badger, and run down a fox, but you cannot get at a man—he has so many doublings and hiding places. Yet the Word of God will dig him out, and seize on him. When the Spirit of God works with the gospel, the man may dodge, and twist, but the preaching goes to his heart and conscience, and he is made to feel it, and to yield to its force.

ILLUSTRATION

The Word Sees Everything

The Word of God gets at the very marrow of our manhood; it lays bare the secret thoughts of the soul. It is "able to judge the reflections and thoughts of the heart." Have you not often, in hearing the Word, wondered how the preacher could so unveil that which you had concealed? He says the very things in the pulpit that you had uttered in your bedchamber. Yes, that is one of the marks of the Word of God, that it lays bare a man's inmost secrets; indeed, it discovers to him that which he had not even himself perceived. The Christ that is in the Word sees everything.

---

13 **to whom we must give our account** However great a revealer the Word may be, however clear a discerner of the thoughts and intents of the heart, the God who gave the Word is even more so.

We should earnestly labor to be right, for no deceptions will avail. The Lord's word lays us bare and opens up our secret selves. Oh, to be clean before the Lord! This we can never be except by faith.

14 **we have a great high priest** All that Israel had under the law we still retain; only we have the substance, of which they had only the shadow. "We have an altar from which those who serve in the tabernacle do not have the right to eat" (Heb 13:10). We have a sacrifice, which, being once offered, forever avails; we have one "greater than the temple" (Matt 12:6), and he is to us the mercy seat and the High Priest. Take it for granted that all the blessings of the law remain under the gospel. Christ has restored that which He did not take away; but He has not taken away one single possible blessing of the law. On the contrary, He has secured all to His people. I look to the Old Testament, and I see certain blessings appended to the covenant of works, and I say to myself by faith, "Those blessings are mine, for I have kept the covenant of works in the person of my Covenant Head and Surety. Every blessing that is promised to perfect obedience belongs to me, since I present to God a perfect obedience in the person of my great Representative, the Lord Jesus Christ." Every real spiritual boon that Israel had, you have as a Christian.

Not only do we read that there is a High Priest, but we read, "We *have* a high priest." It would be a small matter to us to know that such and such blessings existed; the great point is to know by faith that we personally possess them. What is the great High Priest to me unless He is mine? What is a Savior but a word to tantalize my despairing spirit, until I can say that this Savior is mine? Every blessing of the covenant is prized in proportion as it is *had*: "We have a High Priest."

who has gone through the heavens He does not forget us now that He has passed through the lower heavens into the heaven of heavens, where He reigns supreme in His Father's glory. He is still touched with a feeling of our infirmities.

Although He has left behind Him all pain, and suffering, and infirmity, He retains to the full the fellow-feeling that His life of humiliation has developed in Him.

Jesus has triumphed, He has entered into the glory on our behalf, the victory on our account rests with Him; therefore let us follow Him as closely as we can. May He help us, just now, if we are in the least dispirited or cast down, to pluck up courage, and press on our way!

Jesus the Son of God His name is *Jesus*. There is His manhood: He was born of a woman to save His people from their sins. But we read further, "Jesus, *the Son of God*." There is His deity. He is the Only-begotten of the Father: as glorious in His Godhead as He is gracious in His manhood.

let us hold fast to our confession Shall we desert Him now that He has gone into heaven to represent us now that He has fought the fight, and won the victory on our behalf, and gone up to heaven as our representative? God forbid!

15 **For we do not have a high priest who is not able to sympathize** How this ought to draw us to the Savior—that He was made like unto ourselves; that He knows our temptations by a practical experience of them; and though He was without sin, yet the same sins that are put before us by Satan were also set before Him.

with our weaknesses Does not "our" mean yours and mine? Jesus is touched with the feeling of your infirmities and mine. He is not only touched with the feeling of the heroic endurance of the martyrs, but he sympathizes with those of you who are no heroes, but can only plead, "the spirit is willing, but the flesh is weak" (Matt 26:41). While you are entreating the Lord three times to take away the thorn in the flesh He is sympathizing with you. Is it not well that it does not say, touched with the feeling of our patience, our self-denial, our valor? But "with our weaknesses"; that is, our littleness, the points in which we are not strong or happy. Our pain, our depression, our trembling, our sensitiveness; He is touched with these, though He does not fall into the sin that too often comes of them.

tempted in all things in the same way Our Lord could never have fallen the victim of temptation, but through life He was the object of it. He could never have been so tempted as that the sin of a temptation could spot his soul. Far from it. Yet remember that in the wilderness He was tempted to unbelief. The evil one said, "If you are the Son of God" (Luke 4:3). Most of us know how he can hiss that "if" into our ear. Upon our Lord that "if" fell painfully but harmlessly.

Then came the temptation to help Himself and anticipate the providence of God by selfish action: "Order that these stones become bread" (Matt 4:3). We, too, have had this rash act suggested to us. The tempter has said, "You could get out of your difficulties by doing a wrong thing—do it. It is not a very wrong thing either; indeed, it is questionable whether it might not be justifiable under the circumstances. In vain will you wait for the Lord; put out your own hand and provide for yourself. The way of faith in God is slow, and you are in pressing need." Our Lord came just there. When no bread in the house is made the background of a great temptation, remember that our Lord has undergone the counterpart of that temptation.

Next, the Lord Jesus was tempted to *presumption*. Set on the pinnacle of the temple, He heard a voice saying, "If you are the Son of God, throw yourself down from here, for it is written, 'He will command his angels concerning you, to protect you'" (Luke 4:9-10). Are you haunted by a similar suggestion to presume? Is it suggested that you quit your old standing and try the new notions, or that you speculate in business, or that you profess to understand what God has never taught you? Resist earnestly. Ah, dear friends! Your Lord knows all about this, and as He escaped that temptation, you shall do the same.

Then the fiend—how often I have wondered at him!—dared to say to Christ, "I will give to you all these things, if you will fall down and worship me" (Matt 4:9). Picture the Lord of angels, with all the royalty of heaven shining on His brow, and the black fiend daring to say, "Fall down and worship *me*." It may be that a like temptation is coming home to you: live for gold, live for fame, live for pleasure: in some form or other, worship the devil and renounce faith in God. But even though the fiend could fulfill his promise, and all the world should be ours, we are bound to resist unto the death, and we are encouraged to do so by the fact that we are upon the old ground where our Redeemer fought and conquered. He can enter into the distress that this temptation is causing you; for He has felt the same.

without sin Temptation does not necessitate sinning. It did not in the case of our Lord, for He "has been tempted in all things in the same way, without sin." And that which was possible to Him, in His life on earth, can also be made possible to you by Him with whom all things are possible. A man need not fall into avarice because he is tempted to covetousness. A man need not become unchaste because he is tempted to lewdness. Remember the case of Joseph; he was none the less pure because he was so foully tempted. A man need not be false to his convictions because someone tries to bribe him to be so; rather, he may prove the honesty and uprightness of his heart by recoiling from the very touch of the briber.

He who is tempted need not therefore sin, for that God who permits the temptation to come will, with the temptation, make a way of escape for him that he may be able to bear it (1 Cor 10:13). A man may walk in the midst of a furnace of temptation, yet not even the smell of fire shall be upon him (Dan 3:27). He may be "protected by the power of God through faith" unto salvation (1 Pet 1:5), and kept as well amid the most furious temptations as if he lived in a region that was most helpful to his graces. A child of God may be specially, peculiarly, singularly, emphatically tempted, and yet he may be preserved from sin.

16 **Therefore** It is clear from the connection of our text that the interposition of the Lord Jesus Christ is essential to acceptable prayer. As prayer will not be truly prayer without the Spirit of God, so it will not be prevailing prayer without the Son of God. He, the Great High Priest, must go within the veil for us; no, through His crucified person the veil must be entirely taken away. For, until then, we are shut out from the living God.

This glorious God-man Mediator continually presents before His Father His one great sacrifice for sin. There will never be a repetition of it, and it will never need to be offered again, "for by one offering he has perfected for all time those who are made holy" (Heb 10:14), that is, those who are set apart unto Himself. This one sacrifice He perpetually pleads before the throne, and our prayers therefore ascend to God with the merit of Christ's atoning blood giving them acceptance with His Father. So they must have power with God, for they come before Him signed, as it were, with the name of His well-beloved Son. He lays His hand upon each petition, and so leaves the print of the nails upon it, and therefore it must prevail with God.

let us approach with confidence We have a Friend at court; our Bridegroom is on the throne. He who reigns in heaven loves us better than we love ourselves. Come, then, why should we hesitate, why should we delay our approach to His throne of mercy? What is it that we want at this moment? Let us ask for it. If it is a time of need, then we see clearly from this verse that it is a time when we are permitted and encouraged to pray.

ILLUSTRATION
Praying as Children Speak

You who are parents know that you do not make your children offenders for a word. When they first learn to talk to you, they pronounce their words very imperfectly, and make many blunders. They break all the rules of grammar, and their prattle is often so indistinct that strangers who come to your house do not know what they are saying. But you know, mother; you know, father. You understand them all right, and you like to hear them talk like that. It is the natural speech for little children, and there is the accent of love in it that endears it to you.

Well, now, go to your God as your little child comes to you. Tell Him all that is in your heart. Never mind about your words; use such language as your heart dictates, and when you find that you cannot pray as you would, tell him so. Say to him, "O Lord, I cannot put my words together properly; but I ask you to take my meaning, O my Father; do not judge my prayer by my broken, faulty speech, but read the desires of my heart, and grant them if they are in accordance with your gracious will!"

the throne In prayer we come, not only to our Father's feet, but we come also to the throne of the Great Monarch of the universe. The mercy seat is a throne, and we must not forget this. He is the most holy of all kings. His throne is a great white throne, unspotted, and clear as crystal. "The heavens are not clean in his eyes" (Job 15:15), and "he charges his angels with error" (Job 4:18). And you, a sinful creature, with what lowliness should you draw nigh to Him! Familiarity there may be, but let it not be unhallowed. Boldness there should be, but let it not be impertinent.

of grace Lest the glow and brilliance of the word "throne" should be too much for mortal vision, our text now presents us with the soft, gentle radiance of that delightful word—"grace." We are called to the throne of grace, not to the throne of law. It is a throne set up on purpose for the dispensation of grace; a throne from which every utterance is an utterance of grace; the scepter that is stretched out from it is the silver scepter of grace; the decrees proclaimed from it are purposes of grace; the gifts that are scattered down its golden steps are gifts of grace; and He that sits upon the throne is grace itself. It is the throne of grace to which we approach when we pray.

That word "grace" is one of the choicest in the whole description of our great resort for prayer. We might well have trembled if we had been bidden to come to a throne of justice; we might have been afraid to come to a throne of power alone; but we need not hesitate to come to the throne of grace, where God sits on purpose to dispense grace. It would be terrible if we had to pray to a just God if He was not also a Savior; if we could only see the awful glare of Sinai without the blessed attractions of the atonement made on Calvary.

APPLICATION

The Power of the Word

If you seek to do good in this sad world, and want a powerful weapon to work with, stick to the gospel, the living gospel, the old, old gospel. There is a power in it sufficient to meet the sin and death of human nature. All the thoughts of men, use them as earnestly as you may, will be like tickling Leviathan with a straw. Nothing can get through the scales of this monster but the Word of God. This is a weapon made of sterner stuff than steel, and it will cut through coats of mail. Nothing can resist it. "Where the word of a king is, there is power." About the gospel, when spoken with the Holy Ghost sent down from heaven, there is the same omnipotence as there was in the Word of God when in the beginning He spoke to the primeval darkness saying, "Let there be light," and there was light (Gen 1:3).

Oh how we ought to prize and love the revelation of God; not only because it is full of life, but because that life is exceedingly energetic and effectual, and operates so powerfully upon the lives and hearts of men!

Let the Word of God Criticize

Since this book is meant to be a discerner or critic of the thoughts and intents of the heart, *let the book criticize us.* When you have issued a new volume from the press—which you do every day, for every day is a new treatise from the press of life—take it to this great critic, and let the Word of God judge it. If the Word of God approves you, you are approved; if the Word of God disapproves you, you are disapproved. Have friends praised you? In so doing, they may be your enemies. Have other observers abused you? They may be wrong or right, let the book decide. A man of one book—if that book is the Bible—is a *man*, for he is a man of God. Cling to the living Word, and let the gospel of your fathers, let the gospel of the martyrs, let the gospel of the Reformers, let the gospel of the blood-washed multitude before the throne of God, the gospel of our Lord Jesus Christ, be your gospel, and none but *that,* and it will save you and make you the means of saving others to the praise of God.

The Lord Jesus' Sympathy

Sympathy in sin is conspiracy in crime. We must show sympathy with sinners, but not with their sins. If, then, you dream that our Lord Jesus would have derived any gracious power to sympathize with us from Himself sinning, you greatly err. Such sympathy, had it been possible, would have been to the last degree injurious to us. Inasmuch as He had no sin, we can drink in His words of comfort without fear. His oil and wine will bring no evil to our wounds. His holy experience comforts us, and runs us into no risk. It is a blessed thing for a sinner to have the sympathies of one who never sinned. Rejoice, you people of God; rejoice in this, that the sinless One has perfect sympathy with you in your infirmities. He sympathizes all the more graciously because He is without sin.

If our Lord was thus sympathetic, let us be tender to our fellow men. Let us not restrain our tenderer feelings, but encourage them.

Love is the brightest of the graces, and most sweetly adorns the gospel. Love to the sorrowing, the suffering, the needy, is a charming flower, which grows in the garden of a renewed heart. Cultivate it! Make your love practical! Love the poor, not in word only, but in actual gifts to them! Love the sick, and help them to a cure!

Approaching the Throne with Confidence

Take heed of imagining that God's thoughts are as your thoughts, and His ways as your ways. Do not bring before God stinted petitions and narrow desires, and say, "Lord, do according to these," but, remember, as high as the heavens are higher than the earth, so His ways are higher than your ways, and His thoughts than your thoughts (Isa 55:9). Ask, therefore, after a Godlike sort; ask for great things, for you are before a great throne. Oh that we always felt this when we came before the throne of grace, for then He would do for us exceeding abundantly above what we ask or even think (Eph 3:20).

I may add that the right spirit in which to approach the throne of grace is that of *unstaggering confidence*. Who shall doubt the King? Who dares question the imperial word? With our God before us in all His glory, sitting on the throne of grace, will our hearts dare to say we mistrust Him? Shall we imagine either that He cannot, or will not, keep His promise? Banished be such blasphemous thoughts, and if they must come, let them come upon us when we are somewhere in the outskirts of His dominions, if such a place there be, but not in prayer, when we are in His immediate presence, and behold Him in all the glory of His throne of grace. There, surely, is the place for the child to trust its Father, for the loyal subject to trust his monarch; and, therefore, far from it be all wavering or suspicion. Unstaggering faith should be predominant before the mercy seat.

113

HEBREWS 5

HEBREWS
5:1–10

¹ For every high priest taken from among men is appointed on behalf of people in the things relating to God, in order that he can offer both gifts and sacrifices on behalf of sins, ² being able to deal gently with those who are ignorant and led astray, since he himself also is surrounded by weakness, ³ and because of it he is obligated to offer sacrifices for sins, as for the people, so also for himself. ⁴ And someone does not take for himself the honor, but is called by God, just as Aaron also was. ⁵ Thus also Christ did not glorify himself to become high priest, but was appointed by the one who said to him,

> "You are my Son,
>   today I have begotten you,"

⁶ just as also in another place he says,

> "You are a priest forever,
>   according to the order of Melchizedek."

⁷ In the days of his flesh he offered up both prayers and supplications, with loud crying and tears, to the one who was able to save him from death, and he was heard as a result of his reverence. ⁸ Although he was a son, he learned obedience from what he suffered, ⁹ and being perfected, he became the source of eternal salvation to all those who obey him, ¹⁰ being designated by God a high priest according to the order of Melchizedek.

EXPOSITION

1   **every high priest taken from among men** Notice that the high priests were taken from among men, not from among angels. Hence, our Lord Jesus Christ "is not concerned with angels, but he is concerned with the descendants of Abraham"

(Heb 2:16). The Jewish high priests were ordained for men; they acted on behalf of men, and they stood in the place of men. So the Lord Jesus Christ stood in the room, place, and stead of His people, that He might offer to God for them two things—gifts—that is, such offerings as the Jew made when he presented the fine flour, and oil, and other bloodless oblations that were only intended for thanksgiving. Christ offered thanksgiving unto His Father, and that offering was a sweet savor unto God. But besides those gifts, the priests offered sacrifices, and our Lord Jesus Christ did the same, for He was made a sin offering for us, though He Himself knew no sin.

2   **being able to deal gently** When the people of Israel came to them they saw that they were speaking to persons who knew and understood their weaknesses and sorrows, and not to exalted beings who would look down upon them with serene indifference. They felt that they could approach their priest without the awe that creates a freezing distance, as though a yawning crevasse opened between. And when they spoke to their friend, the minister of God, they felt that they could tell him their trials and troubles, for he had felt the same, and therefore was able to console and comfort them.

The Lord Jesus has made all His saints to be priests; we offer no sacrifice of blood, but He has made us kings and priests unto God. And we have to deal with men for God; all of us, I mean, not ministers alone, but all of you who are the Lord's own people. And it ought to be said of all of you who are kings and priests unto God that you are "able to deal gently with those who are ignorant."

But our text concerns our Lord Jesus Christ; so now let me say that I speak not merely of what ought to be, but of what is true of Him. He is a man, brother to every man. He is a man, the friend of all mankind; yes, the friend of His bitterest foe. And he is ever tender toward all the sorrows and the griefs of men. Then He is also a priest in a sense in which you and I are not, a priest above Aaron and all mere earthly priests, the great High Priest in whom all the types unite, and from whom our priesthood is derived.

ILLUSTRATION
Teaching with Patience

Some of our teachers wanted us to learn the big doctrines first, and they did not like it because we could not at once see all the sublime truths of election and predestation. Certain of the old standards who are very orthodox expect all newborn babes to eat meat at once; as soon as ever a person is converted, they would have him know all about the sublapsarian and supralapsarian schemes; and if he does not, they say, "He is a doubtful character. He is not sound."

But that is not the manner of our Lord, who is tender over us as a nurse with a child. He begins by working into our experience a few elementary truths, and then when we get farther on we find out something more, and as we are able to bear it He reveals to us His truth. He does not teach us experimentally all at once any more than He taught the apostles all at once; but by degrees he illuminates our minds.

---

with those who are ignorant As with the high priest of Israel in the olden time, among those who come to our High Priest are *many whose fear and distress arise from ignorance.* If all the ignorant were to come, we should all come, for we are all ignorant. But there are some who fancy it is otherwise with them. They imagine they know all things, and, professing themselves to be wise, they become fools (Rom 1:22). These do not know their need of the great High Priest. Their folly is proved by their light esteem of Him. But among those who come to our great High Priest in heaven, there are none but those who are ignorant.

ILLUSTRATION
We Are All Among the Ignorant

I have seen, at a railway station, gentlemen with first-class tickets walking up and down the platform unable to find a first-class carriage; and if the train was going on they have jumped in the third class so as to get to their journey's end.

If there is any man who does not think that he ought to be put down quite among the ignorant, jump in, brother, because you will get to your journey's end in this compartment; and there is no carriage, just now, for any wise person. There is nothing provided in the train that starts from this text except that which is provided for the ignorant. May the Lord help us personally to rejoice that He can have compassion on the ignorant!

---

and led astray Then there were others who tried the high priest far more even than the ignorant did. They were those who erred from the right path, those who went out of the way, and who continued to do so even after many warnings and much earnest exhortation. The true priest must have patience with people of this sort.

To be out of the way is, in the case of all men, *their natural state*. "All of us have wandered about like sheep; we each have turned to his own way" (Isa 53:6). That is where we are all by nature, and our own way is out of *the* way. Therefore, Christ can have compassion upon all of us who come to Him; for He has learned to deal with those who are out of the way; and such, literally, are we all.

since he himself also is surrounded by weakness It was, in the all-wise providence of God, ordained that the sons of Aaron should be men compassed with infirmity that they might compass others with sympathy. Men admire an iron duke for war, but who could bear an iron priest in the hour of trouble? A brazen wall is good for a defense, but we need a breast of flesh and blood for consolation. Give me for a spiritual comforter and guide, not an infallible pontiff, nor a thrice-crowned spiritual lord, but a brother of my own condition, a friend possessed of a nature like my own.

Christ was not compassed with sinful infirmity, but He was compassed with sorrowful infirmity. His were true infirmities or weaknesses; there was no evil about Him, but still He had the infirmity of misery, and He had it even to a greater extent than we have. The high priest of old was a man like those for whom he stood as a representative, and our great High Priest is like unto us, though without sin.

ILLUSTRATION
Love Will Teach You How to Speak

Nobody, I suppose, teaches the young mother how to manage her first child, and yet somehow or other it is done, because she loves it. It is wonderful to me how a widow with quite a swarm of children somehow provides for them. I cannot tell how, but the love she bears them leads her to make exertions that would seem impossible to anyone else, and the little ones are somehow or other housed and fed and clothed.

If you have love enough, you can win any man to Jesus, by God's grace. If his heart is as hard as a diamond, why then you must have a purpose twice as hard as a diamond, and you will cut him to the heart yet.

3   **he is obligated to offer sacrifices for sins** We know that, being compassed with infirmity and imperfection, the high priests first offered sacrifices on their own account, and then afterward offered them on behalf of the people. Christ, being pure and holy, needed no sacrifice for Himself; but He did offer a complete, and acceptable, and sufficient sacrifice for us.

Do not, therefore, think that He is less sympathetic with us because He had no sins; far from it. Fellowship in sin does not create true sympathy, for sin is a hardening thing. If there are two men who are guilty partners in sin, they never really help each other; they have no true heart of kindness, either of them. But when the time of difficulty comes, each man looks to his own interest. The fact that Christ is free from sin is a circumstance that does not diminish the tenderness of His sympathy with us, but rather increases it.

as for the people, so also for himself What a comfort this is to us, that we have a High Priest through whom we can come to God who is full of compassion toward us, and who, though He had no sinful infirmity about Him, was subject to the infirmities to which flesh is heir!

4   **but is called by God** Men could not constitute themselves high priests, for the appointment was made by God alone.

The high priest was taken from among men that he might be their fellow, and have a fellow-feeling with them. No angel entered into the holy place; no angel wore the white garments; no angel put on the ephod and the breastplate with the precious stones. It was a man ordained of God, who for his brothers pleaded in the presence of the Shekinah.

5   **Christ did not glorify himself to become high priest** Christ was ordained of God from all eternity to stand as the representative of His people before the throne. The Lord has "let fall on him the iniquity of us all" (Isa 53:6). From old eternity He was set apart to be the High Priest and the Redeemer of His

people. In this, can you not see grounds for resting upon Him? What God appoints it must be safe for us to accept.

You are my Son, today I have begotten you The text is quoted from Psalm 2, and it proves that Christ did not arrogate to Himself any position before God. He is God's Son, not merely because He calls Himself so, but because the Father says, "You are my Son, today have I begotten you." He did not take this honor upon Himself, but He was "called of God, as was Aaron."

6   **You are a priest forever according to the order of Melchizedek** Beloved, there is rich comfort for all believers in the fact that Christ is God's appointed and accepted High Priest. God ordained Him to do what He has done, and is doing, and will do; and therefore it is impossible but that God should accept Him and all His work.

When He came into the world the Holy Ghost bore witness to His being the Son of the Highest. At His baptism there came a voice from heaven saying, "You are my beloved Son, in whom I am well pleased" (Matt 3:17; Mark 1:11), and that same voice was thrice heard declaring the same fact. The Father has given further testimony to the mission of Christ, "by raising him from the dead" (Acts 17:31), and has caused Him to enter into the heavenly places on our behalf. Moreover, He has given Him a pledge that as Melchizedek, being both king and priest, He shall sit at His right hand until He has made His enemies His footstool (Psa 110:1). Our Lord Jesus has been chosen, ordained, and glorified as our "great high priest who has gone through the heavens" (Heb 4:14). This is the groundwork of our comfort in our Lord Jesus.

7   **in the days of his flesh** Our blessed Lord was in such a condition that He pleaded out of weakness with the God who was able to save. When our Lord was compassed with the weakness of flesh He was much in prayer. It would be an interesting exercise for the younger people to note all the times in which the Lord Jesus is said to have prayed. The occasions recorded are very numerous; but these are no doubt merely a

few specimens of a far greater number. Jesus was habitually in prayer; He was praying even when His lips did not utter a sound. His heart was always in communion with the Great Father above.

This is said to have been the case "in the days of his flesh." This term is used to distinguish His life on earth from His former estate in glory. The Son of God dwelt with the Father; but He was not then a partaker of human nature, and the eternal ages were not "the days of his flesh." Then He could not have entered into that intimate sympathy with us that He now exercises since He has been born at Bethlehem and has died at Calvary. "The days of his flesh" intend this mortal life—the days of His weakness, humiliation, labor, and suffering. It is true that He wears our nature in heaven, for He said to His disciples after His resurrection, "Touch me and see, because a ghost does not have flesh and bones as you see that I have" (Luke 24:39). But yet we should not call the period of His exaltation at the right hand of the Father "the days of his flesh." He prays still: in fact, He continually makes intercession for the transgressors; but it is in another style from that in which He prayed "in the days of his flesh."

prayers and supplications, with loud crying and tears
This is to prove His infinite sympathy with His people, and how He was compassed with infirmity. Christ prayed. How near He comes to you and to me by this praying in an agony, even to a bloody sweat, with strong crying, and with weeping! Some of you know what that means, but it did, perhaps, seem to you that Christ could not know how to pray just so; yet He did. In the days of His flesh, He not only offered up prayer, but "prayers and supplications"—many of them, of different forms, and in different shapes—and these were accompanied with "strong crying and tears." Possibly you have sometimes had a dread of death; so had your Lord—not a sinful fear of it, but that natural and perfectly innocent, yet very terrible dread that comes to a greater or less extent upon every living creature when in expectation of death. Jesus also comes very

near to us because He was not literally heard and answered. He said, "If it is possible, let this cup pass from me" (Matt 26:39). But the cup did not pass from Him. The better part of His prayer won the victory, and that was, "Nevertheless, not as I will, but as you will." You will be heard, too, if that is always the principal clause in your prayers; but you may not be heard by being delivered from the trouble. Even the prayer of faith is not always literally heard. Sometimes, instead of taking away the sickness or the death, God gives us grace so that we may profit by the sickness, or that we may triumph in the hour of death. That is better than being literally heard; but even the most believing prayer may not meet with a literal answer. He "was heard as a result of His reverence"; yet He died, and you and I, in praying for ourselves, and praying for our friends, may pray an acceptable prayer, and be heard, yet they may die, or we may die.

to the one who was able to save him from death The expression is startling; the Savior prayed to be saved. In His direst woe He prayed thoughtfully, and with a clear apprehension of the character of Him to whom He prayed. It is a great help in devotion to pray intelligently, knowing well the character of God to whom you are speaking. Jesus was about to die, and therefore the aspect under which He viewed the great Father was as "the one who was able to save him from death."

This passage may be read in two ways: it may mean that He would be saved from actually dying if it could be done consistently with the glorifying of the Father; or it may mean that He pleaded to be saved out of death, though He actually descended into it. The word may be rendered either *from* or *out of*. The Savior viewed the great Father as able to preserve Him in death from the power of death, so that He should triumph on the cross, and also as able to bring Him up again from among the dead. Remember how He said in the psalm: "You will not abandon my soul to Sheol; you will not give your faithful one to see the grave" (Psa 16:10). Jesus had faith in God concerning death, and prayed according to that faith. This brings our blessed Lord very near to us; He prayed in faith even as we do. He believed in the power of God to save Him from death, and even when cast down with fear He did not let go of His hold on God. He pleaded just as you and I should plead: impelled by fear and encouraged by faith.

and he was heard To think that it should be said of your Lord that He was heard, even as you, a poor suppliant, are heard. Yet the cup did not pass from Him, neither was the bitterness thereof in the least abated. When we are compelled to bear our thorn in the flesh and receive no other answer than: "My grace is sufficient for you" (2 Cor 12:9), let us see our fellowship with Jesus and Jesus' fellowship with us.

8 **Although he was a son** It is put as if this might have been a case where the rod of the household could have been spared. That there should be suffering for enemies, that there should be sorrow for rebels against God, is natural and proper; but one might have thought that He would have spared His own Son, and that, in His case, there would be no learning of obedience by the things that He suffered. But, according to the text, sonship did not exempt the Lord Jesus Christ from suffering.

he learned obedience Is not that a wonderful thing? As a man, our Savior had to learn. He was of a teachable spirit, and the Lord Himself instructed him. All God's children go to school, for it is written, "All your children shall be pupils of Yahweh" (Isa 54:13). The lesson is practical—we learn to obey. Our Lord took kindly to this lesson: He always did the things that pleased the Father. This is our time of schooling and discipline, and we are learning to obey, which is the highest and best lesson of all. How near this brings our Lord to us, that He should be a Son and should have to learn! We go to school to Christ and with Christ, and so we feel His fitness to be our compassionate High Priest.

from what he suffered He was always obedient, but He had to learn experimentally what obedience meant, and He could not learn it by the things that He did; He had to learn it "from what he suffered." And I believe that there are some of the most sanctified children of God who have been made so, by His grace, through the things that they have suffered. We may not all suffer alike; we may not all need the same kind of suffering; but I question whether any of us can truly learn obedience except by the things that we suffer.

God had one Son without sin, but He never had a son without suffering. We may escape the rod if we are not of the family of God, but the true-born child must not, and would not if he might, avoid that chastisement of which all such are partakers.

ILLUSTRATION

Obedience, Like Anything, Must Be Learned

Obedience has to be learned experimentally. If a man is to learn a trade thoroughly, he must be apprenticed to it. A soldier, sitting at home and reading books, will not learn the deadly art of war. He must go to the barracks, and the camp, and the field of battle if he is to win victories and become a veteran. The dry land sailor, who has never even been in a boat, would not know much about navigation, study hard as he might; he must go to sea to be a sailor.

So obedience is a trade to which a man must be apprenticed until he has learned it, for it is not to be known in any other way. Even our blessed Lord could not have fully learned obedience by the observation in others of such an obedience as He had personally to render, for there was no one from whom He could thus learn.

---

9   **and being perfected** "What," says one, "did Christ need to be made perfect?" Not in His nature, for He was always perfect in both His divine and His human nature; but perfect as a Savior, perfect as a sympathizer—above all, according to

the connection, perfect as a High Priest. "Being perfected, he became the source of eternal salvation to all those who obey him." Christ will not save those who refuse to obey Him, those who will not believe in Him. There must be an obedient faith, rendered unto Him, or else the virtue of His passion and death cannot come to us.

As a high priest He is perfect, because He has suffered to the end all that was needful to make Him like unto His brothers. He has read the book of obedience quite through. He was not spared one heavy stroke of divine discipline. You and I never go to the end of grief. We are spared the utmost depth; but not so our Lord. The Lord sets us a service proportioned to our strength; but what a service was exacted of the Son of God! Ours is a lightened burden; but the Well-Beloved was not spared the last ounce of crushing sorrow. "For it was fitting for him for whom are all things and through whom are all things in bringing many sons to glory to perfect the originator of their salvation through sufferings" (Heb 2:10).

ILLUSTRATION

Jesus Is Our Ship's Pilot

If you were on board a vessel, and had lost your bearings, you would be glad enough to see a pilot. Here he is on board, and you say, "Pilot, do you know where we are?" "Yes," says he, "of course I do. I can tell you within a yard." "It is well, Mr. Pilot, but can you bring us to the port we want to make?" "Certainly," says he. "Do you know the coast?" "Coast, sir! I know every bit of headland, and rock, and quicksand, as well as I know the cut of my face in a looking-glass. I have passed over every inch of it in all tides and all weathers. I am a child at home here." "But, pilot, do you know that treacherous shoal?" "Yes, and I remember almost running aground upon it once, but we escaped just in time. I know all those sands as well as if they were my own children."

You feel perfectly safe in such hands. Such is the qualification of Christ to pilot sinners to heaven. There is not a bay or a creek or a rock or a sand between the Maelstrom of hell and the Fair Havens of heaven but what Christ has sounded all the deeps and the shallows, measured the force of the current, and seen the set of the stream. He knows how to steer so as to bring the ship right away by the best course into the heavenly harbor.

---

he became the source He is the designer, creator, worker, and cause of salvation. By Him salvation has been accomplished: "His right hand and His holy arm have secured His victory" (Psa 98:1); "He has trodden the wine press alone, and of the people there was none with him." He is the author of salvation in this sense: that every blessing comes through Him. All the various departments of salvation, whether they be election, calling, justification, or sanctification, all bless us through Him, according as the Father has chosen us in Him from before the foundation of the world. In Him we are called, in Him preserved, in Him accepted; all grace flows from Him. Christ is all, and in all. Salvation within us is all His work.

ILLUSTRATION
Jesus the Sole Author of the Book of Salvation

Let me compare salvation to a book, of which Jesus is the sole author. No one has contributed a line or a thought thereto. He has never asked any human mind to write a preface to His work; the first word is from His pen. Some of you are trying to preface Christ's work, but your toil is fruitless; He will never bind up your wretched introduction with His golden lines of love. Come to Him without a preface, just as you are.

---

of eternal salvation When the Jewish high priest had offered a sacrifice, the worshiper went home satisfied, for the blood was sprinkled and the offering accepted. But in a short time he sinned again, and he had to bring another sacrifice. Once a year, when the high priest entered within the veil and came out and pronounced a blessing on the people, all Israel went home glad; but next year there must be the same remembrance of sin, and the same sprinkling with blood, for the blood of bulls and of goats could not really put away sin. It was only a type. How blessed is the truth that our Lord Jesus will not need to bring another sacrifice at any time, for He has obtained eternal salvation through His one offering.

Jesus does not save us today, and leave us to perish tomorrow. He knows what is in man, and so He has prepared nothing less than eternal salvation for man. A salvation that was not eternal would turn out to be no salvation at all. Those whom Jesus saved are saved indeed. Man can be the author of temporary salvation; but only He who is "a high priest forever" can bring in a salvation that endures forever.

to all those who obey him Not to some few, not to a little select company here and there, but "to all those who obey him." To obey Christ is in its very essence to trust Him, or believe in Him; and we might read our text as if it said, "The author of eternal salvation to all those who believe in him." If you would be saved, your first act of obedience must be to trust Jesus wholly, simply, heartily, and alone. Recline your soul wholly on Jesus and you are saved now. Is that all? Certainly, that is all! But it says "*obey*"? Precisely so; and do you not know that every man who trusts Christ obeys Him? The moment you put yourself into His hands you must obey Him, or you have not trusted Him.

ILLUSTRATION
Trusting the Doctor Means Obeying

The doctor feels your pulse. "I will send you some medicine," says he, "that will be very useful, and besides that, you must take a warm bath." He comes the next day; you say to him, "Doctor, I thought you were going to heal me. I am not a bit better." "Why," said he, "you do not trust me." "I do, sir; I am sure I have every faith in you." "No," says he, "you do not believe in me, for there is that bottle of medicine untouched; you have not taken a drop of it. Have you had the bath?" "No, sir." "Well, you are making a fool of me; the fact is I shall not come again. You do not believe in me. I am no physician to you."

Every man who believes Christ obeys Him; believing and obeying always go side by side.

10   **according to the order of Melchizedek** It is a glorious mark of our Lord Jesus that He was "called of God a High Priest." He did not assume this office to Himself, but this high honor was laid upon Him by God Himself.

Then the apostle appeared to be going on to enlarge upon the Melchizedek priesthood, but he stopped. Perhaps he recollected what his Master said to His disciples on one occasion, "I have yet many things to say unto you, but you cannot hear them now."

APPLICATION
God Will Not Disappoint His Children

The Good Shepherd will have compassion upon us, and bind up our wounds, and bear with our weaknesses and follies; therefore let us come to Him anew and trust Him more and more. Let us come to Him as He is now, enthroned in the highest heavens, and say, "Jesus, we have heard that you have compassion on the ignorant and those that are out of the way, and such are we. Behold, we trust ourselves with you." Trembling believer, do not be slow to draw near, for His loving heart is unable to refuse you. If you will trust yourselves with the Savior, He cannot betray or deceive your trust. Only do that and your faith will have power over the sacred heart of the Crucified One. You know if a child trusts you—if it is only to buy a penny toy—you do not like to go home without doing it. Men, if your little daughter trusted father to buy her something, you would not like to disappoint her. Well, and God, our blessed Savior, cannot and will not disappoint His trustful children.

People Will Not Follow a Leader Who Lacks Compassion

Men will not long remain with an unloving leader: Even little children in our classes will not long listen to an unsympathetic teacher. Great armies of soldiers must be led by a great soldier, and children must be held in hand by childlike instructors. When human beings surround an uncompassionate personage they soon find it out, and fly off at a tangent as if by instinct. You may collect people for a time by some extraneous means, but unless they perceive that you love them, and that your heart goes out with desires for their good, they will soon weary of you. The multitude still clung to the skirts of Jesus, even to the last, whenever he preached, because they saw that He really desired their good. You, dear friend, must have compassion if you are to keep up the attention of those whom you address. The earth is held together by the force of attraction, and to the men upon it that same power is exercised by love and compassion.

Weakness Is Our Blessing

If you have not had a certain experience, you cannot so well help others who have; but if you were compassed with infirmity in your first coming to Christ, you may use that in helping others to come to Him. *Our grievous temptations* may be infirmities that shall be largely used in our service. "What a blessing it would be to live without temptations!" says one. I do not believe it would be a blessing at all. I think that, being without temptation is more of a temptation than having a temptation. There is no devil that is equal to no devil, for when there seems to be none, we get so very quiet and so very easy, and think that everything is going on well, when it is not. Be glad if you have been tempted.

Our sickness may turn out to be in the same category. Of course we would like to be always well. I think that health is the greatest blessing that God ever sends us, except sickness, which is far better. I would give anything to be perfectly healthy; but if I had to go over my time again, I could not get on without those sick beds and those bitter pains, and those weary, sleepless nights. Oh, the blessedness that comes to us through smarting, if we are ministers and helpers of others, and teachers of the people! I do not say that too much of it is to be desired, but the Lord knows how much is too much, and He will never afflict us beyond what He will enable us to bear. But just a touch of sickness now and then may help you mightily.

Our trials, too, may thus be sanctified. He that has had no troubles, and no trials, what mistakes he makes! He is like the French lady in the time of famine, who said that she had no patience with the poor people starving because of the price of bread. You could always buy a penny bun for a penny, she said; and therefore she thought there need not be any poverty at all. She was one of the rich ones of the earth. I do not suppose that she had ever had a penny bun in her life, or a penny either. Ah, dear friends! You must, if you are ready to help others, be yourself compassed with infirmity.

Our depressions may also tend to our fruitfulness. A heart bowed down with despair is a dreadful thing. "A broken spirit, who may bear it?" (Prov 18:14). But if you have never had such an experience, you will not be worth a pin as a preacher. You cannot help others who are depressed unless you have been down in the depths yourself. You cannot lift others out of despondency and depression unless you yourself sometimes need to be lifted out of such experiences. You must be compassed with this infirmity, too, at times, in order to have compassion on those in a similar case.

Our whole nature as feeble men may be turned to the noblest use if it calls forth our compassion toward others. Let us go, in all our weakness and infirmity, and try to help others who are as ignorant and as out of the way as we once were; and, God blessing us, when we are weak, we shall be strong. When we are less than nothing, the all-sufficiency of God will be all the more manifested.

Jesus Is Our Example in Praying

Those of you who are only now beginning to pray, I would encourage you to remember Jesus as setting you the example of praying. If your prayers have but few words in them, and are mainly made up of crying and tears, yet in this they are like those of your Savior, and so you may hope that they will be accepted. If you are afraid that your prayers are shut out from heaven, remember how the Savior complains in Psalm 22, "O my God, I call by day and you do not answer, and by night but I have no rest." He was heard in the end, but at the first He seemed to plead in vain. Jesus prayed under discouragements: What He did Himself He will help you to do. He knows what the agony of prayer means, and He will cast a brother's eye on you when in the bitterness of your repentance you seek the Lord. How clear it is that we have a suitable High Priest, of tender heart and loving soul!

HEBREWS
5:11-14

¹¹ Concerning this we have much to say, and it is difficult to explain, since you have become sluggish in hearing. ¹² For indeed, although you ought to be teachers by this time, you have need of someone to teach you again the beginning elements of the oracles of God, and you have need of milk, not solid food. ¹³ For everyone who partakes of milk is unacquainted with the message of righteousness, because he is an infant. ¹⁴ But solid food is for the mature, who because of practice have trained their faculties for the distinguishing of both good and evil.

EXPOSITION

11 **Concerning this we have much to say** The apostle was about to allegorize upon Melchizedek. He had intended to set forth that that venerable and priestly king was, so far as scriptural information goes, without father, without mother, without descent, having neither beginning of years nor end of life, and that he was superior to Levi, seeing that Levi's progenitor paid tithes to him and received his blessing. The apostle was about to show that Melchizedek was a type of Jesus, who, as a priest, is without father, without mother, without descent, having neither beginning of days nor end of years, but is a priest forever according to the power of an endless life. But the apostle paused, for he felt that this allegory of Melchizedek was too strong a meat for those who were not full-grown.

We have all heard, I dare say, of the divine who was foolish enough to take the three baskets full of sweet meats that were upon the head of Pharaoh's baker and to say that they represented the Trinity. I have heard of another who preached from this passage in Ezra 1:9—"twenty-nine knives"—and went to show that they were types of the 24 elders. What he did with the surplus five I don't know. Was God's Word ever meant to be a toy for the amusement of childish imagination? Surely, no. The strong meat of allegory must be for half-inspired saints like John Bunyan, and those masters in Israel who are not to be carried away upon the back of every figure, but who can ride their figures like good horsemen, with a bit in the mouth of the allegory, and make it keep in a straight road and bear them safely on to their destination.

you have become sluggish in hearing It is true of many Christians that they learn very little to any purpose, and always need to be going over the ABC's of the gospel. They never get into the classics, the deep things of God; they are afraid of the doctrine of election, and of the doctrine of the eternal covenant, and of the doctrine of the sovereignty of God, for these truths are meant for men of full age, and these poor puny babes have not cut their teeth yet. They want some softer and more childlike food. Well, it is a mercy that they are children of God; it would be better, however, for them to grow so as to become teachers of others.

12   **although you ought to be teachers** They should have become men, but they remain babes in grace. They are sadly slow in reaching the fullness of the stature of men in Christ Jesus. How many are quite unable to bear arms against the foe; for they need to be themselves guarded from the enemy!

you have need of milk, not solid food Do not be frightened, you who have lately been brought into the Lord's family. We are not going to feed you with meat yet; we shall be glad enough to serve you with milk for the present. At the same time, let us all be praying the Lord will make us grow, that we may know more, and do more, and be more what the Lord would have us to be.

13   **because he is an infant** A child is a very beautiful object, an infant is one of the loveliest sights under heaven; but if, after

20 years, your child was still an infant, it would be a dreadful trial to you. We must keep on growing till we come to the stature of men in Christ Jesus.

The babe is perfect in its measure, but it is not perfectly *perfect*. Those limbs must expand; the little hand must get a wider grasp; the trembling feet must become strong pillars for ripening manhood; the man must swell, and grow, and expand, and enlarge, and be consolidated. Now when we are born to God, we have all the parts of the advanced Christian. Faith, hope, love, patience,—they are all there, but they are all little, all in miniature, and they must all grow; and he is of full age whose faith is vigorous, whose love is inflamed, whose patience is constant, whose hope is bright, who has every grace, in full fashion.

ILLUSTRATION
The Full-Grown Christian

The full-grown man is *stronger* than the babe. His sinews are knit; his bones have become more full of solid material; they are no longer soft and cartilaginous; there is more solid matter in them.

So with the advanced Christian; he is no longer to be bent about and twisted; his bones are as iron, and his muscles as steel; he moves himself in stately paces, neither does he need any upon whom to lean. He can plough the soil, or reap the corn; deeds that were impossible to infancy are simplicities to the full-grown man.

---

14 **But solid food is for the mature** Milk you may use as you will. You cannot take too much of it; it will not do strong men any very great amount of good, but it will certainly do them no hurt. But the strong meat must always be accompanied

by a word of caution when it is placed before the uninstruct-
ed and feeble, since such are very apt to do mischief both to
themselves and to others with this strong meat.

Understand, dear friends, that there is no reference here at
all to the age of a person as to human life. The Greek word
is "Men that are perfect"; it signifies, therefore, spiritual men
who have attained to the highest degree of spiritual develop-
ment. Now this is not the result of years, for there are some
gray heads that have no more wisdom than when they first
began; and, on the other hand, there are some youthful believers who are worthy to be called fathers in Israel through the
progress that they have made in grace. Growth in grace does
not run side by side with growth in years.

because of practice have trained their faculties The soul
has senses as well as the body. Men who have had their senses exercised know how to choose between good and evil.
Now, what are these senses? Well, there are our spiritual *eyes*.
Travelers who go to Switzerland for the first time soon discover that they have not had their eyes exercised. At a distance,
young travelers scarcely know which is mountain and which
is cloud. All this is the result of not having the eyes exercised
upon such glorious objects. It is just precisely so in spiritual
things, unless Christians have their eyes exercised. The man,
the eye of whose faith has been tried with bright visions and
dark revelations, is qualified to discern between good and evil
in those great mysteries that would be too high for unexer-
cised believers.

Then there is *the ear*. We hear it said of some that they have no
ear for music. We sometimes hear it said of others that they
have an ear for music, and they can tell when people are singing half a note amiss. But there are some who cannot tell one
note from another. So is it in spiritual things, "Blessed are the
people that know the joyful sound," but many do not know the
difference between the joyful sound and that which is half a
note lower. Why, dear friends, when a Christian is well taught,

he knows when a note goes too high, and he says—"No, no, no; that jars;" or when it goes too low he says—"No, that is out of tune." Happy is he whose ear is well-tuned to discern both good and evil.

Then comes *the nose*, the intention of which sense is to smell things far away. True Christians have smelled the fragrance of Christ's fellowship. "While the king was on his couch, my nard gave its fragrance" (Song 1:12). Advanced Christians know the fragrance of heaven. The spiritual nostril that has been made to perceive the difference between the righteous and the wicked will soon be able to perceive what is true food and what is carrion.

Then there is *the taste*; and this sense needs educating too. There are many who have no taste spiritually. Give them a cup of mingle-mangle, and if it is only warm they will drink it down and say, "Oh! How delightful!" If you give them a cup, on the other hand, that is full of divine purposes, precious promises, and sure mercies of David; if you will only flavor it with a good style of oratory, they will drink that sweet potion too and relish it. The two things may contradict each other flatly, but these people have no discernment—they have not had their senses exercised. But those of you who have been made to taste the sweets of covenant grace, you, especially, who have eaten his flesh and drunk his blood, and you, too, who have been made to drink the wormwood and the gall till your mouth knows every flavor, from the bitterness of death up to the glory of immortality, you may taste the strong meat without any fear, for your senses are exercised.

Lastly, there is the sense of *touch*. Believers have been made to touch the hem of Jesus' garment. They have exercised the sense of feeling by joy, by rapture, perhaps by doubt and by fear, and their touch has become so acute, so keen, that, though their eyes were shut, as soon as they touch a doctrine they would know what was of God and what of man.

ILLUSTRATION

Trained Through Affliction

Have you never noticed how men get their senses clear through affliction? I read in the life of good Dr. Brown that when he first preached he heard two women at the door talking to one another about his sermon. One of them said to the other, "Ah! It was very well, but it was almost all tinsel." A short time after, the good preacher lost his wife. His heart was broken, and his whole nature affected; the roots went deeper down into the solid truth. And when he preached again, the same woman said to her friend, "It is all gold now."

Afflicted Christians come to know the difference between tinsel and gold.

---

for the distinguishing of both good and evil We should desire not only to be saved, and to know the elementary truths, but to be advanced scholars in Christ's school, so as to handle the deeper doctrines, and teach them to others.

APPLICATION

A Rebuke to Those Who Have Not Matured

How long have you been converted to God? How long have you known the Savior? Why, I have known some converts that have been in long clothes for 30 years after they were converted, and are babies still. If you asked them to speak for Christ, they could only say a word or two of mere babble. And as for their confession of faith, it was not a reason; they did declare the hope that was in them, but they did not give a reason for it, for they could not give one.

Then there are some who grow so slowly that their faith is just as weak now as it was 20 years ago. They go tottering along, and cannot run alone yet. They will want always to have preached to them just the simple elements, and if you give them a piece of high doctrine they have not cut their wisdom teeth yet, and therefore they cannot masticate it, much less can they get any comfort out of it. Have I not seen some who ought to have been as patient as Job by this time, as fretful as they can well be?

I must just give you a word of rebuke. It must be gently, and if you be but a babe, yet, if you have life in you, you are saved. But why should you always be a babe? Is it not that you have been too worldly? You have made money; I wish you had made an increase of grace! If you had been as diligent in prayer, if you had been as diligent for your Bible as for your ledger, how much better a Christian you might have been! Do you not see, you have been stinting yourself of food. You do not read the Scriptures, which are the food of the saints. You have stinted yourself of breath, and if a man is short of breath he will not have much to boast over. If you want to grow, you want to pray more. Surely you have attached too little importance to these things; you have not enough considered them. Why not begin to search the Scriptures? Why not try to live nearer to God? Why not pant after a greater conformity to Christ's image? Why, what a Christian you might then be!

HEBREWS 6

HEBREWS
6:1–12

¹ Therefore, leaving behind the elementary message about Christ, let us move on to maturity, not laying again a foundation of repentance from dead works and faith in God, ² teaching about baptisms and laying on of hands, and resurrection of the dead and eternal judgment. ³ And this we will do, if God permits. ⁴ For it is impossible, in the case of those who have once been enlightened, and have tasted the heavenly gift, and have become sharers of the Holy Spirit, ⁵ and have tasted the good word of God and the powers of the coming age, ⁶ and then have fallen away, to renew them again to repentance, because they are crucifying again for themselves the Son of God and holding him up to contempt. ⁷ For ground that drinks the rain that comes often upon it, and brings forth vegetation usable to those people for whose sake it is also cultivated, shares a blessing from God. ⁸ But if it produces thorns and thistles, it is worthless and close to being cursed, whose end is for burning.

⁹ But even if we are speaking in this way, dear friends, we are convinced of better things concerning you, things belonging to salvation. ¹⁰ For God is not unjust, so as to forget your work and the love that you demonstrated for his name by having served the saints and continuing to serve them. ¹¹ And we desire each one of you to demonstrate the same diligence for the full assurance of your hope until the end, ¹² in order that you may not be sluggish, but imitators of those who inherit the promises through faith and patience.

EXPOSITION

1   **let us move on to maturity** Let us go from the school to the university. Let us be done with our first spelling books and

advance into the higher classics of the kingdom. Children are to learn their letters in order that they may go on to higher branches of education, and believers are to know the elements of the faith but are then to advance to the higher attainments and endeavor to understand the deeper mysteries.

not laying again a foundation Let us make sure that the foundation is laid, but let us not have to continually lay it again. Let us go on believing and repenting, as we have done; but let us not have to begin believing and begin repenting. Let us go on to something beyond that stage of experience.

2   **and eternal judgment** Let us take these things for granted and never dispute about them anymore, but go on to still higher matters.

3   **And this we will do, if God permits** We must keep on going forward; there is no such thing in the Christian life as standing still, and we dare not turn back.

4   **For it is impossible** There are some spots in Europe that have been the scenes of frequent warfare, as for instance, the kingdom of Belgium, which might be called the battlefield of Europe. War has raged over the whole of Europe, but in some unhappy spots, battle after battle has been fought. So there is scarce a passage of Scripture that has not been disputed between the enemies of truth and the upholders of it; but this passage, with one or two others, has been the special subject of attack. This is one of the texts that have been trodden under the feet of controversy. There are opinions upon it as adverse as the poles, some asserting that it means one thing, and some declaring that it means another.

It appears to us that the apostle wished to push the disciples on. There is a tendency in the human mind to stop short of the heavenly mark. As soon as ever we have attained to the first principles of religion, have passed through baptism, and understand the resurrection of the dead, there is a tendency in us to sit still; to say, "I have passed from death unto life;

here I may take my stand and rest." Whereas the Christian life was intended not to be a sitting still, but a race, a perpetual motion. The apostle, therefore, endeavors to urge the disciples forward and make them run with diligence the heavenly race, looking unto Jesus. He tells them that it is not enough to have on a certain day passed through a glorious change—to have experienced, at a certain time, a wonderful operation of the Spirit. He teaches them it is absolutely necessary that they should have the Spirit all their lives—that they should, as long as they live, be progressing in the truth of God. In order to make them persevere, if possible, he shows them that if they do not, they must most certainly be lost; for there is no other salvation but that which God has already bestowed on them. And if that does not keep them, carry them forward, and present them spotless before God, there cannot be any other.

concerning those who If you read John Gill, John Owen, and almost all the eminent Calvinistic writers, they all assert that these persons are not Christians. They say that enough is said here to represent a man who is a Christian externally, but not enough to give the portrait of a true believer.

Now, it strikes me that they would not have said this if they had not had some doctrine to uphold; for a child, reading this passage, would say that *the persons intended by it must be Christians.* If the Holy Spirit intended to describe Christians, I do not see that He could have used more explicit terms than there are here. How can a man be said to be enlightened, and to taste of the heavenly gift, and to be made partaker of the Holy Ghost, without being a child of God? With all deference to these learned doctors, and I admire and love them all, I humbly conceive that they allowed their judgments to be a little warped when they said that; and I think I shall be able to show that none but true believers are here described.

have once been enlightened This refers to the enlightening influence of God's Spirit, poured into the soul at the time of conviction, when man is enlightened with regard to his spiritual state, shown how evil and bitter a thing it is to sin against God, and made to feel how utterly powerless he is to rise from the grave of his corruption. He is further enlightened to see that "by the works of the law no person will be declared righteous before him" (Rom 3:20), and to behold Christ on the cross as the sinner's only hope. The first work of grace is to enlighten the soul. By nature we are entirely dark; the Spirit, like a lamp, sheds light into the dark heart, revealing its corruption, displaying its sad state of destitution, and, in due time, revealing also Jesus Christ, so that in His light we may see light.

and have tasted the heavenly gift By which we understand *the heavenly gift of salvation*, including the pardon of sin, justification by the imputed righteousness of Jesus Christ, regeneration by the Holy Ghost, and all those gifts and graces that in the earlier dawn of spiritual life convey salvation. All true believers have tasted of the heavenly gift.

It is not enough for a man to be enlightened; the light may glare upon his eyeballs, and yet he may die. He must taste as well as see that the Lord is good. It is not enough to see that I am corrupt; I must *taste* that Christ is able to remove my corruption. It is not enough for me to know that He is the only Savior; I must taste of His flesh and of His blood, and have a vital union with Him. We do think that when a man has been enlightened and has had an experience of grace, he is a Christian. And whatever those great divines might hold, we cannot think that the Holy Spirit would describe an unregenerate man as having been enlightened, and as having tasted of the heavenly gift. No, if I have tasted of the heavenly gift, then that heavenly gift is mine. If I have had ever so short an experience of my Savior's love, I am one of His. If He has brought me into the green pastures, and made me taste of the still waters and the tender grass, I need not fear as to whether I am really a child of God.

and become sharers of the Holy Spirit It is a peculiar privilege to believers, after their first tasting of the heavenly gift, to be made partakers of the Holy Ghost. He is an indwelling Spirit; He dwells in the hearts and souls and minds of men; He makes this mortal flesh His home; He makes our soul His palace, and there He rests.

5   **and have tasted the good word of God** I will venture to say there are some good Christian people, who have tasted the heavenly gift who have never "tasted the good word of God." I mean by that, that they are really converted, and have tasted the heavenly gift, but have not grown so strong in grace as to know the sweetness, the richness, and fatness of the very Word that saves them. They have been saved by the Word, but they have not come yet to realize, and love, and feed upon the Word as many others have. It is one thing for God to work a work of grace in the soul; it is quite another thing for God to show us that work. It is one thing for the Word to work in us; it is another thing for us really and habitually to relish, and taste, and rejoice in that Word.

and the powers of the coming age All those powers with which the Holy Ghost endows a Christian. And what are they? Why, there is the power of faith, which commands even the heavens themselves to rain, and they rain, or stops the bottles of heaven, that they rain not. There is the power of prayer, which puts a ladder between earth and heaven, and bids angels walk up and down, to convey our wants to God, and bring down blessings from above. There is the power with which God girds His servant when he speaks by inspiration, which enables him to instruct others and lead them to Jesus. And whatever other power there may be—the power of holding communion with God, or the power of patient waiting for the Son of Man—they were possessed by these individuals. They were not simply children, but they were men. They were not merely alive, but they were endued with power. They were men whose muscles were firmly set, whose bones were strong. They had become giants in grace, and had received not only the light but the power also of the world to come. These we say, whatever may be the meaning of the text, must have been, beyond a doubt, none other than true and real Christians.

6 **and having fallen away** *There is a vast distinction between falling away and falling.* It is nowhere said in Scripture that if a man falls he cannot be renewed. On the contrary, "For seven times the righteous will fall, but he will rise" (Prov 24:16). However many times the child of God does fall, the Lord supports the righteous (Psa 37:17). Indeed, when our bones are broken, He binds up our bones again and sets us once more upon a rock.

Moreover, *to fall away is not to commit sin.* Abraham goes to Egypt; he is afraid that his wife will be taken away from him, and he says, "She is my sister." That was a sin under a temporary surprise—a sin, of which, by-and-by, he repented, and God forgave him. Now that is falling; but it is not falling away. A Christian may go astray once, and speedily return again. And though it is a sad and woeful and evil thing to be surprised into a sin, yet there is a great difference between this and the sin that would be occasioned by a total falling away from grace.

Nor can a man who commits *a sin that is not exactly a surprise* be said to fall away. I do believe that there are some Christians, who, for a period of time, have wandered into sin, and yet have not positively fallen away. There is that black case of David—a case which has puzzled thousands. Certainly, for some months David lived without making a public confession of his sin. But doubtless he had achings of heart, for grace had not ceased its work. There was a spark among the ashes that Nathan stirred up, which showed that David was not dead, or else the match that the prophet applied would not have caught light so readily. You may have wandered into sin for a time, and gone far from God; and yet you are not the character here described, concerning whom it is said that it is impossible you should be saved.

Again, falling away is not even *a giving up of profession*. I remember a case in Scripture of a man who denied his Lord and Master before his own face. You remember his name; he is an old friend of yours—our friend Simon Peter! He denied Him with oaths and curses, and said, "I do not know the man" (Matt 26:74). And yet Jesus looked on Simon. He had fallen, but he had not fallen away. Only two or three days after that, there was Peter at the tomb of his Master, running there to meet his Lord, to be one of the first to find Him risen. You may even have denied Christ by open profession, and yet if you repent there is mercy for you. Christ has not cast you away; you shall repent yet. You have not fallen away.

ILLUSTRATION
Falling, or Falling Away

I can use no better illustration than the distinction between fainting and dying. There lies a young creature; she can scarcely breathe; she cannot herself lift up her hand, and if lifted up by anyone else, it falls. She is cold and stiff; she is faint, but *not* dead. There is another one, just as cold and stiff as she is, but there is this difference—she *is* dead.

The Christian may faint, and may fall down in a faint too, and some may pick him up, and say he is dead; but he is not. If he falls, God will lift him up again. But if he falls away, God Himself cannot save him. For it is impossible, if the righteous *fall away*, "to renew them again to repentance."

But someone says, "What is falling away?" Well, there never has been a case of it yet, and therefore I cannot describe it from observation; but I will tell you what I suppose it is. To fall away would be for the Holy Spirit entirely to go out of a person; for His grace entirely to cease. Not to lie dormant, but to cease to be; for God, who has begun a good work, to leave off doing it entirely—to take His hand completely and entirely away, and say, "There! I have half saved you; now I will damn you." That is what falling away is.

to renew them again to repentance If once the real work of grace fails it cannot be commenced again; the case is hopeless forever. Hence the absolute necessity for persevering to the end. To draw back totally would be fatal.

If all the processes of grace fail in the case of any professors, what is to be done with them? If the grace of God does not enable them to overcome the world, if the blood of Christ does not purge them from sin, what more can be done? Upon this supposition, God's utmost has been tried, and has failed. Note that Paul does not say that all this could ever happen; but that, if it could, the person concerned would be like a piece of ground that brought forth nothing but thorns and briers.

they are crucifying again for themselves the Son of God Christ died, and by is death He made an atonement for His own murderers. He made an atonement for those sins that crucified Him once; but do we read that Christ will ever die for those who crucify Him twice? But the apostle tells us that if believers do fall away, they will crucify the Son of God afresh, and put Him to an open shame. Where, then, would be an atonement for that? He has died for me. Although the sins of all the world were on my shoulders, still they only crucified Him once, and that one crucifixion has taken all those sins away. But if I crucified Him again, where would I find pardon?

ILLUSTRATION
God's Warning Keeps Us from Falling

There is a deep precipice; what is the best way to keep anyone from going down there? Why, to tell him that if he did he would inevitably be dashed to pieces. In some old castle there is a deep cellar where there is a vast amount of fixed air and gas that would kill anybody who went down. What does the guide say? "If you go down you will never come up alive." Who thinks of going down? The very fact of the guide telling us what the consequences would be keeps us from it. Our friend puts away from us a cup of arsenic. He does not want us to drink it, but he says, "If you drink it, it will kill you." Does he suppose for a moment that we should drink it? No; he tells us the consequence, and he is sure we will not do it.

So God says, "My child, if you fall over this precipice you will be dashed to pieces." What does the child do? He says, "Father, keep me. Hold me up, and I shall be safe." It leads the believer to greater dependence on God, to a holy fear and caution, because he knows that if he were to fall away he could not be renewed. He stands far away from that great gulf, because he knows that if he were to fall into it there would be no salvation for him. It is calculated to excite fear, and this holy fear keeps the Christian from falling.

7-8   **produces thorns and thistles** If, after having ploughed this ground, and sown it, and after it has been watered by the dew and rain of heaven, no good harvest ever comes of it, every wise man would leave off tilling it. He would say, "My labor is all thrown away on such a plot of ground as this. Nothing more can be done with it, for after having done my utmost nothing but weeds is produced, so now it must be left to itself." You see, if it were possible for the work of grace in your souls to be of no avail, nothing more could be done for you. You have had God's utmost effort expended upon your behalf, and there remains no other method of salvation for you.

I believe that there have been some professors, such as Judas and Simon Magus, who have come very near to this condition, and others who are said, after a certain sort, to have believed, to have received the Holy Spirit in miraculous gifts, and to have been specially enlightened so as to have been able to teach others; but the work of grace did not affect their hearts, it did not renew their natures, it did not transform their spirits, and so it was impossible to renew them to repentance.

When all that is possible is done for a piece of land, and yet it bears no harvest, it must be given up. If, after all, the Holy Spirit's work in a man should prove fruitless, he must be given over to destruction; nothing else remains. Will any truly regenerated man ever come into this condition? The apostle answers this question in the next two verses.

ILLUSTRATION

Hypothetical Situations Teach Us of God's Faithfulness

Suppose you say to your little boy, "Don't you know, Tommy, if I were not to give you your dinner and your supper you would die? There is nobody else to give Tommy lunch and dinner." What then? The child does not think that you are not going to give him his lunch and dinner. He knows you will, and he is grateful to you. The chemist tells us that if there were no oxygen mixed with the air, animals would die. Do you suppose that there will be no oxygen, and therefore we shall die? No, he only teaches you the great wisdom of God in having mixed the gases in their proper proportions. One of the old astronomers says, "There is great wisdom in God, that He has put the sun exactly at a right distance—not so far away that we should be frozen to death, and not so near that we should be scorched." He says, "If the sun were a million miles nearer to us we should be scorched to death." Does the man suppose that the sun will be a million miles nearer, and, therefore, we shall be scorched to death? He says, "If the sun were a million miles farther off we should be frozen to death." Does he mean that the sun will be a million miles farther off, and therefore we shall be frozen to death? Not at all.

Yet it is quite a rational way of speaking, to show us how grateful we should be to God.

So says the apostle. Christian, if you should fall away, you could never be renewed unto repentance. Thank your Lord, then, that He keeps you.

---

9 **we are convinced of better things concerning you** Harsh as the apostle's words may seem, they are not meant for you who are really believers in Christ, and in whom the Holy Spirit has wrought a complete change of heart and life.

and belonging to salvation Our faith does not cause salvation, nor our hope, nor our love, nor our good works; they are things that attend it as its guard of honor. The origin of salvation lies alone in the sovereign will of God the Father, in the infinite efficacy of the blood of Jesus—God the Son, and in the divine influence of God the Holy Spirit.

10 **the love that you demonstrated for his name** If you have proved by your works that the grace of God is within you, God will not forget you. He will not leave you; He will not cast you away. You know the contrast in the speech between different persons concerning this doctrine. One will wickedly say, "If I am a child of God, I may live as I like." That is damnable doctrine. Another will say, "If I am a child of God, I shall not want to live as I like, but as God likes, and I shall be led by the grace of God into the path of holiness, and through divine grace I shall persevere in that way of holiness right to the end." That is quite another doctrine, and it is the true teaching of the Word of God.

11 **demonstrate the same diligence** How peremptory are the words of Christ in John 10:28-29, "I give them eternal life"—not temporal life, which may die—"and they will never perish forever, and no one will seize them out of my hand. My Father, who has given them to me, is greater than all, and no one can

seize them out of the Father's hand." The apostle tells us, in Romans 11:29, that "the gifts and calling of God are irrevocable"; that is, whatever gifts the Lord gives, He never repents of having given them so as to take them back again. And whatever calling He makes of any man, He never retracts it, but He stands to it still. There is no playing fast and loose in divine mercy; His gifts and calling are without repentance.

Keep it up; be as earnest today as you were 20 years ago, when you were baptized and joined the church: "Demonstrate the same diligence unto the end." Still, "work out your own salvation with fear and trembling. For the one at work in you, both to will and to work for his good pleasure, is God" (Phil 2:12).

12   **but imitators of those who inherit the promises** You and I also are patiently to endure, to hold on even to the end, and God's sure promise will never fail us. Those promises we shall inherit most surely, for we shall by grace be enabled to remain faithful until death.

APPLICATION

Hold On, and Trust Christ

There is a cup of sin that would damn your soul, O Christian. What grace is that which holds your arm, and will not let you drink it? There you are, at this hour, like the bird catcher of St. Kilda. You are being drawn to heaven by a single rope; if that hand that holds you let you go, if that rope that grasps you do but break, you are dashed on the rocks of damnation. Lift up your heart to God, then, and bless Him that His arm is not wearied, and is never shortened that it cannot save. Lord Kenmure, when he was dying, said to Rutherford, "Man! My name is written on Christ's hand, and I see it! That is bold talk, man, but I see it!" Then, if that be the case, His hand must be severed from His body before my name can be taken from him; and if it be engraved on His heart, His heart must be rent out before they can rend my name out.

Hold on, then, and trust, believer! You have "an anchor of the soul, both firm and steadfast, and entering into the inside of the curtain" (Heb 6:19). The winds are bellowing, the tempests howling; should the cable slip, or your anchor break, you are lost. See those rocks on which myriads are driving? You are wrecked there if grace leave you. See those depths, in which the skeletons of sailors sleep? You are there, if that anchor fail you. It would be impossible to moor you again, if once that anchor broke; for there is no other anchor; other salvation there can be none, and if that one fails you, it is impossible that you should ever be saved. Therefore thank God that you have an anchor that cannot fail.

HEBREWS
6:13–20

¹³ For when God made a promise to Abraham, since he had no one greater to swear by, he swore by himself, ¹⁴ saying, "Surely I will greatly bless you, and I will greatly multiply you." ¹⁵ And so, by persevering, he obtained the promise. ¹⁶ For people swear by what is greater than themselves, and the oath for confirmation is the end of all dispute for them. ¹⁷ In the same way God, because he wanted to show even more to the heirs of the promise the unchangeableness of his resolve, guaranteed it with an oath, ¹⁸ in order that through two unchangeable things, in which it is impossible for God to lie, we who have taken refuge may have powerful encouragement to hold fast to the hope set before us. ¹⁹ We have this hope like an anchor of the soul, both firm and steadfast, and one that enters into the inside of the curtain, ²⁰ where Jesus entered as forerunner for us, having become a high priest forever according to the order of Melchizedek.

EXPOSITION

13 **For when God made a promise to Abraham** The Lord's transactions with the patriarch Abraham are frequently used in Scripture as types of His dealings with all the heirs of promise. The Lord found him in an idolatrous household, even as He finds all His people far off from Him and strangers to Him. But the Lord separated him by an effectual call, and brought him out from his country and from his father's house, even as He does unto all His people when He visits them in mercy, and says, "Come out from their midst, and be separate, and do not touch what is unclean" (2 Cor 6:17). The Lord, then, was pleased to give to His servant a very gracious promise, the like of which, only yet more clear and bright, He is pleased to

give to every heir of salvation. And after a while, that the patriarch's faith in the midst of his increasing trials might come to a fullness of strength, the Lord was pleased to make a covenant with him, and to confirm that covenant by sacrifice of blood and by solemn oath.

since he had no one greater to swear by, he swore by himself He then who is a believer is certified by the oath of God that in blessing He will bless him. This is sure to all believers, and sure to me and to you if we are believers. As believers, we flee away from ourselves and the covenant of works to the sure covenant of unchanging grace. And our consolation is strong, because God is true.

We see clearly that the Lord does not desire us to be in an unsettled condition, but would put an end to all uncertainty and questioning. As among men a fact is established when an honest man has sworn to it, so "God, because he wanted to show even more to the heirs of the promise the unchangeableness of his resolve, guaranteed it with an oath" (Heb 6:17). Condescending to the weakness of human faith, He Himself swears to what He declares, and thus gives us a gospel doubly certified by the promise and oath of the everlasting God. Surely angels must have wondered when God lifted His hand to heaven to swear to what He had promised, and must have concluded that thenceforth there would be an end of all strife, because of the confirmation that the Lord thus gave to His covenant.

14 **Surely I will greatly bless you, and I will greatly multiply you** His hands are branded with the names of His beloved, and it is not possible that He can forget them. The Lord has a loving memory. He cannot forget His own. Think of words like these—"I remember concerning you the loyal love of your childhood, the love of your betrothal-time" (Jer 2:2); "Israel, you will not be forgotten by me" (Isa 44:21); "For Yahweh your God is a compassionate God; He will not abandon you" (Deut 4:31).

Every blessing that in that covenant was guaranteed to the chosen seed was by the precious blood made eternally secure to that seed. Oh, how I delight to speak about the sureness of that covenant! How the dying David rolled that under his tongue as a sweet morsel! "Yet not so is my house with God"— there was the bitter in his mouth; "for," said he—and there came in the honey—"he has made an everlasting covenant for me, arranging everything. He has secured all my deliverance" (2 Sam 23:5). And this sureness, mark you, lies in the blood; it is the blood of Christ that makes all things secure, for all the promises of God are indeed and amen in Christ Jesus, to the glory of God by us.

15 **he obtained the promise** Here was a faithful God and faithful Abraham bound in an immovable covenant. God trusted Abraham, for He said, "I have chosen him, that he will command his children and his household after him that they will keep the way of Yahweh" (Gen 18:19). And Abraham knew his God, and trusted Him without suspicion; and thus there was firm friendship between them.

16 **For people swear by what is greater than themselves** The Father pledged His honor and His word. He did more; He pledged his oath. He pledged His own word and sacred honor of Godhead that He would be true to His Son, that He should see His seed, and that by the knowledge of Him, Christ should "declare many righteous" (Isa 53:11).

But there was needed a seal to the covenant, and what was that? Jesus Christ in the fullness of time set the seal to the covenant, to make it valid and secure, by pouring out His life's blood to make the covenant effectual once for all. If there be an agreement made between two men, the one to sell an estate, and the other to pay for it, the covenant does not hold good until the payment is made. Now, Jesus Christ's blood was the payment of His part of the covenant; and when He shed it, the covenant stood firm as the everlasting hills, and the throne of God Himself is not more sure than is the covenant of grace. And, mark you, that covenant is not sure merely in its great outlines, but sure also in all its details. Every soul whose name was in that covenant must be saved. Unless God can undeify Himself, every soul that Christ died for He will have. Every soul for which He stood as substitute and surety, He demands to have, and each of those souls He must have, for the covenant stands fast.

17 **he wanted to show even more** Even thus does He reveal Himself to us, unfolding the ancient covenant of grace that He has made with us in Christ Jesus. And He bids us look upon the solemn seal of the Savior's sacrifice, and of the oath of old that the Lord made unto His Son. As He led His servant a stranger in a strange land, but yet surrounded and enriched with innumerable mercies, even so are we sojourners with Him, as all our fathers were, but yet endowed with boundless favor in the blessings of the right hand of the Most High.

to the heirs of the promise Heirs, not according to the power of the flesh, but according to the energy of grace. Ishmael was the heir according to flesh, but he did not obtain the inheritance: "It is not the children by human descent who are children of God" (Rom 9:8). Isaac was born not through his father's or his mother's strength, for they were well stricken in years, but he was the child of promise, the fruit of divine visitation.

Then this excludes those who are heirs according to their own will, who scoff at the mighty work of grace, and believe that their own free choice has saved them! The Lord said unto Moses, "I will have mercy on whomever I have mercy, and I will have compassion on whomever I have compassion" (Rom 9:15). And Paul adds in Romans 9:16, "It does not depend on the one who wills or on the one who runs, but on God who shows mercy."

ILLUSTRATION
Heirs Must Be Sons

The servant in your house, however diligent, is not your heir; a servant claiming to be the heir would not be tolerated for a moment in a court of law. The servant may be able truthfully to say, "I have been in my master's house these many years, neither have I transgressed at any time his commandments; and all that is right for a servant to do, I have done for him from my youth up." But if he were to go on to ask, "What do I yet lack?" the reply would be, "You lack the one thing that is absolutely essential to heirship, namely, sonship."

How this truth cuts at the root of all the efforts of those who hope to win heaven by merit, or to obtain the favor of God by their own exertions! To them, God says what Jesus said to Nicodemus, "You must be born again." Birth alone can make you children, and you must be children if you are to be heirs. If you remain what you are by nature, you may strive to do what you please. But when you have dressed out the child of nature in its finest garments, it is still only the child of nature, finely dressed, but not the child of God. You must be, by a supernatural birth, allied to the living God, for, if not, all the works that you may perform will not entitle you to the possession of the inheritance of the Most High.

18   **in order that through two unchangeable things** The one is God's *promise*, a sure and stable thing indeed. We are very ready to take a good man's promise, but perhaps the good man may forget to fulfil it, or be unable to do so: neither of these things can occur with the Lord. He cannot forget and He cannot fail to do as He has said.

To this sure word is added another divine thing, namely, God's *oath*. I scarcely dare speak upon this sacred topic. God's oath, His solemn assertion, His swearing by Himself! Conceive the majesty, the awe, the certainty of this!

in which it is impossible for God to lie He has done this; He who has not twice destroyed the earth with a flood, notwithstanding all her sins; He who settled the mountains, and fixed the hills in their sockets, has said that the mountains shall depart and the hills be removed, but that His love shall not depart from us, neither shall His covenant be removed from us. He has said it whose power is equal to His truth, whose love, with golden hands, encircles both His power and His faithfulness. He has said it who never knows the shadow of a change, the sun without a parallax, and without a tropic.

The worst possible trial to a believer is to have it suggested to him that the gospel is not true, that pardon through the precious blood is a fiction, and that God is not reconciled through the atoning sacrifice. If we are absolutely certain as to the truth of God's gospel and our own salvation thereby, then all other things are of small concern to us. Therefore has the Lord fixed on a sure basis of promise and oath this cornerstone of our comfort, and set His promise in such a light that it becomes blasphemy to doubt it.

ILLUSTRATION

Our Guilt Makes Us Suspicious

Guilt is very suspicious. When you have done wrong to a man, you cannot believe him. Nothing renders you so full of doubt toward another as your own consciousness of having acted unjustly toward him.

Now, when a sense of guilt comes over the soul, nature begins to say, "Can the Lord be a sin-pardoning Lord? Can He love me as He says he does? Such a base, ungrateful rebel as I, can I really have part in so great a salvation as that which God has provided and set forth?" Knowing the suspicious nature of a guilty heart, God has made His oath and promise to be two sheet-anchors to the soul, that our faith may ride out every storm of doubt.

---

we who have taken refuge Although the original Greek does not quite so plainly refer to a refuge, yet the figure here used is undoubtedly that of the city of refuge to which the man-slayer fled when he was in danger from the avenger of blood.

Observe that fleeing for refuge implies that a man flees from his sin. He sees it and he repents of it, but he flees away to Christ the sin-bearer directly. His thoughts return gloomily to the sad memories of the past, but from all these he flies to Christ. He thinks of himself as under the law, and he soon finds that he cannot keep it, and therefore the law curses him for his failures. He will then have no consolation unless he flees away to Christ who kept the law on our behalf. In Christ is our refuge from the law, and nowhere else. When despair hovers over a man like a black cloud charged with lightning, he must run to Jesus. "How can you be justified?" says the wounded conscience: the answer must be found in Jesus. When we fly to Christ, the fulfiller of the law, despair vanishes at once, for we see that we are righteous in the righteousness of Christ and accepted in the Beloved.

The strong consolation mentioned in the text belongs to those who have fled to Christ for refuge, and surely this is the very beginning of the divine life. It belongs also to those who lay hold upon the hope of the gospel, and this also is a very elementary part of Christian experience. If you have only newly fled to Christ for refuge, and if by a childlike faith you have freshly laid hold upon the hope that is set before you, then the riches of grace are yours, and God's oath and promise are intended to afford you strong consolation.

encouragement to hold fast It seems a great change in this chapter from the sad tone at the beginning to the joyous note at the end. But, indeed, there is no contradiction between the two. Paul is but giving us two sides of the truth—both equally true—the one needful for our warning, the other admirable for our consolation. God will not leave you; He has pledged Himself by covenant to you, and He has given an oath that His covenant shall stand. Why, be of good courage, and press forward in the divine life, for your work of faith and labor of love are not in vain in the Lord; so let us "hold fast to the hope set before us."

the hope set before us We must personally lay hold on the hope. There is the hope, but we are bound to grasp it and hold it fast. As with an anchor the cable must pass through the ring, and so be bound to it, so must faith lay hold upon the hope of eternal life. The original Greek signifies "to lay hold by main force and so to hold as not to lose our hold when the greatest force would pull it from us." We must take firm hold of firm truth.

19 **like an anchor of the soul** The design of an anchor, of course, is to hold the vessel firmly to one place when winds and currents would otherwise remove it. God has given us certain truths, which are intended to hold our minds fast to truth, holiness, and perseverance—in a word, to hold us to Himself.

ILLUSTRATION
Our Glorious Anchor

The ship may not need an anchor in calm waters; when upon a broad ocean a little drifting may not be a very serious matter. But there are conditions of weather in which an anchor becomes altogether essential. When a gale is rushing toward the shore, blowing great guns, and the vessel cannot hold her course, but must surely be driven upon an iron-bound coast, then the anchor is worth its weight in gold. If the good ship cannot be anchored, there will be nothing left of her in a very short time but here and there a spar. The gallant vessel will go to pieces, and every mariner be drowned; now is the time to let down the anchor, the best bower anchor if you will, and let the good ship defy the wind.

Our God does not intend His people to be shipwrecked. Shipwrecked and lost, however, they would be if they were not held fast in the hour of temptation. If every wind of doctrine whirled you about at its will, you would soon be drifted far away from the truth as it is in Jesus, and concerning it you would make shipwreck. But you cost your Lord too dear for Him to lose you. He bought you at too great a price, and sets too great a store by you for Him to see you broken to pieces on the rocks. Therefore He has provided for you a glorious holdfast, that when Satan's temptations, your own corruptions, and the trials of the world assail you, hope may be the anchor of your soul, both sure and steadfast.

---

both firm and steadfast Notice that our hold on the anchor should be a present thing and a conscious matter, for we read, "We *have* this hope." We are conscious that we have it. We have no right to be at peace if we do not know that we have obtained a good hope through grace. May you all be able to say, "We have this hope."

entering into the inside of the curtain Sailors throw their anchors downward; we throw ours upward. Their anchor goes within the veil of the waters into the deeps of the sea; ours goes within the veil of glory, into the heights of heaven, where Jesus sits at the right hand of God.

ILLUSTRATION
Fear, but No Danger

I may say to every believer in Jesus that his condition is very like that of the landsman on board ship when the sea was rather rough. He said, "Captain, we are in great danger, are we not"? As an answer did not come, he said, "Captain, don't you see great fear?" Then the old seaman gruffly replied, "Yes, I see plenty of fear, but not a bit of danger."

It is often so with us; when the winds are out and the storms are raging there is plenty of fear, but there is no danger. We may be much tossed, but we are quite safe, for we have an anchor of the soul both sure and steadfast, which will not start.

20   **the forerunner for us** This title of Forerunner is peculiar to the passage before us. The fact that Christ is the Forerunner of His people may be found, in other words, in the Scriptures, and again and again in this letter. But it is only here that we have the exact expression that Jesus Christ within the veil has gone to be the Forerunner of His people.

The word used here means a person running before: an out-runner, a herald, a guide, one who precedes. Such terms would correctly interpret the Greek word used here. So it means, first, *one who goes before to proclaim, or to declare.* A battle has been fought, and the victory won.

ILLUSTRATION
Jesus Is the Messenger of Victory

A swift young man, out of the ranks of the victors, runs with all speed to the city, rushes through the gate, into the marketplace, and proclaims to the assembled people the welcome news: "Our country is victorious; our commander is crowned with laurels." That young man is the forerunner of the victorious host; the whole army will be back by-and-by, the conquering legions will come marching through the streets, and all eyes will gaze with admiration upon the returning heroes; but this is the first man to arrive from the field of conflict, to report the victory.

Jesus Christ was the Forerunner to report in heaven his own great victory. He did much more than that, as you well know, for He fought the fight alone, and of the people there were none with Him; but He was the first to report in heaven His own victory. On the cross He had met Satan and all the powers of darkness, and there had He fought and overcome them, and shouted the victor's cry, "It is finished" (John 19:30). Who shall report that victory in heaven? Shall some swift-winged angel, one of the many that had hovered round the cross, and wondered what it all could mean, fly like a flame of fire, and pass through the gates of pearl, and say, "He has done it"? No, Jesus must Himself be the first to proclaim His own victory, and the eternal safety of all for whom He died.

a high priest forever The most solemn warnings against apostasy, and the declaration that total apostasy would be fatal, are not inconsistent with the great truth of the safety of all true saints. Safe they are, for the covenant promise and oath guarantee their security, their hope is placed where it cannot fail, and in their name Jesus has gone to take possession of heaven. Has He gone as a forerunner of those who may after all perish on the road? God forbid. Where our Head is, there must the members be before long.

APPLICATION

You Need a Solid Gospel

Some of you people who have never known affliction, you rich people who never knew want, you healthy folks who were never ill a week, you have not half a grip of the glorious hope that the tried ones have. Much of the unbelief in the Christian Church comes out of the easy lives of professors. When you come to rough it, you need solid gospel. A hardworking hungry man cannot live on your whipped creams and your syllabubs—he must have something solid to nourish him. And so the tried man feels that he must have a gospel that is true, and he must believe it to be true, or else his soul will famish.

Now, if God promises and swears, have we not the most solid of assurances? The firmest conceivable faith is no more than the righteous due of the thrice holy and faithful God. Therefore, when greater trouble comes, believe the more firmly, and when your vessel is tossed in deeper water believe the more confidently. When the head is aching, and the heart is palpitating, when all earthly joy is fled, and when death comes near, believe the more. Grow surer and surer yet that your Father cannot lie; indeed, "Let God be true and every human being a liar" (Rom 3:4). In this way, you will obtain the strong consolation that the Lord intends you to enjoy.

The text concludes with this very sweet reflection, that though our hope is out of sight we have a friend in the unseen land where our hope has found its hold. In anxious moments a sailor might almost wish that he could go with his anchor and fix it firmly. That he cannot do, but we have a friend who has gone to see to everything for us. Our anchor is within the veil. It is where we cannot see it, but Jesus is there, and our hope is inseparably connected with His person and work. We know of a certainty that Jesus of Nazareth, after His death and burial, rose from the grave, and that 40 days afterwards, in the presence of His disciples, He went up into heaven, and a cloud received Him. We know this as a historical fact. And we also know that He rose into the heavens, as the comprehensive seed of Abraham, in whom are found all the faithful. As *He* has gone there, *we* shall surely follow, for He is the firstfruits of the full harvest.

The Real Refuge for Sinners

If you would be saved, you must be among those who have fled for refuge to lay hold upon the hope set before you. That is the real refuge for sinners—the laying hold of Christ, the getting a faith-grip of Jesus as the one atoning sacrifice, the looking to Him with tearful but believing eye, and saying, "Jesus, Son of God, I trust in you; I put myself into your hands, and leave myself there, that you may deliver me from 'the wrath to come.'"

I pray you, wherever you are, you who think you are so good, be anxious to get rid of all that fancied goodness of yours. I ask you, if you have any self-righteousness about you, to ask God to strip it off you at once. I should like you to feel as that man did who had a forged bank note and some counterfeit coin in his possession. When the policeman came to his house, he was anxious not to have any of it near him; so shake off your self-righteousness. You will be as surely damned by your righteousness, if you trust in it, as you will by your unrighteousness. Christ alone, the gift of the free grace of God—this is the gate of heaven. But all self-satisfaction, all boasting, all exaltation of yourself above your fellow men, is mischievous and ruinous, and will surely be deadly to your spirit forever.

Consolation in God, not Circumstances

What I want you to note is that *the consolation of the Christian lies wholly in his God*, because the ground of it is that God has sworn, and that God has promised. Never look, therefore, to yourselves for any consolation; it would be a vain search. Flee from yourselves, and lay hold upon the hope set before you. Christian, you lose consolation when you look away from your God. Fasten the eye of faith on Him and never let it glance elsewhere. His promise, His oath, Himself, a true and faithful God, this consideration alone can sustain you.

Remember, too, that your consolation must come *from what God has spoken* and not from His providence. Mind that you do not look to the Lord's providential dealings for your springs of joy, for He may chasten you with the rod of men, and beat you with many stripes, but His promise smiles when His providence frowns. Outward providences change, but the oath never changes; hold on to that. Your comfort must not even depend upon sensible realizations of

God's favor, nor on sweet communions and delights. No, but upon "He has said it and He has sworn it"—those are the two strong pillars upon which your comfort must rest. Not upon what you think He says to your heart, nor upon what you may believe you have felt to be applied to your own soul, but upon the bare word, promise, and oath of God without feeling or evidence to back it. God has said it and sworn it; there is your strong consolation.

Run After the Forerunner

Is He your Forerunner? Then run after him. There can be no forerunner, as I have said before, unless somebody follows. Jesus is our Forerunner, so let us be his after-runners. "Ah!" says one, "but he is so different from us." The beauty of it is that he is *not* different from us, for he was a man like ourselves. "Therefore, since the children share in blood and flesh, he also in like manner shared in these same things" (Heb 2:14). Although in Him was no sin, yet in all other respects He was just such as we are. And it cost Him as much to run as it will cost us to run; indeed, more, for His race was more arduous than ours is. "You have not yet resisted to the point of shedding your blood as you struggle against sin" (Heb 12:4); therefore "consider the one who endured such hostility by sinners against himself, so that you will not grow weary in your souls and give up" (Heb 12:3). Your road may be full of crosses, but they are not such crosses as the one He carried. You have suffered bereavements; yes, and "Jesus wept" (John 11:35). You have to endure poverty; and He had nowhere to lay His head. You are often despised, and He is still "despised and rejected by men" (Isa 53:3). You are slandered; but as they called the Master of the house Beelzebub, what wonder is it that they speak ill of those who are the members of His household?

Jesus Christ ran the very race that you have to run, and He ran it perfectly. That same power that wrought in Him to run until he entered within the veil, and so passed the goal, will help you to run till you reach the same spot. If He is your Forerunner, and He has run the race, it is essential that you should run it too, and should also win the prize. Courage; nothing is too hard for our poor manhood to accomplish through the power of the ever-blessed Spirit. As Christ has conquered, so can we. Sin's assaults can be repelled, for Christ repelled them. The Holy Ghost can lift up "poor human nature"—as we call it—into something nobler and better, transforming it into the likeness of the human nature of the Christ of God, till in that human nature purity and holiness even to perfection shall dwell.

Follow the mighty Runner who has gone before you within the veil, and the best way to follow Him is to put your feet into His footprints. It may seem as if you might get to the goal either this way or that, but the best Christian is one who does not wish for any other path than that which the Master trod. I would like—oh, that I might realize it!—to "follow the Lamb wherever he goes" (Rev 14:4); not to say, "This is not essential, and that might be dispensed with," but, like the Master Himself, to say, "In this way it is right for us to fulfill all righteousness" (Matt 3:15).

Good writing, I think, depends very much upon the little letters. If you want to read a man's letter easily at the first glance, he must write legibly, and mind his p's and q's, and all the other letters of the alphabet, especially those that are nearly alike, such as "c" and "e," or "i" and "l." O Christian, there may be very little difference, to the eye of man, between this letter and that of the believer's alphabet, but you will do best if you follow your Master exactly in all points! No hurt comes of doing that, but great hurt comes of even the least laxity. Follow closely your great Forerunner. Follow at His heels, as a dog follows his master. Just as Christ ran, so may the Holy Ghost help you to run with endurance the race set before you, "fixing [your] eyes on Jesus" (Heb 12:2).

HEBREWS 7

¹ For this Melchizedek, king of Salem, priest of the most high God, who met Abraham as he was returning from the slaughter of the kings and blessed him, ² to whom also Abraham apportioned a tenth of everything—in the first place, his name is translated "king of righteousness," and then also "king of Salem," that is, "king of peace"; ³ without father, without mother, without genealogy, having neither beginning of days nor end of life, but resembling the Son of God—he remains a priest for all time.

⁴ But see how great this man was, to whom Abraham the patriarch gave a tenth from the spoils! ⁵ And indeed those of the sons of Levi who receive the priesthood have a commandment to collect a tenth from the people according to the law, that is, from their brothers, although they are descended from Abraham. ⁶ But the one who did not trace his descent from them collected tithes from Abraham and blessed the one who had the promises. ⁷ Now without any dispute the inferior is blessed by the more prominent. ⁸ And in this case mortal men receive tithes, but in that case it is testified that he lives. ⁹ And, so to speak, even Levi, the one who receives tithes, has paid tithes through Abraham. ¹⁰ For he was still in the loins of his father when Melchizedek met him.

EXPOSITION

1   **this Melchizedek** Consider how great Melchizedek was. There is something majestic about every movement of that dimly revealed figure. His one and only appearance is thus fitly described in the book of Genesis: "And Melchizedek, the king of Salem, brought out bread and wine (He was the priest of God Most High). And he blessed him and said, 'Blessed

be Abram by God Most High, Maker of heaven and earth. And blessed be God Most High who delivered your enemies into your hand.' And he gave to him a tenth of everything" (Gen 14:18–20). We see but little of him, yet we see nothing little in him. He is here and gone, as far as the historic page is concerned, yet he is "a priest forever," (Psa 110:4) and "it is testified that he lives" (Heb 7:8). Everything about him is majestic and sublime.

king of Salem Melchizedek seems to have been, first by name, and then by place of office, doubly designated a king. First, his name is *Melekzedek*, which signifies by interpretation, "king of righteousness." His personal name is "king of righteousness." As a matter of fact, he was also the monarch of some town called Salem. It is not at all likely to have been Jerusalem, although that may have been the case. The interpretation of his official name is "king of peace."

priest of the most high God He was one who worshiped God after the primitive fashion, a believer in God such as Job was in the land of Uz, one of the world's gray fathers who had kept faithful to the Most High God. He combined in his own person the kingship and the priesthood; a conjunction by no means unusual in the first ages.

2   **first** Note well the order of these two, and the dependence of the one upon the other; for there could be no true peace that was not grounded upon righteousness; and out of righteousness, peace is sure to spring up. Righteousness is essential to peace; if it were not first, peace could not be second. If there could be a kind of peace apart from righteousness, it would be dank, dark, deadly, a horrible peace, ending in a worse misery than war itself could inflict. It is needful where an unrighteous peace exists that it should be broken up, that a better peace should be established upon a true foundation that will last forever.

his name is translated "king" Herein he is like our divine Lord, whose name and character can only come to us by interpretation. What he is and who he is and all his character, no angel's tongue could tell. No human language can ever describe to the full what Jesus is. He is King, but that is a poor word for such royalty as His. He reigns, but that word "reigns" is but a slender description of that supreme empire that He continually exercises. He is said to be King of righteousness, but that is by interpretation, by the toning down of His character to our comprehension.

"of righteousness" This Melchizedek, whom we exhibit as a type, is such a king as God is. He is according to divine model. He is priest of the Most High God, and he is like the Most High God, for the Lord Himself is, first, King of righteousness, and after that also King of peace. The great Creator entered the garden of Eden in that sorrowful hour when our parents had rebelled, and were hiding among the trees to escape His call; and He bade them answer for their fault. When they stood trembling before Him in the nakedness of their conscious guilt, they knew Him as their King and their Judge. At that moment he was not first the King of peace to them, but first the King of righteousness.

All over the world, and everywhere, this is God's way of dealing with men. Do not imagine that God will ever lay aside His righteousness for the sake of saving a sinner—that He will ever deal with men unrighteously in order that they may escape the penalty due to their transgression. He has never done so, and He never will. Glorious in holiness is He forever and ever. That blazing throne must consume iniquity; transgression cannot stand before it; there can be no exception to this rule. The Judge of all the earth must do right. Whatever things may change, the law of God cannot alter, and the character of God cannot deteriorate. High as the great mountains, deep as the abyss, eternal as His being, is the righteousness of the Most High. Peace can never come to men from the Lord God Almighty except by righteousness. The two can never be separated without the most fearful consequences. Peace without righteousness is like the smooth surface of the stream before it takes its awful Niagara plunge. If there is to be peace between God and man, God must still be a righteous God, and by some means or other the transgression of man must be *justly* put away; for God cannot wink at it or permit it to go unpunished. Salvation must first of all provide for righteousness, or peace will never lodge within its chambers. The Lord of heaven is King of righteousness first, and then King of peace, so that Melchizedek was such a king as God is.

Today our Lord and Master has gone His way up to the eternal hills where He reigns. But His kingdom, for which we daily pray, is coming; and, mark you, it will come by righteousness. I say no word against those who endeavor to bring peace to the nations by the extension of commerce, facilities for travel, and so forth; but it is not thus that the sword of war shall be broken. I never anticipate the reign of universal peace on earth till first the King of righteousness is acknowledged in every place. I do not think that we shall ever see the fruits without the tree, or the stream without the source, or peace without the enthronement of the principle of righteousness from which it springs. There shall come a day when the lion shall eat straw like the ox, and the wolf shall lie down with the lamb—when they shall hang the useless helmet in the hall, and study war no more. But that reign of the joyous King, that era of plenty, love, and joy, can only commence as a reign of righteousness. It cannot be anything else. Until sin is dethroned, till iniquity is banished, we shall not see the divine fruit of peace upon the face of the earth. Wherever Jesus is King He must be first King of righteousness, and after that King of peace.

So, then, Melchizedek is such a king as God is, and such a king as Jesus is.

and then also "king of Salem" *Salem,* which, brought down to our tongue, signifies "peace," is in reference to a place rather than a person. You see, our Lord Jesus is essentially righteousness; that is interwoven with His name and person. But He gives, bestows, deposits, pours forth peace in a place that He has chosen, and upon a people whom He has ordained, and whom He has brought near unto Himself: so that His kingdom of peace links Him with His redeemed, to whom He has given the peace of God.

that is, "king of peace" In beginning to deal with an apostate race the Lord observed the fitting order of our text: He began with righteousness, and afterward went on to peace. At the gate of the garden the dispensation of mercy and peace commenced, but first of all there was the pronouncing of the sentence that man should eat bread in the sweat of his face, and that unto dust he should return. Substantial righteousness was dealt out to the guilty, and then peace was provided for the troubled. At the fall, God first set up a judgment seat, and then quickly a mercy seat. Righteousness must ever lead the van.

3   **without father, without mother, without genealogy** We find no father or mother mentioned in the case of Melchizedek, because he did not come to the priesthood by natural descent as did the sons of Aaron. In this he is the great type of Jesus, who is not one of a line, but the sole and only priest of His order. As a priest He is "without beginning of days or end of years," neither taking the priesthood from a predecessor, nor passing it on to a successor, nor laying it down because of old age.

So mysterious is Melchizedek that many deeply taught expositors think that he was veritably an appearance of our Lord Jesus Christ. They are inclined to believe that he was not a king of some city in Canaan, as most of us suppose, but that he was a manifestation of the Son of God, such as were the angels that appeared to Abraham on the plains of Mamre, and that divine being who appeared to Joshua by Jericho, and to the three holy ones in the furnace. At any rate, you may well "consider how great this man was" when you observe how veiled in cloud is everything about his coming and going—veiled so as to impress us with the depth of the sacred meanings that were shadowed forth in him.

resembling the Son of God—he remains a priest for all time Melchizedek just passed across the page; he has no predecessor and no successor. We see him in Scripture, and we know nothing of his descent; we know nothing of his death. We only know that he was a priest of the Most High God; and this very silence about him is highly significant and instructive, for in this he is like "the Son of God—he remains a priest for all time." Now consider who this great man was, unto whom even "Abraham the patriarch gave a tenth from the spoils." If Abraham, the father of the faithful, the friend of God, paid tribute to him, how great must he have been, how high his office!

4 **But see how great this man** He was duly appointed both priest and king: king of righteousness and peace, and at the same time priest of the Most High God. It may be said of him that he sat as a priest upon his throne. He exercised the double office to the great blessedness of those who were with him; for his one act toward Abraham would seem to be typical of his whole life; he blessed him in the name of the Most High God. "See how great this man was," that he not only ruled his people with righteousness and brought them peace, but he was their representative toward God and God's representative to them.

If Melchizedek was so great, how much greater is that man whom Melchizedek represents! If the type is so wonderful, what must the Antitype be! I invite you to consider "how great" is He of whom it is written that the Lord "has sworn and he will not change his mind, 'You are a priest forever according to the manner of Melchizedek" (Psa 110:4). I will not say "Consider how great this man *was*," for there is no verb: the "was" is inserted by the translators. We are to consider "how great this man." Say "was" if you will, but read also "*is*," and "*shall be*." Consider how great this man was and is, and is to be, even the man Christ Jesus.

ILLUSTRATION

Consider Jesus as Compared to Alexander and Napoleon

Look at Alexander. He is a great conqueror, but what a pitiful creature he appears when the drunkard's bowl has maddened him. What a poor thing is Napoleon as seen in privacy! In his captivity, he was as petulant as a spoiled child.

Consider the Lord Jesus, and it does not matter where you view Him. In the wilderness He is grandly victorious over temptation; in the crowd He is greatly wise in answering those who would entrap him. Behold Him in his agony in the garden; was there ever such an Agonizer? Behold Him as the crucified; did ever a cross hold such a sufferer? When Jesus is least, He is greatest, and when He is in the direst darkness, His brightness is best revealed. In death He destroys death; in the grave He bursts the sepulcher. "See how great this man was." The field of His life is ample; do not be slow to investigate it.

to whom Abraham the patriarch gave a tenth from the spoils He met Abraham when he was returning as a conqueror from the overthrow of the robber kings; and the victorious patriarch bowed before him and gave him tithes of the best of the spoil. Without a moment's hesitation the man of God recognized the priest of God, and paid to him the tribute of a subject to the officer of a great king.

5 **the sons of Levi who receive the priesthood** In Abraham's bowing all the line of Aaronic priesthood did homage unto Melchizedek. So that all kings in Abraham, and all priests in Abraham, did homage unto this man, who as king and priest was owned to be supreme.

6   **But the one who did not trace his descent from them**
He had no predecessor in his priesthood, and he had no successor. He was not one who took a holy office and then laid it
down; but as far as the historic page of Scripture is concerned
we have no note of his quitting this mortal scene. He disap-
pears, but we read nothing of his death any more than of his
birth. His office was perpetual, and passed not from sire to
son; for he was the type of One "who has become a priest not
according to a law of physical requirement, but according to
the power of an indestructible life" (Heb 7:16).

7   **the inferior is blessed by the more prominent** This great
man yet further blessed the blessed Abraham, and the father
of the faithful was glad to receive benediction at his hands.
No small man this: no priest of second rank; but one who
overtops the sons of men by more than head and shoulders,
and acts a superior's part among the greatest of them.

Therefore, Abraham was less than Melchizedek. He could
not bless Melchizedek, but Melchizedek could bless him.
How great, then, was he! How far greater still is that Lord of
ours of whom Melchizedek was but a type!

8   **but in that case it is testified that he lives** And thus Aaron
was greater than the people, being set apart to a high and
honorable office, into which none else might intrude. He was
God's representative, and so he spoke with the authority of his
office. Today our Savior's intercession in the heavenly places
rises far higher in power and glory than that of any ordinary
intercessor. He blesses in fact, while the greatest saints on
earth and in heaven can only bless in desire.

9   **even Levi, the one who receives tithes, has paid tithes
through Abraham** Before the foundation of the world, when
there was no word concerning a priest of the house of Levi,
our Lord Jesus Christ was looked upon by God as priest and
sacrifice for men. It is not said, "You will be a priest," but "You,
a priest forever." The verb is left out, but the word "are," in the
present tense, is correctly enough supplied by the translators.

"You are a priest forever according to the order of Melchizedek" (Psa 110:4). He was a priest before Aaron and his sons were born or thought of. Moreover, consider that the decree registered by the psalmist in Psalm 110 was published by revelation hundreds of years after the law had been given, so that it was not an old decree invalidated by the law of Moses, but a newly published decree that would overrule in due time that which had gone before.

Even while the law was in its prime, and the priest wore the Urim and the Thummim, there was a note struck in the Psalms of David that intimated the ending of it all, because there was another priest, not of the house of Aaron, who surpassed all of them, being made a priest by oath, even while they were priests without an oath. Whatever priesthood there may have been of God's ordaining under the Old Testament, it was evidently all subordinate to the superior Melchizedek-priesthood of Jesus Christ our Savior, and was predestinated to give place to it.

10 **For he was still in the loins of his father** Thus the old priesthood, the Levitical and Aaronic priesthood, did homage unto the Melchizedek priesthood, which is greater still.

ILLUSTRATION

In Christ, as Levi Was in Abraham

As Abraham was less than Melchizedek, for without doubt the less is blessed of the greater, so also Levi was less than Melchizedek, for he was in the loins of Abraham when Melchizedek met him. As Levi was in the loins of Abraham and paid tithes to Melchizedek, so we were in the loins of Christ and paid the debt due to divine justice, gave to the law its fulfilment, and to wrath its satisfaction.

In the loins of Christ we have passed through the tomb already, and have entered into that which is within the veil, and are made to sit down in heavenly places, even in Him. This day the chosen of God are one with Christ and in the loins of Christ.

APPLICATION

Repent of Sin to Gain Peace with God

If you would have peace with God, you must repent of sin. If you love evil, you cannot love God. There must be a divorce between you and sin, or there can be no marriage between you and Christ. When Jesus comes to a soul, He comes as King of righteousness first, and after that as King of peace. We must have a positive righteousness of life, a cleanness of heart and hand, or we shall not be found at the right hand of the Judge. Let no man deceive himself. "Whatever a person sows, this he will also reap" (Gal 6:7). He that comes to Christ, and takes Christ to be his Savior, must take Christ also to be his Ruler. And, Christ ruling him, there must be in that man's heart an active, energetic pursuit of everything that is good and holy, for without holiness "no one will see the Lord" (Heb 12:14). He that lives in sin is dead while he lives, and knows nothing of the life of God in his soul. Righteousness must hold the scepter, or peace will not attend the court.

Will you give up your sin? For Christ has come to save His people from their sins. If you do not wish to be saved from sinning, you will never be saved from damning. Christ cannot save you while sin is loved and followed after, and has a reigning power in you; for it is an essential of His salvation that He should deliver you from the mastery of evil. But if you say, "I will live in sin, and yet go to heaven," you will never do so. There shall by no means enter into the celestial city anything that defiles. He that takes men to heaven is first King of righteousness, and after that He is King of peace.

No Peace with Unrighteousness

We must so hold and love the truth as to hate every false way; for the way of error is ruinous to the souls of men, and it will go hard with us if even by our silence we lead men to run in it. If any man shall say to you, "Come and let us sin together," reply to him, "I cannot enter into association with you, for I must first be pure and then peaceable, since I serve a Lord who is first King of righteousness, and after that King of peace." "Hold your tongue," says the world. "Do not fight against error. Why do you need to speak so loudly against a wrong thing?" We must speak, and speak sharply too, for souls are in danger. We must lift up the banner of truth, or we shall be meanest of all cowards. God has made us kings, and we must be first kings of righteousness, and after that kings of peace.

God's people are tempted sometimes to be a little too peaceable. Remember that our Lord Jesus has not come to make us live at peace with sin. He has come to set a man against his brother—to divide a household where iniquity holds sway. There can be no peace between the child of God and wrongdoing or wrong thinking of any kind. We must have "war to the knife" with that which would rob God of His glory and men of their salvation. Our peace is on the footing of righteousness, and on no other ground. We are for all that is good and right; but we dare not cry "Peace, peace," where there is no peace (Jer 6:14; 8:11).

Consider the Greatness of Christ

There is an exceeding great reward for any man who will "see how great this man was" (Heb 7:4). I find for myself that the only possibility of my living is living in Christ and unto Christ. Here is a rock beneath my feet: "God was in Christ reconciling the world to himself, not counting their trespasses against them" (2 Cor 5:19). Certain great facts concerning God and His Christ have been made known to us by the Holy Ghost, and these are infallibly sure. God's revelation is true, whatever man's dreams may be. On the basis of revelation there is a foothold. A personal knowledge of Christ revealed by the Spirit is also a sure matter. I get to Jesus, I speak to Him, and meditate upon Him, and He rises before me greater than ever, till in His presence all the learning of men condenses into folly. He is "God only wise." Ah, then I live when He is all in all! My heart is glad and my glory rejoices when I forget all else save Christ Jesus my Lord. Therefore, I say that you shall find a great reward in full often coming near to your Lord, and considering again and again how great He is.

You must carefully consider, or you will miss the blessing. It will not be enough for you to hear or read; you must do your own thinking, and consider your Lord for yourselves. You may even read the Bible itself without profit if you do not *consider* as well as read. The wine is not made by gathering the clusters, but by treading the grapes in the wine vat. Under pressure the red juice leaps forth. Not the truth as you read it, but the truth as you meditate upon it, will be a blessing to you. "Read, mark, learn, and inwardly digest." "See how great this man was." Shut yourselves up with Jesus, if you would know Him. "Go, my people, enter into your chambers and shut your doors behind you; hide for a very little while, until the wrath has passed over" (Isa 26:20). Shelter in Christ there, and the more you consider Him the greater your peace will be. Come and lay your finger into the prints of the nails, and thrust your hand into His side. Commune with the personal Christ, who ever lives; and evermore "see how great this man was."

¹¹ Thus if perfection was through the Levitical priesthood, for on the basis of it the people received the law, what further need is there for another priest to arise according to the order of Melchizedek and not said to be according to the order of Aaron? ¹² For when the priesthood changes, of necessity there is a change of the law also. ¹³ For the one about whom these things are spoken belongs to another tribe from which no one has officiated at the altar. ¹⁴ For it is evident that our Lord is a descendant of Judah, a tribe with reference to which Moses said nothing concerning priests. ¹⁵ And it is still more clear if another priest according to the likeness of Melchizedek arises, ¹⁶ who has become [a priest] not according to a law of physical requirement, but according to the power of an indestructible life. ¹⁷ For it is testified,

> "You are a priest forever
> according to the order of Melchizedek."

¹⁸ For on the one hand a preceding commandment is set aside because of its weakness and uselessness ¹⁹ (for the law made nothing perfect), but on the other hand there is the introduction of a better hope through which we draw near to God. ²⁰ And inasmuch as this was not without an oath (for these on the one hand have become priests without an oath, ²¹ but he with an oath by the one who said to him,

> "The Lord has sworn and will not change his mind,
> 'You are a priest forever' "),

²² by so much more Jesus has become the guarantee of a better covenant.

²³ And indeed many have become priests, because they were prevented by death from continuing in office, ²⁴ but he, because he continues forever, holds the priesthood permanently.

²⁵ Therefore also he is able to save completely those who draw near to God through him, because he always lives in order to intercede on their behalf.

²⁶ For a high priest such as this indeed is fitting for us: holy, innocent, undefiled, separated from sinners, and having become exalted above the heavens, ²⁷ who does not need every day, like the former high priests, to offer up sacrifices for his own sins and then for the sins of the people, because he did this once for all when he offered up himself. ²⁸ For the law appoints men as high priests who have weakness, but the statement of the oath, after the law, appoints a Son, who is made perfect forever.

EXPOSITION

11 **not said to be according to the order of Aaron** The priesthood of Aaron and his successors was intended to be temporary. God did not confirm the priests of old in their offices, because He held in reserve the right to set them aside when He pleased. From the first He intended that their functions should be abolished when the fullness of time should come for another and better priest to take their place. They were candles for the darkness, but the sun was to rise, and then they would not be needed. They were pictorial representations, but when the substance was come they would not be required. He allowed their priesthood to be one of imperfect men, because He intended by-and-by to supersede it by a perfect and enduring priesthood; hence no oath of God attended the ordination of the sons of Aaron.

12 **For when the priesthood changes** The law of the priesthood alters since the person of the priest, the character of the priest, and the very office of the priest had altered too.

13 **another tribe from which no one has officiated at the altar** According to the belief of the Jewish people, the Messiah was to come of the tribe of Judah, yet none of the house of

David or of the tribe of Judah ever presumed to present themselves as priests of the order of God.

14   **our Lord is a descendant of Judah** Therefore our Lord did not receive the priesthood by descent, but, like Melchizedek, his ordination was direct from God.

15   **another priest according to the likeness of Melchizedek** He is the Son of the Highest, as other priests were not. They were men that had infirmity, but He is sinless: they lived and died, and so were changed, but "your throne, O God, is forever and ever" (Psa 45:6). They were ordained to be types and emblems, serving for the time of Israel's infancy, but He came as the "I am," the substance of the whole. They were mere men and nothing more, but Jesus counted it not robbery to be equal with God, though for our sakes He assumed our nature.

16   **a priest not according to a law of physical requirement** Our Lord sprang out of Judah, of which tribe nothing is said concerning the priesthood, that it might be clear that His priesthood is "not according to a law of physical requirement, but according to the power of an indestructible life" (Heb 7:16). Yet he comes of Judah's royal tribe; for He is King.

Further on we find our blessed Lord described as better than Aaron, while His blood is mentioned as speaking better things than that of Abel (Heb 12:24). And He is declared to be the surety of a better covenant, of which it is said that it is established upon better promises.

17   **a priest forever** Christ is never to be changed or superseded. He is a priest *forever*. As we read nothing of Melchizedek's having given up the priesthood, so depend upon it Christ never will lay down His office while there remains a single man to be saved. "Once a priest always a priest" is true of the Lord Jesus Christ, though true of nobody else. Once was He ordained, and none can put Him from His priesthood: as once the Father set Him upon the hill of Zion as King, and the kings of the earth cannot dash Him from His throne.

according to the order of Melchizedek This proves that the priests of the order of Levi were not sufficient: there was need of a still greater priesthood. This is the inspired testimony of David in Psalm 110, where he speaks of the Lord Jesus as his Lord, and salutes Him as king and priest.

The Lord Jesus Christ was ordained to the priesthood, according to Psalm 110, in a manner distinct from all others. His ordination was unique, for neither Aaron, nor his sons, nor any of the priests of the tribe of Levi were ever ordained by an oath. Ceremonies most important, imposing, instructive, and impressive were performed, but there was no oath. God gave promises to the house of Levi, but He expressly stopped short of anything like an oath to them, not because His promise can be broken, but because that promise was conditional, and must not be confirmed by an oath, as though it constituted a perpetual engagement. But our Savior is made a priest by an oath. And it is written, as if to make it exceeding sure, that the Lord "has sworn and will not change his mind" (Psa 110:4); not because God ever can or does repent, or run back from His oath in any case, but for the confirmation of our faith in the immutability of His word it is expressly added, "He will not change his mind." By an oath that stands fast forevermore Christ is made a priest forever after the order of Melchizedek.

18   **a preceding commandment is set aside** The old Levitical law is disannulled; it became weak and unprofitable. Now a higher and better dispensation is ushered in with a greater and undying priesthood.

19   **introduction of a better hope** If God had ever meant that this covenant should be temporary He would never have given His Son to bleed and die as the substance of that covenant. It cannot be that so vast an expense should be laid out upon a transient business. Moreover, Jesus lives, and as long as He lives the covenant must be regarded as a reality. It cannot possibly be that a work should be regarded as a fiction when it has been wrought out by one such as He is. The ever-living Son of

God did not die to perform a mere representation: the abiding essence of the matter is in His work, and He lives to prove that it is so.

20   **priests without an oath** The Levitical priesthood dealt only with the shadows of good things to come, and not with the very substance of the things. So to speak, the sacrificial bull was not actually a sacrifice, but the representation of the sacrifice that was to come. The morning and evening lambs did not take away sin, but only mirrored the great blood-shedding of the Lamb of God, who takes away the sin of the world. In very deed and truth, the men of the house of Aaron who attended at the visible altar were not actual priests before the real altar of the Lord, but only shadows of the truth. The real altar is the person of Christ, the real sacrifice is the death of Christ, and the real priest is Christ Himself.

21   **but he with an oath** I tremble while I speak of the oath of God; for God's lifting His hand to heaven and swearing by Himself, because He can swear by no greater, is something so solemn that one scarcely dares to think of it. The Lord will not hold him guiltless that takes His name in vain. The devout soul is full of awe at the bare thought of God in His most fatherly and ordinary acts, but how shall we think of the Lord wrapped in solemnity, resolute in purpose, stern in truth, as lifting His hand and taking an oath? Surely this is the innermost sanctuary of mystery, the holy of holies. This oath was for the honor of His dear Son as He assumed the sacred priesthood on behalf of the sons of men. The glory of His character, the dignity of His work, the certainty of its accomplishment, and the supreme excellence of His motive in entering upon it, all lift up the priesthood of Christ out of the category of all human priesthoods. Therefore the eternal Father signalizes it by a special mark of distinction, and Himself makes an oath that His only begotten Son is a priest forever after the order of Melchizedek.

ILLUSTRATION
How Much Better Is God's Oath?

An oath for confirmation among men is the end of all strife. When an honest man has sworn to it, the testimony stands in evidence and may not be questioned. When God not only gives His promise and His word, but swears to His declaration, who shall dare to doubt?

22 **Jesus has become the guarantee** We are absolutely certain that the covenant of grace will stand because the Redeemer has come into the world and has died for us. The gift of Christ is a pledge that the covenant, of which He is the substance, cannot be dissolved. Christ has been born into the world, God Himself has become incarnate. That is done and can never be undone; how can the Lord draw back after going so far? More, Christ has died: He bears in His flesh today the scars of His crucifixion. That also is done, and can never be undone.

The priests of the house of Aaron were poor sureties of the former covenant, for they could not keep it themselves. But Christ *has* kept the covenant of grace; He has fulfilled all that was conditional in it, and carried out all that was demanded on man's part. It was conditional that Christ should present a perfect righteousness and a perfect atonement; He has effected this to the full, and now there is no "if" in it. The covenant now reads as a legacy, or a will—the will of God, the New Testament of the Most High. Christ has made it so, and the very fact that there is such a person as Jesus Christ the Son of Man living, bleeding, dying, risen, reigning, is the proof that this covenant stands secure.

ILLUSTRATION
Christ Is No Mere Pattern

The first covenant was typical and shadowy. It was but a school lesson for children. Just as we give to our boys models of churches or models of ships, so was the ceremonial law a model of good things to come, but it did not contain the things themselves. Christ is no surety of a mere model or pattern of things in the heavens, but of a covenant that deals with the heavenly things themselves, with real blessings, with true boons from God.

of a better It is implied in the use of the word "better" that the ordinances of the ceremonial law were good in their place, but Jesus is better than the best of all visible things. The eternal Christ is better than the best of all the temporal arrangements that God has made for the good of people.

covenant Learned men have fought each other very earnestly over this word. Some say that it means "testament"; others answer that in the Septuagint Greek it is used as the interpretation of the Hebrew word that signifies "covenant." I feel quite sure that the combatants are both right. I am always glad when I can conscientiously take both sides in a battle. I do so in this instance, because it matters nothing which of the two conquers, though it would be a loss for either side to be defeated. The word means both testament and covenant. God's covenant of grace has had the conditional side of it so completely fulfilled that it has virtually become a "testament," or a deed of free gift, in which the one party is a donor and the other has become simply a receiver. Although the economy of grace is a covenant under one aspect, under another it is no covenant, now requiring something from each of two parties, but it has become a testament or will as to its practical result.

The first covenant was temporary: It was meant to be so. It was meant in part to teach the coming covenant, and in part to show the weakness of man and the necessity of divine grace, but it was never meant to stand. This covenant of which Christ is the surety stands forever and ever. The everlasting hills may bow, and the heavens themselves be rolled up like a worn-out vesture, but God's covenant shall stand forever and forever while Christ, its surety, lives.

23 **because they were prevented by death** A common priest served from 30 to 50 years of age, and then his work was done. Priests of the house of Aaron, who became high priests, held their office through life. Sometimes a high priest would continue in his office, therefore, for a considerable length of time, but in many cases he was cut off as other men are by premature death; hence there was priest after priest of the order of Aaron to go within the veil for the people.

Our Lord Jesus is not as Aaron, who had to be stripped of his garments on the top of Mount Hor, and to die in the mount; neither is He like to any of the sons of Aaron who in due time suffered the infirmities of age, and at last bowed their heads to inevitable death. He died once, but death has no more dominion over Him; it is witnessed of Him that He lives.

24 **he continues forever** Here is our comfort: We have only *one* priest, and He ever lives. He had no predecessor and He will have no successor, because He ever lives personally to exercise the office of high priest on our behalf. My soul reposes in the faith of His one sacrifice, offered once and no more. There is but one presenter of that one sacrifice, and never can there be another, since the One is all-sufficient, and He never dies. Jesus reads my heart, and has always read it since it began to beat: He knows my griefs and has carried my sorrows from of old, and He will bear both them and me when old age shall shrivel up my strength. When I myself shall fall asleep in death He will not die, but will be ready to receive me into His own undying blessedness.

holds the priesthood permanently I think they reckoned that there were 83 high priests in regular succession from Aaron to the death of Phineas, the last high priest at the siege of Jerusalem. One succeeded another, but this one goes on continually, forever has a nontransferable priesthood.

We know no priests on earth now, save that in a secondary sense the Lord Jesus has made all believers to be kings and priests unto God. We have now no special order of persons set apart to represent their fellows before God. Under the Mosaic dispensation there were many priests not suffered to continue by reason of death; but under the Christian dispensation we have only one priest, who continues ever in a nontransferable priesthood.

ILLUSTRATION
Jesus Is Still Not Divided from Our Nature

If some glorious spirit from on high, angel or archangel, had loved a race of ants, and had condescended for the salvation of these tiny creatures to assume their nature, and if in that nature he had died for them, you would naturally expect that at the conclusion of his labors and sufferings he would lay aside the form of his humiliation and return to the greatness of his former estate.

But our Lord Jesus Christ, whose stoop of condescension when He assumed our nature was greater than any archangel could have achieved, having taken our human nature, and having bled and died in it, continued to wear it after He had said, "It is finished," after He had risen from the dead, and after He had taken His seat at the divine right hand! He has become so wedded to us, so truly one flesh with us, that He will not be divided from us in nature.

25   **Therefore also he is able to save completely** By which we understand that *the uttermost extent of guilt* is not beyond the power of the Savior. Can anyone tell what is the uttermost amount to which a man might sin?

But there is a limit to His purpose to save. If I read the Bible rightly, there is one sin that can never be forgiven. It is the sin against the Holy Ghost. Tremble, unpardoned sinners, lest you should commit that. If I may tell you what I think the sin against the Holy Ghost is, I must say that I believe it to be different in different people; but in many persons, the sin against the Holy Ghost consists in stifling their convictions.

those who draw near to God There is no limitation here of sect or denomination. It does not say the Baptist, the Independent, or the Episcopalian that comes unto God by Jesus Christ, but it simply says *"them,"* by which I understand men of all creeds, men of all ranks, men of all classes, who do but come to Jesus Christ. They shall be saved, whatever their apparent position before men, or whatever may be the denomination to which they have linked themselves.

through him The people who are said to be saved by the great Intercessor are those who come unto God *through Him.* Certain persons talk of coming to God as Creator, and Ruler, and even as Father, but they do not think of His dear Son as their way of approach. They forget or else deny the declaration of our Lord Jesus—"No one comes to the Father except through me" (John 14:6). Yet this saying is true. There is no true way of approach to God except through Jesus Christ, the one Mediator between God and man.

Do you fancy that you will be heard and saved by the great God your Creator, apart from the merits of His Son? Let me solemnly assure you, in God's most holy name, there never was a prayer answered for salvation by God the Creator since Adam fell without Jesus Christ the Mediator.

because he always lives That Man who once died on the cross is alive; that Jesus who was buried in the tomb is alive. Jesus resembles Melchizedek in being both king and priest, in having no predecessor or successor in office, and in being greater than the Levitical priesthood. He is a priest forever by the oath of God, and we who trust in Him have this sweet consolation that our Great High Priest ever lives, is always in power, is always accessible, and always ready to perform His office on our behalf.

to intercede on their behalf The Lord Jesus Christ in His perpetual priesthood lives on purpose to be the Advocate, Defender, Patron, Mediator, and Interposer for His people. You who come to God by Him will highly esteem this constant service rendered to you by your Lord. Whereas Christ by His death provided all that was necessary for your salvation, He, by His life, applies the provision that He made in His death. He lives on purpose to see brought home to you, and enjoyed by you, all those blessed boons and privileges that He purchased upon the tree, when He died in your room and stead.

ILLUSTRATION

The Most Powerful Person Lives for Us

If some influential and powerful person should say to you, "I live to promote your interest. Wherever I go and whatever I do, whatever I seek and whatever I obtain, I live for you," it would show great friendship, and excite in us great expectations. Would it not?

Yet here is the Lord Jesus declaring that He lives for us. For us He appears in the presence of God; for us He has gone to the many mansions of the Father's house; for us He constantly intercedes with God. Oh, the deep debt of gratitude we owe to this glorious One, who having died for us, now lives for us!

---

26 **a high priest such as this indeed is fitting for us** There is no approach unto God except through the intercession of Christ. Does not this teach the grand principle of the evil of sin, and teach it in the plainest manner? The distance that sin puts between the sinner and God, and the necessity of mediation in order that a just God may commune with the imperfect—are not these fully taught by the institution of the perpetual intercession of the Son of God? This is as much a declaration of the righteousness of God as was the substitutionary death on Calvary.

27 **he did this once for all** Jesus Christ, the Son of God, came into the world, and "offered up Himself" as a sacrifice for sin. The great High Priest, who officiated on the occasion of that wondrous and unique sacrifice, was Jesus Christ Himself.

he offered up himself When He bowed His head, it was because He would do it, and willingly yielded up His soul, committing His spirit to the Father—not under constraint, but "he offered up himself." Oh, this makes the sacrifice of Christ so blessed and glorious! They dragged the bullocks and they drove the sheep to the altar; they bound the calves with cords, even with cords to the altar's horn. But not so was it with the Christ of God. None did compel Him to die; He laid down his life voluntarily, for He had power to lay it down, and to take it again.

So far as Christ was Himself alone concerned, there was no necessity that He should die. He was infinitely glorious and blessed. "He offered up himself," but not for Himself; then, for whom did He die? For men. We are told that He took not up angels, but He took up the seed of Abraham—He took up sinful men.

28 **the law appoints men as high priests who have weakness** Our High Priest is of such dignity that none can be compared with Him. He is the Son of the Highest, the equal of the Father. I want you to think of this truth, because it may help you to see how great the merit of the sacrifice must have been when

it was God Himself who "offered up himself." He was no mere delegated or elected priest, but Christ Jesus Himself, in whom "all the fullness of deity dwells bodily" (Col 2:9)—Christ, who is the brightness of His Father's glory, and the express image of His person. He it was who stood at the altar presenting "himself" to God as the one and only sacrifice for sin.

who is made perfect forever If you will not accept this Christ, there will never be another; and if you will not be saved by His redemption, you will never be redeemed at all. And there is this comfort about it—that He only died once because there is no need that He should ever die again. His one death has slain death for all who trust Him. His one bearing of sin has put their sin away forever. God now can justly forgive the believing sinner; and He may well blot out the debt when it has been paid by His Son. Well may He remit the sentence against us now that His Son has stood in our place, and borne the penalty due to our sin. God is therefore just when He justifies those for whom Christ died.

APPLICATION

Christ Must Be Our Mediator

It comes to this: that we must believe in Jesus Christ and take Him to be our priest, or be out of the covenant of grace. God will not deal with us without a Mediator, and "there is one God and one mediator between God and human beings, the man Christ Jesus" (1 Tim 2:5). Will you have Him? Will you have Him, or forever be excluded from the covenant of grace, and consequently condemned under the covenant of works, and cast away forever and ever? Will you, O unbelievers, will you despise the oath of God? I feel a solemn awe at the very mention of the oath of God. Will you give the lie to that oath? Will you say, "You have sworn to Christ that He shall be priest, but He shall never be mine"? This would be the honest expression of what your heart feels if you refuse Jesus; will you venture so to speak? Will you reject heaven's own appointed Savior, and deny the witness of the Lord? See that you do not do this, for the Lord your

God is a jealous God. And if you touch His dignity so far as to strike at His oath, what more atrocious crime can you commit? "The one who does not believe God has made him a liar, because he has not believed in the testimony that God has testified concerning his Son" (1 John 5:10). Will you refuse the ever-living Savior?

Christ Saves to the Uttermost

Christ is able to save you to the uttermost. Are you brought very low by *distress*? Have you lost house and home, friend and property? Remember, you have not come "to the uttermost" yet. Badly off as you are, you might be worse. He is able to save you; and suppose it should come to this, that you had not a rag left, nor a crust, nor a drop of water, still He would be able to save you, for "He is able to save to the uttermost." So with temptation. If you should have the sharpest *temptation* with which mortal was ever tried, He is able to save you. If you should be brought into such a predicament that the foot of the devil should be upon your neck, and the fiend should say, "Now I will make an end of you," God would be able to save you then. And in the uttermost *infirmity* should you live for many a year, till you are leaning on your staff, and tottering along your weary life, if you should outlive Methuselah, you could not live beyond the uttermost, and He would save you then. Indeed, and when your little bark is launched by *death* upon the unknown sea of eternity, He will be with you; and though thick vapors of gloomy darkness gather round you, and you cannot see into the dim future, though your thoughts tell you that you will be destroyed, yet God will be "able to save you to the uttermost."

Then, my friends, if Christ is able to save a Christian to the uttermost, do you suppose he will ever let a Christian perish? Wherever I go, I hope always to bear my hearty protest against the most accursed doctrine of a saint's falling away and perishing. There are some ministers who preach that a man may be a child of God that a man may be a child of God today, and a child of the devil tomorrow; that God may acquit a man, and yet condemn him—save him by grace, and then let him perish—suffer a man to be taken out of Christ's hands, though He has said such a thing shall never take place. How will you explain this? It certainly is no lack of power.

You must accuse Him of a want of love, and will you dare to do that? He is full of love; and since He has also the power, He will never suffer one of His people to perish. It is true, and ever shall be true, that He will save them to the very uttermost.

Our Savior Still Lives for Us

There is an almighty and divine One in heaven who ever lives for our highest benefit. Let us adore him most lovingly. This should show us how great our need is, that we always want a living Savior to interpose for us. A dying Savior was not enough; we still require every moment of our lives a living Savior engrossed with the care of our spirits, interposing on our behalf in all manner of ways, and delivering us from all evil. Our hour of necessity is ever present, for Jesus is ever guarding us, and His work is never a superfluity. Herein should lie our great comfort: we should fall back upon this truth whenever our burden presses too sorely upon our shoulders. Jesus lives: my great Redeemer lives for me: lives in all fullness of power and glory, and devotes that life, with all that pertains to it, to the preservation of my soul from every ill. Can I not rest in this? With such a keeper, why should I be afraid? Must I not be safe when One so vigilant and so vigorous devotes His life to my protection? What innumerable blessings must come to those for whom Jesus spends the strength of His endless life!

The Effects of Christ Offering Himself

It seems to me that, if God appointed Christ to be an atonement for sin, and if He is satisfied with His sacrifice, I may well be content. Surely, if my great Creditor and Judge is appeased by what His Son has offered on my behalf, it is not for me to begin to complain about it. I know how some criticize the great central truth of the atonement. I do not care how they criticize it so long as God has accepted it; and since He has also accepted me in Christ Jesus, my Lord and Savior, my soul feels perfectly content, and understands why.

And how this truth also wins the affections of men! Can you help loving the Christ who offered up Himself for you? And loving Him, do you not desire to honor and glorify Him? Do you not feel that you hate the sin that made Him die? Do you not wish to be like Him, and in everything to give Him pleasure by a life of holiness, and self-denial, and self-sacrifice? I know you do; it must be so. Because Jesus sacrificed Himself for you, you feel that you must love Him with all your heart.

That Christ offered up Himself leads us who accept it to be ready for self-sacrifice. It makes the believing person say, "As He offered himself for me, I must give myself for Him." It teaches the doctrine of the self-sacrifice of men for God, and of men for men. This is the nursery of brave spirits, and the school in which true heroes are trained. None have been bolder for the truth, and for the right, and for the advancement of the ages, and for the glory of God, than those who have enshrined the blood-red cross within their hearts, and who have been prepared for love of it even to die. O Christ of God, you who have offered yourself for us, we offer ourselves to you; accept us now!

HEBREWS 8

¹ Now this is the main point in what has been said: we have such a high priest, who sat down at the right hand of the throne of the Majesty in heaven, ² a minister of the sanctuary and of the true tabernacle, which the Lord set up, not man. ³ For every high priest is appointed in order to offer both gifts and sacrifices; therefore it was necessary for this one also to have something that he offers. ⁴ Now if he were on earth, he would not even be a priest because there are those who offer the gifts according to the law, ⁵ who serve a sketch and shadow of the heavenly things, just as Moses was warned when he was about to complete the tabernacle, for he says, "See to it that you make everything according to the pattern that was shown to you on the mountain." ⁶ But now he has attained a more excellent ministry inasmuch as he is also mediator of a better covenant, which has been enacted upon better promises. ⁷ For if that first covenant had been faultless, occasion would not have been sought for a second. ⁸ For in finding fault with them he says,

"Behold, days are coming, says the Lord,
when I will complete a new covenant
with the house of Israel
and with the house of Judah,
⁹ not like the covenant that I made with their ancestors
on the day I took hold of them by my hand
to lead them out of the land of Egypt,
because they did not continue in my covenant
and I disregarded them, says the Lord.
¹⁰ For this is the covenant that I will decree with the house
of Israel
after those days, says the Lord:
I am putting my laws in their minds

and I will write them on their hearts,
and I will be their God
and they will be my people.
¹¹ And they will not teach each one his fellow citizen
and each one his brother, saying, 'Know the Lord,'
because they will all know me,
from the least of them to the greatest.
¹² For I will be merciful toward their wrongdoings,
and I will not remember their sins any longer."

¹³ In calling it new, he has declared the former to be old. Now what is becoming obsolete and growing old is near to disappearing.

EXPOSITION

1 **we have a high priest such as this** We have all the privileges of the once-favored race. Are they the seed of Abraham? So are we, for He was the Father of the faithful, and we, having believed, have become His spiritual children. Had they an altar? We have an altar whereof they have no right to eat who serve the tabernacle. Had they any high priest? We have a high priest—we have one who has entered into the heavenly. Had they a sacrifice and paschal supper? We have Christ Jesus, who, by His one offering, has forever put away our sin, and who is today the spiritual meat on which we feed. All that they had we have, only we have it in a fuller and clearer sense.

2 **a minister of the sanctuary and of the true tabernacle** The sanctuary was a place in which only one person ever dwelt, and that was God Himself. The mysterious light that they called the Shekinah shone from between the wings of the cherubim; there were the pillar of cloud by day and the pillar of fire by night—the symbols of the divine presence. It was God's house. No man lived with Him; no man could. The high priest went in but once a year, and out he went again to the solemn assembly. But now, in Christ Jesus, in whom dwells all

the fullness of the Godhead bodily, we find a sanctuary to reside in, for we dwell in Him; we are one with Him. God was in Christ, reconciling the world to Himself, not imputing their trespasses unto them; and as God was in Christ, so it is written, "You in me, and I in you" (John 17:23). Such is the union between Christ and His people. Every believer is in Christ, even as God is in Christ.

When a Christian loses the realization of the presence of the Lord Jesus Christ, who is the "minister of the sanctuary and of the true tabernacle that the Lord set up, not man," then it is, above all other seasons, that he sighs and cries for a renewal of communion with Christ. We would envy any, however poor and insignificant they may be, who can maintain unbroken fellowship with their Lord.

3   **to offer both gifts and sacrifices** Go where you may, you will discover that, as soon as ever people begin to say "God," the next thing they say is "sacrifice"; and though their idea of God is often distorted, and their idea of sacrifice is distorted also, yet both ideas are there. Man, however degraded, cannot altogether forget that there is a God; and then, shrinking back from the awful majesty of the divine holiness, he at least hopes that there is a sacrifice by which his sins may be put away. He feels that there must be one if he is ever to be brought into connection with God; and so, in some form or other, the notion of sacrifice crops up wherever there is any religion at all. It may be in the ghastly form of human sacrifice, which is a hideous misinterpretation which has crept in under the darkness and gloom of heathenism or false teaching; or it may appear in the continued sacrifice of bullocks, or lambs, or other victims; but, somehow or other, the idea is there. Man seems to know, in his inmost nature, that he must bring a sacrifice if he would appear before God; and this is, by no means, an error on his part. However erroneous may be the form it takes, in its essence there is truth in it.

was necessary for this one also to have something that he offers If God is to pardon sin, there must be something done by which His law can be honored, His justice can be vindicated, and His truthfulness can be established; in fact, there must be an atonement. That is what it all comes to, or else pardon is impossible, and you and I must be lost forever.

4-5   **who serve a sketch and shadow of the heavenly things** In the tabernacle everything was done according to the pattern seen in the holy mount by Moses; in the temple no sacrifice was presented but according to divine command. The whole Aaronic ritual was very impressive. The priests in their holy robes, pure white linen garments, the golden altar, candlestick, and table, the fire, the smoke, the incense; the whole thing was calculated very much to impress the mind. The first covenant provided a very magnificent service, such as never will be excelled, but for all that, costly, divinely arranged, impressive, yet it could not put away sin; and the evidence of this is found in the fact that after one day of atonement they needed another atonement next year.

God set aside that first covenant. He put it away as an outworn and useless thing; and He brought in a new covenant—the covenant of grace; and in our text we see what is the tenor of it: "I will put my laws into their mind, and write them in their hearts" (Jer 31:33). This is one of the most glorious promises that ever fell from the lips of infinite love. God did not say, "I will come again, as I came on Sinai, and thunder at them." No, but, "I will come in gentleness and mercy, and find a way into their hearts." He did not say, "I will take two great tables of stone, and with my finger write out my law before their eyes." No, but rather, "I will put my finger upon their hearts, and there will I write my law." He did not say, "I will give promises and threats that shall be the safeguard of this new covenant"; but, "I will with my Spirit graciously operate upon their minds and their hearts, and so I will sweetly influence them to serve me—not for reward, nor from any servile motive, but because they know me, and they love me, and they feel it to be their delight to walk in the way of my commandments."

6 **he is also mediator of a better covenant** The old covenant, the old ceremonial law, the old spirit of bondage, and the whole of the old leaven Jesus has purged out of the house, and He has admitted to a new dispensation wherein grace reigns through righteousness unto eternal life.

7 **if that first covenant had been faultless** When God gave to Israel His law—the law of the first covenant—it was such a holy law that it ought to have been kept by the people. It was a just and righteous law, concerning which God said, "You must carry out my regulations, and you must observe my statutes by following them; I am Yahweh your God. And you shall observe my statutes and my regulations by which the person doing them shall live; I am Yahweh" (Lev 18:4–5). The law of the Ten Commandments is strictly just; it is such a law as a man might make for himself if he studied his own best interests and had wisdom enough to frame it aright. It is a perfect law, in which the interests of God and man are both studied. It is not a partial law, but impartial, complete, and covering all the circumstances of life. You could not take away one command out of the ten without spoiling both tables of the law, and you could not add another command without being guilty of making a superfluity. The law is holy, and just, and good; it is like the God who made it. It is a perfect law. Then, surely, it ought to have been kept.

occasion would not have been sought for a second In the economy of grace of which our Lord is the surety no fault can be found, and in it there is no fuel for decay to feed upon. There is nothing about it that is weak and unprofitable, for it is "ordered in all things and sure" (2 Sam 23:5). "He takes away the first" (Heb 10:9), not that He may set up another that shall be removed in its turn, but "in order to establish the second." In this second we have covenant purposes from eternity unalterable, love infinite and changeless, promises sure and inviolable, and pledges given that can never be withdrawn, for the Lord has sworn and will not repent.

8   **I will complete** The tenor of the covenant of grace is, "I will," and "they shall"; there are no ifs or buts in it. It is made up of absolute promises upon God's part, and cannot be put in jeopardy by the acts of man; hence it is sure. The old covenant had an "if" in it, and so it suffered shipwreck. It was, "If you will be obedient then you shall be blessed," and hence there came a failure on man's part, and the whole covenant ended in disaster. It was the covenant of works, and under it we were in bondage until we were delivered from it and introduced to the covenant of grace, which has no "if" in it, but runs upon the strain of promise. It is "I will" and "You shall" all the way through. No longer the law graven upon the tables of stone, but the law written on the heart; no more the Lord's command without man's power and will to obey it, but God will renew our nature, and change our disposition, so that we shall love to do what once we loathed, and shall loathe the sins that we once loved. What a wonderful mass of mercies is included in the covenant of grace!

new covenant with the house of Israel Under the first covenant we are ruined; there is no salvation for us but under this new covenant. For this reason, let us read to our joy and comfort what the promises and provisions of that new covenant are.

9   **covenant that I made with their ancestors** God not only gave a law that ought to have been kept, because of its own intrinsic excellence, but He also gave it in a very wonderful way, which ought to have ensured its observance by the people. The Lord came down upon Mount Sinai in fire, and the mountain was all wrapped in smoke, and "its smoke went up like the smoke of a smelting furnace, and the whole mountain trembled greatly" (Exod 19:18). And the sight that was then seen on Sinai, and the sounds that were heard, and all the pomp and grandeur were so terrible that even Moses—that

boldest, calmest, quietest of men—said, "I am terrified and trembling" (Heb 12:21).

The children of Israel, as they heard that law proclaimed, were so amazed and overwhelmed with God's display of His majesty and might that they were ready enough to promise to keep His commandments. The law of God could not have been made known to mankind in grander or more sublime style than was displayed in the giving of that covenant on Mount Sinai.

they did not continue in my covenant After the giving of the law, did not God affix to it those terrible penalties that should have prevented men from disobeying His commands? "Cursed be the one who does not keep the words of this law, to observe them" (Deut 27:26). "The person, the one sinning, will die" (Ezek 18:20). It was the capital sentence that was to be pronounced upon the disobedient; there could be no heavier punishment than that. God had, as it were, drawn His sword against sin; and if man had been a reasonable being, he ought at once to have started back from committing an act that he might be sure would make God his foe.

Moreover, the blessings that were appended to the keeping of the law ought to have induced men to keep it; look again at those words I quoted just now: "And you shall observe my statutes and my regulations by which the person doing them shall live; I am Yahweh" (Lev 18:5). This did not mean that the man who kept God's law should merely exist; there are some in these degenerate days who seek to make out life to be existence, and death to be annihilation, but there is little likeness between the words, or between what those words mean. "He shall live in them," said the Lord concerning the man who kept His law; and there is a fullness of blessedness couched in that word "live." If men had kept the covenant of the Lord— if Adam, for instance, had kept it in the garden of Eden, the rose would have been without a thorn to tear his flesh, and the enjoyment of life would never have been marred by the bitterness of toil or grief.

Notwithstanding all these solemn sanctions of the ancient covenant, men did not keep it. The promise, "Do this and you will live" (Luke 10:28), never produced any doing that was worthy to be rewarded with life; and the threatening, "Do this, and you will die," never kept any man back from daringly venturing into the wrong road that leads unto death. The fact is that the covenant of works, if it be looked upon as a way of safety, is a total failure.

10 **I am putting my laws in their minds** When God comes to deal with His own chosen people, really to save them, *he makes them to know His law.* The law still stands in the Old Testament, and our blessed Master, the Lord Jesus Christ, has condensed it into one word, "Love." Then He has expanded it throughout the whole of His earthly life to show us how it ought to be kept.

ILLUSTRATION
Learning by Heart

If children have learned a thing by heart, rather than merely by memorization, they have made it their own, and it remains with them. A man with whom God the Holy Spirit deals is one who does not have to go to Exodus 20 to know what the law is. He does not need to stop and ask concerning most things, "Is this right?" or "Is this wrong?" but he carries within him a balance and a scale, a standard and test by which he can try these things for himself. He has the law of his God written upon his heart, so that, almost as soon as he looks at a thing, he begins to perceive whether there is evil in it, or whether it is good.

I will write them on their hearts Although we can read the law in the Scriptures, and see it wrought out in the life of Christ, yet it is needful that the Spirit of God should come and enlighten us with regard to it if we are really to know what it is. Otherwise, a man may hear the Ten Commandments read every Sabbath day and go on breaking them without ever knowing that he is breaking them. He may be keeping the letter of the commandments and yet all the while be violating their spirit. When the Holy Spirit comes to us, He shows us what the law really is.

Take, for instance, the command, "And you shall not commit adultery" (Deut 5:18). "Well!" says one, "I have not broken that commandment." "Stay," says the Spirit of God, "till you know the spiritual meaning of that command, for everyone who looks at a woman to lust for her has already committed adultery with her in his heart" (Matt 5:28). There is, also, the command, "You shall not murder" (Deut 5:17). "Oh!" says the man, "I never killed anybody, I have not committed murder." "But," says the Spirit of God, "Everyone who hates his brother is a murderer" (1 John 3:15).

When the Lord thus writes His law upon our heart, He makes us to know the far-reaching power and scope of the commandment. He causes us to understand that it touches not only actions and words, but thoughts and indeed the most transient imaginations, the things that are scarcely born within us, the sights that pass in a moment across the mind, like a stray passenger who passes in front of the camera when a photographer is taking a view. The Spirit of God teaches us that even these momentary impressions are sinful, and that the very thought of foolishness is sin.

When He writes His law in our heart, He makes us to approve it. An ungodly man wishes to alter God's law. "There," says he, "I do not like that command, 'You shall not steal (Exod 20:15).' I should like to be a little bit of a trickster." Another says, "I do not like that purity of which the minister spoke just now—

I should like to indulge myself a little. Am I to have no plea-sure?" But when the law of the Lord is written in his heart, the man says, "The law is right."

When God writes the law in a man's heart, he takes the law more to himself than he applies it to anybody else. His cry is not, "See how my neighbors sin," but "See how I sin." His clam-or is not against his brother's fault, but against his own fault. No longer does he look out for specks in other men's eyes, but he is most concerned about the beam that he is quite sure is in his own eye, and he prays to the Lord to remove it.

Is it not a wonderful thing that God shall ever make it as natu-ral for us to be holy as once it was natural for us to be unholy, and that then we shall find it as much a joy to serve Him as once we thought it a pleasure not to serve Him, when, indeed, to deny ourselves shall cease to be self-denial? It shall be en-joyment to us to be nothing; it shall be delight to renounce everything of self, and to cling close to God, and to walk in His ways. Then will be fulfilled in our experience the promise of our text, "I will put my laws into their mind, and write them in their hearts."

ILLUSTRATION

Guided by Mr. Recorder Conscience

In a child of God there is a burning and a shining light that reveals the truth concerning sin. There is within him something that cannot be silenced; this is that principle or power that John Bunyan calls in his *Holy War*, "Mr. Conscience, the Recorder of Mansoul." You know that, when the city of Mansoul rebelled against the great King Shaddai and came under the sway of Diabolus, they shut Mr. Recorder Conscience up in a dark room, for they did not want to let him see what was being done. Yet notwithstanding, when the old gentleman had his fits, he used to sorely trouble the inhabitants of the guilty

211

town, so they kept him under lock and key as much as possible. But when Mr. Recorder Conscience gets full liberty, and lifts his brow into the sunlight, then are we guided in a very different way from that of ungodly men who follow their own evil course. Then does the Lord say, "I am putting my laws in their minds and I will write them on their hearts" (Heb 8:10).

The law is there to censure or to cheer; it is there to let us hear it say, "This is the way; walk in it" (Isa 30:21), or it is there to say, "You shall come up to here, but you shall not go further" (Job 38:11), or, "Return, O apostate children, I will heal your backsliding" (Jer 3:22).

---

and I will be their God Where the Spirit of God has come to teach you the divine will, and make you love the divine will, God becomes to you—what? A father? Yes, a loving, tender Father. A shepherd? Yes, a watchful guardian of His flock. A friend? Yes, a friend that sticks closer than a brother. A rock? A refuge? A fortress? A high tower? A castle of defense? A home? A heaven? Yes, all that, but when He said, "I will be their God," He said more than all these put together, for "I will be their God" comprehends all gracious titles, all blessed promises, and all divine privileges.

and they will be my people All flesh belongs to God in a certain sense. All men are His by rights of creation, and He has an infinite sovereignty over them. But He looks down upon the sons of men, and He selects some, and He says, "These shall be my people, not the rest; these shall be my peculiar people." In the great battles and strifes of this world, when God lets loose the dread artillery of heaven His glance is stern upon His enemies, but the tear is in His eye toward His people. He is always tender toward them. "Spare my people," He says, and the angels interpose lest these chosen ones should dash their feet against a stone.

People have their treasures, their pearls, their jewels, their rubies, their diamonds, and these are their peculiar store. Now, all in the covenant of grace are the peculiar store of God. He values them above all things else besides. In fact, He keeps the world spinning for them. The world is but a scaffold for the Church. He will send creation packing when once it has done with His saints. Yes, sun, and moon, and stars shall pass away like worn-out rags when once He has gathered together His own elect, and enfolded them forever within the safety of the walls of heaven. For them, time moves; for them, the world exists. He measures the nations according to their number, and He makes the very stars of heaven to fight against their enemies, and to defend them against their foes. "They will be my people." The favor that is contained in such love it is not for words to express. Perhaps on some of those quiet resting places prepared for the saints in heaven, it shall be a part of our eternal enjoyment to contemplate the heights and depths of these golden lines.

11   **will not teach each one his fellow citizen** Renewed people, people under the covenant of grace, do not constantly need to resort to their Bible to learn what they ought to do, nor go to some fellow Christians to ask instruction. They do not now have the law of God written on a table of stone, or upon parchment, or upon paper; they have the law written upon their own minds. There is now a divine, infallible Spirit dwelling within them, which tells them the right and the wrong, and by this they may speedily discern between the good and the evil. They no longer put darkness for light, and light for darkness, bitter for sweet, and sweet for bitter. Their minds are enlightened as to the true holiness and the true purity that God requires.

they will all know me The more we know of God, of this life, of the life to come, of heaven and hell, of the person of Christ, of the atonement, and of every other subject that is taught us in the Scriptures, the more we see the evil of sin, and the more we see the delights of holiness. Why, at the very first moment of one's conversion, a person is afraid of sin because of what he or she has seen of it. But as that person begins to perceive how sin put Christ to death, how sin dug the pit of hell, how sin brought all the plagues and curses upon the human family, and will continue to curse generations yet unborn, then the person says, "How can I do this great wickedness, and sin against God?" Trained and educated in the school of Christ, the more a person knows, the more he or she delights in the law and the will of God.

ILLUSTRATION
"Holy to Yahweh"

The lawyer always says, "You had better be careful what you say, but when you go to law, never write anything. Hold back from the use of pen and ink, for that which is written remains."

When God writes His law in our hearts, He writes that which will never be blotted out. Once let Him take the pen in His hand, and begin to write, "Holy to Yahweh" (Zech 14:20), right across a man's heart, and the devil himself can never remove that sacred line.

---

12   **I will be merciful toward their wrongdoings** Suppose that you are under a sense of sin. Something has revived in you a recollection of past guilt, or it may be that you have sadly stumbled this very day, and Satan whispers, "You will surely be destroyed, for you have sinned." Now go to the great Father, and open this page, putting your finger on that twelfth verse, and say, "Lord, in infinite, boundless, inconceivable mercy you have entered into covenant with me, a poor sinner, seeing I believe in the name of Jesus. And now, I ask you, have respect unto your covenant. You have said, *I will be merciful toward their wrongdoings*—O God be merciful to mine. *I will not*

remember their sins any longer—Lord, remember no more my sins: forget forever my iniquity." That is the way to use the covenant: When under a sense of sin, run to that clause which meets your case.

I will not remember their sins any longer There is no "if" in the covenant of grace. It runs thus: "I will," and "You shall." That is the tenor of it. Its essence lies in the supreme word, "I will." Therefore, because the conditions of the covenant of grace have been fulfilled it is in no danger of retraction, and Christ Jesus has become the surety of a better covenant.

13   **In calling it new, he has declared the former to be old** So the old covenant has vanished away, with all its types, and symbols, and sacrifices. As the morning mists dissolve upon the rising of the sun—as darkness flies away when the light shines—so has the covenant of works departed forever. In its place stands out the everlasting covenant of God's unmerited mercy to the most guilty and vile of the sons and daughters of men. May He graciously grant to us the privilege of having an interest in that covenant, for His dear Son's sake.

what is obsolete and growing old is near to disappearing The ark was made of long-enduring gopher wood, but it has yielded to time. The veil was one of the most costly and durable fabrics, but it yielded to the strain, and was torn from top to bottom. The temple itself, if it had not been destroyed by the enemy, must have grown gray with age, for time strikes with impartial hand buildings both holy and profane.

But see the doctrine of the cross of Christ! No time affects it. The message of salvation by grace is as fresh today as when Peter preached it at Pentecost. The great command, "Believe and live," has as much life-giving power about it as when it was first applied by the Holy Ghost. No time affects the promise of the Father, the merit of the blood of Jesus, or the energy of the Divine Spirit; hence our faith remains.

APPLICATION

Cry to God for a New Heart

The work of the covenant of grace is not to wash the outside, not to cleanse the flesh, not to pass you through rites and ceremonies and episcopal hands, but to wash the inside; to purge the heart, to cleanse the vitals, to renew the soul. And this is the only salvation that will ever bring a man to enter heaven. You may go tonight and renounce all your outward vices—I hope you will. You may go and practice all church ceremonies, and if they are scriptural, I wish you may. But they will do nothing for you, nothing whatsoever as to your entering heaven, if you miss one thing else—that is, getting the covenant blessing of the renewed nature, which can only be acquired as a gift of God through Jesus Christ, and as the result of a simple faith in Him who died upon the tree.

I press the work of self-examination upon you all; I press it earnestly upon you church members. It is of no avail that you have been baptized; it is of no avail that you take the sacrament. Avail? Indeed, it shall bring a greater responsibility and a curse upon you unless your hearts have been by the Holy Spirit made anew according to the covenant of promise. If you have not a new heart, go to your chambers, fall upon your knees, and cry to God for it. May the Holy Spirit constrain you so to do, and while you are pleading remember the new heart comes from the bleeding heart; the changed nature comes from the suffering nature. You must look to Jesus.

The Law of the Lord in Your Heart

When the Lord once writes His name in your heart, He writes His law within you; and though the devil may batter you, God will claim you as His own. Temptation and sin may assail you, but if the law of the Lord is in your heart, you shall not give way to sin, you shall resist it, you shall be preserved, you shall be kept, for you are the Lord's.

This is the only way of salvation that I know of for any of you. First, you must be washed in the fountain filled with blood; and next, you must have the law of God written in your inward parts. Then shall you be safe beyond fear of ruin. "They will be mine," says the Lord of hosts, "on the day that I am acting, my treasured possession"

(Mal 3:17). Oh, blessed plan of salvation! May it be accepted by every man and woman! And it can only be so by the work of the Spirit of God leading you to a simple trust in the Lord Jesus Christ. Trust Christ to save you, and He will do it, as surely as He is the Christ of God. God help you to trust Him now!

All Things Are Yours if You Are in Covenant with God

Do you want provision? The cattle on a thousand hills are His; it is nothing to Him to give; it will not impoverish Him; He will give to you like a God. Do you want comfort? He is the God of all consolation; He will comfort you like a God. Do you want guidance? There is infinite wisdom waiting at your beck. Do you want support? There is eternal power, the same that guards the everlasting hills, waiting to be your stay. Do you want grace? He delights in mercy, and all that mercy is yours. Every attribute of God belongs to His people in covenant with Him. All that God is or can be—and what is there not in that?—all that you can conceive and more; all the angels have and more; all that heaven is and more; all that is in Christ, even the boundless fullness of Godhead—all this belongs to you, if you are in covenant with God through Jesus Christ.

HEBREWS 9

¹ Now the first covenant had regulations for worship and the earthly sanctuary. ² For a tent was prepared, the first one, in which were the lampstand and the table and the presentation of the loaves, which is called the holy place. ³ And after the second curtain was a tent called the holy of holies, ⁴ containing the golden incense altar and the ark of the covenant covered on all sides with gold, in which was a golden jar containing the manna and the rod of Aaron that budded and the tablets of the covenant. ⁵ And above it were the cherubim of glory overshadowing the mercy seat, about which it is not now possible to speak in detail.

⁶ Now these things having been prepared in this way, the priests enter into the first tent continually as they accomplish their service, ⁷ but only the high priest enters into the second [tent] once a year, not without blood, which he offers on behalf of himself and the sins of the people committed in ignorance. ⁸ The Holy Spirit was making this clear, that the way into the holy place was not yet revealed, while the first tent was still in existence, ⁹ which was a symbol for the present time, in which both the gifts and sacrifices that were offered were not able to perfect the worshiper with respect to the conscience, ¹⁰ concerning instead only food and drink and different washings, regulations of outward things imposed until the time of setting things right.

¹¹ But Christ has arrived as a high priest of the good things to come. Through the greater and more perfect tent not made by hands, that is, not of this creation, ¹² and not by the blood of goats and calves, but by his own blood, he entered once for all into the most holy place, obtaining eternal redemption. ¹³ For if the blood of goats and bulls, and the ashes of a young cow sprinkled on those who are defiled, sanctify them for the ritual purity of the flesh, ¹⁴ how much more will the blood of Christ, who through the eternal Spirit offered himself without blemish to God, cleanse our consciences from dead works to serve the living God?

EXPOSITION

1   **earthly sanctuary** That is to say, a material sanctuary, a sanctuary made out of such things as this world contains. Under the old covenant, there were certain outward symbols. Under the new covenant, we do not have the symbols, but we have the substance itself. The old law dealt with types and shadows, but the gospel deals with the spiritual realities themselves.

2   **For a tent was prepared** All this was by divine appointment. The form of the rooms, the style of the furniture, everything was ordained of God—and that not merely for ornament, but for purposes of instruction. As we shall see farther on, the Holy Ghost intended a significance, a teaching, a meaning, about everything in the old tabernacle, whether it was a candlestick, or a table, or the shewbread.

3   **after the second curtain** The child of God is a priest, and as a priest he is sanctified to enter within the veil. He is now permitted to go into the place that was once within the veil, but which is now not so, because the veil is torn in two.

      the holy of holies The holy of holies was not open to all people, but only to Jews; and not to all Jews, but only to priests; and not to all priests, but to the high priest alone; and not even to him at all times, or indeed at any time, except on one solitary day in the year.

4   **containing the golden incense altar** I will take you for a moment into that which was called the holy place under the old Jewish law, the holy of holies. What was there? Only two things that could be seen. The one was the golden censer, and the other was the mercy seat, and both of these things were instructive.

Now, when you go to the Lord to worship, the first thing you want is somebody to render your worship acceptable. See there, in the person of your Lord Jesus Christ, a golden censer, representing the sweet merit of His prevalent intercession by which you also are accepted. When the high priest went into the holy place, he filled this golden censer and waved it to and fro till the sweet perfumed smoke went up before the mercy seat. That is just what Jesus does in heaven for us. We burn the incense here below, and the sweet perfume of His merit continually ascends before the throne of the Most High and Holy God, and beneath the cloud of the smoke we worship. Jesus becomes a sanctuary for us, and you can never worship God aright till you feel that Jesus' merits go with your worship. If your prayers are perfumed with the incense of your own merits, and you think they will be acceptable, you do not know what you are doing. But if you see that golden censer, and look to God through the smoke of Jesus' merits, then do you really worship, and Christ thus becomes to you a sanctuary.

and the ark of the covenant The presence of God, as you know, in the temple and the tabernacle was known by the shining of the bright light called the Shekinah between the wings of the cherubim over the ark of the covenant. We often forget that the presence of God in the most holy place was a matter of faith to all but the high priest. Once a year the high priest went within the awful veil, but we do not know that even he ever dared to look upon the blaze of splendor. God dwells in light that no man may approach. The smoke of the incense from the priest's censer was needed partly to veil the exceeding glory of the divine presence, lest even those chosen eyes should suffer blindness. No one else went into the hallowed shrine, and only he once in the year.

5   **it is not now possible to speak in detail** Because it was not his main purpose at that time, and he was writing an important letter upon the most vital truths, and it would not do to encumber it with too many explanations.

6   **the priests enter into the first tent** But the high priest could not go within the veil, because he was not perfect. He had to be sprinkled with the blood, and that made him officially perfect. It would not make him perfect merely to put on the breastplate or to wear the ephod; he was not perfect till the

blood had been sprinkled upon him, and then he went within the veil. But when next year came around he was not fit to go within the veil till blood was sprinkled on him again. And the next year, though he was always a sanctified man, he was not always, officially, a perfect man. He had to be sprinkled with blood again. And so, year after year, the high priest who went within the veil needed to be made perfect afresh in order that he might obtain access to God.

We who are the priests of God have a right as priests to go to God's mercy seat that is within the veil, but it would be to our death to go there unless we were perfect. But we *are* perfect, for the blood of Christ has been sprinkled on us, and, therefore, our standing before God is the standing of perfection. Our standing, in our own conscience, is imperfection, just as the character of the priest might be imperfect. But that has nothing to do with it. Our standing in the sight of God is a standing of perfection. Just as the destroying angel passed over Israel, so this day, when He sees the blood, God passes over our sins and accepts us at the throne of His mercy as if we were perfect.

7   **but only the high priest enters into the second tent once a year** None entered the sacred precincts except one man, and he but once a year. The great teaching was, God is hidden from men; sin has made a division between man and God; the way of approach is not yet made manifest. Yet even then there was a hint given that an entrance would be made manifest, for the division was not a piece of brickwork, nor even an arrangement of cedar overlaid with gold. It was a veil that, once in the year, was solemnly lifted, that the high priest might pass beneath. This hinted that sinful men were yet to be permitted to draw nigh unto the Most Holy God through the Christ of God.

not without blood Notice especially those words, "Not without blood." There could be no approach to God under the old dispensation without the shedding of blood, and there is no access to the Lord now without the precious blood of Christ.

Inasmuch as the new covenant was not the type, but the substance, a more precious sacrifice was needed, and nobler blood than any which is found in the veins of bulls or of goats. Jesus the Son of God must die, or the covenant would be unsealed, the testament without force. No covenant blessing comes to us apart from the death of our great sacrifice, for "apart from the shedding of blood there is no forgiveness," (9:22) and forgiveness is one of the earliest of the gifts of grace. If we cannot even begin the heavenly life by receiving forgiveness of sins without coming into connection with the blood, we may be sure that no further blessing can come to us apart from it. It seems to be absolutely necessary that when God comes into communication with guilty people it must be through an atonement, and that atonement must be made by blood, or by the sacrifice of a life.

on behalf of himself The greatest of the Jewish high priests had to admit that they were sinners themselves, for they had to present sin offerings on their own account. But our Lord Jesus has no sin of His own; hence in part His ability to bear our sin.

8   **The Holy Spirit was making this clear** It is from this sentence that I am sure that the Holy Ghost had a signification, a meaning, a teaching, for every item of the ancient tabernacle and temple. We are not spinning fancies out of idle brains when we interpret these types and learn important gospel lessons from them.

the way into the holy place was not yet revealed It was necessary that you should take away the sacred tent, the tabernacle—and take away the temple too—before you could learn the spiritual meaning of them. You must break the shell to get at the kernel. So God had ordained. Hence, there is now no tabernacle, no temple, no holy court, no inner shrine, the holy of holies. The material worship is done away with in order that we may render the spiritual worship of which the material was but the type.

9 **which was a symbol for the present time** Only a figure, and only meant for "the present time." It was the childhood of the Lord's people. It was a time when, as yet, the light had not fully broken in upon spiritual eyes, so they must be taught by picture books. They must have a kind of kindergarten for the little children that they might learn the elements of the faith by the symbols, types, and representations of a material worship. When we come into the true gospel light, all that is done away with; it was only "a symbol for the present time."

were not able to perfect the worshiper with respect to the conscience All these sacrifices and ceremonies, although full of instruction, were not in themselves able to give peace to the conscience of men. The new and better covenant does give rest to the heart by the real and actual taking away of guilt, but this the first covenant could not do.

It is astonishing that there should be any who want to go back to the "miserable elemental spirits" (Gal 4:9) of the old Jewish law, and again to have priests, and an elaborate ritual, and I do not know what besides. These things were faulty and fell short of what was needed even when God instituted them, for they were never intended to produce perfection or to give rest to the troubled conscience. So of what use can those ceremonies be that are of man's own invention, and that are not according to the new covenant at all?

10 **imposed until the time of setting things right** These ordinances were only laid upon the Jews—not upon any other people—and only laid upon them until the better and brighter days of reformation and fuller illumination.

11 **But Christ has arrived** No son of Aaron stands before us, but the Christ, the truly Anointed One, commissioned of the Lord to introduce people to their offended God. Anointed by the eternal Spirit without measure, the Lord Jesus Christ appears in the end of the world to put away sin by the sacrifice of Himself, and then to destroy the separating veil by going in unto the Father.

Up till then religion dealt with externals, such as meats, and drinks, and washings, and carnal ordinances, and priests who could only offer the blood of bulls and of goats. *But* the coming of the Messiah changed all this. We pass from shadow to substance.

as a high priest of the good things to come Things that were in the olden time "things to come" are things present at this hour. Jesus has brought to light the precious things of the covenant, which kings and prophets desired to see. Yet even now there are good things in the future: "Things that eye has not seen and ear has not heard, and have not entered into the heart of man, all that God has prepared for those who love him" (1 Cor 2:9). The Lord Jesus has brought all good things to those who believe in Him, that they may rejoice with joy unspeakable and full of glory. Good things to come find their way here by the Mediator. God Himself has come among men in the person of the Lord Jesus, who has taken our nature into union with His Godhead. Our Immanuel was born at Bethlehem, He dwelled at Nazareth, He died on Calvary, and He has now gone up on high because His work is finished and the reward of it is given.

tent not made by hands That tabernacle was his body, which was not made with hands, nor yet formed by carnal generation as our human tabernacle is. This greater and more perfect tabernacle was made according to the power of an endless life.

12   **by his own blood** The Lord Jesus did not bring before God the sufferings of others or the merits of others, but His own life and death. "He poured his life out to death" (Isa 53:12). Aaron could not do this; the blood he brought was not his own. And if he could, by any strange imagination, be supposed to bring his own blood, yet it could only have been for himself, since his death was due to God as the punishment for his own individual sin. Our Lord owed nothing to the justice of God on His own account; he was "holy, innocent, undefiled, separated from sinners" (Heb 7:26). Therefore, when He took our place,

it was that He might voluntarily offer up His own sacrifice of personal suffering and personal death, yielding up His whole being as a sacrifice in our stead.

ILLUSTRATION

Make Christ Your Solid Foundation

If you go to the top of some mountains such as Snowdon or the Rigi, you will find it all solid and firm enough. But there are some people who want to get a little higher than the mountain, so the people there build a rickety old stage and charge you fourpence or sixpence to go to the top of it. When you get up there, you find it is all shaky and ready to tumble down, and you are alarmed. Well, what need is there to go up there at all? If you would stand on the mountain, that would not shake.

So sometimes we are not content with resting upon Christ as poor sinners and depending on Him. We build a rickety stage of our own experience, or sanctification, or emotions, and I do not know what besides, and then it begins to shake under our feet.

---

he entered once for all The Jewish high priests went once a year into the holy of holies. Each year as it came round demanded that they should go again. Their work was never done; but "he entered once," and only once, "into the most holy place, obtaining eternal redemption." I love that expression, "eternal redemption"—a redemption that really does redeem, and redeems forever and ever. If you are redeemed by it, you cannot be lost. If this redemption is yours, it is not for a time, or for a season, but it is "eternal redemption." Oh, how you ought to rejoice in the one entrance within the veil by our great High Priest who has obtained eternal redemption for us!

What if I say that the inner shrine has expanded itself and taken in the holy place, and now all places are holy where true hearts seek their God? Had our High Priest merely lifted the veil and passed in, we might have supposed that the veil fell back again. But since the veil of the temple was rent in two from the top to the bottom, there can be no need for a new entrance, for that which hinders is taken away. No veil now hangs between God and His chosen people; we may come boldly to the throne of grace. Blessed be the name of our Lord who has entered in "once"!

into the most holy place Christ has entered into the true holy place—not into that which was curtained with a veil, which was but a type, and which was put away when the veil was torn from the top to the bottom as Jesus died. He has entered into the immediate presence of God, and He has entered there once for all, "obtaining eternal redemption."

obtaining eternal redemption When Aaron went in with the blood of bulls and goats, he had not obtained "eternal redemption"; he had only obtained a symbolic and temporary purification for the people, and that was all.

Redemption is deliverance through payment: in this case, ransom through one standing in another's stead and discharging that other's obligations. When the Lord Jesus Christ died, He paid our redemption price. And when He entered within the veil, He entered as one who not only desired to give us redemption, but as one who had "obtained eternal redemption." He has won for us redemption both by price and by power.

And now think of the nature of that redemption; for here is a grand point. He has obtained "eternal" redemption. If you carefully study the verses around the text, you will find the word "eternal" three times: there is "eternal redemption" (v. 12), the "eternal Spirit" (v. 14), and an "eternal inheritance" (v. 15). Why is redemption said to be eternal? It is a long word, that word "eternal." Notwithstanding all the squeezing and cutting that people give to it nowadays, they cannot make it into a limited period, do what they may. He has obtained eternal redemption—a redemption that *entered into eternal consideration*. I speak of the Lord God with great reverence when I say that redemption was from eternity in His thoughts. When our Lord entered in, *he had by his sacrifice also dealt with eternal things*, and not with matters of merely passing importance. He offered Himself by the Eternal Spirit, and by that offering He took off the mortgage from the eternal inheritance and bade us freely enter upon the predestinated possession. Sin, death, hell—these are not temporary things. The atonement deals with these, and hence it is an eternal redemption. Now, look forward into eternity. Behold the vista that has no end! *Eternal redemption covers all the peril of this mortal life*, and every danger beyond, if there be such.

13 **For if the blood of goats and bulls** The atonement was made not only by the blood of sacrifice, but *by the presentation of the blood within the veil*. With the smoke of incense and a bowl filled with blood Aaron passed into the most holy place. Let us never forget that our Lord has gone into the heavenly places with better sacrifices than Aaron could present. His merits are the sweet incense that burns before the throne of the heavenly grace. His death supplies that blood of sprinkling that we find even in heaven. The presenting of the blood before God effects the atonement. The material of the atonement is in the blood and merits of Jesus, but a main part of the atoning act lies in the presentation of these in the heavenly places by Jesus Christ Himself.

ashes of a young cow sprinkled on those who are defiled Under the old law men might be unclean who did not know it. A man might have touched a bone and not be aware of it, yet the law operated just as much: he might walk across a grave and not know it, but he was unclean. I fear that our proud sense of what we think to be our inward cleanness is simply the stupidity of our conscience. If our conscience were more sensitive and tender, it would perceive sin where now we congratulate ourselves that everything is pure. This teaching puts us into a very lowly place, but the lowlier our position the better and the safer for us, and the more shall we be able to prize the expiation by which we draw near to God.

The defilement was frequent, but the cleansing was always ready. At a certain time all the people of Israel brought a red heifer to be used in the expiation. It was not at the expense of one person, or tribe, but the whole congregation brought the red cow to be slain. It was to be their sacrifice, and it was brought for them all. It was not led, however, up to the holy place for sacrifice, but it was brought forth without the camp, and there it was slaughtered in the presence of the priest, and wholly burnt with fire, not as a sacrifice upon the altar, but as a polluted thing that was to be made an end of outside the camp. It was not a regular sacrifice, or we should have found it described in Leviticus. It was an ordinance entirely by itself, as setting forth quite another side of truth.

The red heifer was killed before the uncleanness was committed, just as our Lord Jesus Christ was made a curse for sin long, long ago. Before you and I had lived to commit the uncleanness, there was a sacrifice provided for us. For the easing of our conscience we shall be wise to view this sacrifice as that of a substitute for sin, and consider the results of that expiation. Sin on the conscience needs for its remedy the result of the Redeemer's substitution.

But while this red cow was slaughtered for all, and the blood was sprinkled toward the holy place for all, no one derived any personal benefit from it in reference to his own uncleanness unless he made a personal use of it. When a person became unclean, he procured a clean person to go on his behalf to take a little of the ashes, and to put them in a cup with running water, and then to sprinkle this water of purification upon him, upon his tent, and all the vessels in it. By that sprinkling, at the end of seven days, the unclean person was purified. There was no other method of purification from his uncleanness but this.

It is so with us. Today, the living water of the divine Spirit's sacred influences must take up the result of our Lord's substitution, and this must be applied to our consciences. That which remains of Christ after the fire has passed upon Him, even the eternal merits, the enduring virtue of our great sacrifice, must be sprinkled upon us through the Spirit of our God. Then are we clean in conscience, but not until then.

14 **how much more** Why does he say, "How much more?" First, because it is *more truly purifying*. There was not really and truly anything of purification about the blood of bulls and of goats. Speaking very literally, the blood of bulls and of goats might defile a person. Falling upon any man, it bespattered his garments. Who cared to have a smear of blood upon his brow or on his hands? It was not in itself a thing that could actually purify. All the prescribed purifications were types and shadows of the true propitiation for sin.

Moreover, our Lord Christ offered *a much greater sacrifice*. One reason why the precious blood has such power to put away sin is because it is the blood of Christ—that is, of God's Anointed, God's Messiah, the Sent One of the Most High. Our Lord did not come as an amateur, but He came with a commission. He came with an appointment and unction from the Holy One. If, therefore, the Lord Jesus Christ is offered a sacrifice for us, He is appointed to that end by God Himself, and therefore He must be accepted by God.

the blood of Christ The whole stress is laid upon "*the blood of Christ*," signifying thereby death, death with pain, death as a victim, death with reference to sin. "The life of all flesh is its blood" (Lev 17:14), and "apart from the shedding of blood there is no forgiveness" (Heb 9:22). It is by the blood of Christ that you and I have our consciences purged from dead works. Rejoice in Christ in glory, but put your trust in Christ crucified. Look with longing hope to His second coming; but for your purification rest upon His first coming. See in His agony and His death your joy and life. It is the blood of Christ that alone can make you fit to serve the living and true God.

through the eternal Spirit This does not refer to the Holy Ghost. The meaning is this: that His eternal Godhead gave to His offering of Himself an extreme value that otherwise could not have been attached to it. He by the power of His Godhead offered up Himself without spot.

The Spirit of Christ was an eternal spirit, for it was the Godhead. There was conjoined with His deity the natural life of a perfect man, but the eternal spirit was His highest self. His Godhead willed that He should die, and concurred in the death of the manhood, so that by the eternal spirit He offered Himself. The blood that He shed was the blood of God, for thus we read: "Shepherd the church of God, which he obtained through his own blood" (Acts 20:28). Of course, "blood" as a physical, material thing cannot be the blood of God. But viewing it as what it means—His sufferings, His griefs, His woes—these were consented to by the divine spirit of Christ. And so by the eternal spirit He offered Himself to God.

Once more, I must call to your notice the use of that word "eternal." It gives to the offering of Christ an endless value. It can never cease to operate, for He offered up Himself by the "eternal spirit." There is as much purging power in the death of our Lord today as in that hour when for the first time He appeared in the presence of God for us. The blood of the bull was a temporary thing; the "ashes of a young cow" could not last forever, but the merits of Christ are the merits of one who ever lives. His merits ever abide; they are the merits of an Eternal Person, who by His own spirit offered up Himself a sacrifice for sin.

offered himself What a splendid word that is! Did He offer His blood? Yes, but He offered "himself." Did He offer His life? Yes, but He specially offered "himself." The entire Christ was offered by Christ. "He offered himself"! You cannot put it so strongly by the use of any other word. He "himself bore our sins in his body on the tree" (1 Pet 2:24); "Christ loved the church, and gave himself for her" (Eph 5:25)—not His life on earth, not His life in heaven, nor His abilities and His thoughts and His works; but He gave Himself.

without blemish The sacrificial act by which He presented himself was a faultless one, without spot. There was nothing in what Christ was Himself, and nothing in the way in which He offered Himself, that could be objected to of God: it was "without blemish."

Now you see why it is that it has such purifying power for us. God sent the Christ; this Christ offered up Himself, and He offered Himself without spot. So we for whom this wondrous Christ was sent, for whom He made this matchless offering, for whom He made that offering without spot, we, I say, are accepted in the Beloved, made perfect in His perfection.

to God Need I call your attention to the fact that He offered Himself "to God"? Yes, I must; for of late some have blasphemously said that the sacrifice was made to the devil. To mention such profanity is to condemn it.

cleanse our consciences from dead works In the camp in the wilderness the law was that if a man touched a dead body he was made unclean by that touch; not only so, but if he only trod upon a dead bone in his daily walks, he was polluted by his accidental contact with death. If any person died in the tent, all the family and the tent itself became at once defiled, and they must undergo purgation before the inhabitants could mingle with the rest of the congregation, much less could go up to the holy place of assembly.

We are all under the ban by coming into contact with spiritual death. The apostle does not say, "Purge your conscience from evil works," because he wanted to turn our minds to the type of defilement by death. Therefore he said, "dead works." I think he had a further motive; he was not altogether indicating willful transgressions of the law, but those acts that are faulty because they are not performed as the result of spiritual life.

Even of old there were no fishes presented on his altar, because they could not come there alive: the victim must be brought alive to the horns of the altar, or God could not receive it. We must not bring our dead faith or our dead works as an offering unto God; our prayers without emotion, our praises without gratitude, our testimonies without sincerity, our gifts without love—all these will be dead, and consequently unacceptable. We must present a living sacrifice to the living God, or we cannot hope to be accepted; and for this reason we greatly need the blood of Christ to purge our conscience from dead works.

to serve the living God You who are acquainted with the Greek will find that the kind of service here mentioned is not that which the slave or servant renders to his master, but a worshipful service such as priests render unto God. We who have been purged by Christ are to render to God the worship of a royal priesthood. It is ours to present prayers, thanksgivings, and sacrifice; it is ours to offer the incense of intercession; it is ours to light the lamp of testimony and furnish the table of shewbread. You who are the sons of God are all the sons of Levi this day. Yes, you are the true seed of Aaron, the priesthood is with you, even with you who worship God in the spirit and have no confidence in the flesh. You who believe in Christ, and are made pure by His blood, it is for you to live as if you wore the snow-white robes of the priests of the house of Aaron. Your garments should be vestments, and your conversation a perpetual priesthood unto God.

ILLUSTRATION

Living without Serving God Is Like Being a Fish Out of Water

The service of God is the element in which alone we can fully live. If you had a fish here upon dry land, supposing it possible that it could exist, it would lead a very unhappy life. It would scarcely be a fish at all! You could not tell of what it was capable; it would be deprived of the opportunity of developing its true self. It is not until you put it into the stream that the fish becomes really a fish and enjoys its existence.

It is just so with man. He does exist without God, but we may not venture to call that existence "life," for he "will not see life—but the wrath of God remains on him" (John 3:36). If he lives in pleasure, yet he is dead while he lives. He is so constituted that to develop his manhood perfectly, as God would have it to be, he must addict himself to fellowship with God and to the service of God.

APPLICATION

Our Eternal Redemption

You do not know how much you are to be tempted and tried before the end comes. Perhaps you will live to extreme old age, and you dread the decay of intellect and the increase of infirmity—and well you may. Nevertheless, be glad that He has obtained eternal redemption for you. You cannot possibly outlive the redemption of Christ; neither can any temptation for which He has not provided by any possibility assail you.

When prophecy is all fulfilled and we pass into the dread future, we do not fear death, since our Lord has obtained eternal redemption. "Eternal punishment" is a word of unspeakable terror, but it is met and fully covered by "eternal redemption." Do not be afraid, you who put your trust in the Lord Jesus as your Sacrifice and Priest! There is nothing in the mystery of eternity that need appall you. Fearlessly you may launch into the deep and quit the shores of this present being, since you bear with you eternal redemption. How shall you be lost, for whom an eternal ransom has been paid? Oh, leap for joy, you believers in Jesus; He has obtained eternal redemption for you! He would not go within the veil to His Father until He had fully wrought out your redemption. He stayed here until He could cry exultingly, "It is finished," and then, but not until then, He gave up the ghost and entered into His Father's presence. Rejoice that you have no trifle here but an eternal redemption. This is nothing of today, or tomorrow, but of the eternal past and future.

The Difficulty of Being a Living Sacrifice

You are not at this day likely to die in order to prove your love to God. But if you are ever called to it, you must be prepared to lose your lives for Christ's sake. What you have to do is to "present your bodies a living sacrifice, holy and pleasing to God" (Rom 12:1). Now a living sacrifice is much more difficult of presentation than a slain one. I believe there are thousands of men who could go to the stake and die, or lay their necks on the block to perish with a stroke for Christ, who nevertheless find it hard work to live a holy, consecrated life. The act of one moment, however painful, must be much easier than that service which is to run through a series of years until life itself shall close.

But if the Lord Jesus gave Himself for you, will you not give yourselves for Him? If He died for you by His eternal spirit, will you not live for Him by that new Spirit with which He has quickened you? Are you not under bonds to serve Him? From this time forth, you should not have a pulse that does not beat to His praise, nor a hair on your head that is unconsecrated to His name, nor a single moment of your time that is not used for His glory. Yes, brothers, sisters, it must be a lifelong sacrifice that we now present to Him who lives forever.

Should not our service be rendered in the full strength of our new life? Let us have no more dead works, no more dead singing, no more dead praying, no more dead preaching, no more dead hearing. "Oh," said one, when he heard a sermon, "it was very good, if it had been alive." Dead-and-alive Christianity is poor stuff. No dish ever comes to table that is so nauseous as cold religion. Put it away. Neither God nor man can endure it. Let us have cakes hot from the oven, manna fresh from heaven, living waters leaping from the rock. Stale godliness is ungodliness. Let our religion be as warm and constant and natural as the flow of the blood in our veins. A living God must be served in a living way.

Seek Forgiveness

Did you ever feel the atonement of Christ applied by the Holy Ghost to your conscience? Then I am certain of it that the change upon your mind has been as sudden and glorious as if the darkness of midnight had glowed into the brightness of noonday. I remember well its effects upon my soul at first, how it broke my bonds and made my heart to dance with delight. But I have found it equally powerful since then, for when I am examining myself before God it sometimes comes to pass that I fix my eye on some evil that I have done. I turn it over until the memory of it eats into my very soul like a caustic acid, or like a gnawing worm, or like coals of fire. I have tried to argue that the fault was excusable in me, or that there were certain circumstances that rendered it almost impossible that I could do otherwise, but I have never succeeded in quieting my conscience in that fashion.

Yet I am soon at rest when I come before the Lord and cry, "Lord, though I am your own dear child, I am unclean by reason of this sin. Apply, again, the merit of my Lord's atoning sacrifice, for have you not said, 'If anyone sins, we have an advocate with the Father, Jesus Christ the righteous' (1 John 2:1)? Lord, hear His advocacy and pardon my offenses." The peace that thus comes is very sweet. You cannot pray acceptably before that peace. And you may thank God that you cannot pray, for it is a dreadful thing to be able to go on with your devotions as well under a sense of guilt as when the conscience is at rest. It is an ill child that can be happy while its father is displeased; a true child can do nothing until he is forgiven.

¹⁵ And because of this, he is the mediator of a new covenant, in order that, because a death has taken place for the redemption of transgressions committed during the first covenant, those who are the called may receive the promise of the eternal inheritance. ¹⁶ For where there is a will, it is a necessity for the death of the one who made the will to be established. ¹⁷ For a will is in force concerning those who are dead, since it is never in force when the one who made the will is alive. ¹⁸ Therefore not even the first [covenant] was ratified without blood. ¹⁹ For when every commandment had been spoken by Moses to all the people according to the law, he took the blood of calves with water and scarlet wool and hyssop and sprinkled both the scroll itself and all the people, ²⁰ saying,

> "This is the blood of the covenant that God has commanded for you."

²¹ And likewise, he sprinkled both the tabernacle and all the utensils of service with the blood. ²² Indeed, nearly everything is purified with blood according to the law, and apart from the shedding of blood there is no forgiveness.

EXPOSITION

15 **He is the mediator** It was absolutely needful that guilt should be atoned for, and, therefore, Jesus became a mediator. Nothing short of this could secure the eternal inheritance for those who are called. Take away the atonement and you have robbed our Lord of His greatest reason for being a mediator at all. We love and live upon the truth of His atoning death.

new covenant Whether it be a covenant or a testament, death is necessary to make it valid. God's covenants have ever been sanctioned and ratified with blood, and the covenant or the testament of eternal grace is ratified with the blood of the Surety and Testator.

eternal inheritance When you come to deal with Christ, you have to do with eternal things. There is nothing temporary about Him, or about His work. It is eternal redemption that He has obtained for us, it is an "eternal inheritance" that He has purchased for us.

16 **it is a necessity for the death of the one who made the will** The covenant was not in force in the olden times until there had been a sacrifice to confirm it, and a will does not stand until the death of the testator has been proved to make it valid. The heart's blood of Jesus is, as it were, the establishment of His last will and testament. Jesus, the great testator, has died, has made an end of sin, and His blood is the great seal of His testament, and makes it valid to us.

Jesus has made His testament in the character of a sin-atoning sacrifice, and we can only share in it by regarding Him under that character. If I am not a sinner, I have no interest in the legacy of a bleeding Redeemer. The blood-mark proves that the testament was made for those who need atonement by blood, and that its legacies are bequeathed to sinners. This is one of the most humbling and yet most blessed of all truths. It casts down, and yet lifts up. If I have any grace or any covenant blessing, it did not come to me because I was heir to it by nature, or because I had purchased it, or because of any right intrinsic in myself, but because Jesus, when He died, had a right to make His will as He pleased, and He so made it that He would give Himself and all that He had to such a poor, needy, empty, lost, and guilty sinner as I am. Not because of any good in us do these blessings come to us, but all of our Lord's good will who made the testament of love and sealed it with His heart's blood.

17 **it is never in force when the one who made the will is alive**
Until the blood of Jesus had been shed, the covenant was not
signed, and sealed, and ratified. It was like a will that could
only become valid by the death of the testator. It is true that
there was such perfect unity of heart between the Father and
the Son, and such mutual foreknowledge that the covenant
would be ratified in due time, that multitudes of the chosen
ones were welcomed to heaven in anticipation of the redemption that would actually be accomplished by Christ upon the
cross. But when Jesus took upon Himself the likeness of men,
and in our human nature suffered and died upon the accursed
tree, He did, as it were, write His name in crimson characters
upon the eternal covenant, and thus sealed it with His blood.
It is because the blood of Jesus is the seal of this covenant that
it has such power to bless us, and is the means of lifting us up
out of the prison pit where there is no water.

18 **not even the first covenant was ratified without blood**
Aversion and shrinking crosses most minds at the thought
of blood. One feels sickened and saddened. The sight of murdered Abel must have been terrible indeed to Adam and Eve,
unused as they were to gaze on blood. If it would be so to them
after the fall, what would the sight have been to them had they
remained pure and perfect beings?

In proportion to purity will be the shock to the mind in the
presence of death and blood. Cruel men might gloat over a
battlefield, but to most of us the sight of a single violent death
would be horrible to the last degree. Humanity, until it is bru-
talized, has the greatest possible aversion to the sight of blood;
it is as though God had selected as the token of atonement that
which would show to us His antipathy to sin. He would move
us to aversion toward evil from a sight of its painful and deadly consequences. He as good as tells us that while a thing is
stained with evil He will sooner destroy it than have it in His
sight. Man, the masterpiece of the divine creation, shall sooner be slain and his life flow out on the ground than be allowed
to wallow in iniquity. It was intended that even while we are

being pardoned we should feel horror at having been defiled with sin.

But this aversion must not be used sinfully, as some have used it. I have heard of persons saying, when I preach of the blood of Christ, "I could not bear to hear so much about blood! It quite disgusted me." I want you to feel shocked because your sin requires such an awful cleansing, but you must not be shocked at the great sacrifice itself.

ILLUSTRATION
Our Need for a Sacrifice

It is not possible that any sin should ever be forgiven to any man without shedding of blood. This has been known from the very first. As soon as man had sinned, God taught him that he needed a sacrifice. Adam and Eve, after they had sinned, tried to clothe themselves with fig leaves, but that was not a sufficient covering. God must kill some animals, shedding their blood, and in their skins our first parents must be clothed.

When Cain and Abel had grown up, the only sacrifice that God could accept was the slain lamb. To Cain and his sacrifice of the fruits of the earth, God had no respect. Job is, perhaps, the earliest of the patriarchs, but he offered sacrifice for his children lest they should have offended God while they were feasting. He did not think, nor did any of those ancient men who feared God think, of finding acceptance with Him, and remission of sin, without shedding blood.

This belief has been almost universally held; there is scarcely to be found a tribe of men who have not believed in this. Wherever explorers go, they find that, wherever there is any conception of God, there is a sacrifice in some form or other.

---

19 **he took the blood of calves with water and scarlet wool and hyssop** Under the law, some things were purified by fire or by water; but "almost all things" were "purged with blood;" and there was, and still is, no remission of sin "without shedding of blood" (Heb 9:22).

sprinkled both the scroll itself Oh, how delightful this Bible looks to me when I see the blood of Christ sprinkled upon it! Every leaf would have flashed with Sinai's lightnings, and every verse would have rolled with the thunders of Horeb, if it had not been for Calvary's cross. But now, as you look, you see on every page your Savior's precious blood. He loved you, and gave Himself for you, and now you who are sprinkled with that blood, and have by faith rested in Him, can take that precious book and find it to be green pastures and still waters to your souls.

and all the people The drops fell upon them all. As Moses took the basin and scattered the blood over the whole crowd, it fell upon all who were assembled at the door of the tabernacle.

Have you had a sprinkling with the precious blood? If you have, you shall live forever. But if you have not, the wrath of God abides on you. Do you ask how you can have the blood of Christ sprinkled on you? It cannot be done literally, but faith does it. Faith is the bunch of hyssop that we dip into the basin, and it sprinkles man's conscience from bad works.

It is by the sprinkling of the blood, then, that we are saved. We must have the blood of Christ upon us in one way or the other. If we do not have it upon us to save us, we shall have it upon us to destroy us. "His blood be on us and on our children" (Matt 27:25) said the Jews to Pilate in their madness, and the siege of Jerusalem was the answer to the cry. Worse than the siege of Jerusalem was to the Jews shall be the death of those who have contempt for the Spirit of grace and despise the blood of Jesus. But happy shall they be who, giving up every other confidence, come to the blood of the covenant and put their trust there, for it shall not deceive them.

20 **This is the blood of the covenant** Long before this round world was made or stars began to shine, God foresaw that He would make man. He also foresaw that man would fall into sin. Out of that fall of man, His distinguishing grace and infinite sovereignty selected a multitude that no man can number to be His. But, seeing that they had offended against Him, it was necessary, in order that they might be saved, that a great scheme or plan should be devised by which the justice of God should be fully satisfied, and yet the mercy of God should have full play. A covenant was therefore arranged between the persons of the blessed Trinity. It was agreed and solemnly pledged by the oath of the eternal Father that He would give unto the Son a multitude whom no man could number who should be His, His spouse, the members of His mystical body, His sheep, His precious jewels. These the Savior accepted as His own, and then on His part He undertook for them that He would keep the divine law, that He would suffer all the penalties due on their behalf for offenses against the law, and that He would keep and preserve every one of them until the day of His appearing. Thus stood the covenant, and on that covenant the salvation of every saved man and woman hangs.

To show you that salvation is not by human merit, God was pleased to cast it entirely upon covenant arrangements. In that covenant, made between Himself and His Son, there was not a word said about our actions having any merit in them. We were regarded as though we were not, except that we stood in Christ, and we were only so far parties to the covenant as we were in the loins of Christ on that august day. We were considered to be the seed of the Lord Jesus Christ, the children of His care, the members of His own body.

21 **he sprinkled both the tabernacle and all the utensils** If God is to dwell in the midst of sinful men, it can only be through the blood of the atonement. Twice seven times were the holy place and the tabernacle to be sprinkled with blood, as though to indicate a double perfectness of efficacy of the preparation for God's dwelling among sinful men.

I like that thought. I like to come up to God's house and say, "Well, I shall worship God today in the power and through the merit of the precious blood. My praises will be poor, feeble things, but then the sweet perfume will go up out of the golden censer, and my praises will be accepted through Jesus Christ. My preaching—oh! How full of faults; how covered over with sins! But then the blood is on it, and because of that, God will not see sin in my ministry, but will accept it because of the sweetness of His Son's blood."

22 **nearly everything** In one case only was there an apparent exception, and even that goes to prove the universality of the rule, because the reason for the exception is so fully given. The trespass offering, referred to as an alternative in Lev 5:11, might, in extreme cases of excessive poverty, be a bloodless offering. If a man was too poor to bring an offering from the flock, he was to bring two turtledoves or young pigeons. But if he was too poor even for that, he might offer the tenth part of an ephah of fine flour for a sin offering, without oil or frankincense, and it was cast upon the fire. That is the one solitary exception through all the types. In every place, at every time, in every instance where sin had to be removed, blood must flow. Life must be given.

is purified with blood I suppose that the outer court of the Jewish temple was something worse than an ordinary slaughterhouse. If you will read the lists of the multitudes of beasts that were sometimes slain there in a single day, you will see that the priests must have stood in gore, and have presented a crimson appearance—their snow-white garments all splashed over with blood as they stood there offering sacrifice from morning till night. Every man who went up to the tabernacle or to the temple must have stood aside for a moment, and have said, "What a place this is for the worship of God! Everywhere I see signs of slaughter."

according to the law Some things under the Jewish law might be cleansed by water or by fire, but in no case where absolute sin was concerned was there ever purification without blood, teaching this doctrine: that blood, and blood alone, must be applied for the remission of sin. Indeed, the very heathen seem to have an inkling of this fact. Do not I see their knives gory with the blood of victims? Have I not heard horrid tales of human immolations, of holocausts, of sacrifices? And what do these mean but that there lies deep in the human breast, deep as the very existence of man, this truth: that "apart from the shedding of blood there is no forgiveness"?

God intended this to be so. It was the great lesson that He meant to be taught to the Jewish people, that sin was a loathsome and a detestable thing, and that it could only be put away by the sacrifice of a great life—such a life as had not then been lived—the life of the Coming One. The life of the eternal Son of God, who must Himself become man, that He might offer His own immaculate life upon the altar of God to expiate the guilt, and put away the filth and the loathsomeness of human transgression.

apart from the shedding of blood there is no forgiveness
There is no truth more plain than this in the whole of the Old Testament, and it must have within it a very weighty lesson to our souls. There are some who cannot endure the doctrine of a substitutionary atonement. Let them beware lest they be casting away the very soul and essence of the gospel. It is evident that the sacrifice of Christ was intended to give ease to the conscience, for we read that the blood of bulls and of goats could not do that. I fail to see how any doctrine of atonement except the doctrine of the vicarious sacrifice of Christ can give ease to the guilty conscience. Christ in my stead suffering the penalty of my sin—that pacifies my conscience, but nothing else does.

All the repentance in the world cannot blot out the smallest sin. If you had only one sinful thought cross your mind, and you grieved over that all the days of your life, still the stain of that sin could not be removed even by the anguish it cost you. Where repentance is the work of the Spirit of God, it is a very precious gift, and is a sign of grace; but there is no atoning power in repentance. In a sea full of penitential tears, there is not the power or the virtue to wash out one spot of this hideous uncleanness. Without the blood-shedding, there is no remission.

Jesus Christ Himself cannot save us apart from His blood. It is a supposition that only folly has ever made, but I must refute even the hypothesis of folly when it affirms that the example of Christ can put away human sin, that the holy life of Jesus Christ has put the race on such a good footing with God that now He can forgive its faults and its transgression. Not so— not the holiness of Jesus, not the life of Jesus, not the death of Jesus, but the blood of Jesus only, for "apart from the shedding of blood there is no forgiveness."

ILLUSTRATION
Christ Crucified, Not Merely Christ Glorified

Who among us can tell all the perils of this mortal life? I remember reading a work in which there were collected together numerous instances of the simple means by which men have died, such as the swallowing of a fruit stone, or the sticking of a small bone in the throat, the breathing of some invisible noxious gas, or the failure of some almost imperceptible organ in the body to perform its usual functions. How suddenly death often comes!

You must often have heard of the death of friends, and someday people will tell the survivors that you too are gone. With unforgiven sin upon you, you know where you will go, do you not? I need not tell you where they are driven whose sin has never been forgiven, and whose sin never will be forgiven, as they have passed out of this world unwashed in the precious blood of Jesus.

APPLICATION

Another Clause in the Redeemer's Will

Whenever you read a precious promise in the Bible, you may say, "This is a clause in the Redeemer's will." When you come to a choice word, you may say, "This is another codicil to the will." Recollect that these things are yours, not because you are this or that, but because the blood makes them yours. The next time Satan says to you, "You do not believe as you ought, and therefore the promise is not sure," tell him that the sureness of the promise lies in the blood, and not in what you are or in what you are not.

There is a will, proved in heaven's court of probate, whose validity depends upon its signatures, and upon its witnesses, and upon its being drawn up in proper style. The person to whom the property is left may be very poor, but that does not overthrow the will; he may be very ragged, but that does not upset the will; he may have disgraced himself in some way or other, but that does not make the will void. He who made the will and put His name to the will makes the will valid, and not the legatee to whom the legacy was left. And so with you this covenant stands secure, this will of Christ stands firm. In all your ups and downs, in all your successes and your failures, you, poor needy sinner, have nothing to do but to come and take Christ to be your all-in-all, and put your trust in Him, and the blood of the covenant shall make the promises sure to you.

Remission of Sins for the Lost

Do you feel yourself to be lost? I am so glad of it; for there is remission by the blood-shedding. O sinner, are there tears in your eyes? Look through them. Do you see that man in the garden? That man sweats drops of blood for you. Do you see that man on the cross? That man was nailed there for you. Oh, if I could be nailed on a cross this morning for you all, I know what you would do: you would fall down and kiss my feet, and weep that I should have to die for you. But sinner, lost sinner, Jesus died for you—*for you*. And if He died for you, you cannot be lost.

Christ died in vain for no one. Are you, then, a sinner? Are you convinced of sin because you do not believe in Christ? I have authority to preach to you. Believe in His name and you cannot be lost. Do you say you are no sinner? Then I do not know that Christ died for you. Do you say that you have no sins to repent of? Then I have no Christ to preach to you. He did not come to save the righteous; He came to save the wicked. Are you wicked? Do you feel it? Are you lost? Do you know it? Are you sinful? Will you confess it? Sinner, if Jesus were here this morning, He would put out His bleeding hands and say, "Sinner, I died for you. Will you believe me?" He is not here in person; He has sent His servant to tell you. Won't you believe him? "Oh," but you say, "I am such a sinner." "Ah!" says He, "that is just why I died for you, because you are a sinner." "But," you say, "I do not deserve it." "Ah!" says He, "that is just why I did it." You say, "I have hated Him." "But," says He, "I have always loved you." "But, Lord, I have spat on your minister and scorned your word." "It is all forgiven," says He, "all washed away by the blood that ran from my side. Only believe me; that is all I ask. And that I will give you. I will help you to believe."

Fly to the Blood

If you are in any measure failing as to holiness, fly to the blood for help. Perhaps you have not thought enough of late of the dying love of your Lord. His death has a living power about it to breed and nourish holiness within you. Remember, there is no slaying sin but by nailing it to the cross. The lance that pierced the heart of Jesus alone can kill the love of sin. You must overcome through the blood of the Lamb; other victory there is none. You will never avoid sin merely by believing it to be your duty to do so; law points the way, but cannot bear us along it. A sense of the great love of Christ to you in bearing your sin in His own body on the tree, and so removing it from you, will give you power to rise superior to temptation.

It is charged against some of us, as preachers, that we do not urge men enough to their duties. We deny the charge, and yet we claim that we do better, for we touch secret springs that nerve to duty, and we point to the strength by which virtuous deeds are done. The acceptance of the atonement is the great source of virtue. The grace of God is seen in the atonement of Jesus, by which sin is put away, and thus the heart is won to God and led by gratitude to obey Him. The blood of Jesus is the strongest restraint from transgression. We say to the pardoned, "Will you so dishonor the blood that cleanses you as to go and live in sin? Will you go back to that from which you have been redeemed by the death of your Savior? Will you roll again in that foul mire out of which Christ has lifted you, and so dishonor the blood that cleanses you, and make it to be to you as an unholy thing?" It must not be. Let but the heart feel the power of the blood of Jesus, and it will growingly aspire after holiness and increasingly attain to it.

²³ Therefore it was necessary for the sketches of the things in heaven to be purified with these sacrifices, but the heavenly things themselves to be purified with better sacrifices than these. ²⁴ For Christ did not enter into a sanctuary made by hands, a mere copy of the true one, but into heaven itself, now to appear in the presence of God on our behalf; ²⁵ and not in order that he can offer himself many times, as the high priest enters into the sanctuary year by year with blood not his own, ²⁶ since it would have been necessary for him to suffer many times from the foundation of the world; but now he has appeared once at the end of the ages for the removal of sin by the sacrifice of himself. ²⁷ And inasmuch as it is destined for people to die once, and after this, judgment, ²⁸ thus also Christ, having been offered once in order to bear the sins of many, will appear for the second time without reference to sin to those who eagerly await him for salvation.

EXPOSITION

23 **it was necessary for the sketches of the things in heaven to be purified** These things down below are only the patterns, the models, the symbols of the heavenly things; they could therefore be ceremonially purified with the blood which is the symbol of the atoning sacrifice of Christ.

ILLUSTRATION

Not Perfect until the Blood Is on Us

God could not accept any sacrifice that was touched with the golden tongs or that lay upon the brazen altar so long as those golden tongs and the brazen altar were imperfect. What was done to make them perfect? Why, they were sprinkled with blood; but they had to be sprinkled with blood ever so many times—once, twice, thrice, multitudes of times, because continually they needed to be made perfect.

Now you and I are this day, if we are consecrated persons, like the vessels of the sanctuary. Sometimes we are like the censer: God fills us with joy, and then the smoke of incense ascends from us. Sometimes we are like the slaughter-knife that the priest used: we are enabled to deny our lusts, to deny ourselves, and put the knife to the neck of the victim. And sometimes we are like the altar: upon us God is pleased to lay a sacrifice of labor, and there it smokes acceptably to heaven. We are made like sanctified things of His house. But we, though we are sanctified, and He has chosen us to be the vessels of His spiritual temple, are not perfect until the blood is on us.

the heavenly things themselves Was the heavenly place itself defiled? No, that cannot be. But if you and I had gone there without atonement by blood, heaven would have been defiled. Look at the crowds of once sinful men and women who are daily entering there to dwell with God. How could they come there if the heavenly places had not been prepared for them? Look at the multitude of our prayers and praises that are daily going up there! Are they not all in a measure impure, and would it not have defiled heaven to accept them? But the Lord has gone there, and has sprinkled His blood upon the mercy seat, so that our prayers and praises—indeed, and ourselves also—may enter without hindrance.

better sacrifices than these The blood of bulls would suffice to purge the types, but the realities must have a richer sacrifice to cleanse them.

In the tabernacle everything was done according to the pattern seen in the holy mount by Moses. In the temple no sacrifice was presented but according to divine command. The whole Aaronic ritual was very impressive. The priests in their holy robes, pure white linen garments, the golden altar, candlestick and table, the fire, the smoke, the incense—the whole thing was calculated very much to impress the mind. The first covenant provided a very magnificent service, such as never will be excelled. But for all that, costly, divinely arranged, impressive, yet it could not put away sin. The evidence of this is found in the fact that after one day of atonement they needed another atonement next year.

24 **For Christ did not enter into a sanctuary made by hands** He never went within the veil in the Jewish temple; that was but the symbol of the true holy of holies. He has gone "into heaven itself, now to appear in the presence of God on our behalf."

on our behalf Jesus, as our representative, is a hiding place to us from all the winds that would come to us by the way of the sepulcher. We are not afraid to die, for Jesus lives; and He said to His disciples, "Because I live, you also will live" (John 14:19). He has also gone up into heaven; in His glorified body, He ascended up on high, there to appear in the presence of God for us. So, whenever you have any dread about the future, recollect that you will be where He is. If you are a believer in Him, you must ascend to heaven even as He has done; and as He sits upon His throne, even so shall you; and as He is perfected in glory, even so must you be.

ILLUSTRATION

Our Legal Representative in the Heavenly Places

Christ has gone to heaven to put in an appearance on our behalf. As in a court of law, when a man appears by his attorney, or legal representative, he is in the court, even though he may be miles away.

So are we, today, in possession of our eternal inheritance through Him, who has put in an appearance for us. God sees His saints in heaven in the person of their glorious representative. In Him we are raised up together, and made to sit together in the heavenly places.

25 **not in order that he can offer himself many times** No, there is not a repeated offering of Christ to God, nor a repeated taking possession of heaven on our behalf. "Once for all" (Heb 10:10) the work is done. Jude 3 tells us that "once and for all" the faith was delivered to the saints: it is a final act, which is so complete that it needs no repeating. The entrance of our Lord once for all into the holy place has secured the entrance of His people. It was once, and it cannot be twice, because it was so effectual. This is set forth by the Evangelists, for when our Lord entered the holy place, the veil was torn. The holy of holies was laid open: its enclosure was thrown down.

If any of His work were left undone, He would return to the earth that He might finish it, for He never did leave a work incomplete, and He never will. Christ effected the redemption of His people by one stroke: coming here, and living, and dying. He put away sin; He did not merely try to do it, but He actually accomplished the stupendous work for which He left His glory-throne above.

as the high priest enters into the sanctuary year by year What Aaron could not do by entering into the holy place year after year, Christ has done by entering into heaven once.

There is no more need of a sacrifice for sin, and they are grossly guilty who pretend to offer Christ over again. The great work of redemption is finished; sin is put away, and there is no more remembrance of it. In the sight of God, Christ's one sacrifice has completed the expiation of sin; glory be to His holy name!

ILLUSTRATION

Christ Has Done the Work

I have told you before of the bricklayer who fell off a scaffold, and was taken up so injured that it was seen that he must soon die. A good clergyman, bending over him, said, "My dear man, you had better make your peace with God." The poor fellow opened his eyes and said, "Make my peace with God, sir? Why, that was done for me more than eighteen hundred years ago by Him who took my sin and suffered in my stead."

Thank God for that! I hope that many of you could say the same; you would not then talk about making your peace with God, or about doing something to reconcile you to God. The very thought of adding anything to Christ's finished work is blasphemy. Believe that He has done all that is required, and rest in it, and be happy all your days.

---

26 **since it would have been necessary for him to suffer many times** For Christ once to die a shameful death upon the cross on Calvary has made an indelible mark upon our heart, as though it had been burned with a hot iron. I have sometimes half said to myself, "God forbid that His dear Son should ever have died!" The price seemed too great even for our redemption. Should He die, the Holy One and the Just, the glorious, and blessed Son of God? The answer to that question is that he

has died. Thank God, he can never die again! It would be horrible to us to think that it should be possible that He should ever be called upon to bear our sins a second time.

Every man's death day is his doomsday; all is settled then. So Jesus, when He died, finished His atoning work, and nothing remains for Him but to come a second time, no more to die, to take His great reward.

but now he Who is this that has appeared to put away sin? I will not delay for a moment, but tell you at once that He that appeared was *very God of very God*. He against whom sin had been committed, He who will judge the quick and the dead—He it was who appeared to put away sin.

Who is it that appeared? It is He, *the commissioned of the Father*. Christ did not come as an amateur Savior, trying an experiment on His own account. He came as the chosen Mediator, ordained of God for this tremendous task. "He appeared," He who was *pledged in covenant* to do it—for, of old, before the world was, He became the Surety of the covenant on behalf of His people. He undertook to redeem them. His Father gave Him a people to be His own, and He declared that He would do the Father's will and perfect those whom the Father had given Him.

has appeared He could not sit in heaven and do this great work. With all reverence to the blessed Son of God, we can truly say that He could not have saved us if He had kept His throne, and not left the courts of glory; but he appeared.

once at the end of the ages Our Lord has once for all made an atonement, and all attempts to tamper with His finished work is treason such as shall be answered for in the court of heaven. Terrible shall be the doom of those who have dishonored Christ in the point where He is most jealous of his honor. Christ's being in heaven today is a proof that there is nothing to divide a sinner from God on God's part.

for the removal of sin "Sin." It is a very little word, but it contains an awful abyss of meaning. "Sin" is transgression against God, rebellion against the King of kings, violation of the law of right, commission of all manner of wrong. Sin is in every one of us. We have all committed it; we have all been defiled with it. Christ came to put away sin. You see, the evil is put in one word, as if wrongdoing was made into one lump, all heaped together, and called, not "*sins*," but "*sin*." Can you catch the idea? All the sinfulness, all the omissions, all the commissions, and all the tendencies to rebel that ever were in the world are all piled together, hill upon hill, mountain upon mountain, and then called by this one name, "sin."

Christ was revealed to *put away* sin. He did not come into the world to palliate it merely, or to cover it up, but He came to put it away. Observe, He not only came to put away some of the attributes of sin, such as the filth of it, the guilt of it, the penalty of it, the degradation of it; He came to put away sin itself. For sin, you see, is the fountain of all the mischief. He did not come to empty out the streams, but to clear away the fatal source of the pollution. He appeared to put away sin itself, sin in its essence and being.

You know what the modern babblers say. They declare that He appeared to reveal to us the goodness and love of God. This is true, but it is only the fringe of the whole truth. The fact is that He revealed God's love in the provision of a sacrifice to put away sin. Then they say that He appeared to exhibit perfect manhood and to let us see what our nature ought to be. Here also is a truth, but it is only part of the sacred design. He appeared, say they, to manifest self-sacrifice and to set us an example of love to others. By His self-denial He trampled on the selfish passions of man. We deny none of these things, and yet we are indignant at the way in which the less is made to hide the greater. To put the secondary ends into the place of the grand object is to turn the truth of God into a lie. It is easy to distort truth by exaggerating one portion of it and diminishing another, just as the drawing of the most beautiful face may soon be made a caricature rather than a portrait by neglect of proportion. You must observe proportion if you would take a truthful view of things. In reference to the appearing of our Lord, His first and chiefest purpose is "the removal of sin by the sacrifice of himself."

ILLUSTRATION

Christ Put Away Sin as the Israelites Put Away Leaven

The Israelites were commanded on the Feast of the Passover to put away all leaven out of their houses, and to this day they are very scrupulous about the fulfillment of that command at the time of that great festival. The house is very carefully swept lest a crumb of common leavened bread should remain. The cupboards are ransacked, drawers emptied carefully and swept with a little brush, and then the master of the house will go through every department of the house to see that no trace of leaven should remain. All leaven must be put away that they may keep the feast with unleavened bread.

Now Jesus Christ in this same way has put away sin. There might have been a sin left in some secret region of my heart or soul or conscience or memory, hidden in a dark department of my nature, and that little sin would have ruined me. But Jesus put it all away; every crumb and particle of the horrible leaven Christ has swept right out.

---

by the sacrifice of himself There was never any way of putting away sin except by sacrifice. The Bible never tells us of any other way; human thought or tradition has never discovered any other way. Find a people with a religion, and you are sure to find a people with a sacrifice. It is very strange, but, wherever our missionaries go, if they find God at all thought of, they find sacrifices being offered. It must be so; for man has this law written upon his very conscience.

Christ offered Himself alone. He put away sin by the sacrifice of *Himself*—not by the sacrifice of his Church, not by the sacrifice of martyrs, not by the offering of wafers and consecrated wine, but by the sacrifice of Himself alone. You must not add anything to Christ's sacrifice. Christ does not put away sin through your tears, and your grief, and your merit, and your almsgiving. No, He put away sin by the sacrifice of *Himself*—nothing else. You must take nothing from Christ's sacrifice, and you must add nothing to it.

ILLUSTRATION

Rejoice That Help Is on the Way

If your house were on fire, you would rejoice to hear that the fire engines were coming down the street. You would feel an absolute certainty that they were coming to you, because your house was in a blaze if no one else's might be. If there were appointed today a commissioner for the relief of such traders as might be in difficulties, whose capital was little, and whose liabilities were great, if you were in that condition you would feel at once that a hope was held out to you, because the commissioner's office supposes a condition of circumstances in which you are found.

The news of Christ's coming into the world to put away sin sounds like the joy blasts of the silver trumpets of jubilee to those who know themselves to be full of sin, who desire to have it put away, who are conscious that they cannot remove it themselves, and are alarmed at the fate that awaits them if the sin is not by some means blotted out.

---

27 **it is destined for people to die once** A man dies once, and after that everything is fixed and settled, and he answers for his doings at the judgment. One life, one death—then everything is weighed, and the result declared: "after this, judgment." So Christ comes, and dies once; after this, for Him also the result of what He has done, namely, the salvation of those who look for Him. He dies once, and then reaps the fixed result, according to the analogy of the human race, of which He became a member and representative. Men do not come back here to die twice. Men die once, and then the matter is decided, and there comes the judgment. So Christ dies; He does not come back here to die again, but He receives the result of His death—that is, the salvation of His own people.

28 **Christ, having been offered once** He came the first time with, "I delight to do your will, O my God" (Psa 40:8). He comes a second time to claim the reward and to divide the spoil with the strong. He came the first time with a sin offering; that offering having been once made, there is no more sacrifice for sin. He comes the second time to administer righteousness. He was righteous at His first coming, but it was the righteousness of allegiance. He shall be righteous at His second coming with the righteousness of supremacy. He came to endure the penalty, He comes to procure the reward. He came to serve, He comes to rule. He came to open wide the door of grace, He comes to shut the door. He comes not to redeem but to judge; not to save but to pronounce the sentence; not to weep while He invites, but to smile while He rewards; not to tremble in heart while He proclaims grace, but to make others tremble while He proclaims their doom.

will appear for the second time The appearing will be of the most open character. He will not be visible in some quiet place where two or three are met, but He will *appear* as the lightning is seen in the heavens. At His first appearing He was truly seen: Wherever He went He could be looked at and gazed upon, and touched and handled. He will appear quite as plainly by-and-by among the sons of men. The observation of Him will be far more general than at His first advent, for "every eye will see him" (Rev 1:7). Every eye did not see Him here when He came the first time, for He did not travel out of Palestine, save only when, as an infant all unknown, He was carried down into Egypt. But when He comes a second time all the nations of the world shall behold Him. They that are dead shall rise to see Him (1 Thess 4:16), both saints and sinners, and they that are alive and remain when He shall come shall be absorbed in this greatest of spectacles.

without reference to sin That is to say, He will bring no sin offering with Him, and will not Himself be a sacrifice for sin. What need that it should be so? We have seen that He once offered Himself without spot to God, and therefore, when He comes a second time, His relation to human guilt will finally cease. He will then have nothing further to do with that sin that was laid upon Him.

Our sin, which He took to Himself by imputation, He has borne and discharged. Not only is the sinner free, but the sinner's Surety is free also, for He has paid our debt to the utmost farthing. Jesus is no longer under obligation on our account. When He comes a second time, He will have no connection of any sort with the sin that once He bore. He will come, moreover, without those sicknesses and infirmities that arise out of sin. At His first advent, He came in suffering flesh, and then He came to hunger and to thirst, to be without a place to lay His head (Matt 8:20). He came to have His heart broken with reproach, and His soul grieved with the hardness of men's hearts. He was compassed with infirmity; He came unto His God with strong crying and tears; He agonized even unto bloody sweat, and so He journeyed on with all the insignia of sin hanging about Him. But when He comes a second time it will be without the weakness, pain, poverty, and shame that accompany sin. There will then be no marred visage nor bleeding brow. He will have reassumed His ancient glory. It will be His glorious appearing.

to those who eagerly await him for salvation At His coming He will set His foot upon the dragon's head and bruise Satan under our feet. He will come to have all His enemies put under His feet. Today we fight, and He fights in us. We groan and He groans in us, for the dread conflict is raging. When He comes again the battle will be ended. He shall divide the spoil of vanquished evil and celebrate the victory of righteousness.

I will tell you what it is to look for that second appearing. It is to love the Lord Jesus, to love Him so that you long for Him as a bride longs for her husband. Why are His chariots so long in coming? Come quickly, Lord Jesus! Strong love hates separation, it pines for union. It cries, "Come, Lord! Come, Lord!" Longing follows on the heels of loving. To look for His coming is to prepare for Him.

ILLUSTRATION

Prepare for Christ to Come

If I were asked to visit you tomorrow evening, I am sure you would make some preparations for my call—even for one so commonplace as myself. You would prepare, because you would welcome me. If you expected the Queen to call, how excited you would be! What preparation you would make for a royal visitor!

When we expect our Lord to come, we shall be concerned to have everything ready for Him. I sometimes see the great gates open in front of the larger houses in the suburbs, and it means that they are expecting company. Keep the great gates of your soul always open, expecting your Lord to come.

APPLICATION

Sin Has Been Put Away

You and I live in a period when the putting away of sin has been perfectly accomplished. Sin is put away. We do not have to exercise the faith of a Noah, or an Isaac, or a David, in looking forward to the expiation as a blessing yet to come. The testimony of the Holy Ghost is that Jesus has once for all finished transgression, and made an end of sin, and brought in everlasting righteousness. Jesus has been led like a lamb to the slaughter; the Passover is slain, the propitiation is made. It is a recorded fact; it is a fact that never can be blotted from the annals of time, that redemption is finished. Sin is put away by the one great sacrifice, and we may come to God, who is reconciled through the death of His Son.

If, in the earliest ages, you had come in the faith that this atonement would be offered, you would have been accepted. But how can you linger when the atonement is already presented? Once, in the end of the ages, the work of grace has been done. You have not to wait until the bridge spans the gulf; you have not to enquire who shall roll away the stone. Behold, one greater than an angel has descended and rolled away the stone from heaven's gate and opened the kingdom of heaven to all believers. There are no barriers now between a seeking soul and God, except such as unbelief shall set up. I pray you build no barricades to exclude yourself from happiness. Christ has dashed down all the partition walls that your sin had erected, and there is a straight path from your present position right up to God's greatest glory. Come now, even now, unto the Lord, believing in the atonement that is achieved.

Put Your Confidence in Christ

"How may I share in this blessed result of the putting away of sin?" The answer is that the way for us to enjoy a share in it must evidently be one in which we do not, even by implication, seem to claim a part in the putting away of sin. If you think you can get a part in this gracious result by your own feelings or doings, you dishonor the perfect work of Christ, and so you make a gulf between you and Christ. The only test as to whether Christ put your sin away is this: Have you done with all idea of putting the sin away yourself? Are you willing that He should have the whole, sole, and entire glory of putting it away? Will you now trust Him with your whole heart to put your sin away?

Well, soul, there never was a man yet who gave up confidence in everything but Christ, and relied unfeignedly and heartily upon Christ, but who had in that fact an assurance that Jesus loved him and gave himself for him. "Oh," said one, "I have done that, then, years ago." Rejoice, then, be glad, and out of love to Jesus go and perform works of holiness, to honor Him by whom you are saved. Rejoice all your days, and praise the name of Him who has washed you. Do not, O you pardoned ones, kneel down every Lord's day, night and morning, and wail out the cry that you are "miserable sinners!" You ought not to be miserable sinners now that you are forgiven, justified, adopted, and made one with Christ. You are sinners, but why miserable? To those believers who call themselves "miserable sinners," the Lord might well reply, "You do not then believe me. Have I not pardoned you and declared that there is no condemnation to you?"

No Sins Can Be Held to Your Charge

Look back during the past week. Has there not been a great deal in your life that you have to mourn over? Do you live a single day in which you go to your rest contented with the review of your character or your conduct? I must acknowledge I never spent such a day, and I am afraid I never shall till I get home to heaven. Sins and sorrows multiplied pollute the day, to my shame and my horror. But when I come to look to Jesus Christ my Lord and trust in Him, shall I feel dismayed on account of my sins? No, they are all forgiven; they are all forgiven! Yes, that particular sin—you know what it is—that has caused you so much trouble this week is forgiven. There is no sin that you have fallen into, as a believer in Jesus, that can be laid to your charge.

Come, then, let us shake off these fears. We who know that our debt is paid would be foolish to be troubled about the debt, and we who know our sin is forgiven may have, should have, ought to have, peace with God through Jesus Christ our Lord. God will help me, I hope, to live more and more in the atmosphere of peace with God.

I do believe the devil often worries us when there is no cause whatever for our being troubled. Sin is always to be hateful to us; we are always to loathe it. But when washed in the precious blood of Jesus we are to endeavor to realize that through His blood we are clean, and that, with His spotless vesture on, we are holy as the Holy One. Notwithstanding the depravity of our old nature, and the workings of the flesh against which we strive, yet we are accepted in the Beloved. We are justified by faith that is in Christ Jesus.

Believe in the Second Coming

As you really believe in the first coming and the one great sacrifice, so really believe in the second coming without a sin offering to the climax of your salvation. Standing between the cross and the crown, between the cloud that received Him out of our sight and the clouds with which He will come with ten thousands of His saints to judge the living and the dead (1 Pet 4:5), let us live as people who are not of this world, strangers in this age that darkly lies between two bright appearings, happy beings saved by a mystery accomplished, and soon to be glorified by another mystery that is hasting on. Let us, like her in the Revelation, have the moon under our feet (Rev 12:1), keeping all sublunary things in their proper place. May we even now be made to sit together with Christ in the heavenlies!

Now all this must be strange talk to some of you. I wish it would alarm those of you who once made a profession of true religion and have gone back to the world's falsehood. How will you face Him, you backsliders, in that day when He shall appear, and all else shall vanish in the blaze of His light, as stars when the sun shines out? What will you do when your treachery shall be made clear to your consciences by His appearing? What will you do, who have sold your Master, and given up your Lord, who was and is your only hope for the putting away of your sins? I pray you, as you love yourselves, go to Him as He appears in His first coming. And then, washed in His blood, go forward to meet Him in His second coming for salvation.

HEBREWS 10

¹ For the law, possessing a shadow of the good things that are about to come, not the form of things itself, is never able year by year, by means of the same sacrifices that they offer without interruption, to make perfect those who draw near. ² For otherwise, would they not have ceased to be offered, because the ones who worship, having been purified once and for all, would no longer have any consciousness of sins? ³ But in them there is a reminder of sins year by year. ⁴ For it is impossible for the blood of bulls and goats to take away sins.

⁵ Therefore, when he came into the world, he said,

"Sacrifice and offering you did not want,
but a body you prepared for me;
⁶ you did not delight in whole burnt offerings and [offerings] for sins.
⁷ Then I said, 'Behold, I have come—
in the roll of the book it is written about me—
to do your will, O God.' "

⁸ When he says above,

"Sacrifices and offerings and whole burnt offerings and offerings for sin
you did not want, nor did you delight in,"

which are offered according to the law, ⁹ then he has said,

"Behold, I have come to do your will."

He takes away the first in order to establish the second. ¹⁰ By this will we are made holy through the offering of the body of Jesus Christ once for all.

¹¹ And every priest stands every day serving and offering the same sacrifices many times, which are never able to take away

sins. ¹² But this one, after he had offered one sacrifice for sins for all time, sat down at the right hand of God, ¹³ from now on waiting until his enemies are made a footstool for his feet. ¹⁴ For by one offering he has perfected for all time those who are made holy. ¹⁵ And the Holy Spirit also testifies to us, for after saying,

> ¹⁶ "This is the covenant that I will decree for them
> after those days, says the Lord:
> I am putting my laws on their hearts,
> and I will write them on their minds,"

¹⁷ he also says,

> "Their sins and their lawless deeds I will never remember again."

¹⁸ Now where there is forgiveness of these, there is no longer an offering for sin.

EXPOSITION

1 **For the law** This refers to the old ceremonial law, under which the Jews lived so long. They always had to go on, year after year, offering the same kind of sacrifices, because the work of atonement was never done perfectly. Men were not cleansed or saved by it, so the process had to be constantly repeated.

possessing a shadow of the good things Ceremonies under the old dispensation were precious because they set forth the realities yet to be revealed, but in Christ Jesus we deal with the realities themselves. This is a happy circumstance for us, for both our sins and our sorrows are real, and only substantial mercies can counteract them. In Jesus, we have the substance of all that the symbols set forth. He is our sacrifice, our altar, our priest, our incense, our tabernacle, our all in all. The law had "the shadow of good things to come," but in Christ we have "the form of things itself."

to make perfect those who draw near Those that were sprinkled with the blood of the Old Testament sacrifices did not feel that their sin was forever put away. They went back, after the victim had been offered, with a certain measure of rest and relief, but not with that perfect rest which is the accompaniment of the pardon that Jesus gives to those who come unto God through Him.

2   **would they not have ceased to be offered** Why offer any more, if you are a perfect man? Now mark: the Jewish sacrifice was never intended to make the Jews' moral character any better, and it did not. It had no effect upon what we call his sanctification; all the sacrifice dealt with was his justification.

Now that is the meaning of the word "perfect" here. It does not mean that the sacrifice did not make the man perfectly holy, and perfectly moral, and so forth. The sacrifice had no tendency to do that; it was quite another matter. It means that it did not perfectly make him justified in his own conscience and in the sight of God, because he had to come and offer again.

Now, here comes a man who is troubled in his conscience. He comes to the temple, and he must speak to the priest. He says to the priest, "I have committed such-and-such a sin." "Ah," says the priest, "You will never have any ease to your conscience unless you bring a sin offering." He brings a sin offering, and it is offered, and the man sees it burn and goes away. He has got faith—faith in the great sin offering that is to come—and his conscience is easy. A day or two after, the same feelings arise; and what does he do? He goes to the priest again. "Ah!" says the priest, "you must bring another offering; you must bring a trespass offering." He does that, and his conscience grows easier for a time. But the more his conscience gets quickened, the more he sees the unsatisfactory character of the offering he brings.

God well knew that the sacrifices were themselves imperfect, only a shadow of the great substance, and that His people would need to have the service renewed, not only every year, but every day; not only every day, but every morning and every evening.

would no longer have any consciousness of sins There would have been no need to bring another lamb to be offered if the one which was presented had put away sin; there would have been no need of another day of atonement if the sacrifice on the one day had really made atonement for sin.

3   **But in them there is a reminder of sins year by year** Their blood was only a picture, an emblem, a type of far more precious blood—the shadow of the real atonement that was afterward to be offered.

There was a lamb slain every morning, and that sacrifice must have reminded at least some of them that a perpetual atonement was provided. But, as with an undertone of thunder, it also reminded them all that such an atonement was still needed; that, after a thousand years of the offering of lambs, sacrifices were still required. There was ordained a day of atonement with especially solemn ceremonies, but what did that day say to the Jews? That atonement was provided? No, but that an atonement was still needed. For, as soon as ever that year was up, the atonement had not been made, and they must have another day of atonement.

4   **For it is impossible for the blood of bulls and goats to take away sins.** There was a perpetual remembrance of sin in every one of the offerings under the ceremonial law. They were intended—the most of them, at any rate—continually to remind men that sin was not washed away. Thus all the ceremonies drew up a handwriting, and said to the Jews, and to us too, "You need an atonement by blood; you are guilty, and there is no hope of your ever coming to God except by a sacrifice, which these rams and bullocks represent, but the place of which they cannot possibly fill."

5   **Sacrifice and offering you did not want** When once the life is gone out of the best symbolism, the Lord abhors the carcass,

and even a divinely ordained ritual becomes a species of idolatry. When the heart is gone out of the externals of worship, they are as shells without the kernel. Habitations without living tenants soon become desolations, and so do forms and ceremonies without their spiritual meaning. Toward the time of our Lord's coming, the outward worship of Judaism became more and more dead; it was time that it was buried. It had decayed and waxed old, and was ready to vanish away. And vanish away it did, for our Lord set aside the first, or old, that He might establish the second, or new.

What did God require of man? Obedience. He said by Samuel, "To obey is better than sacrifice; to give heed than the fat of rams" (1 Sam 15:22). He says in another place, "He has told you, O mortal, what is good; and what does Yahweh ask from you, but to do justice, and to love kindness, and to walk humbly with your God?" (Mic 6:8). The requirement of the law was love to God and love to men. This has always been God's great requirement. He seeks spiritual worship, obedient thought, holy living, grateful praise, devout prayer—these are the requirements of the Creator and Benefactor of men.

but a body you prepared for me The whole body of Christ was prepared for Him and for His great work. To begin with, it was a sinless body, without taint of original sin, else God could not have dwelt in it. It was a body made highly vital and sensitive, probably far beyond what ours are, for sin has a blunting and hardening effect even upon flesh. And His flesh, though it was in the "likeness of sinful flesh" (Rom 8:3), was not sinful flesh, but flesh that yielded prompt obedience to His spirit, even as His whole human nature was obedient to death, even the death of the cross. His body was capable of great endurance, so as to know the griefs and agonies and unspeakable sorrows of a delicate, holy, and tender kind, which it was necessary for Him to bear.

The human nature of Christ was taken on Him in order that He might be able to do for us that which God desired and required. God desired to see an obedient man—a man who would keep His law to the full, and He sees Him in Christ. God desired to see one who would vindicate the eternal justice and show that sin is no trifle. Behold our Lord, the eternal Son of God, entering into that prepared body, was ready to do all this mighty work by rendering to the law a full recompense for our dishonor of it!

6   **you did not delight in whole burnt offerings and offerings for sins** The Lord God had no desire for matters so trivial and unsatisfactory. They were good for the people, to instruct them, if they had been willing to learn. But they fulfilled no desire of the heart of God. He says, "Do I eat the flesh of bulls, or drink the blood of goats?" (Psa 50:13). By the prophet Micah He asks, "Will Yahweh be pleased with thousands of rams, with myriads of rivers of oil?" (Mic 6:7).

A clean sweep has been made of all the ancient rites, from circumcision up to the garment with its fringe of blue. These were for the childhood of the Church, the pictures of her first schoolbooks. But we are no longer minors, and we have grace given us to read with opened eyes that everlasting classic of "the glory of God in the face of Jesus Christ" (2 Cor 4:6). Now has the brightness of the former dispensation been quite eclipsed by the glory that excels.

7   **Then I said, 'Behold, I have come'** Observe *when* he says this. *It is in the time of failure.* All the sacrifices had failed. The candle flickered and was dying out, and then the great light arose, even the eternal light, and like a trumpet the words rung out, "Behold, I have come." All this has been of no avail; now I come. It is in the time of failure that Christ always does appear. The last of man is the first of God; and when we have come to the end of all our power and hope, then the eternal power and Godhead appears with its "Behold, I have come."

The infinite *Ego* appears: "Behold, *I* have come." No mere man could talk thus and be sane. No servant or prophet of God would ever say, "Behold, I have come." Saintly men do not talk so. God's prophets and apostles have a modest sense of their true position. They never magnify themselves, though they magnify their office. It is for God to say, "Behold, I have come." He who says it takes the body prepared for Him and comes in His own proper personality as the I AM. "In him all the fullness of deity dwells bodily" (Col 2:9). He comes forth from the ivory palaces to inhabit the tents of manhood. He takes upon Himself the body prepared for Him of the Lord God, and He stands forth in His matchless personality ready to do the will of God. "He was well pleased for all the fullness to dwell in him" (Col 1:19). Everything is stored up in His blessed person, and we are complete in Him.

in the roll of the book it is written about me When our Lord comes, it is with the view of filling up the vacuum that had now been sorrowfully seen. God does not desire these things; God does not require these things. But He does desire and He does require something better, and behold, the Christ has come to bring that something. That awful gap that was seen in human hope when Moses had passed away, and the Aaronic priesthood and all the ordinances of it were gone, Christ was born to fill. It looked as if the light of ages had been quenched, and God's glorious revelation had been forever withdrawn. Then, in the dark hour, Jesus cries, "Behold, I have come!" He fills the blank abyss; He gives to man in reality what he had lost in the shadow.

to do your will, O God His own will was absorbed in the divine will. It was His pleasure to say, "Not my will but yours be done" (Luke 22:42). It was His meat and His drink to do the will of Him that sent Him, and to finish His work. Although He was Lord and God, He became a lowly servant for our sakes. Although high as the highest, He stooped low as the lowest. The King of kings was the servant of servants that He might save His people. He took upon Himself the form of a servant, and girded Himself, and stood obediently at His Father's call.

8 **offerings for sin you did not want** If we had to render to God something by which we should be accepted, we should be always in jeopardy. But now, since we are accepted "in the beloved" (Eph 1:6), we are safe beyond all hazard. Had we to find that with which we should appear before the Most High God, we might still be asking, "Shall I approach him with burnt offerings, with bull calves a year old? Will Yahweh be pleased with thousands of rams, with myriads of rivers of oil?" (Mic 6:6–7).

nor did you delight in An end was made of the types and shadows of the ceremonial law, that the real substance might be introduced by Christ. Never imagine that the old Jewish ceremonial law is to drag on its existence and to be inter-mingled with the Christian dispensation. No! As the shad-ows of the night vanish when the sun arises, as the lamps in the street are put out when daylight returns, so was it with all the types and shadows of the ancient law when the great Antitype appeared.

9 **Behold, I have come to do your will** He came cheerfully among the sons of men. You who are sent from Christ must al-ways go gladly to your service; never look as if you were driv-en to the field like oxen that do not love the plough. God does not delight in a slavish spirit. If we serve Christ because of the yoke of duty, we shall serve badly. But when our service is our pleasure, when we thank God that to us is this grace given that we should "proclaim the good news of the fathomless riches of Christ to the Gentiles" (Eph 3:8), then we shall labor wisely, zealously, and acceptably.

He takes away the first in order to establish the second He takes away the type because the great Antitype has come. He abolishes the offering of bullocks, and goats, and lambs, because He has come whom they all foreshadowed.

There is a first in order that there may be a second. The first has to be taken away when it has fulfilled its design in order that then we may enter upon the second. Some lower good precedes the higher. When the lower good has educated us for the higher, then it is removed and the greater blessing fills its place.

ILLUSTRATION
God Gives His Mercies Little by Little

It would never do for weak eyes to have the full light of the sun pouring down upon them. Often, when men are faint and nearly dying of hunger, they would be killed outright if strong meat were at once set before them. They must be gently fed as they are able to bear it.

So God, knowing the feebleness of His creatures, and especially the feebleness of His sinful creatures, is pleased to bestow His mercies with great wisdom and prudence. Little by little, first a very little it may be, and then rather more, and then still more, and then much more, and then most of all, until He exceedingly abounds in mercy toward us according to the riches of His grace.

---

10 **by which will** It is an eternal will. We have no vacillating deity, no fickle God. He wills change, but He never changes His will. "But he is alone, and who can dissuade him? And whatever he desires, Indeed, he does it" (Job 23:13). The will of God is invincible as well as eternal. We are told in Ephesians 1:11 that He works all things according to the counsel of His will. "There is not one who can hold back His hand, or ask Him, 'What are you doing?' " (Dan 4:35). The good pleasure of His will is never defeated; there cannot be such a thing as a vanquished God. "'My plan shall stand,' and 'I will accomplish all my wishes' " (Isa 46:10). In fact, the will of God is the motive force of all things. "For he himself spoke and it came to pass. He himself commanded and it stood firm" (Psa 33:9). His word

is omnipotent because His will is at the back of it and it puts force into it.

we are made holy We have "passed over from death to life" (1 John 3:14). We have escaped from under the dominion of law into the kingdom of grace. We have come from under the curse, and we dwell in the region of blessing. We have believed on Him who justifies the ungodly, and our faith is "credited for righteousness" (Rom 4:5). There is now no condemnation to us, for we are in Christ Jesus our Lord, and "do not live according to the flesh but according to the Spirit" (Rom 8:4).

ILLUSTRATION
Our Joy in Serving

Suppose that one of the Queen's enemies, who has sought her life and has always spoken against her, were to say, "I mean to be one of her servants; I will go into her palace and I will serve her," having all the while in his heart a rebellious, proud spirit. His service could not be tolerated—it would be sheer impudence.

Even so, "But to the wicked God says, what right have you to recite my statutes?" (Psa 50:16). A wicked man pretending to serve God stands in the position of Korah, Dathan, and Abiram trying to offer incense. He is not purified and not called to the work, and has no fitness for it. But now you who are in Christ are called to be His servants. You have permission and leave to serve Him. It ought to be your great joy to be accepted servants of the living God.

through the offering of the body of Jesus Christ It was the will of God the Father, but it was carried out by the divine Son when He came into the world. A body was prepared for Him, and into that body, in a mysterious manner that we will not attempt even to conceive of, He entered, and there He was the incarnate God. This incarnate God, by offering His own blood, by laying down His own life, by bearing in His own body the curse, and in His own spirit enduring the wrath, was able to effect the purpose of the everlasting Father in the purging of His people, in the setting of His chosen apart, and making them henceforth holy unto the Lord (Zech 14:21).

once for all "It is finished" (John 19:30). Does the divine law require for our acceptance perfect submission to the will of the Lord? He has rendered it. Does it ask complete obedience to its precepts? He has presented the same. Does the fulfilled will of the Lord call for abject suffering, a sweat of blood, pangs unknown, and death itself? Christ has presented it all, whatever that "all" may be. Just as, when God created, His word effected all His will, so when God redeemed His blessed and incarnate Word has done all His will. In every point, as God looked on each day's work and said "It is good," so, as He looks upon each part of the work of His dear Son, He can say of it, "It is good." The Father joins in the verdict of His Son that it is finished; all the will of God for the sanctification of His people is accomplished.

ILLUSTRATION
Christ the Meeting Place of Sin

You may have seen a deep mountain lake that has been filled to the brim by innumerable streamlets from all the hillsides round about. Here comes a torrent gushing down, and there trickles from the moss that has overgrown the rock a little drip, drip, drip, which falls perpetually. Great and small tributaries all meet in the black tarn, which after the rain is full to the brim and ready to burst its banks.

That lone lake pictures Christ, the meeting place of the sin of His people. It was all laid on Him so that from

Him the penalty might be exacted. At His hands the price must be demanded for the ransom of all this multitude of sins.

---

11   And every priest stands There were many priests at the same time—the sacrifices of the temple were too numerous to have been all of them performed by one man. All the descendants of Aaron were set apart to this work, and even then they required the aid of the Levites in certain inferior duties. And as there were many priests at one time, so there were many in succession. As a priest died, he was succeeded by his sons. By reason of infirmity, they were not able to continue in their office even through the whole of their lifetime; there was a certain period at which they were commanded to surrender their office to younger men. By reason of mortality the priesthood was perpetually changing—one high priest died, and was succeeded by another.

Now the reason for the existence of many priests was this: no one priest had accomplished the work of expiation. The good man has gone to his fathers and offered up the last of the morning lambs—but the morning lambs must still be offered. The high priest is dead, and there shall be no more opportunity for him to enter into that which is within the veil, but there must be a new high priest appointed, for the work is not finished.

offering the same sacrifices many times The sacrifice was offered once, but sin was not put away, and therefore had to be offered again. The great day of atonement came every year, when sin was afresh brought to remembrance. There was a day of atonement last year, but the people are unforgiven, and there must be a day of atonement this year. When that day is over and the priest has come forth in his holy and beautiful apparel, with the breastplate gleaming in the light of God, Israel may rejoice for a while, but there is one thought that will sadden her: there must be an atonement day next year. Sin still remains on Israel, despite all that the house of Aaron can do by all their sacrifices.

which are never able to take away sins There was the lamb for the morning; the innocent victim was slaughtered and burned. But the morning sacrifice did not put away the day's sin, for as the sun began to descend in the west, another victim must be brought, and so on each morning and each night. Victim, victim, victim, sacrifice, sacrifice, sacrifice, because the expiation was always incomplete. But our blessed Lord, "the Lamb of God who takes away the sin of the world" (John 1:19), was sacrificed but once, and that one sacrifice has completed His expiatory work. In every truth, His was a sacrifice of nobler name and richer blood than theirs.

How could the blood of bulls and of goats put away sin? What conceivable connection can there be, except in symbol, between the death pangs of a beast and the sin of a man before God? The principle of substitution was by the legal sacrifices clearly set forth, but that was all. Those offerings did not and could not provide the actual substitute. The principle of vicarious sacrifice they plainly unfolded, but they provided no real sin offering. How could they? Where but in the Christ of God could a propitiation be found? Where else is there one who could in our nature make recompense to the injured law of God?

12 **But this one** You see the stars and the moon in their brightness, but suddenly they are all eclipsed and lost in a superior light. What can this glory be that has paled their fires? It is the sun rising in His strength. So while we are beholding the priesthood of Aaron with all its excellence, it suddenly ceases to shine, because of the glory that excels—the radiant presence of one for whom, like heaven's manna, it is not easy to find one fully descriptive name. Shall we call Him "man"? Blessed be His name; He is so, our near kinsman, the "Son of Man." Shall we call Him "priest"? He is so. Blessed be His name; He is the

true Melchizedek. Shall we call Him "God"? Well may we do so, for He counts it not robbery to be equal with God. But this one divinely mysterious person, this unique and solitary high priest, accomplishes what the many priests of Aaron's race could not. They were weak, but He is all-sufficient. He has wrought out eternal redemption, and made an end of sin.

after he had offered What a blessed doctrine this is—that the one offering of Christ has done what the tens of thousands of offerings under the old law never could accomplish! All the work of man is but the spinning of a righteousness that is undone as quickly as it is spun. But Christ has finished the seamless and spotless robe of His righteousness that is to last forever. By His one sacrifice, He has ended all the fruitless labor of the ages. And now as many of us as have received Him have all the benefits of His perfect work.

one sacrifice for sins for all time On Him their sins were laid, and He was numbered with the transgressors. There He, in their stead, suffered what was due to the righteousness of God and made atonement to divine justice for the sins of His people. This was done, not by many offerings, but by one sacrifice, and that one alone. Jesus offered no other sacrifice: He had never made one before, nor since, nor will He present another sacrifice in the future. His sin offering is one.

sat down at the right hand of God Our Lord sits down because there is no more sacrificial work to do. Atonement is complete; He has finished His task. There were no seats in the tabernacle. Observe the Levitical descriptions and you will see that there were no resting places for the priests in the holy place. Not only were none allowed to sit, but there was nothing whatever to sit upon. According to the rabbis, the king might sit in the holy places, and perhaps David did sit there; if so, he was a striking type of Christ sitting as king. A priest never sat in the tabernacle. He was under a dispensation that did not afford rest and was not intended to give it, a covenant of works that gives the soul no repose. Jesus sits in the holy of holies, and herein we see that His work is finished.

ILLUSTRATION
Obedience because of Love

Men will do far more from love than we might dare to ask as a matter of duty. Napoleon's soldiers frequently achieved exploits under the influence of fervid attachment for him that no law could have required them to attempt. Had there been cold-blooded orders issued by some domineering officer who said, "You shall do this and you shall do that," they would have mutinied against such tyranny. Yet when the favorite little corporal seized the standard and cried, "Come on," they rushed even to the cannon's mouth out of love to the person of their gallant leader.

This is the difference between the law and the gospel. The law says, "You shall or you shall be punished;" but the gospel says, "I have loved you with an everlasting love (Jer 31:3); I have forgiven all your trespasses; now my love shall sweetly constrain you, and the influence of inward principle shall guide you in my ways, my law shall be written not upon stone but upon the fleshy tablets of your hearts."

---

13 **his enemies are made a footstool for his feet** They are crushed already. Sin, which is the sting of death, has been removed, and the law, which was the strength of sin, has been satisfied. Sin being put away by Christ's death, He has effectually broken the teeth of all His enemies. When Jesus Christ offered Himself unto God He fulfilled that ancient promise, "The offspring of the woman will strike the serpent's head"

(Gen 3:15). Christ has set His foot upon the old dragon's head and crushed out His power. Still, however, a feeble fight is kept up. Feeble, I say, for so it is to Christ, though to us it seems vigorous. Sin and Satan within us, and all Christ's enemies without us, including death itself, are vainly raging against the Christ of God, for every day they are being put beneath His feet. Every day as the battle rages the victory turns unto the enthroned Christ.

14 **For by one offering he has perfected** Those for whom Christ has died were perfected by His death. It does not mean that He made them perfect in character, so that they are no longer sinners, but that He made those for whom He died perfectly free from the guilt of sin. When Christ took their sins upon Himself, sin remained no longer upon them, for it could not be in two places at one and the same time. If it was on Christ, it was not upon them. They were acquitted at the bar of God when Christ was, on their behalf, "counted with the transgressors" (Isa 53:12). When Jesus suffered the penalty due to His people's sins to the last jot and tittle, then their sins ceased to be, and the covenant was fulfilled: "I will forgive their iniquity and their sin I will no longer remember" (Jer 31:34). There was a clean sweep made of sin. He has "put an end to the transgression and sealed up sin" (Dan 9:24), and that for all His people. They need no other washing, no further purging, as far as pardon of sin and acceptance with God in the matter of justification are concerned, for they are all perfected by His sacrifice.

for all time those who are made holy You must beware of misunderstanding that word as though it meant those who are made perfectly holy in character. The word implies an inward work of grace, but it means a great deal more. The passage should be read "He has perfected for all time those who are being made holy," for it is in the present in the Greek. The text is not to be made to say that those who are perfectly sanctified are perfected—that would be a commonplace, self-evident truth—but the Great High Priest perfected forever those who are being sanctified. Now, sanctification means, primarily, the setting apart of a people by God to be holy to Himself. Election is sanctification virtually; all God's people were sanctified—set apart and made holy to the Lord—in the eternal purpose and sovereign decree before the earth was. Christ has by His death perfected all who were sanctified or set apart in election.

ILLUSTRATION
God's Chosen Vessels

In the sanctuary there were persons who did nothing else but wait upon the Lord. These were consecrated to their offices, for God chose the tribe of Levi, and out of the tribe of Levi he chose the house of Aaron. These persons were chosen, and then they were prepared. They underwent certain ceremonies, and washings, and so they were made ceremonially holy. These priests were therefore sanctified persons, because they were set apart, dedicated, and reserved to the special service of the Lord God.

Now that is just what you and I are, and what we ought to be. We are sanctified persons; that is to say, we are chosen by God to be the peculiar vessels that He will use in pouring out His mercy, and to be the special priests whom He shall employ in His divine worship in this world.

---

15   **the Holy Spirit also testifies to us** And what more veritable witness can we have? That to which the Holy Ghost bears testimony must never be questioned by us.

16   **"This is the covenant that I will decree for them after those days, says the Lord: I am putting my laws on their hearts** What the law could not do with its iron fetters, the gospel has done with its silken bonds. If God had thundered at

you, you would have grown proud like Pharaoh when he said, "Who is Yahweh that I should listen to his voice?" (Exod 5:2). But when the Lord Jesus spoke softly to you, you bowed before Him, and said, "He is my Lord and my God" (John 20:28). The blustering wind of the law made you bind about yourself the cloak of your sins, but the genial warmth of the sun of the gospel constrained you to cast away the garments of your sin, and fly to the Savior.

and I will write them on their minds Oh, what a blessed covenant this is! Christ's death has established a covenant of grace in which there is no flaw, and no possibility of failure, for the one condition of the covenant has been fulfilled by Christ and now it stands as a covenant of "shalls" and "wills" on God's part from which He will never run back. It is not, "If they do this, and if they do that, I will do the other," but it is all "I will."

17 **their lawless deeds I will never remember again** What a wonderful covenant that is—not that He will bless you if you keep the law, but that you shall be enabled to keep it, and that He will lead you to do so by putting His law, not on tables of stone, where your eye can see it, but on the fleshy tablets of your heart, where your soul shall feel its force and power, so that you shall be obedient to it. Meditate on those glorious words: "Their sins and their lawless deeds I will never remember again."

Once in the end of the world God Himself descended from the skies and was veiled in our inferior clay. Here on earth God's eternal Son lived and dwelt like one of us. In the fullness of time, when the sins of all His people had been laid upon Him, He was seized by the officers of justice and was taken away as having our sins upon His own person. On the tree was He fastened that He might die, the just for the unjust that He might bring us to God. Christ stood in the place of His people, and when God's wrath fell upon sin it fell upon Him and spent itself upon His person. There is no wrath left in God's heart now against those for whom the Savior died. Christ has suffered all.

ILLUSTRATION

God Forgives the Prodigal

When the prodigal is received and forgiven, he is not put at the end of the table, below the salt, or sent into the kitchen with the servants, as if his faults were forgiven but yet remembered. He is invited to the table, and he feasts there upon the best the house affords. The fatted calf is killed, the ring is on his finger, and there are music and dancing for him—as sweet music and as joyous dancing as for the constantly obedient elder son. Not only so but more, for there is more joy over him than over the son who did not go astray.

God in this sense forgets His people's sins.

18 **no longer an offering for sin** If the sins themselves have gone, and God will remember them no more, no further sacrifice is required for them. What need do you have of cleansing if you are so clean that God Himself sees no sin in you? O glorious purgation by the atoning sacrifice of Christ! Rejoice in it, and praise the Lord for it forever and ever.

APPLICATION

We Are God's Accepted Servants

Because Jesus Christ by the offering of His body once has perfected the Father's will, and has sanctified us, therefore what we do is now accepted with God. We might have done whatever we would, but God would not have accepted it from a sinner's hands—from the hands of those that were out of Christ. Now He accepts anything from us. You dropped a penny into the box: it was all that you could give, and the Lord accepted it. It dropped into His hand. You offered a little prayer in the middle of business this afternoon because you heard an ill word spoken, and your God accepted that prayer. You went down the street and spoke to a poor sick person; you did not say much, but you said all you could—the great God accepted it. Acceptance in the Beloved, not only for our persons, but for our prayers and our work, is one of the sweetest things I know of. We are accepted. That is the joy of it. Through that one great, bloody sacrifice, offered once for all, God's people are forever accepted, and what His people do for Him is accepted too. And now we are privileged to the highest degree, being sanctified—that is to say, made into God's people, God's servants, and God's accepted servants.

Every privilege that we could have had, if we had never sinned, is now ours, and we are in Him as His children. We have more than would have come to us by the covenant of works; and if we will but know it, and live up to it, even the very privilege of suffering and the privilege of being tried, the privilege of being in want, should be looked upon as a great gift. You are favored sons of Adam, you who have become sons of God. You are favored beyond cherubim and seraphim in accomplishing a service for the manifestation of the riches of the grace of God, which unfallen spirits never could accomplish. Rejoice and be exceedingly glad that this one offering has put you there.

Christians Are to Rest

I want you to gather from the text the true posture of every believer in Christ. "This one, after he had offered one sacrifice for sins for all time, sat down" (Heb 10:12). If I am a believer, that is my posture; if you are a believer, that is yours—you are to sit down. Under the law there was no sitting down. Even at the Passover the Israelites stood with their loins girded and their staffs in their hands. There was no sitting down. It is only at the gospel supper that our proper posture is that of recumbency, reclining, or sitting down, because our warfare is accomplished. They that have believed have entered into rest. Jesus has given us rest—we are not traversing the wilderness, we are come unto Mount Zion, unto the glorious assembly of the church of the first born whose names are written in heaven. Our justifying work is finished, finished by Christ.

Sit down, Christian; sit down and rest in your Lord. There is much to be done as to fighting your sins, much to be done for Christ in the world. But so far as justification and forgiveness are concerned, rest is your proper place, peace in Christ Jesus your lawful portion.

Look Only to Jesus

See in the text the position out of which you should labor to escape. It is the position of those who stand daily ministering and daily offering sacrifices that can never put away sin. You are seeking mercy, and I know what you are doing: you are going about to establish a righteousness of your own. You thought, "I will pray very regularly." You have done so for months, but prayers can never put away sin. What is there in prayer itself that can have merit in it to make atonement for sin? You have read the Scriptures regularly, for which I am most glad, but this you always ought to have done. If you now do it most commendably, in what way will that put away sin? "I have been a regular attendant at a place of worship." It is well you should, for "faith comes by hearing" (Rom 10:17), but I see no connection between the mere fact of your sitting in a place of worship and the putting away of sin. You know it has not eased your conscience yet, but has even increased your sense of sin. Perhaps some of you have for years been trying to save yourselves, and you have got no further—you feel as if you were further off than you ever were. "Why do you weigh out money for what is not food, and your labor for what cannot satisfy" (Isa 55:2)? Why do you stand daily at the altar offering that which can never put away sin? It would be infinitely wiser to flee to the sacrifice that can atone.

If you would have peace of heart, you must get it only from this one glorious person, the Christ of God. I tell you solemnly, you will damn yourself by your prayers, and your tears, and your repenting, and your going to church as easily as by blasphemy and fornication, if you trust in them. For if you make a Savior and an idol of your best works, they are accursed. Although your idol may be of purest gold, it is as much an abomination to the living God as if you had made it of filth. There must be no looking anywhere but to Jesus, not in any measure or degree.

Beware Unbelieving Repentance

Why is it that you and I are sometimes desponding in spirit concerning past sin? It is right of us to hate it, to sorrow over it, but it is not right for us to fear and tremble as to the punishment of that sin. Why do we? I will tell you. It is because we forget the cross. The repentance that does not look to the cross is a legal repentance, and it will breed misery.

Brothers and sisters, beware of an unbelieving repentance, for God cannot accept it, but seek to get repentance at the foot of the cross. If you have an eye to sin, take care to have an eye to the atonement too. Let your eyes be full of tears, but let those tears act like magnifying glasses to make the cross appear a grander and a dearer thing than ever. Never let your sin shake your confidence in Christ, for if you are a great sinner, glorify Him by believing Him to be a great Savior. Do not diminish the value of the blood while you magnify the intensity of your sin. Think as badly of sin as you can, but think right gloriously of Christ, for there is no sin, however hellish or devilish, which the blood of Jesus cannot take away. And if the concentrated essence of everything that is diabolical in iniquity be found in you, yet "the blood of Jesus his Son cleanses us from all sin" (1 John 1:7), and herein we must—indeed, and will—rejoice.

¹⁹ Therefore, brothers, since we have confidence for the entrance into the sanctuary by the blood of Jesus, ²⁰ by the new and living way that he inaugurated for us through the curtain, that is, his flesh, ²¹ and since we have a great priest over the house of God, ²² let us approach with a true heart in the full assurance of faith, our hearts sprinkled clean from an evil conscience and our bodies washed with pure water. ²³ Let us hold fast to the confession of our hope without wavering, for the one who promised is faithful. ²⁴ And let us think about how to stir one another up to love and good works, ²⁵ not abandoning our meeting together as is the habit of some, but encouraging each other, and by so much more as you see the day drawing near.

EXPOSITION

19 **Therefore, brothers, since we have confidence for the entrance** There was under the law this ordinance—that no man should ever go into the holiest of all, with the one exception of the high priest, and he but once in the year, and not without blood. If any man had attempted to enter there he must have died, as guilty of great presumption and of profane intrusion into the secret place of the Most High. Who could stand in the presence of Him who is a consuming fire? This ordinance of distance runs all through the law; for even the holy place, which was the vestibule of the holy of holies, was for the priests alone.

into the sanctuary by the blood of Jesus Those who refuse Jesus refuse the only way of access to God. God is not approachable except through the rending of the veil by the death of Jesus. There was one typical way to the mercy seat of old, and that was through the turning aside of the veil; there was no other. And there is now no other way for any of you to come into fellowship with God except through the torn veil, even the death of Jesus Christ, whom God has set forth to be the propitiation for sin. Come this way, and you may come freely. Refuse to come this way, and there hangs between you and God an impassable veil. Without Christ you are without God, and without hope.

20 **by the new and living way that he inaugurated for us**
The precept to keep back is abrogated, and the invitation is, "Come to me, all of you who labor and are burdened" (Matt 11:28). "Let us draw near" is now the filial spirit of the gospel. How thankful I am for this! What a joy it is to my soul! Some of God's people have not yet realized this gracious fact, for still they worship afar off. Much prayer is to be highly commended for its reverence but it has in it a lack of childlike confidence. I can admire the solemn and stately language of worship that recognizes the greatness of God, but it will not warm my heart nor express my soul until it has also blended with the joyful nearness of that perfect love that drives out fear (1 John 4:18) and ventures to speak with our Father in heaven as a child speaks with its father on earth.

through the curtain In the East, men express their sorrow by tearing their garments. The temple, when it beheld its Master die, seemed struck with horror and tore its veil. Shocked at the sin of man, indignant at the murder of its Lord, in its sympathy with Him who is the true temple of God the outward symbol tore its holy vestment from the top to the bottom. Did not the miracle also mean that from that hour the whole system of types and shadows and ceremonies had come to an end? The ordinances of an earthly priesthood were rent with that veil.

The veil has not been merely lifted up for a while, and then dropped down again; it is not rolled up ready for future use;

it is torn in two, destroyed. Since Jesus has died, there is no separation now between the believer and his God except by means of such a veil as our base unbelief may please to hang up. The crimson way of Christ's shed blood lies open to all believers; therefore, "let us approach with a true heart in the full assurance of faith, having our hearts sprinkled clean from an evil conscience, and our bodies washed with pure water" (Heb 10:22).

that is, his flesh Whoever beneath the wide heavens is conscious of the plague of his own heart, or has anything that plagues him or anything that troubles him, may turn his eyes toward Christ, the true temple, with a certainty that God will hear his prayer and answer his request and send to him deliverance. "We have an altar" (Heb 13:10), and that altar is our Lord's own blessed person; we have but one, and we tremble for those who set up another, but to that one we look with confident hope, being assured that the sacrifice once offered there has made our peace with God, and procured acceptance for our supplications.

Let us never try to pray without Christ; never try to sing without Christ; never try to preach without Christ. Let us perform no holy function, nor attempt to have fellowship with God in any shape or way, except through the tear that He has made in the veil by His flesh, sanctified for us, and offered upon the cross on our behalf.

21 **and since we have a great priest over the house of God** The Israelite could not pass through the veil that hid from public gaze the glory of the Shekinah, and Jesus Christ's humanity was a veil that somewhat concealed the glory of His deity. But the flesh of Christ having been crucified, the veil has been torn, and now we may come right up to the throne of God without trembling. We may come even with holy boldness and familiarity, and speak to God without alarm. Having such a privilege as this, let us not neglect it. It was denied to prophets and kings in the olden time; but now that it is given to us, let us avail ourselves of it.

22   **let us approach with a true heart** We come before God in our station, not in our character. Therefore, we may come as perfect at all times, knowing that God sees no sin in Jacob and no iniquity in Israel. In this sense, Christ has perfected forever every consecrated vessel of His mercy. Is this not a delightful thought: that when I come before the throne of God, I feel myself a sinner, but God does not look upon me as one? When I approach Him to offer my thanksgiving, I feel that I am unworthy in myself, but I am not unworthy in that official standing in which He has placed me. As a sanctified and perfected thing in Christ, I have the blood upon me; God regards me in my sacrifice, in my worship, and in myself as being perfect.

Jesus is the great Priest, and we are the sub-priests under him, and since He bids us come near to God, and Himself leads the way, let us follow Him into the inner sanctuary. Because He lives, we shall live also. We shall not die in the holy place unless He dies. God will not smite us unless He smites Him.

ILLUSTRATION

Let Us Use the Consecrated Way

When a new road is opened, it is set apart and dedicated for the public use. Sometimes a public building is opened by a king or a prince, and so is dedicated to its purpose.

Beloved, the way to God through Jesus Christ is dedicated by Christ, and ordained by Christ for the use of poor believing sinners such as we are. He has consecrated the way toward God and dedicated it for us that we may freely use it. Surely, if there is a road set apart for me, I may use it without fear, and the way to God and heaven through Jesus Christ is dedicated by the Savior for sinners. It is the King's highway for wayfaring men who are bound for the City of God; therefore, let us use it.

---

in the full assurance of faith God cannot talk with an imperfect being. He could talk with Adam in the garden, but he could not talk with you or with me, even in paradise itself, as imperfect creatures. How, then, am I to have fellowship with God, and access to his throne? Why, simply thus: "For by one offering he has perfected for all time those who are made holy" (Heb 10:14). Consequently, we have access with boldness to the throne of the heavenly grace, and may come boldly in all our time of need. And what is better still, we are always perfect, always fit to come to the throne, whatever our doubts, whatever our sins.

Trembling though it be, our faith is true; and though it does not always work in us all the fruit we would desire, yet it does operate in a very blessed way upon our walk and conversation. We believe that Jesus is the Christ, and our trust for eternal life is in Him alone.

our hearts sprinkled clean It is the washing that enables us to draw near. We shrink, we tremble, we find communion impossible until we are made clean.

ILLUSTRATION
With Jesus, For Jesus, Like Jesus

To me it is a solemn memory that I professed my faith openly in baptism. I vividly recall the scene. It was the third of May, and the weather was cold because of a keen wind. I see the broad river, and the crowds that lined the banks, and the company on the ferry boat. The word of the Lord was preached by a man of God who is now gone home; and when he had done so, he went down into the water, and we followed him, and he baptized us. I remember how, after being the slave of timidity, I rose from the liquid grave quickened into holy courage by that one act of decision, consecrated henceforth to bear a lifelong testimony. It was by burial with Christ in baptism that I confessed my faith in his death, burial, and resurrection. By an avowed death to the world I professed my desire henceforth to live with Jesus, for Jesus, and like Jesus.

---

23   **Let us hold fast to the confession of our hope** We have a blessed hope—a hope most "firm and steadfast, and entering into the inside of the curtain" (Heb 6:19). If I begin to describe our hope, I must begin with what, I think, is always the topmost stone of it: the hope of the second advent of our Lord and Savior Jesus Christ; for we believe that when He shall appear, we shall also appear with Him in glory (Col 3:4).

Hope in Christ, and in His coming, and in the victory of the truth. If the storms lower, believe that there is fair weather yet ahead; and if the night darkens into a sevenfold blackness, believe that the morning comes despite the darkening glooms. Do you have faith and trust in Him who lives, and was dead, and is alive for evermore? Let your hope begin to hear the hallelujahs, which proclaim the reign of the Lord God omnipotent; for reign He must, and the victory shall be unto Him and to His truth. Hold fast your faith. Hold fast your hope.

without wavering Not only hold it, but hold it fast without wavering. Let us never have a question about it. God grant that we may have an unquestioning, unstaggering faith! To hold fast the profession of our faith seems enough, but to hold it fast without wavering is better still; and so we ought to do.

ILLUSTRATION
Remember How You First Loved Jesus

I remember well going to speak to the minister and telling him that I hoped I had found the Savior, and begging him to ask me such questions as he thought fit to test me.

The true pilgrim never wishes to enter the house Beautiful if he does not have a right to be there; he is afraid that he may be guilty of intrusion, and he therefore hopes the porter at the gate will only admit him when he feels quite sure that he is a pilgrim such as the Lord of the way would permit to enter his house. It was a day of great trembling, but of great joy, when first we avowed our faith in Jesus! What we said we meant. We salted our words with our tears. We felt it such an honor to be numbered with the people of God! If we had been promised a seat on the floor, or had been allowed only to hear the gospel in the draftiest corner of the building, we should then have been fully content.

We want soft cushions now; we cannot stand to hear a sermon now, nor travel very far, especially in damp weather. It is very strange that we should have become so delicate, but it is so. How many miles we could walk when first we knew the Lord; the miles have grown much longer lately, or else our love has grown much shorter!

---

for the one who promised is faithful God gives us no cause for wavering, for He never wavers. If He were an unfaithful God, we might naturally be an unbelieving people; but "He who promised is faithful." Therefore, "let us hold fast the profession of our faith without wavering."

24 **stir one another up to love and good works** I am afraid there are some who consider one another to provoke in quite a different spirit from this—who watch to find out a tender spot where a wound will be most felt. They observe the weakness of a brother's constitution, and then play upon it, or make jests about it. All this is evil, so let us avoid it; let us all seek out the good points of our brothers, and consider them, that we may afterward be the means of guiding them to those peculiar good works for which they are best adapted.

I do not know how we can do that better than by being very loving and very full of good works ourselves, for then others will be likely to say, "If these people are helped by God's grace to love like this, and to labor like this, why should we not do the same?" A good example is often better than a very proper precept.

25 **not abandoning our meeting together** Christian fellowship is helpful to us, and we are helpful to others by it. A Christian is not meant to be a solitary being. Sheep are gregarious, and so are the sheep of the Lord Jesus Christ. Let us not be solitary pilgrims along the road to heaven, but join that glorious host of God's elect who march beneath the guidance of our great Master.

ILLUSTRATION

Staying at Home to Read a Sermon

There are some who make a bad use of what ought to be a great blessing—namely, the printing press and the printed sermon—by staying at home to read a sermon because, they say, it is better than going out to hear one. It is a bad example for a professing Christian to absent himself from the assembly of the friends of Christ. There was a dear sister who used to attend here with great regularity, although she could not hear a word that was said; but she said it did her good to join in the hymns, and to know that she was worshiping God with the rest of His people.

I wish that some who stay away for the most frivolous excuses would think of this verse: "Not abandoning our meeting together, as is the habit of some."

---

but encouraging each other, and by so much more as you see the day drawing near. It is not the work of the minister alone to exhort, but the brothers, and the sisters, too, should exhort one another and seek to stir each other up in the faith and fear of God.

APPLICATION

We Have Boldness to Enter God's Presence

We cannot die in the holy place now, since Jesus has died for us. The death of Jesus is the guarantee of the eternal life of all for whom He died. We have boldness to enter, for we shall not perish. *We may have this boldness of entering in at all times*, because the veil is always rent, and is never restored to its old place. "And Yahweh said to Moses, 'Tell your brother Aaron that he should not enter at any time into the sanctuary behind the curtain in front of the atonement cover that is on the ark, so that he might not die" (Lev 16:2). But the Lord does not say so to us. Dear child of God, you may at all times have "boldness to enter in." The veil is torn both day and night.

Indeed, even when your eye of faith is dim, still enter in; when evidences are dark, still have "boldness to enter in"; and even if you have unhappily sinned, remember that access is open to your penitent prayer. Come still through the torn veil, sinner as you are. Although you have backslidden, though you are grieved with the sense of your wanderings, come even now! "Today, if you hear his voice, do not harden your hearts" (Heb 3:15), but enter at once; for the veil is not there to exclude you, though doubt and unbelief may make you think so. The veil cannot be there, for it was torn in two from the top to the bottom.

Be a Blessing

The high priest, if you recollect, after he had communed and prayed with God, came out and blessed the people. He put on his garments of glory and beauty, which he had laid aside when he went into the holy place (for there he stood in simple white, and nothing else), and now he came out wearing the breastplate and all his precious ornaments, and he blessed the people. That is what you will do if you have the boldness to enter into the holiest by the blood of Jesus: you will bless the people that surround you. The Lord has blessed you, and He will make you a blessing. Your ordinary conduct and conversation will be a blessed example; the words you speak for Jesus will be like dew from the Lord. The sick will be comforted by your words; the despondent will be encouraged by your faith; the lukewarm will be recovered by your love. You will practically be saying to each one who knows you, "May Yahweh bless you and keep you; May Yahweh make his face shine on you and be gracious to you" (Num 6:24–25). You will become a channel of blessing: "Out of your belly will flow rivers of living water" (John 7:37). May we each one have boldness to enter in, that we may come forth laden with benedictions!

Hold Fast to the Profession of Your Faith

You are Christians, not for a time, but for eternity. Your new birth is not into a dying existence but into life everlasting. Continue your confession, and never conceal it.

There are times when you will be inclined to put your flag away into the canvas case and hide your coat of arms in the cellar. Then you may fitly judge that the devil is getting advantage over you, and that it is time that you ceased to be beguiled by his sorceries. Tear up the wrappings, throw the bag away, and nail your flag aloft where every eye can see it. Whenever you feel inclined to be ashamed of Christ, do not deliberate but say, "This is wrong. There is coming over me something that I must not endure. If I were in a right state of mind I should never feel like this." Never yield to shameful cowardice; scorn such detestable meanness.

Perhaps you may have to go into a certain company where you do not want to have it known that you are a Christian. It is imperative that you break through that snare and put the case beyond debate. If I were you, I would make my profession known in that very company, because the idea that you must not be known to be a Christian will be very dangerous to you. I cannot exactly tell in what way it may endanger you, but it will surely do so. Therefore, whenever the thought of concealment crops up, down with it, and come out clear and straight for Jesus. Only when you are out-and-out for Jesus can you be in a right condition. Anything short of this is full of evil. Since Satan tempts you to hide your faith, feel that he seeks your harm, and therefore come out all the more decidedly.

²⁶ For if we keep on sinning deliberately after receiving the knowledge of the truth, there no longer remains a sacrifice for sins, ²⁷ but a certain fearful expectation of judgment and a fury of fire that is about to consume the adversaries. ²⁸ Anyone who rejected the law of Moses dies without mercy on the testimony of two or three witnesses. ²⁹ How much worse punishment do you think the person will be considered worthy of who treats with disdain the Son of God, and who considers ordinary the blood of the covenant by which he was made holy, and who insults the Spirit of grace? ³⁰ For we know the one who said,

"Vengeance is mine, I will repay,"

and again,

"The Lord will judge his people."

³¹ It is a terrifying thing to fall into the hands of the living God.
³² But remember the former days in which, after you were enlightened, you endured a great struggle with sufferings, ³³ sometimes being publicly exposed both to insults and to afflictions, and sometimes becoming sharers with those who were treated in this way. ³⁴ For you both sympathized with the prisoners and put up with the seizure of your belongings with joy because you knew that you yourselves had a better and permanent possession. ³⁵ Therefore, do not throw away your confidence, which has great reward. ³⁶ For you have need of endurance, in order that after you have done the will of God, you may receive what was promised. ³⁷ For yet

"a very, very little while,
and the one who is coming will come and will not delay.
³⁸ But my righteous one will live by faith,
and if he shrinks back, my soul is not well pleased with him."

> [39] But we are not among those who shrink back to destruction, but among those who have faith to the preservation of our souls.

EXPOSITION

26 **if we keep on sinning deliberately** It would have been better for you never to have had any knowledge of the truth, than to have known it, and then sinned willfully against it, and so, after all, to be a castaway. If you are a true child of God, though a wanderer from His ways, you will be brought back to Him, and I pray that you may be brought back to Him this very hour. But if you are an apostate, a backslider in heart, you will be filled with your own ways. Having filled up the measure of your iniquity, you will be driven from God's presence into the place of woe where hope and mercy never can come.

after receiving the knowledge of the truth How foolish you are who are looking for signs and wonders or else you will not believe. May the Spirit of God show you that Jesus is now able and willing to save you, and that all you have to do is to take what He has done, and simply trust Him, and you shall be saved, completely saved, perfected through His one sacrifice. There remains no more to be done by the Redeemer. He sits down, and He will not rise for any further sacrifice.

there no longer remains a sacrifice for sins How can there be? Do you think when you are in hell that Christ will come a second time to die for you? Will He pour out His blood again to bring you from the place of torment? Have you so vain an imagination as to dream that there will be a second ransom offered for those who have not escaped the wrath to come, and that God the Holy Ghost will again come and strive with sinners who willfully rejected Him?

All the atonement that could save me in 10 years' time is here now. All that I can ever rely upon if I postpone all thoughts of faith—all is here already. There will be no improvement in Christ. He has perfected His work. Oh, poor troubled soul, rest on Him now.

ILLUSTRATION
Rejecting an Invitation to the Feast

Have you ever considered how much you insult God the Father by rejecting Christ? If you were invited to a feast and you should come to the table and dash down every dish, and throw them on the ground, and trample on them, would not this be an insult? If you were a poor beggar at the door, and a rich man had bidden you into his feast out of pure charity, what would you deserve if you had treated his provisions in this way?

And yet this is just your case. You were not deserving of God, you were a poor sinner without any claim upon Him, and yet He has been pleased to prepare a table. His oxen and His fattened cattle have been killed, and now you will not come. You do worse: you raise objections to the feast; you despise the pleasant land and the goodly provision of God. Just think at what an expense the provision of salvation has been made.

---

27 **but a certain fearful expectation of judgment** Here the truth taught is that, if a Christian apostatizes, if he renounces his faith and goes back to the world, it is impossible to reclaim him. A backslider may be restored, but anyone who should willfully, after receiving the truth, reject it, has rejected the only Savior. He has rejected the only regeneration, and consequently, he is without the pale of the possibilities of restoration. The question is, "Will any true child of God so apostatize?" That question is answered in this very chapter; but the truth here taught is that, if he does, he goes into a state of absolute hopelessness.

What, then, is our hope? Why, that we shall never be permitted to do so; that the grace of God will keep us so that, although we may fall like Peter, we shall not fall away like Judas; that—though we may sin—there shall not be that degree of studied willfulness about it that would make it to be the sin unto death, a deliberate act of spiritual suicide. The doctrine of the final perseverance of the saints derives great glory from this other truth that, if they did not persevere, there is no second means of grace, no other plan of salvation. No man was ever born again twice; no man was ever washed twice in the precious blood of Jesus. The one washing makes us so clean that "the one who has bathed only needs to wash his feet" (John 13:10), for which Jesus provides by daily cleansing. But the one grand atoning act never fails. If it did fail, there would remain "no more sacrifice for sins" (Heb 10:26).

28-29 who treats with disdain the Son of God Everything lies in the bowels of this sin—the rejecting of Christ. There is murder in this; for if the man on the scaffold rejects a pardon, does he not murder himself? There is pride in this; for you reject Christ, because your proud hearts have turned you aside. There is rebellion in this; for we rebel against God when we reject Christ. There is high treason in this; for you reject a king. You put far from you Him who is crowned king of the earth, and you incur therefore the weightiest of all guilt. Oh, to think that the Lord Jesus should come from heaven—to think for a moment that He should hang upon the tree—that there He should die in extreme agonies, and that from that cross He should this day look down upon you, and should say, "Come to me, all of you who labor and are burdened" (Matt 11:28), that you should still turn away from him—it is the unkindest stab of all. What more brutish, what more devilish, than to turn away from Him who gave His life for you?

If this does not mean that unbelief is a sin, and *the* sin that, above all others, damns men's souls, they do not mean anything at all. But they are just a dead letter in the Word of God. Now, adultery and murder, and theft, and lying—all these are damning and deadly sins; but repentance can cleanse all these, through the blood of Christ. But to reject Christ destroys a man hopelessly. The murderer, the thief, the drunkard, may yet enter the kingdom of heaven, if, repenting of his sins, he will lay hold on the cross of Christ. But with these sins, a man is inevitably lost, if he does not believe on the Lord Jesus Christ (Acts 16:31).

29 **who considers ordinary the blood of the covenant** Did Jesus die as His people's substitute? That is the question; and there are some, I grieve to say it, to whom this text is applicable. This is the chief aim of the enemy's assaults: to get rid of Christ, to get rid of the atonement, to get rid of His suffering in the room and place and stead of men. They say they can embrace the rest of the gospel; but what "rest" is there? What is there left? A bloodless, Christless gospel is fit neither for the land nor for the dunghill; it neither honors God nor converts the sons of men.

30 **Vengeance is mine, I will repay** God's fire is in Zion, and His furnace in Jerusalem. If a man tries nothing else, he will test his gold; and if no others shall be judged, yet certainly those will be who say that they are the Lord's people. In that dread day, He will separate the goats from the sheep, the tares from the wheat, and the dross from the gold; His fan will be in His hand, and He will thoroughly purge His floor; He will sit as a refiner of silver, and He will purify the sons of Levi; He shall be like a refiner's fire, and like fuller's soap. Woe to those, in that day, who are a defilement to His Church and an adulteration to the purity of His people!

31 **It is a terrifying thing** It must be a fearful thing for impenitent sinners to fall into God's hand when we remember the character of God as revealed in His judgments of old. Taking the Scriptures as our guide, we see in them a revelation of God differing very widely from that which is so current nowadays. The God of Abraham, as revealed in the Old Testament, is as different from the universal Father of modern dreams as he

is from Apollo or Bacchus. Let me remind you that ever since the day when Adam fell, with but two exceptions, the whole of the human race have been subjected to the pains of sickness and of *death*. If you would behold the severity of Him who judges all the earth, you have only to remember that this whole world has been for ages a vast burying place.

to fall into the hands of the living God What a terrible verse is that! It is a text that ought to be preached from by those who are always saying that the punishment of the wicked will be less than, according to our minds, the Word of God leads us to expect it to be.

Upon such a subject we cannot afford to trifle. Besides, the mystery of Calvary indicates to us that sin must deserve at God's hand a terrible penalty. Did Jesus suffer so bitterly to save men, and will not the unsaved endure bitterness indeed? Must the eternal and holy Son of God, upon whom sin was only an imputed thing—must He bleed, and die, and offer up His life, with His soul exceedingly heavy even unto death—and is *the world to come* a thing about which men can afford to sport or idly dream?

ILLUSTRATION
Preaching That There Is No Hell

I like the remark of the people who were requested to accept a Universalist as a minister. They said, "You have come to tell us that there is no hell. If your doctrine is true, we certainly do not need you; and if it is not true, we do not want you. Either way, we can do without you."

It is a most dreadful fact that there is no provision made for the future restoration of the lost; not a word said about it, except that for them remains the blackness of darkness forever.

---

32   **But remember the former days** Some of you can "remember the former days" when you joined the church, when you had to run the gantlet for Christ's sake. Then, in your early Christian life, you feared nothing and no one so long as you could glorify God. Then, you had great enjoyment, sweet seasons of communion with your Lord: "Remember the former days."

33   **being publicly exposed both to insults and to afflictions** In your early Christian days, you were pointed at, and regarded as quite singular for being servants of Christ. Or possibly, it was not yourselves so much as your pastors, your leaders, your friends who were prominent in the church at whom the arrows of the adversaries were aimed. They shot at you through them; and, sometimes, that pained you much more than when they distinctly attacked you. Altogether, it was "a great struggle with sufferings" (Heb 10:32) that you had to endure.

34   **put up with the seizure of your belongings with joy** The early Christians had to suffer for their faith. They were exposed to great ridicule and enmity: they were, indeed, the byword, the laughingstock, and the derision of all mankind. Nor did it end in ridicule: they were deprived of their goods. Ruinous fines were exacted from them. They were driven from city to city, and not thought worthy to dwell among the sons of men. They were made a spectacle to all men, both in their lives and deaths. Very frequently they were not put to death as other condemned persons were, but their execution was attended with circumstances of cruelty and scorn, which made it still harder to bear: they were daubed with pitch and set up in the gardens of Nero to be burned alive to light that tyrant's debaucheries, or taken to the Amphitheater, there to fight with beasts and to be torn in pieces. Everything that could be invented that was at once degrading and cruel their persecutors devised for them: malice exhausted its ingenuity upon believers in Christ.

a better and permanent possession If between here and heaven you had nothing to bear but the cruelty of men, and the unkindness of the enemies of Christ, you should bear it right manfully, and even joyfully, because you can say, "I know in myself that I have in heaven a better and an enduring substance. Even here I have a life that the world did not give me, and cannot take from me; therefore I hold to it still, and I comfort myself with this sweet thought, that it is mine, the gift of God to me. It bears me up amid seas of grief. 'My flesh and my heart failed, but God is the strength of my heart and my reward forever'" (Psa 73:26).

35 **do not throw away your confidence** If it was intimated to you that tomorrow morning you must go out to be burned to death in the great square of the city, or to be torn to pieces in the amphitheater by wild beasts, would you be quite sure that the promise of God was faithful and true? Yet, beloved, that is the kind of faith we must have, for God deserves it. He cannot lie; He has promised that those who trust in Him shall never be forsaken or confounded (Deut 31:6), world without end.

Be like the brave Spartan who would never lose his shield, but would come home either with it or on it. "Do not throw away your confidence." You trusted in God in those early days, and nothing seemed to daunt you then. "Do not throw away your confidence." Rather, get more to add to it. Let there be no thought of going back, but may there rather be a distinct advance!

ILLUSTRATION

Do Not Turn Back Now

I have known a man begin to build his house, and he has spent a great deal of money on it. At length, he has thought, "I do not quite like the situation. Shall I finish the building?" One strong argument for going on has been this: "I have spent so much money on it; I must go through with it."

Now, some of you have spent much upon your faith; by God's grace, you have been pressing on to know the Lord for years. You bore the troubles of your early youth when, perhaps, father and mother were against you, and you were bold then for Christ. Some of you have been known as Christian workers for years, and you have encountered the chaff of the workshop for many a month, and yet you have not gone back. Well, you have spent a good deal upon your faith: never give it up, my brother, never give it up. If, for your Lord's sake, you have had the honor to be abused and scandalized, do not turn your back now.

---

which has great reward The day will come when the King will review His troops as the squadrons come back from the battle. The day will come when He shall come down our ranks and look at every one of us. If we have been faithful in this evil day, it will repay us for anything we suffered if He shall say to us, "Well done!" Oh, those two words! These would be enough to make us eternally happy, but hear the rest: "Well done, good and faithful servant; enter into the joy of your master" (Matt 25:23).

36 **For you have need of endurance** This is sweet counsel for you, O pilgrim, bound to Zion's city. When you were young and strong, you walked many a weary mile with that staff of promise. It helped you over the ground. Don't throw it aside as useless now that you are old and infirm. Lean upon it. Rest upon that promise, in your present weakness, which lightened your labor in the days of your vigor.

ILLUSTRATION

We Become Impatient with Nothing to Do

We are never so subject to impatience as when there is nothing we can do. While the farmer is occupied with plowing, harrowing, tilling, drilling, hoeing, and the like, he is too busy to be fretful. It is when the work is done, and there is nothing more to occupy his hands, that the very leisure he has to endure gives occasion to secret qualms and lurking cares.

So it ever is with us. While "we are God's fellow workers" (1 Cor 3:9), our occupation is so pleasant that we little heed the toil of hard service. But when it comes to a point where we have no activity, for it is "God who is causing it to grow" (1 Cor 3:7), we are apt to be grievously distrustful; our unbelief finds full play. It is after our fight is fought, after our race is run, after our allotted task is finished, there is so much need of patience—of such patience as waits only on God and watches unto prayer, that we may finish our course with joy and the ministry we have received from the Lord Jesus.

after you have done the will of God, you may receive what was promised There must first be the doing of the will of God, and then the reward will come afterward. God will not give to His people their full reward yet. Patience, then, brother; patience, sister. Saturday night will come one of these days; your week's work will then be over, and you will be more than repaid for anything you have done for your Lord.

37 **the one who is coming will come and will not delay.** Then shall the Bridegroom's attendants rejoice with unspeakable joy, because the Bridegroom Himself has come. The day of His marriage has arrived. I ask you, if you have been silent, and hung your harps on the willows, take them down at once, and

sing and give praise to God for the glory which is yet to be revealed in us. Give praise for the precious things that are laid up for them that love Him, which eye has not seen, nor ear heard, but the certainty of which He has revealed unto us by His Spirit.

38 **But my righteous one will live by faith** The ground of the sinner's acceptance in the first moment of his faith is the finished work of Christ, and, after 50 years of earnest service, that must still be the sole cause of his acceptance with God, and the only rock upon which his soul must dare to build. The act of simple faith, looking out of self, and looking alone to Christ, is a thing for your penitent tax collector when first he beats his breast (Luke 18:13). It is also for your dying David, when he knows that the covenant is ordered in all things and sure.

The righteous man will carry his faith into his ordinary life. He will live by faith. All the actions of his life that have in them any decree of moral or spiritual aspect—all of these shall be conspicuously ruled by his confidence in God. Even the lowliest and commonest affairs in which he takes a part shall be subdued and elevated by the dignity of his trust and the fidelity of his adherence. He shall live by faith. Not alone in the study and in the closet, not alone in the assembly of the saints and at the table of fellowship, but in the market and on the exchange, in the shop and the counting-house, in the parlor or the drawing room, at the plough-tail or at the carpenter's bench, in the senate house or at the judgment hall. The just man, wherever his life is cast, shall carry his faith with him; indeed, his faith shall be in him as part of his life; he shall live there by faith.

ILLUSTRATION

Can a Sinner Sink through a Rock?

There was a good old soul whose minister called to see her when she was dying. Among other things he said to her, "My sister, you are very weak; don't you feel yourself sinking?" She looked at him, and gave no answer, but said, "Did I understand you, minister? Please tell me what you said—I hope you didn't say what I thought I heard." "Why," said he, "my dear sister, I said to you, don't you feel yourself sinking?" And then she said, "I did not think my minister would ever ask me such a question as that! Sinking? Did you ever know a sinner sink through a rock? I am believing in Jesus Christ; if I were resting anywhere else I might sink, but as I am resting upon Him, did you ever know a sinner sink through a rock?"

That is just the point. God assures us that if we believe, we have gotten onto a rock, that if we believe, we shall live. We shall live by our faith under all circumstances and difficulties.

---

39 **But we are not among those who shrink back to destruction** Our old evil nature, though it may have lost some of its strength, yet is capable of wonderful outbursts of power, and the world outside of us is full of grief. We must expect to be tempted in many fresh ways between here and the celestial city. But there is no lulling temptation in them all, for the just shall live by his faith. Empty your quiver, O enemy of souls, but this divine shield shall catch every arrow and quench its fire, and blunt those points, and save and deliver us from them all.

I look with admiration upon brothers who have remained faithful to God for 60 or 70 years. It seems to me that the length of the Christian's life is, in itself, oftentimes a very severe trial. A man might stand at the stake and burn for a few minutes, but hanging up over a slow fire—who can bear that? To do one brave and generous action, this seems simple enough; but to stand on the watchtower day and night, always vigilant; watching, lest the foe surprise us; watching, lest our hearts betray us; watching unto prayer, that we may keep ourselves in the love of God. Oh, this is a work—this is a labor that only grace can help us to perform. But here is the comfort. No length of days can exhaust the believer's patience or peril his spiritual life, because the just shall live by faith.

but among those who have faith to the preservation of our souls What a blessed truth this is! Christian, as you see the danger that lies before you if you did prove to be an apostate, bless that sovereign grace that will not allow you to do so, even as Paul wrote to the Philippians, "I am convinced of this same thing, that the one who began a good work in you will finish it until the day of Christ Jesus" (Phil 1:6).

APPLICATION

Falling into the Hands of the Living God

What could there be that would terrify and alarm the soul in falling into the hands of the living God? Let me remind you. You sinners, when you begin to think of God, feel uneasy. In a future state you will be compelled to think of God. God is not in all your thoughts now—it is the only place where He is not. But when you enter the future state, you will not be able to escape from the thought of God; you will then realize the words of David, "If I make my bed in Sheol, look! There you are" (Psa 139:8). That thought will torment you. You will have to think of God as one to whom you were ungrateful. You will feel remorse, but not repentance, as you recollect that He did honestly invite you to come to Him, that He called and you refused, that He stretched out His hand and you did not regard Him. As you think of the happiness of those whose hearts were given to Him, it will make your miseries great to think of what you have lost. You will hate Him, and here it seems to me will be your misery.

Well may the wicked gnash their teeth, as they note the overthrow of evil and the establishment of good! Ungodly men, both here and hereafter, hate God just because He is good, just as of old the wicked hated the saints because they were saints. And they hate Him all the more because He is so powerful that they cannot defeat Him or frustrate His designs. Those sins of yours will feed the flame within your conscience and will be an undying worm within your heart.

Turn to Him, for to turn *from* Him is to be unhappy! To love God is heaven; to hate Him brings hell. You are so made that you cannot sin and be happy. It was right of God to make you such a creature that holiness and happiness should go together; it was right of Him to make you such a creature that sin and sorrow must go together, and if you will have sin, you must have sorrow. Turn from it, while you may. May God's Spirit turn you now before you enter into that world where there is no turning, but where the die is cast and the road is chosen. As the arrow, once shot, speeds onward in its course and does not turn from it, so must you speed on in holiness and happiness or in sin and sorrow, for there is no turning from the course.

Reward for Followers of Christ

Believe me, kings and mighty men who have rolled in riches and yet were enemies to Christ will hear Christ say, "Well done!" to His poor people. They will think themselves accursed that they were not martyrs, and that they did not lie in prison, or at least suffer reproach for Christ. The enemies of Christ laugh today, but they will laugh on the other side of their faces before long. Let them laugh, for *we* shall win. The day shall come when shame shall be the promotion of fools, but the royal robe shall be put upon each man's back who dared to be a fool for Christ. The scars of suffering saints shall shine like diamonds, and those who were most abused shall be the brightest of the shining ones. Gladdest of all will be those who have the ruby crown of martyrdom to cast at the Savior's feet. Each one of you who have boldly held on to Christ, though despised and rejected, and dared to suffer slander for His dear name's sake, you shall be among the first and brightest who wear the white robe, and share their Master's victory. By the palm and by the white robe, by the crown unfading, by the harps of angels, and the streets of gold, do not cast away your confidence, for it has great recompense of reward.

You who do not know Christ, and have no confidence in Him, beware! He is coming—coming to call you to judgment. Beware, for in the day of His appearing He will look upon you, and He will know that you never trusted Him, and never suffered for Him, but chose the broad road that leads to destruction (Matt 7:13). Oh, how you will tremble then, and with what agony will you cry to the mountains, "Hide us from the face of the one who is seated on the throne" (Rev 6:16). God grant that you may not thus be carried away with terror, but may you believe your Lord, and then have a full confidence in Him.

No Sin Too Big for God

Do not let the adversary say to you, "You must not come, because you have walked contrary to God." O poor backslider, although sin may hide God from you, and take away your comfortable sense of His love, yet if you believe in Him, His love is toward you. He has not cast you away (Psa 51:11), you will live as long as there is faith in you. If there be so little faith that we have to rake up the ashes and have to go down on our knees and blow that little spark, yet the Lord knows how to fan it, and to put the match to it, and to make a great blaze very speedily. Before you hardly know it, you who were crawling along the road shall be like the chariots of Amminadab, flying along as on mighty wings. Never doubt God's power to lift you out of the ditch into which you have fallen. Still hold to it: "Though he kill me, I will hope in him" (Job 13:15); though you be black with sin, and ashamed of yourself, and dare not look up, but feel that you deserve to be cast into the lowest hell, yet still do not doubt that the precious blood can wash you and make you whiter than snow.

Is there a grander verse in the whole Bible, is there anything in the compass of Scripture that ever glorified God more, than that notable expression of David when he had been sinning with Bathsheba, and made himself as foul and as filthy as the very swine of hell? And yet he cries, "Be gracious to me, O God, according to your loyal love. According to your abundant mercies, blot out my transgressions. Wash me thoroughly from my iniquity, and from my sin cleanse me"

(Psa 51:1–2). "Wash me"—that is the cry—"Wash me, the most scarlet and the blackest of hell-deserving sinners. Only wash me, and I shall be whiter than snow." Believe in the omnipotent power of the atonement. Still believe, and hold fast to Christ. Cling to His skirts, and if He even seem to frown upon you, hold to Him, like the woman whom He called a dog, and yet she said, "The dogs eat the crumbs" (Matt 15:27). Do not believe that which you think you hear Him say, for He cannot say otherwise than this: That everyone who believes in Him is not condemned. He that believes in Him, even if he dies, will live (John 11:25). Out of your very death believe Him. From your very hell of sin believe Him. Wherever you may be, still believe Him. Never doubt Him, for the just shall live by faith.

HEBREWS 11

¹ Now faith is the realization of what is hoped for, the proof of things not seen. ² For by this the people of old were approved. ³ By faith we understand that the worlds were created by the word of God, in order that what is seen did not come into existence from what is visible.

⁴ By faith Abel offered to God a greater sacrifice than Cain, by which he was approved as righteous because God approved him for his gifts, and through it he still speaks, although he is dead. ⁵ By faith Enoch was taken up, so that he did not experience death, and he was not found because God took him up. For before his removal, he had been approved as having been pleasing to God. ⁶ Now without faith it is impossible to please him, for the one who approaches God must believe that he exists and is a rewarder of those who seek him. ⁷ By faith Noah, having been warned about things not yet seen, out of reverence constructed an ark for the deliverance of his family, by which he pronounced sentence on the world and became an heir of the righteousness that comes by faith.

EXPOSITION

1   **faith is the realization of what is hoped for** Although the "things" are only "hoped for" and "not seen" at present, the eye of faith can see them, and the hand of faith can grasp them. Faith is mightier than any of our senses or than all our senses combined.

the proof of things not seen We do see by faith. We see by faith what cannot be seen by our eyes; we grasp by faith what cannot be grasped with our hands. A strange mystery is the simple act of faith.

2 **For by this the people of old were approved** So it was written, in the olden time, that believers "were approved." This second verse shows that they were approved by their faith. The best part of the report about them is that they believed their God, and believed all that was revealed to them by His Word and His Spirit.

ILLUSTRATION

The Leap of Faith

Suppose there is a fire in the upper room of a house and the people gather in the street. A child is in the upper story; how is he to escape? He cannot leap down—he would be dashed to pieces. A strong man comes beneath, and cries, "Drop into my arms." It is a part of faith to know that the man is there; it is another part of faith to believe that the man is strong. But the essence of faith lies in the dropping down into the man's arms. That is the proof of faith, and the real pith and essence of it.

So, sinner, you are to know that Christ died for sin; you are also to understand that Christ is able to save, and you are to believe that. But you are not saved unless in addition to that you put your trust in Him to be your Savior and to be yours forever.

---

3 **By faith we understand the worlds were created by the word of God** The facts about creation must be the subject of faith. It is true that they can be substantiated by the argument from design and in other ways; still, for a wise purpose, as I believe, God has not made even that matter of the creation of the universe perfectly clear to human reason, so there is room for the exercise of faith. People like to have everything laid down according to the rules of mathematical precision, but God desires them to exercise faith. Therefore, He has not acted according to their wishes.

Reason is all very well, but faith mounts upon the shoulders of reason and sees much farther than reason with her best telescope will ever be able to see. It is enough for us who have faith that God has told us how He made the world, and we believe it.

in order that what is seen did not come into existence from what is visible Things that we see were not made out of things that we see. They were brought out of the unseen by the word of God. The word of God is the foundation of everything that has been formed by Him; and, after all, things material—created and seen—are not truly substantial. They are but shadows; the real substance is that which never can be seen, even the ever-blessed God, whose voice—whose word—created the heavens and the earth.

4   **By faith Abel** The first of the long line of martyrs triumphed by faith. If you are to be strong to bear witness for God, you must be made strong by the same power that wrought so effectually in Abel. If, like his, your life is to be a speaking life—a life that will speak even out of the grave—its voice must be the voice of faith.

Faith works differently in each one of these mighty men. It is the same living principle in all of them; but they are different men, and their faith is seen in very different circumstances. Faith is able to work in all manner of ways; it is good at everything. There is nothing that God calls us to do but faith can enable us to accomplish it. In Abel's case, we see that faith is grand at worshiping. Faith brings a right sacrifice, brings it in the right way, and speaks even after she is dead, for the blood of Abel cried out of the ground. Oh, that all of us might so live that, even out of our graves, there might come a voice speaking for God!

offered to God a greater sacrifice than Cain Abel taught the need of approaching the Lord with sacrifice, the need of atonement by blood. He laid the lamb upon the altar and sealed his testimony with his own blood. Atonement is so precious a truth that to die for its defense is a worthy deed, and from the very first it is a doctrine that has secured its martyrs, who being dead yet speak.

God approved him through his gifts There is no worshiping God aright, except by faith. The most gorgeous ceremonies are as nothing in His sight; it is the faith of the heart that He accepts.

he still speaks, although he is dead He spoke by faith when he lived. Faith makes him speak now that he is dead. What wonders faith can work. The first saint who entered heaven entered there, it is certain, by faith. It was faith that enabled him to present an acceptable sacrifice, and it was faith that presented him to heaven. If the first who entered heaven entered there by faith, rest assured that will be true to the last, and none will enter there but those who believe.

5   **By faith Enoch** Then came Enoch, whose life went beyond the reception and confession of the atonement, for he set before men the great truth of communion with God. He displayed in his life the relation of the believer to the Most High, and showed how near the living God condescends to be to His own children.

ILLUSTRATION

A Boy Walking with His Father

The boy is not afraid of missing his way; he trusts implicitly his father's guidance. His father's arm will screen him from all danger, and therefore he does not so much as give it a thought. Why should he? If care is needed as to the road, it is his father's business to see to it, and the child, therefore, never dreams of anxiety. Why should he? If any difficult place is to be passed, the father will have to lift the boy over it, or help him through it—the child meanwhile is merry as a bird. Why should he not be?

Thus should the believer walk with God, resting on eternal tenderness and rejoicing in undoubted love. A believer should be unconscious of dread, either as to the present or to the future. Beloved friend in Christ, your Father may be trusted; He will supply all you need.

---

was taken up Mark that this holiest of men, whose walk with God was so close and unbroken that he was permitted to escape the pangs of death, nevertheless did not attain to this high position by his own works, but by faith.

so that he did not experience death It is faith that muzzles the mouth of death and takes away the power of the sepulcher. If any man, who had not been a believer, had been translated as Enoch was, we should have been able to point to a great feat accomplished apart from faith. It has never been so; for this, which was one of the greatest things that was ever done—to leap from this life into another, and to overleap the grave altogether—was only achieved "by faith."

Now, if there is any man in the world that shall never die, it is he who walks with God. If there is any man to whom death will be as nothing, it is the man who has looked to the second advent of Christ and gloried in it. If there is any man who, though he pass through the iron gates of death, shall never feel the terror of the grim foe, it is the man whose life below has been perpetual communion with God. Do not go about by any other way to escape the pangs of death, but walk with God, and you will be able to say, "Where, O death, is your victory? Where, O death, is your sting?" (1 Cor 15:55).

and he was not found Now, if a man is not found, it shows that somebody looked after him. When Elijah went to heaven, you remember 50 men of the sons of the prophets went and searched for him. I do not wonder that they did; they would not meet with an Elijah every day, and when he was gone away, body and all, they might well look for him. Enoch was not found, but they looked after him. A good man is missed.

We do not want so to live and die that nobody will care whether we are on earth. Enoch was missed when he was gone, and so will they be who walk with God.

God took him up A very remarkable expression. Perhaps He did it in some visible manner. I should not wonder. Perhaps the whole of the patriarchs saw him depart, even as the apostles were present when our Lord was taken up. However that may be, there was some special rapture, some distinct taking up of this choice one, to the throne of the Most High.

he had been approved as having been pleasing to God The way to please God, then, is to believe in Him—and if there is any possibility of entering heaven without seeing death, faith alone can point the way. You cannot be like Enoch unless you please God, and you cannot please God unless you have faith in Him.

If we cannot get a translation as Enoch did, let us not be content without getting God's good pleasure as he did. Oh, that it may be said of us that we pleased God! Then we shall, one way or another, conquer death; for if we do, we shall triumph over the grave. And if Christ shall come before we die, we shall triumph in the coming of Christ. Anyhow, faith shall be more than a match for the last enemy.

6   **Now without faith it is impossible to please him** See here how faith has learned the secret art of pleasing God. God is the thrice-holy One; He is a jealous God, and a very little sin greatly provokes Him. But faith knows how to please Him. I do not wonder that Enoch did not die; it was a less thing to be

translated to heaven than it was to please God. To live for 300 years, in constant communion with God, as he did, to be ever pleasing God, was a mighty triumph for faith. May God grant that, during all the years that we live, whether they are few or many, we may so live as always to please Him!

If Enoch had been pleasing to God by virtue of some extraordinary gifts and talents, or by reason of marvelous achievements and miraculous works, we might have been in despair. But if he was pleasing to God through faith—that same faith that saved the dying thief (Luke 23:43), that same faith that has been wrought in you and in me—then the wicket gate at the head of the way in which men walk with God is open to us also. If we have faith, we may enter into fellowship with the Lord. How this ought to endear faith to us!

If we please God, we shall have realized the object of our being. It is written concerning all things that for His pleasure they are and were created (Rev 4:11), and we miss the end of creation if we are not pleasing to the Lord. To fulfill God's end in our creation is to obtain the highest joy. If we are pleasing to God, although we shall not escape trial—for even the highest qualities must be tested—yet we shall find great peace and special happiness. He is not an unhappy man who is pleasing to God. God has blessed him, indeed, and he shall be blessed. By pleasing God we shall become the means of good to others: our example will rebuke and stimulate; our peace will convince and invite.

ILLUSTRATION
Fair-Weather Christians

Many Christians resemble the nautilus, which in fine smooth weather swims on the surface of the sea in a splendid little squadron, like the mighty ships. But the moment the first breath of wind ruffles the waves, they take in their sails and sink into the depths.

Many Christians are the same. In good company, in evangelical drawing rooms, in pious parlors, in chapels and vestries, they are tremendously religious. But if they are exposed to a little ridicule, if some should smile at them and call them some name of reproach, it is all over with their religion until the next fine day. Then when it is fine weather, and religion will answer their purpose, up go the sails again, and they are as pious as before.

---

one who approaches God The way of acceptance described in Scripture is, first, the man is accepted, and then what that man does is accepted. It is written: "He will purify the children of Levi, and he will refine them like gold and like silver, and they will present to Yahweh offerings in righteousness" (Mal 3:3). First, God is pleased with the person, and then with the gift, or the work. The unaccepted person offers of necessity an unacceptable sacrifice. If a man be your enemy, you will not value a present that he sends you. If you know that he has no confidence in you, but counts you a liar, his praises are lost upon you; they are empty, deceptive things that cannot possibly please you.

must believe that he exists We must believe that there is a God—that these things that we see do not spring of themselves, or come by chance, or in any way whatever except that there is a personal God, who created all things, and by whom all things consist. If you do not believe that, you certainly will never come to God. How is it possible for a man to come to One whose very existence he doubts? That matter must be settled, or there cannot be any real coming to God.

More than that, if we come to God we must believe that there is but one God, that the God of Abraham, of Isaac, and of Jacob is the only living and true God. If we are to come to God—to the God of the Old and the New Testament—we must accept Him as He is there pleased to reveal Himself. We must not try to fashion a god such as we would like to have, for that would be idolatry; we must accept God as He is made known in the Scriptures, and especially as He has manifested Himself in Christ Jesus, for it is in Him that God has revealed Himself to us for the practical purpose of our reconciliation. If we wish really to come to God, it must be by the way in which He has come to us—that is, through His Son, Jesus Christ. Neither, let me add, shall we ever come to God in the right way unless we ask for the assistance of the Holy Spirit, the third Person of the blessed Trinity in Unity.

But the devils believe and tremble, and yet they are not pleasing to God, for more is wanted. Believe that God *is* in reference to yourself, that He has to do with your life and your ways. Many believe that there is a hazy, imaginary power, which they call God. But they never think of Him as a person, nor do they suspect that He thinks of them, or that His existence is of any consequence to them one way or another. Believe that God *is* as truly as you are; and let Him be real to you. Let the consideration of Him enter into everything that concerns you. Believe that He is approachable by yourself, and is to be pleased or displeased by you. Believe in Him as you believe in your wife or your child whom you try to please. Believe in God beyond everything, that "He is" in a sense more sure than that in which anyone else exists. Believe that He is to be approached, to be realized, to be, in fact, the great practical factor of your life.

ILLUSTRATION

Christ Has the Key

A minister was one day going to preach. His attention was arrested by a woman standing at her door, who, upon seeing him, came up to him with the greatest anxiety, and said, "Oh sir, have you any keys about you? I have broken the key of my drawers, and there are some things that I must get." He said, "I have no keys." She was disappointed, expecting that everyone would have some keys. "But suppose," he said, "I had some keys. They might not fit your lock, and therefore you could not get the articles you want. But," said he, wishing to improve the occasion, "have you ever heard of the key of heaven?"

"Yes," she said, "I have lived long enough, and I have gone to church long enough, to know that if we work hard and get our bread by the sweat of our brow, and act well toward our neighbors, and behave, as the catechism says, lowly and reverently to all our betters, and if we do our duty in that station of life in which it has pleased God to place us, and say our prayers regularly, we shall be saved."

He said, "My good woman, that is a broken key, for you have broken the commandments, and you have not fulfilled all your duties. It is a good key, but you have broken it." "But sir," she said, believing that he understood the matter, and looking frightened, "What have I left out?" "Why," said he, "the all-important thing, the blood of Jesus Christ. Don't you know it is said, the key of heaven is at His belt; He opens and no man shuts; He shuts and no man opens?" And explaining it more fully to her, he said, "It is Christ, and Christ alone, that can open heaven to you, and not your good works."

---

and is a rewarder When we believe in the Lord Jesus, the Lord God accepts us for His Beloved's sake, and in Him we are made kings and priests, and permitted to bring an offering that pleases God. As the man is, such is his work. The stream is of the nature of the spring from which it flows. He who is a rebel cannot gratify his prince by any fashion of service; he must first submit himself to the law. All the actions of rebels are acts done in rebellion. We must first be reconciled to God, or it is a mockery to bring an offering to His altar. Reconciliation can only be effected through the death of the Lord Jesus, and if we have no faith in that way of reconciliation we cannot please God.

ILLUSTRATION
Professing Belief without Demonstrating It

You say that he is "a rewarder of those who seek him"; do you despise the reward? Are you content with having made a profession of religion? Some professing Christians remind me of the reply of the child who was asked at the Sunday school about her father, who never went to any place of worship. "Is your father a Christian, Jane?" "Yes," she replied, "but he has not worked much at it lately."

There are many professing Christians of that sort. They are like certain tradesmen who have a notice on their door to say that they have gone out for two weeks. They will not make a fortune in that way, I am persuaded; such a method of doing business generally ends in bankruptcy. What can I say of some professedly Christian people? They have no stock, they are doing no business for their Master, and their chief employment is that of asking, "Do I love the Lord, or no?"

---

of those who seek him The Greek word means not only seek Him, but "seek Him out"—that is, seek Him until they find Him, and seek Him above all others. It is a very strong word; we hardly know how to transfer its meaning into English, for though it does not say "diligently," it implies it. We must seek, and seek out, that is, seek until we really find. Those who with their hearts follow after God shall not be losers if they believe that He will reward them. You have to believe God so as to seek His glory.

We seek Him, first, when we begin by prayer, by trusting to Jesus, and by calling upon the sacred name, to seek salvation. "Everyone who calls on the name of the Lord shall be saved" (Joel 2:32). That is a grand promise, and it teaches how we come to God: by calling upon His name. Afterward, we seek God by aiming at His glory—by making Him the great object for which we live.

Although we deserve nothing at His hands but wrath, yet we perceive from the gospel that if we seek Him through His Son, we shall be so well-pleasing to Him as to get a reward from His hands. This must be of grace—free, sovereign grace! And what a reward it is! Free pardon, graciously bestowed; a change of heart, graciously wrought; perseverance graciously maintained, comfort graciously poured in, and privilege graciously awarded.

ILLUSTRATION

God's Goodness to His People

If a mistress has a large number of maids, somebody might ask them, "What kind of mistress do you have?" They might all say, "Oh, she is a most delightful person," and so on, because they were afraid to speak the truth. But if there should be a dozen of them, eventually one would be found in the street who would say, "You heard what those maids said, but it was not true, for she is a termagant." The truth would ooze out somehow; and if our God were not faithful, one or other of his servants would be sure to tell of it; but none of us have anything to complain of.

---

7   **By faith Noah** "Enoch walked with God, and he was no more for God took him" (Gen 5:24), and we read that Noah also

"walked with God" (Gen 6:9). These two spent their lives in such constant communion with the Most High that they could be fully described as walking with God.

Noah is the picture of one who is the Lord's witness during evil days and lives through them faithfully, enduring unto the end. It was his to be delivered from death by death. The ark was, so to speak, a coffin to him: he entered it and became a dead man to the old world; within its enclosure, he was floated into a new world to become the founder and father of a new race. As in the figure of baptism we see life by burial, so it was with this chosen patriarch; he passed by burial in the ark into a new life. In Enoch we see a type of God's people who will go home peacefully before the last closing struggle. Before the first clash of swords at Armageddon, such Enochs will be taken from the evil to come. But in Noah we see those who will engage in the conflict and bear themselves bravely amid backsliding and apostasy until they shall see the powers of evil trodden under their feet as straw is trodden for the dunghill.

Noah believed in God in his ordinary life. Before the great test came, before he heard the oracle from the secret place, Noah believed in God. We know that he did, for we read that he walked with God, and in his common conduct he is described as being "a righteous man, without defect in his generations" (Gen 6:9). To be righteous in the sight of God is never possible apart from faith, for "the righteous shall live by his faithfulness" (Hab 2:4). It is a great thing to have faith in the presence of a terrible trial, but the first essential is to have faith for ordinary everyday consumption.

ILLUSTRATION

Saving Faith and Niagara Falls

The stupendous falls of Niagara have been spoken of in every part of the world. But while they are marvelous to hear of, and wonderful as a spectacle, they have been very destructive to human life when by accident any have been carried down the cataract. Some years ago, two men, a bargeman and a collier, were in a boat, and found themselves unable to manage it. They were being carried so swiftly down the current that they must both inevitably be borne down and dashed to pieces. Persons on the shore saw them, but were unable to do much for their rescue. At last, however, one man was saved by a rope floated to him, which he grasped. The same instant that the rope came into his hand, a log floated by the other man. The thoughtless and confused bargeman, instead of seizing the rope, laid hold of the log. It was a fatal mistake; they were both in imminent peril, but the one was drawn to shore because he had a connection with the people on the land. The other, clinging to the log, was borne irresistibly along, and never heard of afterward.

Do you not see that here is a practical illustration? Faith is a connection with Christ. Christ is on the shore, so to speak, holding the rope of faith. If we lay hold of it with the hand of our confidence, He pulls us to shore. But our good works, having no connection with Christ, are drifted along down the gulf of fell despair. Hold on to them as tightly as we may, even with hooks of steel, they cannot benefit us in the least degree.

---

having been warned about things not yet seen He had listened to the terrible threat that God would destroy all living things with a flood; his faith believed both the warning and the promise. If he had not believed the threat, he would not have prepared an ark, and so would not have received the promise. Men do not prepare an ark to escape from a flood unless they believe that there will be a flood.

out of reverence Noah had a loyal reverence of God. He feared Him as the King of kings and Lord of lords, and when he went about through the wicked world Noah often said to himself,

"I wonder the Judge of all the earth does not destroy these rebels, who dare to be so vile and violent." When he saw their gluttony, their infidelity, their lasciviousness, their oppression of one another, the preacher of righteousness had a holy fear of judgment. Often his righteous spirit indignantly cried, "Cut it down! Why should it even exhaust the soil?" (Luke 13:7). He wondered how God could be so longsuffering. When it was revealed to him that God was going to destroy the whole race from the face of the earth by a flood, he said to himself, "I thought He would." He felt exceedingly afraid, for he knew that when God once makes bare His arm for vengeance, the pillars of the earth must shake, and the stars of heaven cease their shining. Thus the holy man of God passed the time of his sojourning here in fear.

Fear and faith may sometimes dwell together. There is a holy, humble fear that perfect love never casts out, but entertains and cherishes. This is the kind of fear that Noah possessed: "having been warned about things not yet seen, out of reverence constructed an ark." Noah was a practical lifesaver—an ark-builder. He became the second father of the human race—a sort of new Adam—and that simply by his faith. What is there that is impossible to the man who believes in God? "All things are possible for the one who believes" (Mark 9:23).

constructed an ark *Noah obeyed at all costs.* To build the huge vessel must have cost Noah a great deal of money and labor. He could not get everybody to work at the absurd task of building a vessel on dry land. As they would be laughed at, his workmen would be sure to demand extra pay. Possibly he had to pay double wages to everyone employed on the ark. The patriarch was content to sink all his capital and all his income in this singular venture. It was a poor speculation—so everybody told him—and yet he was quite willing to put all his eggs into that one basket. God had bidden him build, and build he would, feeling that the divine command insured him against risk. Can we do the same?

Noah went on obeying under daily scorn. The men of that generation mocked him. He went out and preached to them, but many would not hear him, for they thought him mad. Those who did listen to him said to each other, "He is building a vessel upon dry land—is he sane? We are scientific, and therefore we know how absurd his preaching is; no one ever heard of the world being drowned by a flood." I cannot reproduce the letters that were written about the sturdy patriarch, nor can I recount the spiteful things that were said by the gossips, but I have no doubt they were very clever, and very sarcastic. Those productions of genius are all forgotten now, but Noah is remembered still. For all the scorning of many he went on obeying his God: he stuck to the lines on which God had placed him, and he could not be turned to the right hand or to the left, because he had a real faith in God.

for the deliverance of his family Many were called, but only the eight were chosen. Noah had preached apparently in vain, and yet he believed with no less dogged resolve. The old man was not to be moved. That ark of his would float; he knew it would. The world would be destroyed; he was sure of it as sure as if he had seen it. "Things not seen" (Heb 11:1) were to his faith substantial and evident.

by which he pronounced sentence on the world I do not read that Noah ever entered into any dispute with the men of his times. He never argued, much less did he wish them ill; he simply believed and told them the truth. He kept his own faith intact and went on building his ark, thus practicing what he believed. In this way he condemned those who criticized him.

So you see that faith has a condemning power toward an ungodly world. You do not need to be constantly telling worldly people that they are doing wrong; let them see clearly the evidence of your faith. That will bear the strongest conceivable witness against their unbelief and sin, even as Noah, by his faith, "pronounced sentence on the world and became an heir of the righteousness that comes by faith."

and became an heir of the righteousness that comes by faith God declared him righteous—not righteous by his works, although his works, following upon his faith, proved him to be righteous. He was righteous by his faith. He believed God, and found grace in the eyes of the Lord. He received the righteousness that God gives through Jesus Christ to all who believe. Wrapped in this, he stood before the Lord, justified and approved. By faith he was adopted and became a son, an heir. For him the promise of the woman's seed, though it was all the Bible that he had, was quite enough. The woman's seed, and the Lamb's sacrifice, which Abel had seen, these were almost all the revelation he had known. He had no Pentateuch, no Psalms, no Gospels, no Epistles, but he so believed that little Bible of his that he expected that Christ in him would bruise the serpent in the world. God honored his faith, and he condemned the world. He lived when the rest perished; he was secure in his ark when the myriads were sinking in the deluge. He became "heir of the righteousness that comes by faith" when others were condemned.

APPLICATION

Do You Have Faith?

Do you have faith? Do you believe on the Lord Jesus Christ with all your heart? If so, you may hope to be saved. Yes, you may conclude with absolute certainty that you will never see perdition. Do you have faith? Shall I help you to answer that question? I will give you three tests:

He who has faith has renounced his own righteousness. If you put one atom of trust in yourself, you have no faith; if you place even a particle of reliance upon anything else but what Christ did, you have no faith. If you trust in your works, then your works are antichrist, and Christ and antichrist can never go together. Christ will have all or nothing; He must be a whole Savior, or none at all.

Then true faith may be known by this: *it begets a great esteem for the person of Christ.* Do you love Christ? Could you die for Him?

Do you seek to serve Him? Do you love His people? If you do not love Christ, you do not believe in Him, for to believe in Christ begets love.

And yet more: *he who has true faith will have true obedience.* If a man says he has faith, and has no works, he lies. If any man declares that he believes on Christ, and yet does not lead a holy life, he makes a mistake. For while we do not trust in good works, we know that faith always begets good works. Faith is the father of holiness. God's blessings are blessings with both His hands. In the one hand He gives pardon, but in the other hand He always gives holiness. No man can have the one unless he has the other.

Believe, and Be Pleasing

Some of you are always fashioning fresh nets of doubt for your own entanglement. You invent snares for your own feet, and are greedy to lay more and more of them. You are mariners who seek the rocks, soldiers who court the point of the bayonet. It is an unprofitable business. Practically, morally, mentally, and spiritually, doubting is an evil trade. You are like a smith who wears out his arm in making chains with which to bind himself. Doubt is sterile—a desert without water. Doubt discovers difficulties that it never solves: it creates hesitancy, despondency, despair. Its progress is the decay of comfort, the death of peace. "Believe!" is the word that speaks life into a man, but doubt nails down his coffin.

If you can believe that Jesus Christ bore the guilt of sin upon the cross, and by His death has made atonement to the insulted government of God—if you can so believe in Him as to cast yourself just as you are at His dear feet—you will be pleasing to God. I entreat you to look up and see the pierced hands, and feet, and side of the dear Redeemer. Read eternal mercy there; read full forgiveness there, and then go away in peace, for you are well-pleasing to God. The sinner who believes God's testimony concerning His Son has begun to please Him, and is Himself well-pleasing to the Lord.

Oh, that you would now trust Him who justifies the ungodly and passes by the iniquities of sinful men! He will receive you graciously and love you freely. Oh, come to Him, for He is a rewarder of those who diligently seek Him. God help you to do so at once. But without faith you cannot please Him. Do what you may, feel what you like, you will labor as in the very fire, and nothing will come of it but eternal despair.

Reward in Eternity

You may say that there are many of God's people who serve Him faithfully, and they do not get any reward; they are very poor and needy. Yet they will tell you that they are more than satisfied with the way their Lord has treated them; moreover, they will tell you that they are strangers and pilgrims here, and that their chief reward is yet to come. They are looking, by faith, for the everlasting remunerations that will follow the life of holiness, when this poor world and all its joys shall have melted like the morning mist and gone forever. Eternity, eternity, eternity—we shall soon know, brothers and sisters, what it will be like to be in eternity. There is not one of us who can live here forever. When a very few years have gone, we shall all have departed.

Imagine yourselves in the future state. If you have not lived for God, but have lived for the world, for yourself, what is your portion? Endless darkness; infinite despair; unutterable woe. But if you have lived for God—if, by His grace, you have put your trust in Jesus Christ—what is your portion? You stand on glittering hills in the midst of the white-robed host, and Christ is with you. You are looking back upon what you suffered for His sake on earth, and you say, "It was nothing at all. I wish I had suffered far more for Him who suffered so much for me!" As for what you did for Him, you will say, "That is not worth mentioning. Oh, that I had lived more intensely for Him!" As for what you gave for Him, you will say, "I never gave a thousandth part of what I would give now if I had it. I reckon that I wasted what was not spent upon His kingdom. I reckon that I lost the time that I did not use for glorifying Him." Then you will see, from before the throne of God, that "he exists and is a rewarder of those who seek him."

Have Everyday Faith

Do you have faith in God as to your daily bread? Do you have faith as to your children and your house? Do you have faith about your trade and business? Do you have faith in the God of providence? Faith in the God who answers prayer? Is it habitual with you to roll your burden upon the Lord? If it is not so with you, what will you do when the floods break forth? Faith will not come to you all of a sudden in the dark night if you have shut it out through all the bright days. Faith must be a constant tenant, not an occasional guest.

I have heard of Latter-day Saints, and I do not think much of them; I far more admire Every-day Saints. You need faith on Sunday: have it, and come to the communion table with it. But you need faith on Monday, when the shutters are taken down to begin another six days' trading. You will need faith the next day, for who can tell you what will happen? To the end of the week you will need to look to the hills from which comes your help (Psa 121:1). You need faith anywhere and everywhere. A man of God alone in his room still needs faith, or solitude may be a nest for temptation. When the servant of Christ is at his ease, and has no work pressing upon him, he needs faith to keep him, lest, like David, he fall into temptation and commit folly.

Rest days or work days, we always need faith. By faith Noah did everything before he entered the ark. This is an important observation, though it may appear a very simple one. I could not omit it, for I feel that a practical workaday faith is what we need most of all. Men think that they need faith in building a temple, but faith is also needed in building a haystack. We need faith for plowing, for buying, for selling, for working, quite as much as for praying, and singing, and preaching. We need faith on the market as well as in the prayer meeting. We wish everywhere to please God, and we cannot do it anywhere unless we have genuine faith in Him. The Lord teach us to have faith seven days a week!

⁸ By faith Abraham, when he was called to go out to a place that he was going to receive for an inheritance, obeyed and went out, not knowing where he was going. ⁹ By faith he lived in the land of promise as a stranger, living in tents with Isaac and Jacob, the fellow heirs of the same promise. ¹⁰ For he was expecting the city that has foundations, whose architect and builder is God. ¹¹ By faith also, with Sarah, he received the ability to procreate even past the normal age, because he regarded the one who had promised to be faithful. ¹² And therefore from one man—and he being as good as dead—these were born, as many as the stars of heaven in number and like the innumerable sand by the shore of the sea.

¹³ These all died in faith without receiving the promises, but having seen them from a distance and welcoming them, and admitting that they were strangers and temporary residents on the earth. ¹⁴ For those who say such things make clear that they are seeking a homeland. ¹⁵ And if they remember that land from which they went out, they would have had opportunity to return. ¹⁶ But now they aspire to a better land, that is, a heavenly one. Therefore God is not ashamed of them, to be called their God, for he has prepared for them a city.

¹⁷ By faith Abraham, when he was tested, offered Isaac, and the one who received the promises was ready to offer his one and only son, ¹⁸ with reference to whom it was said, "In Isaac your descendants will be named," ¹⁹ having reasoned that God was able even to raise him from the dead, from which he received him back also as a symbol. ²⁰ By faith also Isaac blessed Jacob and Esau concerning things that were going to happen. ²¹ By faith Jacob, as he was dying, blessed each of the sons of Joseph and worshiped, leaning on the top of his staff. ²² By faith Joseph, as he was dying,

made mention concerning the exodus of the Israelites and gave instructions about his bones.

EXPOSITION

8   **By faith Abraham** What a mighty sway faith has over a man, and how greatly it strengthens him. Faith was to the patriarch his authority for starting upon his strange journey, an authority that enabled him to defy alike the worldly wisdom that advises and the worldly folly that scoffs. Perhaps they said to him, "Why will you leave your relatives, Abraham?" but he replied, "God bids me." That was a sufficient warrant for him; he needed no further argument. This also became to him the guide of his steps. If any said, "But, strange old man, how can you journey when you do not know the way?" He replied, "I go where the Lord bids me." Faith found in God chart, compass, and polestar, all in one.

when he was called Perhaps we have said, "If I heard a voice speaking from the sky I would obey it," but the form in which your call has come has been better than that. Peter in his second epistle tells us that he himself heard a voice out of the majestic glory when he was with our Lord on the holy mountain, but he adds, "We possess as more reliable the prophetic word" (2 Pet 2:19). It is as if the testimony that is written, the light that shines in the darkness (John 1:5), which beams forth from the word of God, was more sure than even the voice that he heard from heaven.

obeyed to go out There is no hint of hesitation, parleying, or delay. When he was called to go out, he went out. Would to God that such conduct were usual, indeed, universal; with many, the call alone is not enough to produce obedience. "Many are called, but few are chosen" (Matt 22:14). The Lord's complaint is, "I called out and you refused me" (Prov 1:24). Such calls come again and again to many, but they turn a deaf ear to them; they are hearers only, and not doers of the word (James 1:22). Worse still, some are of the same generation as that which Zechariah spoke of when he said, "They turned a stubborn shoulder and stopped their ears from listening" (Zech 7:11). Even among the most attentive hearers, how many there are to whom the word comes with small practical result in actual obedience.

Abraham was prepared for instant obedience to any command from God; his journey was appointed, and he went. He was bidden to leave his country, and he left it; to leave his friends, and he left them all. Gathering together such substance as he had, he exiled himself that he might be a sojourner with his God, and took a journey in an age when traveling was infinitely more laborious than now. He did not know the road that he had to take, nor the place to which his journey would conduct him; it was enough for him that the Lord had given him the summons.

ILLUSTRATION

Adding More to Your Load

The man who waits until he shall find it easier to bear the yoke of obedience is like the woodman who found his bundle of wood too heavy for his idle shoulder. Placing it upon the ground, he gathered more wood and added to the bundle, then tried it. But finding it still an unpleasant load, he repeated the experiment of heaping on more, in the vain hope that by-and-by it might be of a shape more suitable for his shoulder.

How foolish to go on adding sin to sin, increasing the hardness of the heart, increasing the distance between the soul and Christ, and all the while fondly dreaming of some enchanted hour in which it will be easier to yield to the divine call and part with sin.

Delayed obedience is disobedience. I wish some Christians, who put off duty, would remember this. Continued delay of duty is a continuous sin. If I do not obey the divine command, I sin. Every moment that I continue in that condition, I repeat the sin. This is a serious matter. If a certain act is my duty at this hour, and I leave it undone, I have sinned; but it will be equally incumbent upon me during the next hour. And if I still refuse, I disobey again, and so on till I do obey.

to a place that he was going to receive for an inheritance
When men emigrate, they wish to know the nature of the country in which they are to live. If it is a richer country than their own, although it is with some reluctance, they spread the sail and speed across the waters. It may be, after they have settled there a little while, their mother country is almost forgotten, and they find a settled dwelling place in their adopted land. But Abraham knew nothing of the country to which he was about to move; he had simply God's promise that it should be his inheritance.

Prudent consideration of consequences is superabundant, but the spirit that obeys, and dares all things for Christ's sake— where is it? The Abrahams of today will not go out from their kindred; they will put up with anything sooner than risk their livelihoods. If they do go out, they must know where they are going, and how much is to be picked up in the new country.

he went out, not knowing where he was going That is, surely, the very masterpiece of faith. God bade Abraham go forth from his native land; he believed that God knew where he was to go, though he did not himself know. He left the direction of his wanderings entirely in the Lord's hands, and obeyed, and "went out, not knowing where he was going." We are not to ask for full knowledge before we will be obedient to the will of the Lord; but we are to obey God in the dark, even as Abraham did.

He was self-exiled from his home—a wanderer upon the face of the earth. Yet, when called of God, it mattered not to him where he was bidden to go. He seemed to say, "Appoint my way, great God. It is for me not to ask the reason why, but to obey your command."

9   **By faith he lived in the land of promise** God had given it to him and to his seed by a covenant of salt, and yet he possessed not a foot of it except what he bought from the sons of Heth for a burying place. That is all he had. So today, in this world, perhaps all that some of you will ever have is about six feet of earth for a burying place; and yet it is all yours. You are living in the land of promise. "The meek shall inherit the earth." Those who fear the Lord are the true possessors of the world; the day shall come when even this poor world itself, brought into subjection to the Christ of God, shall be ours. Indeed, it is ours already.

as a stranger It is one thing to walk up and down among idolaters, and quite another thing to be in the same family with them. Abraham was safe enough from idolatry when he moved about among the Canaanites and saw their obscene worship. He was not safe from it in a decent, respectable household like that of his father, where the teraphim were slyly adored and the worship of false gods was carried on without the disgusting abominations that were common in Canaan.

I think, also, that Abraham was sent to Canaan as a stranger to be a witness for God. These people were soon to be destroyed, but their iniquity was not yet full. They had another chance in the living of a man of God, a prophet of God, among them. You, my Christian friend, are a stranger here, and you are living here for the good of those around you. It may be that you may snatch some brand from the burning. Be content to stay if such is the case.

ILLUSTRATION

Sit Loose by This World

All things here pass away. I cannot tell you the strange joy I felt after the earthquake at Menton, France. I had been to see many of the houses that had been shaken down, and the two churches that were greatly injured, and I was full of the earthquake. I had quite realized its terrors and its power, and when I went up the stairs of my hotel, I thought, "Well, at any moment this may all come down with a run. When I go to bed, it may all slip away." I felt a great delight in thinking that I actually realized, not in a dream, but as a matter of fact, the shakiness of this poor earthquaky world. Everything in it is without foundation, but is just a mere tent that might come down at any moment; a gust of wind might blow it over. When we are most comfortable in it, we may hear a voice saying, "Up and away: Pack up your tent and journey somewhere else." Sit loose by this world, I pray you.

living in tents with Isaac and Jacob Here is Abraham, who lives in a tent, and has the happiness of *finding his best company in his own family*. I suppose that he lived with Isaac about 75 years. If you calculate, you will find that that is about the time. Did he live with Jacob? Yes, he must have lived at the same time as Jacob for about 15 years. He saw his dear son Isaac married, and twin children born, and he marked their life long enough to see that Jacob was of that kind that would make a plain man dwelling in tents; and Abraham found the sweetest company with his own dear family.

the fellow heirs of the same promise It is one of the great evidences of true faith for her to keep on, to continue, to abide, without any visible signs or tokens of what she knows is hers. The life of faith is wonderful, but so also is the walk of faith.

Her walk has much about it that is mysterious; she knows that the land she treads on belongs to her. And yet, in another sense, she cannot claim a solitary foot of it. She knows that she is at home, even as Abraham was in his own land; yet like him, she knows herself to be a sojourner in a strange land, and is quite content to be so.

10 **For he was expecting the city** He was only a sojourner in the land of promise; he knew that even the promised land was only a tenting-ground for him and his descendants. He also knew that he was on his way to a divinely planned and divinely built city—not like the temporary cities of earth, which shall all perish and pass away, but a city with everlasting foundations—a city that will last as long as God Himself exists. And he was content to be a pilgrim and wanderer until he should reach that city; he was quite willing to dispense with all present comfort for the sake of that glorious future that God set before the eyes of his faith.

Children of God have an eye to the world to come. They do not live "like dumb, driven cattle," but they think of the changeless state into which death, or Christ's coming, may speedily plunge them, and they live with an eye to that state.

that has foundations, whose architect and builder is God Abraham used to pull up the tent pins, and his men would take down the big tent pole, and roll up the canvas, and they were soon away, always moving about that country with their flocks and herds. The tents had no foundations, but Abraham was looking for a city that had foundations. There is nothing on earth that really has a foundation. Even those buildings that seem most firm will be dissolved, and burned up in the last general fire.

11 **By faith also, with Sarah** This holy woman is enrolled among these saintly ones. Her faith was not all it ought to have been, but God saw that it was true faith, and He loved it, and He wrote the record of it.

he regarded the one who had promised to be faithful
And that was good judgment, was it not? There is no mistake
about that. Whatever difficulties may lie in the way, we may
always know that he is faithful who has promised. You are not
past age, my brother. God will bless you in seeking to do good.
You are not past age, my sister. Have faith in God, and then
in your old age you may bring many to the Savior's feet. He is
faithful who has promised.

12   **he being as good as dead** Perhaps the reference is to Abraham,
who was as good as dead, being so old; or to Isaac, who was as
good as dead, for he was laid upon the altar, and was practically "offered up" as a sacrifice unto the Lord. There were many
deaths to work against the life of faith, yet life triumphed over
death after all.

13   **These all died in faith** They did die, although they had faith,
for faith is not given to us that we should escape death, but
that we may die in faith. God will not in every case hear our
prayers for restoration to health. It is not true that if we gather together and pray for a sick man he will always be restored.
No believer would die if that were the case, for every Christian
man would find some friends in Christ to pray for his recovery.

Saints die as well as sinners. David dies as well as Saul. He who
leaned on the bosom of Jesus lived long, but died at last—died
as surely as Judas did, though in a better style. "It is destined
for people to die once" (Heb 9:27). Two have entered into glory
by another way, but only two. There shall come a day when
we who are alive and remain shall not see death, but that day
is not yet.

without receiving the promises They had received a great
deal, but they had not received the fullness of the promises.
Abraham had not beheld his seed so many as the sands upon
the seashore. Neither Isaac nor Jacob had ever seen the Shiloh,
in whom all the nations of the earth are blessed. No, they had
not received the promises.

And you and I have not received all the promises. We have received a great deal, but there are certain promises that we have not received yet. The coming, the glorious coming, which is the brightest hope of the church, when the Lord "will descend from heaven with a shout of command, with the voice of the archangel and with the trumpet of God" (1 Thess 4:16)—we have not received that as yet. And heaven itself, with all its splendor, its white robes and palms of victory, we have not yet received. We are looking for these. We do not die in the fruition of these. We die in faith, expecting that we shall enter upon the fulfillment of these promises.

but seeing them from a distance They saw them from a distance. Faith touched their eyes with salve so that Abraham could see his seed in Egypt—his seed coming out of the land of Zoan. He could see the people traveling through the wilderness. He could see them entering Canaan and taking possession of the land. Indeed, our Lord said, "Abraham saw my day" (John 8:56). He saw the babe in Bethlehem. He saw the Son of God, who was the Son of Man, and the son of Abraham too.

and welcoming them Although the promises could only be seen from a distance, faith has such long arms that it embraced them, clung to them as loving relatives cling to one another, and would not let them go. So may we see the promises, and be persuaded that they belong to us, and embrace them as we clasp to our bosom those who are nearest and dearest to us!

ILLUSTRATION
Salute God's Promises from Afar

In the clear atmosphere of Menton, France, I have sometimes stood on quite a lofty mountain and seen a friend down in the valley. I have spoken his name, and at first it was greatly to my astonishment when he replied, "Where are you?" I held a conversation with him readily.

I could not have actually reached him for a long time, but
I saluted him from afar.

At times, we can see God's promises from a distance,
and we salute them.

---

they were strangers and temporary residents They owned
that they were not at home here. Abraham never built a
house; Isaac never lived anywhere but in a tent, and though
Jacob tried to dwell in a settled habitation, he got into trouble through it, and he was bound still to be a tent dweller.
The reason why they lived in tents was because they wanted
to show to all around them that they did not belong to that
country. There were great cities with walls that, as men said,
reached to heaven, but they did not go to dwell in those cities. You remember that Lot did, yet he was glad enough to get
out again—"saved, but so as through fire" (1 Cor 3:15)—but
Abraham, Isaac, and Jacob kept away from other men, for they
were commanded to dwell alone, and not to be numbered
among the nations. Nor were they; they kept themselves apart
from other people as strangers and sojourners here below, so,
for that very reason, God is not ashamed to be called their God.

Remember how David says to the Lord, "I am an alien with
you, a sojourner like all my ancestors" (Psa 39:12). That is a
very singular expression: "an alien *with* you." Blessed be God
that it is not "an alien *to* you," but "an alien *with* you." That is
to say, God is a stranger here. It is His own world, and He made
it, but when Christ, who is the Son of God, and the Creator of
the world, came into it, "He came to his own, and his own did
not receive him" (John 1:11). They soon made him feel that the
only treatment that He would receive at their hands was this:
"This is the heir. Come, let us kill him and the inheritance will
be ours" (Mark 12:7). There was no man who ever lived who
was a truer man than was Christ the Lord, but there never was
a man who was more unlike the rest of men. He was a homely
man, a home-loving man to the last degree, yet He was never

at home. This world was not His rest; He had nowhere even to lay His head, and what was true naturally was also true spiritually. This world offered Christ no rest whatsoever.

14   **they are seeking a homeland** If they were seeking a country, might they not have gone back to their own country from which they came out? No; true believers know nothing about going back. We are bound to go forward to the better land that is before us. Almighty grace will not permit the people of God to turn aside and find their rest anywhere else. We are bound for the kingdom and, by the grace of God, we shall not rest until we enter it, to go out no more forever.

15   **they would have had opportunity to return** The people of God were not forced to continue because they could not return. If they had been mindful of the place from where they came, they might have found opportunities to return. Frequent opportunities came in their way. There was communication kept up between them and the old family house at Paddan-Aram. They had news concerning the family house. More than that, there were messages exchanged; servants were sometimes sent. There was also a natural relationship kept up. Did not Rebekah come from there? And Jacob, one of the patriarchs, was driven to go down into the land, but he could not stay there. He was always restless until at last he stole a march upon Laban and came back to the proper life, the life that he had chosen—the life that God had commanded him to live—of a pilgrim and stranger in the land of promise.

You see, then, they had many opportunities to have returned, to have settled down comfortably and tilled the ground, which their fathers did before them. But they continued to follow the uncomfortable life of wanderers of the weary foot, who dwell in tents, who own no plot of land. They were aliens in the country that God had given them by promise.

True pilgrims never think of going back; they know that whatever difficulties and trials lie ahead of them, there are far greater ones in "that land from which they went out."

Bunyan's Christian was quite resolved not to go back to the City of Destruction whatever perils he might have to face on his way to the Celestial City.

ILLUSTRATION

Keep with Christ at the Crossroads

Two men are going along a road, and they have a dog behind them. I do not know to whom that dog belongs, but I'll tell you directly. They are coming to a crossroads. One goes to the right, the other goes to the left. Now, which man does the dog follow? His master.

Now, when Christ and the world go together, you cannot tell which a man is following. But when there is a separation, and Christ goes one way, and your interest, your pleasure seems to go the other way, if you can part with the world, and keep with Christ, then you are one of His.

---

16 **But now they aspire to a better land, that is, a heavenly one** I felt greatly encouraged when I read this, "Now they aspire to a better"—the word "land" has been inserted by translators—they desire something better. I know I do. I do not always enjoy something better. Dark is my path. I cannot see my Lord; I cannot enjoy His presence; and though it may be a little thing to desire, let me say a good desire is more than nature ever grew. Grace has given it. It is a great thing to desire: they desire a better country. And because we desire this better thing, we cannot go back and be content with things that gratified us once.

More than that, if ever the child of God gets entangled, for a while he is uneasy in it. Abraham's slips—for he made one or two—were made when he had left the land and gone down among the Philistines. But he was not easy there; he must come back again. And Jacob, he had found a wife—no, two—in Laban's land, but he was not content. No; no child of God can be.

Therefore God is not ashamed If a man believes in God, trusts him—believes that His promise is true and that He will keep it, believes that God's command is right and therefore ought to be obeyed—God is never ashamed to be called that man's God. He is not the God of unbelievers, for they act contrary to His will. They set up their own will in opposition to His; many of them even doubt His existence, they deny His power, they distrust his love; therefore, He is not called their God. But when a man comes to trust God, and to accept His Word, from that moment God sees in that man the work of His grace, which is very precious in His eyes, and He is not ashamed to be called that man's God.

I see, then, why it is written that "God is not ashamed of them, to be called their God": because they are content to live without having received the promises, but to keep on patiently waiting, with a holy, joyful confidence, until the hour of God's gracious purpose shall arrive, and the promise shall be fulfilled.

ILLUSTRATION
God Is Not Ashamed of His People

We have sometimes heard of a brother who has become great and rich in the world. He has some poor brother or some distant relative, and when he sees him in the street he is obliged to speak to him and own him. I dare say he wished him a long way off, especially if some rich acquaintance happened to be with him who should say, "Why, Smith, who was that wretched seedy-looking fellow that you spoke to?" He does not like to say, "That is my relation," or "That is my brother."

But we find that Jesus Christ, however low His people may sink, and however poor they may be, is not ashamed to call them brothers, nor to let them look up to Him in all the depths of their degradation and call Him "a brother [who] is born for adversity" (Prov 17:17). "He is not ashamed to call them brothers" (Heb 2:11). And one reason seems to me to be because He does not judge them by what they are, but by what He has prepared for them.

---

for he has prepared for them a city He might be ashamed to be called their God if He had unsettled them and made them long for another city, and yet had never prepared one for them. The longings of the saints are but prophecies of the benediction of God. That which He makes us hunger for is prepared. The bread of life shall be given us, and the country that He makes us seek exists and will be found by us.

17 **When he was tested, offered Isaac** It may be that Isaac, though a gift from God, began to usurp God's place. An Isaac may become an idol. The dearest thing we have, the most precious, the most beloved, may still become an abomination by being made an idol to keep us away from God. Some people worship gods of mud, others worship gods of gold, but there is no difference in the idolatry, whether the image is made of mire or of the most precious metal.

Do you have any idols, dear friends? I will not press the question too closely, but whatever your idols may be, they will bring you a world of trouble, for you must love nothing in comparison with God. He must be first, and everything else far away in the background. He will endure no rivals. He will permit no Dagon to stand in the place where the ark of the covenant abides. So God tests Abraham to see who has most of his heart's love.

ready to offer his one and only son How beautifully do we see the spirit of consolation exhibited in the character of Abraham, who, with all his troubles, as a stranger in a strange land, walks among men as a king! Have you never envied that quiet dignity with which, believing in God, he seemed also to master all around him without any sign of agitation of mind? Oh, that you had such comfort as he had when he took his son, his only son, whom he loved, to offer him up for a sacrifice! You never have had such a trial as that, and probably you never will; but in all that time of testing, what solid comfort he had! There were no written Scriptures then, yet how grand is the consolation that the Scripture describes him as having!

18   **In Isaac your descendants will be named** However puzzled Abraham may have been by the command to offer up the son in whom his seed was to be called, his plain duty was to obey that command and to leave the Lord to fulfill His own promise in His own way. Perhaps he had also learned, through his mistake concerning Ishmael, that God's way of fulfilling His promise might not be his way, and that God's way was always best.

The faith that was undismayed when the promise of a son was uttered was still undaunted when the Lord demanded the life that He had so strangely given. Perhaps God gave it such a supreme test because of its very grandeur. The trial was terrible, but still Abraham believed. Possibly he did not understand the trial; he did not want to understand. He believed, and he took God at His word, and he would do what God bade him do, whatever that might be, and he would leave the Lord to extricate him out of any difficulties into which his obedience might bring him. Thus God tried his faith.

19   **having reasoned that God was able even to raise him from the dead** See how faith consecrates natural affection. See also how faith laughs at impossibilities. Abraham expects that God will raise his son from the dead, or do something equally wonderful, so that the promise He had given shall be fulfilled.

It was not Abraham's business to keep God's promise for Him; it was God's business to do that for Himself, and He did it. You remember how Rebekah tried to make God's promise come true for Jacob, and what a mess she made by her plotting and scheming. When we give our attention to keeping God's precepts and leave Him to fulfill His own promises, all will be well. It was Abraham's part to offer up his son; it was God's part to fulfill the promise to His seed according to the covenant that He had made.

from which he received him back also as a symbol See how Abraham spied out the great doctrine of the resurrection. Although almost driven to desperation, he would not give up his faith in God. He was bidden to believe two apparently opposite things: first, that in Isaac should his seed be called, and second, that he must offer up Isaac. He bridged the two by believing another grand truth: that God was able to raise up Isaac, "even from the dead." Whenever there are two things revealed to you in Scripture that you cannot quite reconcile, you may always believe that between them there lies something more glorious still, which your dim eyes as yet are scarcely able to perceive.

20 **By faith also Isaac blessed Jacob and Esau** He was old and blind, so that he did not know which of his sons came for the first blessing, yet he could see into the future sufficiently to bless both his sons "concerning things that were going to happen." What wondrous power there is in faith even when it is exercised by very imperfect individuals!

concerning things that were going to happen He looked into the future, although he was blind. He was a poor old man, lying upon his bed, with his eyes so dim that he could not tell one of his sons from another. But he could yet look into the future, and bless his sons "concerning things that were going to happen." Oh, what sharp eyes faith has, even when the eyes of bodily vision have become dim! We may see far more by faith than we can by sight.

21   **By faith Jacob, as he was dying** If only by faith can a dying Jacob bless his descendants, so only by faith can we bless the sons of men. Have faith in God, and the instruction that you give shall really edify, the prayers you offer shall bring down showers of mercy, and your endeavors for your sons and daughters shall be prospered. God will bless what is done in faith; but if we do not believe, our work will not be established. Faith is the backbone and marrow of the Christian's power to do good. We are weak as water until we enter into union with God by faith, and then we are omnipotent.

blessed each of the sons of Joseph and worshiped Faith can bless other people as well as believers themselves. It not only brings good cheer into believers' own hearts, but it enables them to speak words of love and consolation to their children. Dying Jacob pronounces living blessings upon his sons, and upon their sons, generation after generation.

His legacies were all blessings that he possessed by faith only. He gave to Ephraim and Manasseh a portion each—but where and what? Did he fetch out a bag from the iron safe and say, "Here, young men, I give you the same portion of ready money as I give my sons"? No, there does not seem to have been a solitary shekel in the case. Did he call for the map of the family estates and say, "I give over to you, my boys, my freehold lands in such a parish, and my copyhold farms under such a manor"? No, no, he gave them no portion in Goshen, but each had a lot in Canaan.

Did that belong to him? Yes, in one sense, but not in another. God had promised it to him, but he had not yet a foot of land in it. The Canaanites were swarming in the land; they were dwelling in cities walled up to heaven, and held the country by the right of possession, which is nine points of the law. But the good old man talks about Canaan as if it was all his own, and he foresees the tribes growing into nations as much as if they were already in actual possession of the country. He had, as a matter of fact, neither house nor ground in Palestine, and yet he counts it all his own, since a faithful God had promised it to his fathers.

leaning on the top of his staff That staff of his!—you know why he used it. I believe he loved it, because it made him remember the brook Jabbok where "he was limping because of his hip" (Gen 32:31). It had long been his companion, for he said, "With only my staff I crossed this Jordan" (Gen 32:10). But it became more necessary to him than ever after he had won that victory and had also learned his own weakness. And now, as if in memory of the God who had blessed him, he leans upon the top of his staff and blesses the sons of Joseph.

22 **By faith Joseph, as he was dying** Death is a great tester of a man's sincerity, and a great shaker down of bowing walls and tottering fences. Men have thought that it was all well with them, but when the swellings of Jordan have been about them, they have found matters quite otherwise. Here we see Joseph so calm, so quiet, that he remembers the covenant, falls back upon it, and rejoices in it. He speaks of dying as though it were only a part of living, and comparatively a small matter to him. He gives no evidence of trepidation whatsoever. No fear distracts him, but he bears his last witness to his brothers who gather about his bed concerning the faithfulness of God and the infallibility of his promise.

gave instructions about his bones A sure proof that he believed they would come out of Egypt. He would not be buried among the pharaohs, though a prominent place would have been assigned to him there; but he would have his bones lie with those of his ancestors—Abraham and Isaac and Jacob.

He wished his unburied body to share with the people of God in their captivity and their return. He was so certain that they would come out of the captivity that he postpones his burial until that glad event, and so makes what would have been but a natural wish a means of expressing a holy and gracious confidence in the divine promise.

ILLUSTRATION
Joseph's Bones a Testimony

Every time an Israelite thought of the bones of Joseph, he thought, "We are to go out of this country one day." Perhaps he was a man prospering in business, laying up store in Egypt, but he would say to himself, "I shall have to part with this; Joseph's bones are to be carried up; I am not to be here forever." And then, while it acted as a warning, his body would serve also as an encouragement, for when the taskmasters began to afflict the people and their tally of bricks was increased, the despondent Israelite would say, "I shall never come up out of Egypt." But the others would say, "Joseph believed we should; there are his bones still unburied. He has left us the assurance of his confidence that God would in due time bring up His people out of this house of bondage."

It seems to me that Joseph had thought of this device as being the best thing on the whole he could do to keep the Israelites perpetually in remembrance that they were strangers and sojourners, and to encourage them in the belief that in due time they would be delivered from the house of bondage and settled in the land that flowed with milk and honey. True faith seeks to propagate herself in the hearts of others. She is earnest, eager, and intense, if by any means she may scatter a handful of holy seed that may fall in good soil and bring forth glory to God. It is a good proof of your own faith when you lay yourself out to promote the faith of others.

APPLICATION

Separate from the World and Living in It

It is a hard task to a man of loving soul to put long leagues of distance between himself and those he loves, and to become a banished man. Yet in order to attain salvation, we must be separated from this untoward generation. Not that we have to take our journey into a far country, or to forsake our kindred—perhaps it would be an easier task to walk with God if we could do so—but our calling is to be separate from sinners and yet to live among them. We must be strangers and pilgrims in their cities and homes. We must be separate in character from those with whom we may be called to grind at the same mill, or sleep in the same bed. This I warrant you is by no means an easier task than that which fell to the patriarch's lot.

If believers could form a secluded settlement where no tempters could intrude, they would perhaps find the separated life far easier, though I am not very sure about it, for all experiments in that direction have broken down. There is, however, for us no "garden walled around," no "island of saints," no Utopia. We journey among those whose ungodly lives cause us frequent grief, and the Lord Jesus meant it to be so, for He said, "Behold I am sending you out like sheep in the midst of wolves" (Matt 10:16). Come, now, are you willing to be one of the separated?

God's People Are Strangers on Earth

Don't wonder if you have discomforts here. If you are what you profess to be, you are strangers. Don't expect the people of this world to treat you as one of themselves—if they do, be afraid. Dogs don't bark when a person goes by that they know—they bark at strangers. When people slander and persecute you no longer, be afraid. If you are a stranger, they naturally bark at you. Don't expect to find comforts in this world that your flesh would long for. This is our inn, not our home. We tarry here a night; we are away in the morning. We may bear the discomforts of the evening and the night, for the morning will break so soon. Remember that your greatest joy while you are a pilgrim is your God. So the text says, "God is not ashamed of them, to be called their God" (Heb 11:16). Do you want a greater source of consolation than you have? Here is one that can never be diminished, much less exhausted. When the creature streams are dry, go to this eternal fountain, and you will find it ever springing up. Your God is your true joy—make your joy to be in your God.

Now what shall be said to those who are not strangers and foreigners? You dwell in a land where you find some sort of repose, but I have heavy tidings for you. This land in which you dwell, and all its works, must be burned up. The city of which you, who have never been converted to Christ, are citizens, is the City of Destruction, and as is its name, such shall be its end. The king will send his armies against that wicked city and destroy it, and if you are citizens of it you will lose all you have—you will lose your souls, and you will lose yourselves. You must do as Lot did when the angels pressed him and said, "Flee to the mountains lest you be destroyed" (Gen 19:17).

The mountain of safety is Calvary. Where Jesus died, there you shall live. There is death everywhere else, but there is life in His death. Trust Him. God gave His Son, equal with Himself, to bear the burdens of human sin, and He died a substitute for sinners—a real substitute, and an efficient substitute for all who trust in Him. If you will trust your soul with Jesus, you are saved. Your sin was laid on Him. It is forgiven you. It was blotted out when He nailed the handwriting of ordinances to His cross. Trust Him now and you are saved. That is, you shall become a stranger and a pilgrim, and in the better land you shall find the rest that you never shall find here.

Pining After Heavenly Things

Do you have a life within you that makes you pant and pine after heavenly things? Whatever you have in this world, do you hold it with a loose hand? Do you feel that it is not your real riches—it is not your true treasure? You know that Abraham, Isaac, and Jacob were all rich men. God blessed them, and gave them a great increase to all that they had. But still, they did not live simply to gather riches; they did not make them their chief delight. If you had asked them, they would have told you that they were inheritors of a mysterious covenant, by which God had bound himself to be their God, and the God of their seed; and in that covenant was included the promise that Christ Himself should come out of their loins, and for

Him they waited, and He was the hope of their spirit. Now, if that be the case with you also, you can understand the meaning of the text, "Therefore God is not ashamed of them, to be called their God" (Heb 11:16).

Days of Brightness Are Coming

Although one after another we shall pass away, there are not dark days for our descendants, but days of brightness are on the way. "Let your work be visible to your servants, and your majesty to their children" (Psa 90:16). "It is necessary for him to reign until he has put all his enemies under his feet" (1 Cor 15:25). The kings of the isles shall yet acknowledge Him, and the wanderers of the desert shall bow down before Him. Jesus the Christ of God must be King over all the earth, for God has sworn it, saying, "All flesh will see the salvation of God" (Luke 3:6). "And the glory of Yahweh shall be revealed, and all humankind together shall see it, for the mouth of Yahweh has spoken" (Isa 40:5). With such thoughts as these upon our minds, we may well close our eyes in death with a song upon our lips.

And then we have another and brighter hope to die with, if die we must before it is fulfilled: Christ Jesus the Son of God will visit His people. The glad hope of the second advent of our Lord Jesus Christ may light up the chamber of death with hope. As Joseph said, "God will certainly visit you" (Gen 50:24). The time will come when the Lord shall descend from heaven with a shout, with the trumpet of the archangel and the voice of God (1 Thess 4:16). Let our dying testimony be to the effect that surely He comes quickly and His reward is with Him (Rev 22:12). We do not have to look forward as the Jew did; he expected the first advent, and we watch for the second coming. This shall cheer us even in our departure, for if we die before He comes we shall yet share in the splendor, for the dead in Christ shall rise.

We may add to all this a hope concerning our bones. We may tell our weeping kindred, as they gather round our bed, to give our bones a decent sepulcher. They need not blazon our names, or write our fancied virtues on stone. We will tell them that we shall rise again, and that we commit ourselves to the bosom of our Father and our God, with the full conviction that our dust shall yet be quickened anew.

²³ By faith Moses, when he was born, was hidden for three months by his parents, because they saw the child was handsome, and they were not afraid of the edict of the king. ²⁴ By faith Moses, when he was grown up, refused to be called the son of Pharaoh's daughter, ²⁵ choosing rather to be mistreated with the people of God than to experience the transitory enjoyment of sin, ²⁶ considering the reproach of Christ greater wealth than the treasures of Egypt, for he was looking to the reward. ²⁷ By faith he left Egypt, not fearing the anger of the king, for he persevered as if he saw the invisible one. ²⁸ By faith he kept the Passover and the sprinkling of blood, in order that the one who destroyed the firstborn would not touch them. ²⁹ By faith they crossed the Red Sea as if on dry land; the Egyptians, [when] they made the attempt, were drowned. ³⁰ By faith the walls of Jericho fell down after they had been marched around for seven days. ³¹ By faith Rahab the prostitute did not perish with those who were disobedient, because she welcomed the spies in peace.

EXPOSITION

23 **By faith** The stress in these passages of sacred biography should be laid upon the words "by faith." The mighty deeds of heroes and the obedient acts of pilgrim fathers are only told to us because they spring out of faith. It is to commend the root that the fruits are mentioned. The children are named one by one that the mother may have the praise, for faith is the mother of all virtues.

The Lord is not praising the natural affection, but the supernatural faith. A very strong current is seen when nature and faith both set the same way, yet it is not nature but faith that bears the sway. Sometimes faith has to go against nature, as in the case of Abraham when he was bidden to offer up his son (Heb 11:17), and then faith wins the victory. Here, though faith and nature ran together and so made the current stronger, still the text does not say, "By the force of nature, by the natural love of parents for their child, Moses was hidden for three months." No, but they did it "by faith."

hidden for three months by his parents Both the parents of Moses believed, and both acted by faith in disobeying the cruel order of the king. If they had not agreed about it, I do not see how Moses could have been concealed. But they both went together in the hiding of the child, and how well it will be if we all go together in the endeavor to bring our children to Christ. If our prayers are united, if our example is one, if our teaching is never contradictory, if both parents are with like earnestness seeking the salvation of their little ones, we may rest assured the promise will be kept, "Train the child concerning his way; even when he is old, he will not stray from it" (Prov 22:6).

they saw the child was handsome Stephen says in his speech that the child was "exceeding fair"; and if you look at Stephen's speech you will see that the KJV translators have put in the margin, "Or 'fair to God'" (Acts 7:20). So it may run, "they saw that the child was handsome to God." Now, I gather from that expression that the child was exceedingly beautiful, beyond the common run of children. There was a charm about his features, a remarkable glory about his face, and something superhuman, probably, since he was fair to God. A *spiritual* air floated about the child's face, as if he bore some glimmerings of the glory of Sinai, of the wondrous shepherd-lawgiver who led the people 40 years through the wilderness. In the babe's face there were prophecies of the man of God. Surely among those who have been born of women there has not been born a greater than Moses; and about him as a child there was a something so striking, so marvelously beautiful, that his parents were fascinated by him.

and they were not afraid of the edict of the king Their faith made them hide him, for that faith laid hold of God, and they were not afraid of the king's commandment. Faith makes a person wise. It is one of the notable points about faith that it is sanctified common sense. That is not at all a bad definition of faith. It is not fanaticism; it is not absurdity. It is making God the grandest asset in our account, and then reckoning according to the soundest logic. It is not putting my hands into boiling water with the impression that it will not scald me; it is not doing foolish and absurd things. Faith is believing in God and acting toward God as we ought to do. It is treating Him, not as a cipher, but as a grand overtopping numeral in all our additions and subtractions. It is realizing God—that is what it is. And in that sense, faith is the truest reason, spiritualized and lifted up out of the ordinary sphere in which godless men choose to indulge in it. It is sanctified reason, enlightened from on high.

ILLUSTRATION
Faith to Disobey

The Israelites in Egypt had no doubt caught very much the spirit of the Egyptians, and the spirit of the Egyptians was the exact opposite of the spirit of a true-born Englishman. We rejoice that we are free. We are in the habit of discussing laws and criticizing statutes, and if there were an unjust edict passed we should not scruple for a single moment to break it. We should even feel a pleasure in putting our foot through an unrighteous act of parliament, for we have been trained for centuries in the habits and ways of liberty, and think and speak for ourselves.

But it has never been so in Egypt, and especially was it not so in those days. Then they might well swear by the life of Pharaoh, for they all lived by the permission of Pharaoh. They belonged to him—their lands and everything. Hence it must have taken a good deal for Moses' parents, son and daughter of Levi, to feel that they could go against the king's commandment.

---

24   **By faith Moses** What was the source of Moses' decision? Scripture says it was faith, otherwise some would insist that it was the force of blood. We know right well that the sons of godly parents are not led to adore the true God by reason of their birth. Grace does not run in the blood; sin may, but righteousness does not. It was faith, not blood, that impelled Moses in the way of truth.

when he was grown up, refused to be called the son of Pharaoh's daughter The faith of Moses was what ours must be: a faith that worked by love—love to God, and love to His people. It was no mere belief of a fact, but that fact had an overpowering influence upon his life. Moses believed, believed firmly and intensely, believed for himself, so that he took fast hold of that which is invisible. Moses showed the reality of his faith in his life by what he refused to do and by what he chose to do. Both the negative and the positive poles were made right by his faith. Everything about Moses proved the truth and the vigor of his faith in God.

25   **choosing instead to be mistreated with the people of God** Moses believed that the Israelites were the chosen people of God. This, of course, he had learned from his parents, and he heartily believed it, though it certainly did not look to be true. It was the solemn conviction of Moses that the living and true God had chosen the seed of Abraham to be his people, and had taken them into covenant with himself. They were the election of grace. For this cause Moses loved them, and desired to be numbered with them. Certainly, they were not in themselves a very lovable people: there was much about them that

must have saddened the heart of Moses. They were ignorant, while he was educated. They had been debased by slavery, while he was of that brave disposition which is nourished in freedom. When he himself attempted to be their champion, they did not receive him.

rather than to experience the transitory enjoyment of sin He perceived the pleasures of sin to be but for a season. He said to himself, "I may have but a short time to live, and even if I live to a good old age, life at the longest is still short. When I come to the close of life, what a miserable reflection it will be that I have had all my pleasure, it is all over, and now I have to appear before God as a traitorous Israelite who threw up his birthright for the sake of enjoying the pleasures of Egypt."

26 **endured for the sake of Christ** And, then, again, he thought within himself that even the pleasures, which did last for a season, while they lasted were not equal to the pleasure of being reproached for Christ's sake. But Christ was not there. Christ as yet had not been born into the world. How could the reproach of Israel in Egypt be the reproach of Christ? This shows us that Christ was always one with His people. Even as the church is the body of Christ now, so were the Lord's people the body of Christ of old. The Lord Christ so sympathized with Israel in Egypt that what they bore, He bore.

Christ suffers in the least of His people. The poorest and the most obscure of them, when ridiculed and put to scorn for His sake, is not alone in his grief—the head suffers in the members. The reproach of believers is really the reproach of Him in whom they believe. The reproach of Israel is the reproach of Christ, and Moses believed this. He said, "Whatever they say against these people, and whatever they do against them, they are really saying and doing against the Lord's anointed."

for he was looking to the reward Adding all things up and making a deliberate calculation of the whole business, he believed that it must be right and wise to stand on that side that was in agreement with the living God. He made up his mind that he would be where the Lord was.

These days you have read or heard the plausible arguments of the deceivableness of unrighteousness, which in these last days teaches men to do evil that good may come. Moses cared for none of these things. He knew his duty, and did it, whatever might be the consequences. Every Christian man's duty is to believe the truth, and follow the truth, and leave results with God.

27 **By faith he left Egypt** Moses was an Israelite indeed, and he would not conceal his nationality nor renounce it by becoming a naturalized Egyptian. Although it should tear the heartstrings of his foster mother, and be even as a sentence of death to himself, yet he would take his stand. Moses thus proved his faith to be stronger than that of many who are mastered by family ties, and held captive by the bonds of earthly love.

not fearing the anger of the king Faith can do what unbelief must not attempt to do. And when unbelief tries to follow in the footsteps of faith, it becomes its own destroyer. You must have real faith in God, or you cannot go where faith would take you; but with faith you may go through the cloud or through the sea, and find yourself safe on the other side.

for he persevered as if he saw the invisible one This is what you and I must do: feel that it is but common sense, sanctified common sense, to be looking out for that which will endure forever, and to let these temporary things go, if it be needful that they go, that we may win the crown that does not fade away.

28 **By faith he kept the Passover** Here, again, you have the obedience of faith, taking God's precepts and carrying them out.

29 **By faith they crossed the Red Sea** There you have the difference between faith and presumption: faith goes through the sea, presumption is drowned in the sea.

There are two redemptions: redemption by price and redemption by power. Redemption by price was typified in the paschal lamb and the Passover. Redemption by power was typified in the passage of the Red Sea, when the children of Israel went through it dry-shod and the Egyptians were drowned.

30 **By faith the walls of Jericho fell down** On they went with steady tramp, and though they saw no corpses blocking up their pathway, though their arms were not red with blood, though they heard no shriek of those that fly, and could utter no shout of victory, yet they were as confident as they were when actually the walls began to rock, and the dust and smoke went up to heaven, and the shrieks of the slain made glad the foeman's ear. We must encompass this city in full faith.

after they had been marched around for seven days You could not see faith at work on those solid walls. Those huge ramparts and battlements seemed to stand fast and firm, yet they "fell down, after they had been marched around seven days." No battering rams played upon them, but faith can do better work than battering rams or dynamite.

31 **By faith Rahab the prostitute did not perish** All the other persons mentioned here were doubtless saved by faith. But I do not find it especially remarked concerning any of them that they did not perish through their faith, while it is particularly said of this woman that she was delivered amidst the general destruction of Jericho purely and only through her faith. And, without doubt, her salvation was not merely of a temporal nature, not merely a deliverance of her body from the sword, but redemption of her soul from hell.

That she was really saved in a gospel sense, as well as temporally, seems to me to be proved from her reception of the spies. This was an emblem of the entrance of the word into the heart, and her hanging out of the scarlet thread was an evidence of faith, not inaptly picturing faith in the blood of Jesus the Redeemer.

with those who were disobedient It is right to conclude that if there had been other believers there, either the city would have been spared for the sake of ten righteous, or else there would have been means found for their preservation; but she was the only one there. If we could have taken a bird's eye view of the city of Jericho, and had been informed that there was one believer there, I warrant you we should not have looked to Rahab's house. She would have been about the last person that we should have supposed had been a possessor of faith in the true God. God has a people where we little dream of it, and He has chosen ones among a sort of people whom we dare not hope for. Who would think that grace could grow in the heart of one who was a harlot by name, as though her sin was openly known to all? Yet it did grow there.

because she welcomed the spies in peace This woman said, "If I must die for these men, I will; I am prepared, bad name as I have, to have a worse name still. I am prepared to be handed down to infamy as a traitor to my country, if it is necessary, for taking in these spies. For I know it is God's will it should be done, and I will do it at all costs."

Do not trust your faith unless it has self-denial with it. Faith and self-denial, like Siamese twins, are born together, and must live together, and the food that nourishes one must nourish both. But this woman, poor sinner as she was, would deny herself. She brought her life, even as that other woman who was a sinner, brought the alabaster box of precious ointment and broke it on the head of Christ.

ILLUSTRATION

Faith vs. Probability

I have heard of a church clergyman who was once waited upon by his churchwarden, after a long time of drought, and was requested to pray for rain. "Well," said he "I will offer it, but it's not a bit of use while the wind's in the east, I'm sure."

There are many who have that kind of faith: they believe just so far as probabilities go with them, but when the promise and the probability part, then they follow the probability and part with the promise. They say, "The thing is likely, therefore I believe it." But that is not faith; it is sight. True faith exclaims, "The thing is unlikely, yet I believe it."

APPLICATION

Faith in the Ordinary

When the Holy Spirit says, "By faith Moses ... was hidden for three months by his parents," it makes the simple and the natural action glow with an unusual glory, like the bush in Horeb, which was only a bush, but yet the Lord appeared in it. Here is the point of it, dear friends—mothers, daughters, sisters, and all of you engaged in common life—do you not see how you can make faith tell about ordinary things?

When you are ill, you can lie and cough by faith without being impatient. You can keep your temper sweet with a provoking husband, or a disobedient child, by faith. You can do all sorts of things by faith. It rides the whirlwind, but it threads a needle; it climbs up to the throne of God, and yet it stands by a baby's cradle. It can obtain the promises, but it can sit down and twist bulrushes, and boil bitumen, and stir a tar pot to coat a little ark within and without with pitch, if it be necessary.

There is nothing that faith cannot make noble when it touches it. You need not say, "I want to get away from my daily business, or from my domestic concerns, in order to show my faith." No, no; stop where you are and show it. If a soldier wants to be brave, and asks his captain what he can do, he will tell him, "You keep rank in the day of battle; you fire your gun when the word is given." In order to be a brave man you need not leave the ranks or run up to the cannon's mouth out of mere bravado. Soldier of Christ, just keep your place. Do the work appointed by the great Lord, trusting in Him, and believing in His power to help you. So shall you make your life sublime, however commonplace it may appear to carnal eyes.

Lessons from Moses' Decision

We ought all of us to be ready to part with everything for Christ; and if we are not, we are not His disciples: "He that loves son or daughter more than me is not worthy of me" (Matt 10:37). "Every one of you who does not renounce all his own possessions cannot be my disciple" (Luke 14:33). Jesus may not require you actually to leave anything, but you must be ready to leave everything if required.

We also ought to abhor the very thought of obtaining honor in this world by concealing our sentiments or by making compromises. If there is a chance of your being highly esteemed by holding your tongue, speak at once and do not run the risk of winning such dishonorable honor. If there is a hope of people praising you because you are so ready to yield your convictions, pray God to make you like a flint never to yield again. What more damning glory could a man have than to be applauded for disowning his principles to please his fellow men? From this may the Lord save us!

Third, we ought to take our place with those who truly follow God and the Scriptures, even if they are not altogether what we should like them to be. The place for an Israelite is with the Israelites; the place for a Christian man is with Christian men. The place for a thoroughgoing disciple of the Bible and of Christ is with others who are such, and even if they should happen to be the lowest in the land, and the poorest of the poor, and the most illiterate and uneducated persons of the period, what is all this if their God loves them and if they love God? Weighed in the scales of truth, the least one among them is worth ten thousand of the greatest ungodly men.

Lastly, we must all look to our faith. Faith is the main thing. You cannot make a thorough character without sincere faith. If you are not a believer in Christ, if you do not believe in the one God, may the Lord convert you, and give you now that precious gift! To try and raise a character that shall be good without a foundation of faith is to build upon the sand, and to pile up wood and hay and stubble. Wood, hay, and stubble are very good things as wood, hay, and stubble, but they will not bear the fire—and as every Christian character will have to bear fire, it is well to build on the rock, and to build with such graces and fruits as will endure trial. You will have to be tried. And if you have, by sneaking through life as a coward, avoided all opposition and all ridicule, ask yourself whether you really are a disciple of that Master of the house whom they called Beelzebub, whether you are truly a follower of that crucified Savior who said, "Whoever does not carry his cross and follow me cannot be my disciple" (Luke 14:27). Suspect the smooth places; be afraid of that perpetual peace that Christ declares He came to break. He says, "I have not come to bring peace, but a sword" (Matt 10:34). He came to bring fire upon the earth; and "what will I," said He, "if it be already kindled?" (Luke 12:49).

Be the Lord's, without Reserve

If you are a believer in Christ, *give yourself up to God without reserve.* Say, "I will follow you, my Lord, through flood or flame. I will follow wherever the Lord shall lead the way." Say this in your soul. Take God for your all in poverty and disgrace. Take God on the bleak winter's day, and say: "I am resolved, God helping me, to do His will."

If you do this, you cannot tell what God has in store for you, nor do you need to give it a consideration. Moses, after all, was not a loser by his self-denial. He became king in Jeshurun, and was more than a monarch in the wilderness. He refused to be Pharaoh's son, but in the book of Exodus God said to him: "See, I have made you a god to Pharaoh" (Exod 7:1). Egypt's haughty monarch feared his plagues and entreated his intercession. The Lord made Moses so great that among those who are born of woman he ranks among the first unto this day. Even in heaven he is remembered; for they sing "the song of Moses, the slave of God, and the song of the Lamb" (Rev 15:3). If you give yourself to the Lord you can little guess what He will do with you. What you lose will be a mere trifle compared with what you will gain. As to honor, all honor and glory lie in the service of the Most High.

I am come to this pass—whether I sink or whether I swim, I am the Lord's! By His grace I will believe His Word and cling to its inspiration, whether the Lord shall roll away my reproach. I would say with the three holy children, "Our God, whom we serve, is able to rescue us from the furnace of blazing fire. And from your hand, O king, let him rescue us. And if not, let it be known to you, O king, that we will not serve your gods, and the statue of gold that you have set up we will not worship" (Dan 3:17-18). With Job my heart has said: "Though he kill me, I will hope in him" (Job 13:15).

Bring Your Family under the Flag

Love them as she might, Rahab could not save her family unless she got them under the red flag. If any of them stopped in the streets when the Israelites were slaying the people, they might say, "We belong to Rahab." The reply would be, "We cannot help that. The oath we took was to spare all in the house where the red line was in the window, and if you are not there, you cannot be spared."

It will be of no use when you die to say, "Spare me, avenging angel! My mother prayed for me, and my sister agonized for my conversion." No, you must personally get into Christ yourself, and have a real faith in Him, or no prayers of others can be of any help to you. But the mercy was that somehow Rahab was helped by God to bring all her family in. Her father did not say, "No, my girl, I do not believe in it." Some of you have fathers who do say that. Pray hard for them. And the mother did not say, "My child, you are mad. I have always thought you a little affected in the brain. Do not come teaching your mother." No, but mother came too.

When the Israelites marched around the city six days, and the people of Jericho laughed and said, "What fools they were to think they were going to make the walls tumble down by walking round them," she still confided in God. But I dare say she had some difficulty in persuading her lively sisters and her argumentative brothers to believe too. They would say, "Rahab, are you quite clear about this? Is it not all a mere farce?" Somehow, such was the influence God gave her, such was the power of her faith, that they all remained in the house, and with their families were saved. The house, I dare say, was filled as full as could be from top to bottom, and Rahab was glad to see it. God grant I may have all my family thus preserved. I am sure every child of God is breathing the same prayer: "God of Rahab, give me my father and my mother, and my brothers and my sisters, and all my family."

HEBREWS 11:32–40

³² And what more shall I say? For time would fail me to tell about Gideon, Barak, Samson, Jephthah, David, and Samuel and the prophets, ³³ who through faith conquered kingdoms, accomplished justice, obtained what was promised, shut the mouths of lions, ³⁴ extinguished the effectiveness of fire, escaped the edge of the sword, were made strong from weakness, became mighty in battle, put to flight enemy battle lines. ³⁵ Women received back their dead by resurrection. But others were tortured, not accepting release, in order that they might gain a better resurrection. ³⁶ And others experienced mocking and flogging, and in addition bonds and imprisonment. ³⁷ They were stoned, they were sawed in two, they died by murder with a sword, they wandered about in sheepskins, in goatskins, impoverished, afflicted, mistreated, ³⁸ of whom the world was not worthy, wandering about in deserts and mountains and caves and holes in the ground. ³⁹ And although they all were approved through their faith, they did not receive what was promised ⁴⁰ because God had provided something better for us, so that they would not be made perfect without us.

EXPOSITION

32   **Barak** Look at Barak; after he has once believed in the power of God, he marches to the fight and wins the victory, and is commemorated in soul-stirring words by the poetess, "Wake up, wake up, Deborah! Wake up, wake up, sing a song! Get up, Barak! Take captive your captives, O son of Abinoam" (Judg 5:12). Mighty to conquer was the man who was timid to fight. When faith gave him courage, it made him triumph. Carry a

vial of strong faith along with you, and a good dose of it will drive off fainting fits.

Samson There are some names in this chapter that we should hardly have expected to see there, the characters mentioned having been so disfigured by serious faults, and flaws, and failings. But the distinguishing feature of faith was there in every instance, especially in the case of Samson. Perhaps there was no more childlike faith in any man than there was in him. Who but a man full of faith would have hurled himself upon a thousand men with no weapon in his hand but the jawbone of a donkey? There was a wondrous confidence in God in that weak, strong man, which, though it does not excuse his faults, nevertheless puts him in the ranks of the believers. Happy is the man or woman who believes in God.

ILLUSTRATION

Faith Loves a Challenge

I would compare faith to an emperor who summoned his counselors and judged whether he should go to war by their opinion, but he did it in the following manner: If they warned him that it would be a very fearful war, if they said that the enemy's cities would never be taken, that the armies on the other side were too numerous to be conquered, and the provinces too extensive to be held, he would reply, "We will do it then, for if there is anything that you gentlemen think to be easy, it is beneath the dignity of the emperor and the troops whom he commands. But if you reckon it impossible, there is a clear field for honor." And was it not a man fit to be a soldier of such a prince who, when told that the Persian arrows were so numerous that they would obscure the light of the sun, replied, "We shall fight splendidly in the shade"? Surely he was akin to Alexander, who, when they said that the Persians were like the sands on the seashore, replied, "One butcher is not afraid of a whole flock of sheep."

So let it be with us. Let us feel that we are men of another mold than to be afraid, that believing in God we do not know how to spell "cowardice." As to fear of defeat or fear of man, we give that up for the craven dogs who slink at their master's heels, and wear their master's collar, and eat the garbage that his bounty throws to them. We do not care for the things that are seen; we have learned to live on an angel's diet and to eat the bread that comes down from heaven.

---

33   **through faith** All these were men of faith. Others mentioned in Scripture have done something, but God did not accept them. Men have humbled themselves, and yet God has not saved them. Ahab did, and yet his sins were never forgiven. Men have repented, and yet have not been saved, because theirs was the wrong repentance. Judas repented and went and hanged himself, and was not saved. Men have confessed their sins and have not been saved. Saul did it. He said to David, "I have sinned! Come back, David my son" (1 Sam 26:21), and yet he went on as he did before. Multitudes have confessed the name of Christ, and have done many marvelous things, and yet they have never been pleasing to God, from this simple reason: They did not have faith.

conquered kingdoms I take the meaning of these texts to be not a laudation of the acts themselves so much as an honor put upon faith itself by the Holy Spirit. If you read of those who conquered kingdoms, that is not the point: others have conquered kingdoms, but it is "who *through faith* conquered kingdoms." If you read of those who escaped the edge of the sword; many have done that, but none are recorded here but those "who *by faith* escaped the edge of the sword." "Put to flight enemy battle lines": many have done that by valor and strength, but to do it *by faith*—that is the thing. Many have endured flogging and bonds and imprisonment, and have wandered about destitute, afflicted, tormented, but such sufferings are nothing unless they are borne by faith.

accomplished justice Is that as great an exploit as subduing kingdoms? Yes, that it is. To have, by faith, preserved a holy character, in such a world of temptation as this, is a far grander achievement than to have conquered any number of kingdoms by force of arms.

obtained what was promised The promises of God are to the believer an inexhaustible mine of wealth. Happy is it for him if he knows how to search out their secret veins and enrich himself with their hidden treasures. They are to him an armory containing all manner of offensive and defensive weapons. Blessed is he who has learned to enter into the sacred arsenal, to put on the breastplate and the helmet, and to lay his hand to the spear and to the sword.

ILLUSTRATION

Promises upon Promises

God sometimes gives His people fresh promises by faith just before a trial is about to come upon them. It was so with Elijah. God said to him, "Go to the Wadi Kerith; I have commanded the crows to sustain you there" (1 Kings 17:4). This was at the beginning of the famine. There he stayed, and God fulfilled the promise, for by faith Elijah had obtained it. Acting upon faith, still dependent upon God, he abides at Kerith, and as the result of this faith, God gives him a fresh promise: "Get up and go to Zarephath—I have commanded a widow there to sustain you" (1 Kgs 17:9). The faith that received the first promise obtained the honor of a second.

So it is with you and with me. If we have had a little promise, and until now have realized it, if we have lived upon it and made it the stay and support of our souls, surely God will give us another and a greater one. And so, from promise to promise speeding our way, we shall find the promises to be rungs of the ladder that Jacob saw, the top which shall reach to heaven.

---

shut the mouths of lions Remember Daniel in the lions' den, and then ask yourself, "What is there that faith cannot do?"

34 **extinguished the effectiveness of fire** Think of Shadrach, Meshach, and Abednego, and remember how the fierceness of Nebuchadnezzar's fire was quenched for them.

were made strong from weakness Do you notice how, every now and then, there is the mention of a feat that seems altogether beyond you, but then there follows one in which you can be a partaker with these heroes and heroines of faith? It may be that you have never "extinguished the effectiveness of fire," yet, often enough, it has been true of you that, by faith, "out of weakness" you have been "made strong."

They were quite as weak as the weakest of us, but by their faith they laid hold of heavenly strength until they could do all things. There was nothing in the range of possibility, or, I might say, nothing within the lines of impossibility, that they could not have performed. They achieved everything that was necessary in the form of service, and they bore up gloriously under the most fearful pressure of suffering, simply and only by faith in God, who became their Helper. You and I may be very weak at this time, but we can be made strong out of just such weakness.

ILLUSTRATION
Faith Makes Strong

Just as we sometimes see a strong and healthy person growing pale and wan, losing appetite and falling into sickness until he becomes a mere skeleton because a general sapping and undermining of the constitution has come upon him, so have I seen it with Christians. They do not lose life, but they do lose all their energy and become listless and lifeless. Then they can scarcely walk, much less run, and mounting with wings as eagles is quite out of the question. Such persons will bear witness that the only way of recruiting their strength is by faith. They must come again to the first principles, and trust their souls anew with Jesus, believing over again with a novelty of energy the old doctrines of the gospel.

became mighty in battle It is well to be humble; it is never well to be weakly fearful. Some are always afraid. They dare not try this, and dare not try that, and if they happen to be placed in office where they can influence others by their counsels, they are shockingly bad officers, because they are always keeping the church back from Victory by a fear of defeat.

35 **Women received back their dead by resurrection** Such is the power of faith when it uses the weapon of all prayer: even the gates of the grave cannot prevail against it.

But others were tortured, not accepting release They flung their lives away without a sigh, not accepting deliverance, that they might obtain a better resurrection. And they were no fools; they gained by their losses. The ruby crowns they wear today and forever are the full reward of all their sufferings: "Seek first his kingdom and righteousness" (Matt 6:33).

that they might gain a better resurrection What wondrous faith it was that sustained the saints under the awful tortures to which they were subjected! The story harrows one's heart even to read it; what must it have been actually to endure?

36 **And others experienced mocking** Is this also a feat of faith? Yes; instead of showing their faith by putting their enemies to flight, they prove it by enduring all manner of tortures without shrinking.

37 **They were stoned, they were sawed in two** It is wonderful how God takes care that the victories of faith shall somehow or other be kept in mind. There was a period after the prophets had ceased to prophesy, and before Christ came, in which the Israelite church had to contend against antichrist and other enemies. In the Apocrypha you have the account of some few of the martyrdoms of those who held fast to God and to His truth. Those who were stoned and sawed in two for the truth's sake shall not be forgotten. If the details be not given they shall yet be recorded in the gross, on the sacred page.

ILLUSTRATION

Tuned for Heaven's Harmonies

If you have been in a piano factory, did you go there for the sake of music? Go into the tuning room, and you will say, "This is a dreadful place to be in; I cannot bear it; I thought you made music here." They say, "No, we do not produce music here. We make the instruments, and tune them here, and in the process much discord is forthcoming."

Such is the church of God on earth. The Lord makes the instruments down here, and tunes them, and a great deal of discord is easily perceptible, but it is all necessary to prepare us for the everlasting harmonies up yonder.

---

38   **wandering about on deserts and mountains** The gracious characters of which we read in Scripture were not created by favorable circumstances. They owed nothing to their position, or age, their character was formed from within. Their faith was not produced by the tenderness of providence; they were not put into a conservatory like fair flowers that cannot endure the frost. Rather might we say that they were helped to their robustness by the rough winter blasts that swept over them. They were warriors of peace: pilgrims who traveled armed to the teeth, making no holiday march, but contending with giants and dragons.

39   **they did not receive what was promised** It lay in the future to them far more than it does to us, for Christ has now come, and we look back to that glorious appearing of our Lord and Savior, but they had altogether to look forward. But since then, equally noble exploits have been performed by the heroes and heroines of faith. The Christian martyrs have shown the extremity of human endurance when they have been sustained by faith; and the catalog of Christian heroes, since their Lord ascended to heaven, is longer and even brighter than that of the faithful ones who came before them in the earlier dispensation.

40   **they would not be made perfect without us** It never was God's intention that any part of His church should be able to do without the rest of it. Those who lived before the time of Christ cannot do without us; neither can we do without them.

Is it not wonderful that we, who bring up the rear of the army of faith, are necessary to its completeness? It cannot be perfect without us. Yes, heaven itself will not be complete without us who are on the road to it. There would be empty seats in the holy orchestra, gaps in the sacred circle; we who believe must all come there to make them perfect.

The new dispensation is necessary to complete the old. The New Testament is the complement of the Old Testament, and New Testament saints join hands with Old Testament elders. Let us all be worthy of our high pedigree, and may God grant that, if the saints of these latter days are to perfect the history of the Church of Christ, the end may not be less heroic than the beginning was! A true poem should gather force as it grows, and its waves of thought should roll in with greater power as it nears its climax; so should the mighty poem of faith's glorious history increase in depth and power as it gets nearer to its grand consummation, that God may be glorified yet more and more through all His believing children.

APPLICATION

Called to Endure

Few, if any, are without sorrow, and many saints have a double portion of grief in their pilgrimage. Sitting here with your brothers in Christ, you look very cheerful, but I may be addressing those whose life is one protracted struggle for existence. Assuredly, you will not hold out without true faith, and much of it. You must endure, "as seeing him who is invisible." You must joy in God, or you will not joy at all. Earthly comforts are not yours, but if you grasp the spiritual and the eternal, you will not repine. If in this life only you had hope, you would be of all men most miserable, but having that hope, you are among men most happy. The solitary place shall be glad for you, and the desert shall rejoice and blossom as the rose. Commend me to firm faith for power to bear the daily cross. He who believes has everlasting life, and the joys which come of it. Trust in your God, in His love to you, in His care of you, and then you will be as the lilies, which do not toil or spin (Matt 6:28), and yet are clothed; or as the ravens, which have no storeroom nor barn, and yet God feeds them (Luke 12:24). Behold you, by faith, the heaven prepared for you, and know with certainty that you will soon be there among the angels. You will defy cold, and hunger, and nakedness, and shame, and everything else. Your faith out of weakness shall make you strong.

Meditate on God's Promises

There are promises that are like grapes in the winepress: If you will tread them, the juice will flow. Many a time a believer, when he is like Isaac walking in the fields, meditating in the cool of the day upon a promise, unexpectedly meets his Rebekah. The blessing that had tarried long comes suddenly home. He sought retirement to meditate upon a promise, and "on the way" (Gen 24:27) God met with him. Thinking over the hallowed words will often be the means of fulfilling them. "I was in the Spirit on the Lord's day," says John, "and I heard behind me a great sound like a trumpet" (Rev 1:10). It was his being in the Spirit, his meditating upon spiritual things, that made him ready to behold the King in his beauty and to hear what the Spirit says to the churches.

Meditate much especially upon those promises that relate personally to Christ. While you are thinking them over, the faith that you are seeking will insensibly come to you. The word that says, "The blood of Jesus his Son cleanses us from all sin" (1 John 1:7)— think that over, chew and digest it, and in the very act of meditation faith will be born in your soul.

I think it is Martin Luther who says that some passages of Scripture are like trees that bear fruit, but the fruit does not easily drop. You must get hold of the tree, shake it, and shake it again and again. Sometimes you will need to exhaust all your strength, but at the last shake, down drops the luscious fruit. Do so with the promise: shake it to and fro by meditation, and the apples of gold will fall.

Made Strong from Weakness

Some of you are going through a present personal difficulty. You are embarrassed in money matters, or a child is sick, or your wife is dying, or some other providential trial is vexing you. You are saying, "I cannot bear it!" I will not pray with you that you may be comforted in that sinful weakness, but I will and do ask you to ask for faith in the Father's hand that wields the rod that you may get out of the weakness and may now be made strong to suffer with holy patience what your loving Father's wisdom appoints for you. I will ask that, knowing your duty, you may rise out of that weakness by believing that God will help you to obey, and so out of weakness you may be made strong.

Some of you are called where you live to contend earnestly for God and for His truth. You have many adversaries; now your weakness makes you withhold your testimony. Instead of bringing out all the truth you have given up the corners of it. I shall not ask that you may have any comfort in such weakness. May you be ashamed of having been ashamed of Christ and of His cross, but I do plead with God for you that, believing the very sweepings of truth to be precious, and the very cuttings of the diamond of the gospel to be worth fighting for, you may escape from your weakness and be made strong in life and death to declare God's truth boldly.

Some of you are always doubting your Father's love, the faithfulness of Christ, and your own interest in Him; I will not comfort you in such a state. I will not pray God to comfort you while you are in it, but I do ask you to pray that you fly from such weakness. Do not doubt your God until you have cause to doubt Him. If you will never distrust the Lord Jesus until He gives you an occasion for distrust, and until there is something in His character that should rationally excite your suspicion, you will never disbelieve again. I pray you seek more faith, and you will rise out of your fears.

You who are afraid of dying, shall I ask that you may be made strong while in that weakness? No, I dare not. Jesus Christ did not come to give you comfort while you are under the fear of death; He came to deliver those who through fear of death are all their lifetime subject to bondage. The plea shall be, therefore, that you may have such faith in God and such a view of the Canaan on the other side of the river that you may look forward with delight, or at least with resignation, to the time when you shall pass the river and be forever with the Lord.

The text says "from weakness," and may God grant that some of you who have been lying spiritually on a sick bed may be made to take up your bed and walk. May all weakness be left behind even as the child leaves the little garments of the nursery behind him when he becomes a man.

HEBREWS 12

¹ Therefore, since we also have such a great cloud of witnesses surrounding us, putting aside every weight and the sin that so easily ensnares us, let us run with patient endurance the race that has been set before us, ² fixing our eyes on Jesus, the originator and perfecter of faith, who for the joy that was set before him endured the cross, disregarding the shame, and has sat down at the right hand of the throne of God. ³ For consider the one who endured such hostility by sinners against himself, so that you will not grow weary in your souls and give up. ⁴ You have not yet resisted to the point of shedding your blood as you struggle against sin.

EXPOSITION

1 **such a great cloud of witnesses surrounding us** We can have no doubt about the great truths that we believe, for we are encompassed with a cloud of witnesses. The previous chapter gives us the names of many of these glorious bearers of testimony, who all by faith achieved great wonders and so bore witness to the truth of God.

putting aside every weight We cannot win if we are weighted. The pace will have to be very swift, and we cannot get to it, or keep it up, if we have weights to carry. Unloaded, we shall find the race taxing all our powers; weighted, we shall be doomed to failure.

and the sin that so easily ensnares us Even when the weights are laid aside, there is a garment about us that will assuredly twist about our feet and throw us down. Sin, as well as care, must be laid aside. It easily besets us, and therefore we must be more careful to be rid of it. Our original sin, our natural tendencies, our constitutional infirmities—these must be laid aside as garments unsuitable for men who are running the heavenly race. Heaven is for the holy: "Every unclean thing and one who practices detestable things and falsehood will never enter into it" (Rev 21:27). Darling sins must go first; these, as they are most loved, will have the most power to hinder. Every kind of sin must be watched against, struggled against, and mastered. "Sin will not be master over you" (Rom 6:14). We hope to see all our tendencies to sin killed and buried—buried so deep that not even a bone of a sin shall be left above ground. This will be heaven to us.

let us run with patient endurance All through the chapter he keeps up the idea of the great Olympic games, and represents the saints as occupied with spiritual athletics in the presence of God, the angels, and glorified men. In those games, those who ran and wrestled wore very little clothing, or often nothing at all. A runner might lose the race through being entangled by his scarf, so he laid aside everything that might hinder or hamper him.

the race that has been set before us If every weight of care must be laid aside, and every rag of sin, who is sufficient for these things? How can we poor limping mortals run in such a race as this? Even the starting is beyond us; how much more must perseverance in it outreach our strength! See how we are driven to free grace, how we are driven to the power of the Holy Spirit! The race that has been set before us most clearly reveals our helplessness and hopelessness apart from divine grace. The race of holiness and patience, while it demands our vigor, displays our weakness. We are compelled, even before we take a step in the running, to bow the knee and cry unto the strong for strength. We do not dare to retreat from the contest, but how can we begin a struggle for which we are so unfit? Who will help us? To whom shall we look? Does not all this very admirably introduce the next verse—"Fixing our eyes on Jesus, the originator and perfecter of faith"?

2   **fixing our eyes** The Greek word for "looking" is a much fuller word than we can find in the English language. It has a preposition in it that turns the look away from everything else. You are to look from all else to Jesus. Do not fix your gaze on the cloud of witnesses; they will hinder you if they take away your eye from Jesus. Do not look at the weights and the besetting sin—these you have laid aside; look away from them. Do not even look at the racecourse, or the competitors, but look to Jesus and so start in the race.

on Jesus The instructive original has in it the word "*eis*," which is translated "on," but in addition has the force of "into." We shall do well if we look on Jesus, but better still if we are found "*looking into* Jesus." I want you, when you begin your divine life, to take care that you look to Jesus with so penetrating a gaze that your "on" grows to an "into."

ILLUSTRATION

Fix Your Eyes for the Race

I have read of a competition of certain young plowmen who were set to plow for a prize. Most of them made very crooked work of it. After they had ended, one of the judges said, "Young man, where did you look while you were ploughing?"

"I kept my eyes on the plow handles, sir, and saw what I had to hold."

"Yes," the judge said, "and your plow went in and out, and the furrow is all crooked." He asked the next plowman, "Where did you look?"

"Well, sir," he answered, "I looked at my furrow, I kept my eye always on the furrow that I was making. I thought I should make it straight that way."

"But you did not," answered the judge. "You were all over the place." To the next he said, "What did you look at?"

"Well, sir," he said, "I looked between the two horses to a tree that stood in the hedge at the other end of the field, right in front of me." Now that man went straight because he had a fixed mark to guide him. This helps us to appreciate the wisdom of the text, "Fixing our eyes on Jesus." Looking to Jesus means life, light, guidance, encouragement, and joy; never cease to look on Him who ever looks on you.

---

the originator We must fix our eye on "the originator of our faith." If we do not begin by looking to Him, however quickly we may hurry along, we shall run in vain and labor in vain. To what purpose will your running be if the umpire determines that you started improperly? By bearing the cross, He has removed your heaviest weights, and by His death has destroyed your entangling sin. He can renew your nature by His resurrection power, and save you from the dominion of sin by His glorious reign. If you look alone to Him, you start well; but not otherwise.

and perfecter of faith As Jesus is at the commencement of the course, starting the runners, so He is at the end of the course, the rewarder of those who endure to the end. Those who would win in the great race must keep their eyes upon Him all along the course, even until they reach the finish line.

who for the joy that was set before him The joy that was set before Jesus was principally the joy of saving you and me. I know it was the joy of fulfilling His Father's will, of sitting down on His Father's throne, of being made perfect through suffering—but still I know that this is the grand, great motive of the Savior's suffering: the joy of saving us.

It was this joy that made Christ strong to endure in the day of His sorrow, and joy must make you also strong to endure unto the end. He had the joy of anticipated victory. It "was set before Him," and so He "endured the cross, disregarding the shame." He ran with a heavy cross on His back, and yet He ran faster than you or I have run. He ran because He had more joy than we have. So let us live in the joy of heaven; let us live in the joy of ultimate victory, and this will enable us to bear all the toils and trials of our present life.

endured the cross Ours is a trifling cross compared with that which pressed Him down, but He endured it. He took it up willingly, and carried it patiently. He never rebelled against it, and never relinquished it. He bore the cross until the cross bore Him, and then He bore death upon it. He could say, "It is finished."

Let us do the same. Are you persecuted, are you poor, are you sick? Take up the appointed cross. Christ ran with a cross on His shoulder, and so must we run. Do not try to escape trouble; the followers of the Crucified must be familiar with the cross. Endure it patiently, joyfully, in the strength of God. "Fixing your eyes on Jesus," behold His cross whenever you begin to faint under your own.

ILLUSTRATION
Royalty Despised

Perhaps there is nothing so heartrending as royalty despised. There is a story of an English king who was taken out by his cruel enemies to a ditch. They seated him on an anthill, telling him that was his throne, and then they washed his face in the filthiest puddle they could find.

But think of the King of kings and Lord of lords, having for His adoration the spittle of guilty mouths, for damage the smitings of filthy hands, for tribute the jests of brutal tongues! Was there ever shame like yours, you King of

kings, you emperor of all worlds, flouted by the soldiers
and smitten by their menial hands?

---

disregarding the shame Shame is a terrible thing to endure,
and many of the proudest natures have been subdued when
once they have been subjected to it. In the Savior's case, shame
would be peculiarly shameful. The nobler a man's nature, the
more readily does he perceive the slightest contempt, and the
more acutely does he feel it. That contempt which an ordinary
man might bear without suffering, he who has been bred to be
obeyed, and who has all his life long been honored, would feel
most bitterly. Beggared princes and despised monarchs are
among the most miserable of men, but here was our glorious
Redeemer, in whose face was the nobility of Godhead itself,
despised and spit upon and mocked.

has sat down He takes His rest because He has completed His
work. Here on earth He was filled with shame, but in glory He
is full of honor, for He is set down "at the right hand of God."
Here He was bound and led captive; there He is King of kings
and Lord of lords, for He sits at the right hand of the throne
of God.

at the right hand of the throne of God Here on earth we
see His manhood, born in a manger, living in poverty, dying
the ignominious death of the cross. There we adore His divine
glory, for He is "at the right hand of the throne of God." Think
of your Savior as your God, clothed with all power and authority. Surely this should urge you to quicken your pace, and
never to become weary or faint. You began by looking to Him
as a sufferer; persevere by looking to Him as a victor. "Have
courage," said He, "I have conquered the world" (John 16:33).
In that fact He gives you an assurance of your own victory.
The seed of the woman has bruised the serpent's head, and
therefore the Lord will tread Satan under your feet shortly.
The death of Christ is our death for sin, but the life of Christ

is our life unto holiness. The shame of Christ was our shame, and the triumph of Christ is our triumph. Therefore let us run, looking unto Jesus.

3   **For consider the one** What sort of a Savior is Jesus Christ, a little Savior or a great one? Is He not the Son of God, and Himself God? What need is there of a divine person to be a propitiation for limited sin? It was the infinity of sin that required the Godhead itself to become incarnate, in order that human guilt might be put away.

who endured such hostility Luther says, "When I think of what Christ suffered, I am ashamed to call anything that I have endured suffering for his sake." He carried His heavy cross, but we only carry a sliver or two of it; He drank His cup to the dregs, and we sip a drop or two at the very most. Consider how He suffered far more than you can ever suffer, and how He is now crowned with glory and honor. And as you are to be like Him, descend like Him into the depths of agony, that with Him you may rise to the heights of glory.

The believer under persecution should remember that he is suffering no strange thing, but is only enduring that which fell upon his Master before him. Should the disciple expect to be above his Lord? "If they have called the master of the house Beelzebul, how much more the members of his household" (Matt 10:25)? If they had received Christ, they would have received us, but since they reject both Christ and His sayings, the followers of Christ must expect that both their persons and their doctrines will be lightly esteemed.

ILLUSTRATION

Endure False Accusations as Jesus Did

We are sometimes apt to think that a charge that is unfounded is very cruel to us. I have heard people say sometimes, and I have laughed when I have heard them say it, "Mr. So-and-so has charged me with such-and-such a thing, but I am quite innocent. I should not have minded if I had been guilty." I have thought, "Then you ought to have minded it, but being innocent you have no cause to mind it at all." But is it not so that the more unfounded a charge is, the more deeply it seems to cut us from the very wantonness of its cruelty?

Well, then, you know how innocent the Savior was. The next time you feel innocent when you are thus accused "consider the one who endured such hostility by sinners against himself" (Heb 12:3), and who had to suffer both gross charges and unfounded ones.

---

by sinners against himself No personal animosity ever ruffled the serenity of our great Master's spirit. Moreover, He was never moved to take the slightest revenge upon His foes; even for those who nailed Him to the wood, He had no return but the prayer, "Father, forgive them, for they do not know what they are doing" (Luke 23:34). And, as He had no vengeance against them, so they exerted no evil influence upon Him. He persevered in His life work just as much as if He had never been opposed. Like the sun that goes on in its strength whether clouds hide it or whether it shines out of the blue serene, Christ continued in His heavenward way.

We ought to admire the patient serenity with which He so beautifully held His peace, but ought we not also to admire the way in which He unswervingly kept His course? Many a man would have turned either to the right hand or to the left, but the heroic Savior keeps right on.

ILLUSTRATION

"The Anvil Breaks Many Hammers"

There was a crest and motto that some of the old Reformers used to use, and that I commend to any of you who are under trial. It was an anvil with a number of hammers, all broken, lying around; and this was the motto when translated, "The anvil breaks many hammers." And how does it do this? Not by striking: oh, no! The anvil simply endures the blows, keeps its place, and lets the hammers fall, fall, fall until they are broken upon their handles.

This is exactly what the Savior did. They, the accusers, were the hammers; He was the anvil. Who shall say that the anvil did not break the hammers into pieces, that the silence of the Savior was not far more eloquent than all the clamor of the evil multitude? "He was silent" (Matt 26:63), it is said of Him. May it also be said of you and of me. When we have to suffer similar trials, may we bear them, like the Savior, in silence.

so that you will not grow weary in your souls and give up Think how He wrestled; think how He ran. And let your consideration of Him nerve you for your struggle, and brace up every muscle of your spirit, so that you will be determined that, as He won, so will you by the divine help of Him who is "the originator and perfecter of our faith" (Heb 12:2).

4 **You have not yet resisted to the point of shedding your blood** Your battles have been nothing yet; you think yourselves martyrs. What have you done? What have you suffered? What have you endured, compared with your Lord, compared with the saints of old?

APPLICATION

Jesus Sustains Us for the Race

We are helped to run to the end, not only by what Jesus has done for us, but by what Jesus is doing in us. Beloved, you who are in the middle of the race, remember that Jesus sustains you. Every atom of your strength for running comes from your Lord. Look to Him for it. Do not take a step in creature strength, nor seek after any virtue, or growth, or progress apart from His life and grace. He says, "Your fruit comes from me" (Hos 14:8). He works all our works in us, and because He works in us to will and to do of His own good pleasure, therefore we work out our own salvation with fear and trembling.

We are not only sustained by looking unto Jesus, but we are inspirited thereby. If we win a glance from His eye, our feeble knees are confirmed. We take breath as we behold Him on the throne, and dash forward again. Those dear eyes of His are to us as stars are to the mariner. Jesus says to us, "Come on—I am victorious, and so shall you be." A sight of the exalted Leader fires the zeal of each believer, and makes them run like a doe or a young hart.

Looking unto Jesus, you will get many a direction, for as He sits at the finish line, His very presence indicates the way. If our eyes are up to Him, as the eyes of a servant to her mistress, we shall run well. "Do not be as the horse or like a mule, without understanding; that needs his tackle—bridle and rein—for restraint" (Psa 32:10); but say with David, "You will guide me with your eye" (Psa 32:8). A look from the eye of Jesus is enough for a saint. If you are indeed "fixing your eyes on Jesus," you will avoid crooks and turns, and will take the shortest road to holiness and eternal glory. Consider Him who endured such contradiction of sinners against Himself, and you will not grow weary; neither will you miss your way.

Suffer for Him Who Suffered for Us

When the love of Christ is shed abroad in our hearts, then we feel that if the stake were present we would stand firmly in the fire to suffer for Him who died for us. I know our poor unbelieving hearts would soon begin to quail at the crackling wood and the furious heat. But surely this love would prevail over all our unbelief. Are there any of you who feel that if you follow Christ you must lose by it, lose your station, or lose your reputation? Will you be laughed at if you leave the world and follow Jesus? And will you turn aside because of these little things, when He would not turn aside, though all the world mocked Him, until He could say, "It is finished" (John 19:30)? No, by the grace of God, let every Christian lift his hands to the Most High God, to the maker of heaven and earth.

"For me to live is Christ and to die is gain" (Phil 1:21). Living I will be His; dying I will be His. If He will help me, I will live to His honor and serve Him wholly. And if He needs it, I will die for His name's sake.

When Faced with Your Sin, Consider Him

I can well believe that some of you are grievously oppressed with the sense of the greatness of God. You have lived for years negligent of the God who created you and supplied your wants. But now you have been awakened and aroused to the fact that there is a God, a God whom you have spitefully treated, whom you have shamefully disregarded. And you are shocked to find that it is so, for now you have a sense of the greatness of God, and you are afraid that He will crush you. You know the justice of God, and you are sure that He must avenge the injuries you have done to His holy law, and, therefore, you go about every day with a dreadful sound in your ears, crying, "Where shall I go from His presence, and how shall I escape from His vengeance?" You are surrounded with God, and in Him you live and move and exist (Acts 17:28), and this everywhere-present God is your enemy, for you have made Him so by your rebellions against Him.

Now as a cure for all this, I have to say to you: "Consider him" (Heb 12:3)—Christ Jesus. You are afraid of God because He hates sin. Your fears are based on truth. God hates sin infinitely. If there were only one grain of sin in the whole universe, He would burn it to ashes to get rid of that grain of sin, for it is such a detestable thing in His sight. But now consider Christ Jesus, for sin was laid on Him. If you will come now and put your trust in Jesus, you may be sure that your sin was laid on Christ, and the wrath of God concerning sin was spent upon Him.

Christ Suffers with You

You are by yourself now, a solitary protester in the midst of a multitude who are going astray. But the tables shall be turned soon. You shall not then be in a minority, but in a great majority, in the day when shouts of triumph shall be heard for the truth and for the right, and when shame and confusion of face shall be the portion of those who are now the despisers. They shall then wonder and perish and ask the rocks to hide them and the hills to cover their confusion. He endured, and yet He mounted to His throne amidst the shouts of angels and acclamations of heaven. So also shall you; therefore consider Him in this light lest you be weary and faint in your minds.

Then you must consider that He who went through this to get to His crown is very man, akin to us all. He loves us tenderly. He considers us now. He knows all the sorrows that tempt men, for He has felt the same. You are not alone; He is with you. Three of you in the furnace? No, there is a fourth, and that fourth is the Son of God. Into your grief He enters, for His own grief have put into His hand a master-key to fit the wards of every human grief that can ever be known. He can comfort us with all consolation, seeing that He Himself has passed through all tribulation. He is never forgetful of you. He is with you now. If you smart, He smarts. If you are despised, He suffers. "Saul, Saul, why are you persecuting me" (Acts 9:4)? Why, it was but a few poor men and women being hauled away to prison or to be scourged in the synagogue, but Christ takes it as being done to Himself. "Why are you persecuting me?" Oh, Christian, with such nearness to Christ, and such sympathy flowing from Him, be of good courage still. Hear Him say, "In all their distress, there was not distress, and the messenger of His presence saved them" (Isa 63:9). So may you lift up the hands that hang down, and strengthen the weakened knees (Heb 12:12), and go on your way rejoicing in Him!

⁵ And have you completely forgotten the exhortation that instructs you as sons?

> "My son, do not make light of the Lord's discipline,
> or give up when you are corrected by him.
> ⁶ For the Lord disciplines the one whom he loves,
> and punishes every son whom he accepts."

⁷ Endure it for discipline. God is dealing with you as sons. For what son is there whom a father does not discipline? ⁸ But if you are without discipline, in which all legitimate sons have become participants, then you are illegitimate and not sons. ⁹ Furthermore, we have had our earthly fathers who disciplined us, and we respected them. Will we not much rather subject ourselves to the Father of spirits and live? ¹⁰ For they disciplined us for a few days according to what seemed appropriate to them, but he does so for our benefit, in order that we can have a share in his holiness. ¹¹ Now all discipline seems for the moment not to be joyful but painful, but later it yields the peaceful fruit of righteousness for those who are trained by it.

EXPOSITION

5   **And have you completely forgotten** Our trials are little compared with those of the martyrs of the olden times. Take courage, these are small matters to faint about!

ILLUSTRATION

God's Providence Works Both Ways

If a grandfather of ours should die and leave us 500 pounds, what a merciful providence that would be! If by something strange in business we were suddenly to accumulate a fortune, that would be a blessed providence! If an accident happens, and we are preserved, and our limbs are not hurt, that is always a providence.

But suppose we were to lose 500 pounds; would that not be a providence? Suppose our establishment should break up, and business fail; would that not be a providence? Suppose we should during the accident break our leg; would that not be a providence? There is the difficulty. It is always providence when it is a good thing. But why is it not providence when it does not happen to be just as we please? Surely it is so; for if the one thing is ordered by God, so is the other. It is written, "I form light and create darkness; I make peace and I create evil; I am Yahweh; I do all these things" (Isa 45:7).

My son, do not make light of the Lord's discipline God's people can never by any possibility be punished for their sins. God has punished them already in the person of Christ; Christ, their substitute, has endured the full penalty for all their guilt, and neither the justice nor the love of God can ever exact again that which Christ has paid. Punishment can never happen to a child of God in the judicial sense. He can never be brought before God as his Judge, as charged with guilt, because that guilt was long ago transferred to the shoulders of Christ, and the punishment was exacted at the hands of His surety.

But yet, while the sin cannot be punished, while the Christian cannot be condemned, he can be chastised. While he shall never be arraigned before God's bar as a criminal and punished for his guilt, yet he now stands in a new relationship—that of a child to his parent. As a son, he may be chastised on account of sin. Folly is bound up in the heart of all God's children (Prov 22:15), and the rod of the Father must bring that folly out of them (Prov 13:24).

It is essential to observe the distinction between punishment and chastisement. Punishment and chastisement may agree as to the nature of the suffering. The one suffering may be as great as the other: the sinner who while here is punished for his guilt may suffer no more in this life than the Christian who is only chastised by his parent. They do not differ as to the nature of the punishment, but they differ in the mind of the punisher and in the relationship of the person who is punished. God punishes the sinner on His own account, because He is angry with the sinner. His justice must be avenged, His law must be honored, and His commands must have their dignity maintained. But He does not punish the believer on His own account; it is on the Christian's account—to do the believer good. He afflicts us for our profit. He lays on the rod for His children's advantage. He has a good design toward those who receive the chastisement.

or give up when you are corrected by him Note the two evils of which we are in danger: either of making light of God's discipline, or else of giving up under it—either of thinking too little or too much of them. Happy is the Christian who takes the middle course, and never despises the discipline of the Lord, nor ever faints under it.

6   **For the Lord disciplines the one whom he loves** What comfort there is here! Whenever we are under the scourging hand of God, how we ought to be cheered with the thought that this is a part of the heritage of the children. There are those who spoil their children. God is not one of them. He does not spare the rod (Prov 13:24), and the more He loves, often the more He corrects.

ILLUSTRATION

Pruned by the Vinedresser

A tree of common fruit may be let alone so long as there is some little fruit on it, but the very best fruit gets the sharpest pruning. I have noticed that in those countries where the best wine is made, the vinedressers cut the shoots right close in, and in the winter you cannot tell that there is a vine there at all unless you watch very carefully. They must cut them back sharp to get sweet clusters.

The Lord does thus with His beloved. It is not anger. Afflictions are not always anger. They are often tokens of great love.

With doting parents it is not so. Often the child whom his mother loves is allowed to do as he pleases and to escape chastening; but this is folly. The love of God is higher and wiser than the partialities of parents. It is a token of His favor to us that He takes the trouble to remove our love of sin by sharp and bitter pain.

and punishes every son whom he accepts Here is another noble reason for patience. That same trial which, on the one hand, comes from man, viewed in another way comes from God, and is a chastening. Let us accept it at His hands, regarding it as a token of sonship.

God will not spare His children when they need to be chastened. They shall have some blows as hard as He can well lay them—that is to say, as hard as such a loving heart as His will permit Him to give. They shall have such blows that each one of them shall have to cry out, "I am broken in two; my heart is smitten and withered like grass." And this is to be the treatment for every son whom God receives; not for some of them, but for all.

ILLUSTRATION
Those Whom God Is Chastising

We despise the chastening of the Lord *when we despise those that God chastens.* You say, "Poor old Mrs. So-and-so. The last seven years she has been bedridden; what is the good of her in the church? Would it not be a mercy if she were dead? We always have to be keeping her— someone or other giving her charities. Really, what is the good of her?" Many will go to see her, and they will say, "Well, she is a very good sort of woman, but it would be a happy release if she were taken." They mean it would be a happy release for them, as they would not have to give her anything. But if you think little of those whom God is chastising, you are despising the God who chastens them.

7 **God is dealing with you as sons** What a bright light this sheds upon all affliction: that it is for our profit, that it is thereby we are made partakers of the holiness of God. While you feel the weight of God's hand upon you, never forget that it is your Father's hand. Whatever form your trial may take— whether it is the loss of a child or of a parent, or the withdrawal of temporal prosperity, or the smiting of the body with aches and pains—the rod is never in any hand but the paternal one, and even while the Father smites He loves. Let this be your comfort, that it is not the hand of an enemy that is upon you. You are not suffering from a crushing blow from the foe's mailed hand, but the stroke, whether it is heavy or light, is wholly caused by your loving Father's hand.

8 **all legitimate sons have become participants** Yet no one should pray for troubles, or be anxious because he is without them: they will come fast enough and thickly enough before long, and when they do, a blessing will be in them.

then you are illegitimate and not sons None of us would wish to have that terrible name truthfully applied to us. I should greatly prefer to come into the condition of the apostle when he said, "Therefore rather I will boast most gladly in my weaknesses, in order that the power of Christ may reside in me" (2 Cor 12:9).

ILLUSTRATION

Taking Up Sonship Through Sickness

I know an old friend who used to tell me that for 60 years he had never known a day's illness. A splendid healthy old man he was, but about three months ago he took typhoid fever. I went to see him, and when he got better he came to see me. He said, "Well, sir, you see I am not the man I was, but I have made a great advance through this sickness. I have never known any weakness before, but now I have been brought very low. The Bible says: 'If you are without discipline, in which all legitimate sons have become participants, then you are illegitimate and not sons' (Heb 12:8). I am not a bastard after all. I have had my chastening, and I hope I shall take up my sonship more than I ever did before."

God grant that every chastened child may gather assurance from the covenant rod!

---

9   **Furthermore, we have had our earthly fathers who disciplined us** There was, possibly, much of their own temper mixed with their chastisements; they let off their wrath upon us sometimes by the medium of chastisement. But God never chastens His children merely out of anger.

and we respected them Should we not give Him reverence when we are chastened, instead of murmuring and complaining against Him, thus calling Him to account at our judgment seat? Let us be in willing subjection to Him; and the more willingly subject we are, the less painful will the chastisement be. Our bitterest sorrow will be found at the root of our self-will; and when our self-will is gone, the bitterness of our sorrow will be past.

Will we not much rather subject ourselves to the Father
There is a kind of fear toward God from which we must not wish to be free. There is that lawful, necessary, admirable, excellent fear, which is always due from the creature to the Creator, from the subject to the king, and from the child toward the parent. That holy, filial fear of God, which makes us dread sin and constrains us to be obedient to His command, is to be cultivated. This is the fear of the Lord which is "the start of wisdom" (Prov 9:10). To have a holy awe of our most holy, just, righteous, and tender parent is a privilege, not a bondage.

ILLUSTRATION
Sin Makes Cowards

We never find Adam afraid of God or of any manifestation of deity while he was in paradise as an obedient creature. But no sooner had he touched the fatal fruit than he found that he was naked, and hid himself. When he heard the voice of the Lord God walking in the garden in the cool of the day, Adam was afraid and hid himself from the presence of the Lord God among the trees of the garden.

Sin makes miserable cowards of us all. See the man who once could hold delightful conversation with his Maker, now dreading to hear his Maker's voice and skulking in the grove like a felon, who knows his guilt, and is afraid to meet the officers of justice.

---

10 **according to what seemed appropriate to them** Sometimes Christ may hide Himself in absolute sovereignty, but I am always concerned lest we should charge God foolishly. You are so apt to put too many saddles on that stalking horse. There are such multitudes of Christians who would even excuse their sins upon the plea of a divine sovereignty that exposed them to temptation, that I scarcely like to mention it. I believe that God does not afflict the children of men willingly or arbitrarily. Neither does Christ hide His face from His people for nothing; your sins have separated you and your God. He does not chastise us as silly parents may do, out of mere anger or whim, or to please themselves.

he does so for our benefit The heavenly Father's heart is never angry so as to smite in wrath. It is in pity, and gentleness, and tenderness that He afflicts His sons and daughters. "You in faithfulness have afflicted me." See what a blessed state this is to be brought into, to be made children of God, and then in our prayers to be praying, not like serfs and servants, but as children who cry, "Abba, Father" (Rom 8:15).

God is the Father of our spiritual nature, so, if He pleases to chasten us for our profit, shall we not humbly yield ourselves up to Him, and let Him do with us whatever He wills?

share in his holiness Is there no way for us to "share in his holiness" but through chastening? It would seem so from the wording of this verse. The Lord, as our loving Father, makes use of the rod so that He may make us to be truly holy.

ILLUSTRATION

Throw Yourself into the Battle

He who stands in the thickest part of the battle shall have the highest glory at last. The old warriors would not stand and skirmish a little on the outside of the army, but would say, "To the center, men! To the center!" And they cut through thick and thin until they reached the place where the standard was, and the hotter the battle, the more glory the warrior felt. He could glory when he had been where shafts flew the thickest, and where lances were hurled like hail. "I have been near the standard," he could say; "I have struck the standard-bearer down."

Count it glory to go into the hottest part of the field. Do not fear; your head is covered in the day of battle. The shield of God can easily repel all the darts of the enemy. Be bold for His name's sake.

---

11   **Now all discipline seems for the moment** Carnal reason judges in the present light, which happens to be the very worst light in which to form a correct estimate. Suppose that I am under a great tribulation today—let it be a bodily affliction—the head is aching, the heart is palpitating, the mind is agitated and distracted. Am I in a fit state to judge the quality of affliction with a distracted and addled brain? With the scales of the judgment lifted from their proper place, how can I sit and form a just idea of the wisdom of God in his dispensations? All that flesh and blood can discover of the quality of affliction is but its outward superficial appearance. We are not able by the eye of reason to discover the real virtue of sanctified tribulation; this discernment is the privilege of faith.

not to be joyful but painful If affliction *seemed* to be joyous, would it be a chastisement at all? I ask you, would it not be a most *ridiculous* thing if a father should so chasten a child that the child came away laughing, and smiling, and rejoicing? Joyful? Instead of being at all serviceable, would it not be utterly *useless*? What good could a chastisement have done if it was not felt? It is the blows of the wound, says Solomon, that will cleanse evil (Prov 20:30); and so if the chastisement does not come home to the bone and flesh, what good end can it have served?

It might even work the other way and be *hurtful*, for if those very gentle blows were enough, with one or two soft chiding words, to express parental hatred of sin, the child would surely think that the parent only played with it and that disobedience was a trifle. If only the mockery of discipline were given, the child would be hardened in sin, and even despise the authority that it ought to respect. If God sent us trials such as we would wish for, they would be no trials.

ILLUSTRATION
God Refines Us Like Metal

A man takes a mass of metal. It appears to you very pure, and very beautiful to look at. It is alloyed. He puts it into his refining pot, he heats the coals, and he begins to stir it. You say to him, "What are you doing? You are spoiling that precious metal. See how foul the surface is! What a scum floats up." The natural effect of the fire is to make the scum show itself. A skillful hand is needed, for the fire cannot do the refiner's work. He himself must skim the base metal off the top.

Affliction only makes the sin rise to the surface. It makes the devil in us come up; it makes us, while we are boiling in affliction, worse than we were before. It is the supernatural work of the Holy Spirit, and of our blessed Lord and Master, when He sees it on the top, then to skim it off. The affliction does not do us any good in itself; the natural fruit of affliction is rebellion. If God chastens me, can I love Him for that? Not naturally. If He strikes me, can I yield Him homage for that? No, naturally I rebel against Him, and I say, "Who are you that you should smite me this way, and what have I done that I should be tormented by you?" To kiss the hand that smites is something more than nature; it is grace.

---

later it yields the peaceful fruit of righteousness Affliction really does to the Christian, when the time comes, bring forth fruit. This is the object of Christ in sending it. In His sweet prayer for the elect, He prayed that His people might bring forth fruit. He said, "My Father is glorified by this: that you bear much fruit, and prove to be my disciples" (John 15:8). He assured them that every branch of the true vine that brought forth fruit would be purged, that it might bring forth more fruit. So far as this world is concerned, God gets His glory out of us, not by our being Christians, but by our being fruitful Christians.

APPLICATION

Where Do You Get Your Comfort From?

Let me ask those who are afflicted and have no religion where they get their *comfort* from. Christians derive it from the fact that they are children of God, and they know that the affliction is for their good. Where do you get comfort from? It has often puzzled me how poor tried worldly people get on. I can somewhat guess how they can be happy when the glass is full, when hearts are glad and joyous, when hilarity and mirth sparkle in their eyes, when the board is covered and the family is well. But what does the worldly man do when he loses his wife, when his children are taken away, when his health departs and he himself is near death? I leave him to answer. All I can say is, I wonder every day that there are not more suicides, considering the troubles of this life, and how few there are who have the comforts of religion.

Poor sinner, even if there were no heaven and hell, I would recommend to you this religion. For even if in this life only we had hope, we should be of all men most *happy*, really, in our spirits, although we might seem to be "of all people most pitiable" (1 Cor 15:19). I tell you, if we were to die like dogs, if there were no second world, so happy does the Christian religion make the heart that it would be worthwhile having it for this life alone. The secularist who thinks of this world only is a fool for not thinking of Christianity, for it confers a benefit in this world as well as in that which is to come.

It makes us bear our troubles. What would break your backs are only feathers to us; what would destroy your spirits are to us "momentary light afflictions" (2 Cor 4:17). We find light enough in our hearts in the depth of darkness. Where you find darkness, we have light, and where you have light, we have the brilliance of the sun. May God put you in the number of His saved family, and then if He chastens you, I ask whether you will not think His rod light when compared with the sword that you deserve to have smitten you dead. God grant you, if you are chastened now, that you may be chastened and not killed, that you may be chastened with the righteous and not condemned with the wicked.

"Nevertheless Afterwards!"

See where the believer's hope mainly lies; it does not lie in the seeming. He may seem to be rich, or seem to be poor, seem to be sick, or seem to be in health; he looks upon all that as the seeming. He notices that the thing seen is the thing that *seems*, but the thing believed is the thing that *is*. He knows that what his eye catches is only the surface, what his finger touches is only the exterior, but what his heart believes is the depth, the substance, the reality. So he finds all his joy in the "but later" (Heb 12:11).

Christians often learn their best lessons about heaven by contrast. If a man should give me a black book printed in the old black letter, and should say, "You want to know about happiness? That book is written about misery; learn from the opposite," I would thank him just as much for that as if the book were on happiness. So believers take their daily trials and read them the opposite way. Trial comes to a believer and says, "Your hope is dry." "My hope is not dry," the believer says. "While I have a trial I have a ground of hope." "Your God has forsaken you," says tribulation. "My God has not forsaken me," the believer says, "for He says that in the world you shall have tribulation, and I have it. I have a letter from God in a black envelope, but as long as it came from Him I do not mind what kind of envelope it comes in. He has not forgotten me—has not given me up—He is still gracious to me."

And so Christians begin to think about heaven, "For," a Christian says, "this is the place of work, that is the place of rest; this is the place of sorrow, that is the place of joy; here is defeat, there is triumph; here is shame, there glory; here it is being despised, there it is being honored; here it is the hiding of my Father's face, there it is the glory of his presence; here it is absence in the body, there it is presence with the Lord; here weeping, and groaning, and sighing, there the song of triumph; here death—death to my friends and death to myself—there the happy union of immortal spirits in immortality." So a believer learns to sing not of the seeming but of the "but later," with sweet hope, as a harp of many golden strings.

HEBREWS
12:12–17

¹² Therefore, strengthen your slackened hands and your weakened knees, ¹³ and make straight paths for your feet, so that what is lame will not be dislocated, but rather be healed. ¹⁴ Pursue peace with everyone, and holiness, without which no one will see the Lord. ¹⁵ Take care that no one falls short of the grace of God, lest some root of bitterness growing up causes trouble, and by it many become defiled; ¹⁶ lest anyone be a sexually immoral or totally worldly person like Esau, who for one meal traded his own birthright. ¹⁷ For you know that also afterward, when he wanted to inherit the blessing, he was rejected, because he did not find an occasion for repentance, although he sought it with tears.

EXPOSITION

12 **Therefore strengthen your slackened hands** Come, children of God, do not be despondent because of your tribulations. You are in a race, so run; even while you are smarting from your chastisements, still run, and keep on running until you win the prize. Look at chastisement then in the divine light, and be comforted, be strengthened, be healed of the infirmity of your weakness; be strong in the Lord and in the might of His strength (Eph 6:10).

and your weakened knees Cheer the heart when the limbs are weak. Tell the doubting that God is faithful. Tell those that feel the burden of sin that it was for sinners Christ died. Tell the backsliders that God never does cast away His people. Tell the desponding that the Lord delights in mercy. Tell the distracted that the Lord does devise means to bring back His banished. Covet the character of Barnabas. He was a son of encouragement. Study the sacred art of speaking a word in season. Apprentice yourself to the Comforter. Acquaint yourself with the sacred art of comforting the sad. Let your own troubles and trials qualify you to sympathize and relieve. You will be of great value in the Church of God if you acquire the art of compassion, and are able to help those that are bowed down.

13   **and make straight paths for your feet** We are to make straight paths because of lame people. You cannot heal the man's bad foot, but you can pick all the stones out of the path that he has to pass over. You cannot give him a new leg, but you can make the road as smooth as possible. Let there be no unnecessary stumbling blocks to cause him pain.

The Lord Jesus Christ, the great Shepherd of the sheep, evidently cares for the lame ones. The charge He gives is a proof of the concern He feels. He bids us to be considerate of them, because He Himself takes a warm interest in their welfare.

ILLUSTRATION

Our Patience Should Model Christ's

In *Pilgrim's Progress*, when Mr. Greatheart went with Miss Much-afraid and Mr. Feeble-mind on the road to the Celestial City, he had his hands full. He says of poor Mr. Feeble-mind that, when he came to the lions, he said, "Oh, the lions will have me!" And he was afraid of the giants, and afraid of everything on the road. It caused Greatheart much trouble to get him on the road.

It is so with you. You must know that you are very troublesome and hard to manage. But then our Lord Jesus is very patient; He does not mind taking trouble. He has laid down His life for you, and He is prepared to exercise all His divine power and wisdom to bring you home to His Father's house.

so that what is lame will not be dislocated There are some believers with strong and vigorous faith. Soaring high, they can mount up with wings as eagles. Fleet of foot, they can run, and not be weary; or, with steady progress, they can walk, and not faint. But all are not so highly privileged. I suppose there is seldom a family that has no sickly member. However hale and hearty most of the sons and daughters may be, there is likely to be some weak one among them. So it certainly is in the spiritual household.

Some Christian people seem to be so inconsiderate and un-sympathizing that they treat all the lame of the flock with harshness. You may be strong and vigorous in your physi-cal constitution, strangers to nervousness and depression of spirits. Be thankful, then, but do not be presumptuous. Do not despise those who suffer from infirmities that have never come upon you. Your turn may come before long.

rather be healed The good that will come out of their trouble will abundantly recompense them. They are not to expect to see that good at once. It will come later—not yet. No reason-able man expects the harvest at the same time that he sows. You must wait a while. Bear with patience; have confidence in God, and all your trials will end well.

14 **Pursue peace with everyone** Peace is to be studied, but not such a peace as would lead us to violate holiness by conform-ing to the ways of unregenerate and impure men. We are only so far to yield for peace's sake as never to yield a principle. We are to be peaceful so far as never to be at peace with sin: peace-ful with men, but contending earnestly against evil principles.

ILLUSTRATION

Pursue Peace Perseveringly

Often the Alpine hunter, when pursuing the antelope, will leap from crag to crag, will wear out the live-long day, will spend the night upon the mountain's cold brow. He then descends to the valleys and up again to the hills as though he could never tire, and could never rest until he has found his prey.

So perseveringly, with strong resolve to imitate your Lord and Master, follow peace with all.

---

and holiness The holiness meant is evidently one that can be followed like peace; and it must be transparent to any ingenuous man that it is something that is the act and duty of the person who follows it. We are to follow peace; this is practical peace, not the peace made for us, but "the fruit of righteousness ... sown in peace among those who make peace" (Jas 3:18). We are to follow holiness—this must be practical holiness, the opposite of impurity, as it is written, "God did not call us to impurity, but in holiness" (1 Thess 4:7). The holiness of Christ is not a thing to follow—I mean, if we look at it imputatively. We have it at once. It is given to us the moment we believe. The righteousness of Christ is not to be followed; it is bestowed on the soul in the instant it lays hold of Christ Jesus. This is another kind of holiness. It is, in fact, as everyone can see who chooses to read the connection, practical, vital holiness that is the purport of this admonition. It is conformity to the will of God and obedience to the Lord's command.

Some who have aimed at holiness have made the great mistake of supposing it needful to be morose, contentious, faultfinding, and censorious with everybody else. Their holiness has consisted of negatives, protests, and oppositions for opposition's sake. Their religion mainly lies in contrarieties and singularities; to them the text offers this wise counsel: follow holiness, but also follow peace. Courtesy is not inconsistent with faithfulness. It is not needful to be savage in order to be sanctified. A bitter spirit is a poor companion for a renewed heart. Let your determination for principle be sweetened by tenderness toward your fellow men.

Now, if our text said that, without perfection of holiness, no man could have any communion with Christ, it would shut every one of us out. No one who knows His own heart ever pretends to be perfectly conformed to God's will. It does not say, "perfection of holiness," but "holiness." This holiness is a thing of growth. It may be in the soul as the grain of mustard seed, and yet not developed. It may be in the heart as a wish and a desire, rather than anything that has been fully realized—a groaning, a panting, a longing, a striving. As the Spirit of God waters it, it will grow until the mustard seed shall become a tree.

without which no one will see the Lord In the Greek there are no less than three negatives in this passage, as though it said, "No never, no man shall see the Lord."

Surely He who would not spare Satan, the bright archangel, will not admit polluted man to heaven. He who put His Son to death to bring His own elect to heaven by purifying them from sin, will not bring any of us there if we remain unholy and do not submit ourselves to the gospel of Jesus Christ. This is the object of election: God "chose us in him before the foundation of the world, that we should be holy" (Eph 1:4). This is the very end of our calling.

15   **Take care** The word is *"episkopountes,"* a word that signifies overseeing, being true bishops, looking diligently as a man on the watchtower watches for the coming foe.

ILLUSTRATION

As the Sentry Watches

See the sentry pace the rampart. He looks in one direction and he sees the brushwood stirred; he half thinks it is the foe, and suspects an ambush there. He looks to the front, across the sea—does he not discern a sail in the distance? The attack may be from the seaboard. He looks to the right, across the plain, and if even a little dust should move he watches lest the foe should be on foot.

So in the church of God each one should be on his watchtower for himself and for others, watching diligently lest any man fail of the grace of God.

---

that no one falls short of the grace of God Under the means of grace, there are many who do "fall short of the grace of God." They get something that they think is like grace, but it is not the true grace of God, and they ultimately fall from it, and perish. What we need is to have unfailing grace, and power so to hold on that, at the last, we may inherit the crown of life. But we must look diligently for this, for the best of us has shrewd cause to suspect himself. And in church fellowship we ought to be very watchful lest the church as a whole should fail through lack of the true grace of God, and especially lest any root of bitterness springing up among us should trouble us, and thereby many be defiled.

We must remember that though we are saved by grace, yet grace does not stupefy us, but rather quickens us into action. Although salvation depends upon the merits of Christ, yet those who receive those merits receive with them a faith that produces holiness.

that no one growing up like a root of bitterness causes trouble Sin is a bitter thing and a defiling thing; and unless we look diligently, it will grow in our hearts like the weeds grow in our gardens after a heavy rain. It will spring up before we are aware of it.

and by it many become defiled The first person who is likely to fail in this church is myself. Each one ought to feel that; the beginning of the watch should therefore be at home. Depend upon it, if there is anyone likely to fall into sin it is you. Although I say "you," I mean myself as well. Each of us is most in danger.

ILLUSTRATION

Sin Springs from a Hidden Root

In the center of my lawn, horseradish will sprout up. After the smallest shower of rain, it rises above the grass and proclaims its vitality. There was a garden there once, and this root maintains its old position. When the gardener cuts it down, it resolves to rise again. Now, if the gardener cannot get it quite out of the ground, it is his business constantly to cut it down.

Even when associated in church fellowship, each one brings his own particular poisonous root, and there are sure to be bad roots in the ground. We are to watch diligently lest any of these bitter poisonous roots spring up; for if they do, they will trouble us.

---

16   **that no one be a sexually immoral or totally worldly person** Does it not seem strange that after speaking to us about being God's sons and favored with His love, yet even then, in that clear blaze of light, there comes in this caution against fornication and profanity. How near a foul spot may be to lily-like whiteness! How Judas may sit side by side with favored and true-hearted apostles, and may be near the Master too. "The one who thinks that he stands must watch out lest he fall" (1 Cor 10:12). And if at any time the pottage should seem very sweet and we should be very hungry, if the world's gain should be almost necessary to our livelihood, and we are tempted to do an unrighteous thing to get it, let us take care. Esau could not undo the terrible act of selling his birthright; neither could we if we were permitted to do so. God grant we may be spared from such a dreadful crime!

Esau, who for one meal traded his own birthright He was thus guilty of spiritual fornication, preferring his meat to his Maker, thinking more of one morsel of meat than of his birthright.

Those who seek the pleasures of the flesh rather than the pleasures of a higher world are here put side by side with Esau. Now Esau sold the right to his future heritage for a present mess of pottage. There are many who do something very like that: sell their souls for a little Sunday trading, or for a little carnal company, a little of that fool's mirth which is like the crackling of thorns under a pot. They are willing to damn themselves to all eternity because they cannot bear the jeers and sneers of a ribald world. Let us not be like them or like Esau!

17   **when he wanted to inherit the blessing** He could not get his father to change his mind concerning Jacob; on the contrary, he said, "I blessed him. Moreover, he will be blessed" (Gen 27:33). His many tears did not avail; they were not repenting tears, but only selfish ones. He did not repent that he had bartered his birthright for a mess of pottage; he regretted that he had lost the blessing, and that was all.

he did not find an occasion for repentance He never repented of his sin, but only of the consequences of it. He never sought pardon of God, but only sought to inherit the blessing. And there will be many who have lived for this world, and loved it, who, when they wake up in another world, will begin to seek the blessing, but they will be rejected. This may happen even in this world. If they only seek to die the death of the righteous, and do not seek the pardon of their sin, they shall hear the Lord say to them, "Because I called out, and you refused me, I stretched out my hand, yet there is none who heeds. You have ignored all my counsel, and my reproof you are not willing to accept. I will also laugh at your calamity; I will mock when panic comes upon you" (Prov 1:24–27).

although he sought it with tears Esau wanted to have this world, and the next too. He wanted to have the pottage and the birthright; he wanted to be a fine gentleman among the Hittites and yet have the blessing. He wanted to have his wife of a fine noble Philistine family and be thought a famous fellow among them, and yet at the same time have the blessing that belonged to the separate people of God. With tears he sought to get that blessing, but he could not have it.

ILLUSTRATION

Passion and Patience

It is like John Bunyan's parable of Passion and Patience in *Pilgrim's Progress*. Passion would have his best things first; Patience would have his best things last. Passion had all his best things, and laughed at Patience as Patience sat there. But after a while, Passion had used up all his best things and then he had nothing left. But Patience had his best things last, and, as Bunyan says, "There is nothing after the last, so the good things of Patience lasted forever and ever."

So it is with the good things of Jacob, when he chose the good part and sought after it. Even with all his sin, it lasted, and his name is in the covenant, and he rejoices at this day before the throne of God.

APPLICATION

The Ministry of Strengthening the Weak

See to it that you are not negligent of this ministry of love. Remember how high a reputation Job got in his day for the care he bestowed on those who were frail and infirm. Eliphaz the Temanite said of him, "You have instructed many, and you have strengthened the weak hands. Your words have raise up the one who stumbles, and you have strengthened knees giving way" (Job 4:3-4). And do not forget the reproof that the Lord gave to the shepherds of Israel: "The weak you have not strengthened, and the sick you have not healed, and with respect to the hurt you have not bound them up, and you have not brought back the scattered" (Ezek 34:4). Above all, consider the example of our Lord Jesus. His eye was always quick to spy out the lame and the blind, and His hand was always stretched out immediately for their relief. He "went about doing good and healing all who were oppressed by the devil, because God was with him" (Acts 10:38). And if you and I walk with God, and God be with us, our godliness will show itself in the pity we feel, and the kindness we show to the feeble and the faulty, the cross-grained and the crippled.

The Comparative Pleasure of Sin

What is the pleasure of sin contrasted with the results it brings in this life? And what is this pleasure compared with the joys of godliness? Little as you may think I know of the joys of the world, yet so far as I can form a judgment, I can say that I would not take all the joys that earth can ever afford in a hundred years for one half-hour of what my soul has known in fellowship with Christ. We who believe in Him do have our sorrows; but, blessed be God, we do have our joys. They are such joys, with such substance in them, and such reality and certainty, that we could not and would not exchange them for anything except heaven in its fruition.

And what are all these pleasures when compared with the loss of your soul? There is a gentleman, high in position in this world, with fair lands and a large estate, who, when he took me by the button-hole after a sermon—and he never hears me preach without weeping—said to me, "It does seem such an awful thing that I should be such a fool!" "And what for?" I asked. "Why," he said, "for the sake of that court, and of those gaieties of life, and of mere honor, and dress, and fashion, I am squandering away my soul. I know," he said, "I know the truth, but I do not follow it. I have been stirred in my heart to do what is right, but I go on just as I have done before. I fear I shall sink back into the same state as before. What a fool I am to choose pleasures that only last a little while, and then to be lost forever and forever!" I pleaded hard with him, but I pleaded in vain; there was such intoxication in the gaiety of life that he could not leave it.

If we had to deal with sane men, our preaching would be easy; but sin is a madness, such a madness that, when men are bitten by it, they would not be persuaded even though one should rise from the dead. "Without holiness, no one will see the Lord."

Exercise Watchfulness over Yourself and Others

Each man is himself most in danger. If you say, "I do not think so," then there is the more reason that you should think so. If upon hearing of anyone falling into sin you have said, "I do not understand it; I know I never should have done so," it is very likely you will, before long, fall into the same or equally vile sin. You are just the man. "The one who thinks that he stands must watch out lest he fall" (1 Cor 10:12). You who lie low on your faces before God in self-distrust, feeling your liability to err, and asking to be kept every day, you are the least likely to fall of any. But those who say in Pharasaic confidence, "What fools others are to be led astray in that way! I am not one of them," they are fools themselves. God help you when you are self-reliant, for your feet have almost gone, if not to any other sin, at all events in the direction of pride. And remember a man may as easily be damned by pride as by dishonesty.

Then, next, exercise watchfulness over others. How many persons might be saved from backsliding by a little oversight! If we would speak to the brother kindly and considerately, when we think he is growing a little cold, we might restore him. We need not always speak directly to him by way of rebuke, but we may place a suggestive book in his way, or speak generally on the subject. Love can invent many ways of warning a friend without making him angry, and a holy example will also prove a great rebuke to sin. The very presence of some men is a check and guide to others. In the church we ought to bear one another's burden, and so fulfill the law of Christ, exercising the office of bishops over one another, and watching diligently lest any man fail of the grace of God.

¹⁸ For you have not come to something that can be touched, and to a burning fire, and to darkness, and to gloom, and to a whirlwind, ¹⁹ and to the noise of a trumpet, and to the sound of words, which those who heard begged that not another word be spoken to them. ²⁰ For they could not endure what was commanded: "If even an animal touches the mountain, it must be stoned." ²¹ And the spectacle was so terrifying that Moses said, "I am terrified and trembling."

²² But you have come to Mount Zion, and to the city of the living God, to the heavenly Jerusalem, and to tens of thousands of angels, to the festal gathering ²³ and assembly of the firstborn who are enrolled in heaven, and to God the judge of all, and to the spirits of righteous people made perfect, ²⁴ and to Jesus, the mediator of a new covenant, and to the sprinkled blood that speaks better than Abel's.

EXPOSITION

18 **you have not come to something that can be touched**
We are joyfully reminded that we are *not* come to Mount Sinai and its overwhelming manifestations. After Israel had kept the feast of the Passover, God was pleased to give His people a sort of Pentecost, and more fully to manifest Himself and His law to them at Sinai. They were in the wilderness, with the solemn peaks of a desolate mountain as their center; and from the top thereof, in the midst of fire, and blackness, and darkness, and tempest, and with the sound of a trumpet, God spoke with them.

Upon the believer's spirit there rests not the slavish fear, the abject terror, the fainting alarm, which swayed the tribes of Israel; for the manifestation of God that the believer beholds, though not less majestic, is far more full of hope and joy. Over us there does not rest the impenetrable cloud of apprehension; we are not buried in a present darkness of despair; we are not tossed about with a tempest of horror; and, therefore, we do not exceedingly fear and quake. How thankful we should be for this!

and to a burning fire God's presence made the mountain melt and flow down. "And Yahweh thundered from the heavens, and the Most High uttered his voice with hail and coals of fire" (Psa 18:13). Sinai was "all wrapped in smoke" (Exod 19:18); innumerable lightnings flashed forth around the summit of the hill.

and to darkness, and to gloom The cloud on Sinai was so dark as to obscure the day, except that every now and then the lightning flash lit up the scene. What are we come to in contrast to that darkness? "To God the judge of all" (Heb 12:23). Possibly it does not strike you with joy when I mention it, but this is perhaps the most joyous of all the clauses of the passage. "God is light, and there is no darkness in him at all" (1 John 1:5). What a contrast to the darkness of the law is a reconciled God! "But," you say, "he is there as the Judge of all, and that makes us tremble." Why? Why? It makes me stop trembling when I think that I have come "to God the judge of all," that Christ has brought me near, even to the Judge, so that I have nothing to dread from Him.

and to a whirlwind All over the top of Sinai there swept fierce winds and terrible tornadoes, for the Lord was there. All heaven seemed convulsed when God rent it and descended in majesty upon the sacred mount. But what do you and I see? The very reverse of tempest: "The spirits of righteous people made perfect" (Heb 12:23)—serenely resting. What more is there for them to do? They are perfect. They have fought the fight, they have run the race (2 Tim 4:7), they are crowned, and they are full of ecstatic bliss. The light of God is on their brows, and the glory of God is reflected from their faces. Everything like a tempest is far gone from them; they have reached the fair haven, and are tossed with tempest no more.

19   **and to the noise of a trumpet** Clarion notes most clear and shrill rang out again and again the high commands of the thrice-holy God. You are not come to that. Instead of a trumpet, which signifies war and the stern summons of a king, you are come to "Jesus the Mediator of the new covenant" (Heb 12:24), to the silver tones of "Come to me, all of you who labor and are burdened, and I will give you rest" (Matt 11:28).

those who heard begged that not another word be spoken Together with the trumpet there sounded out a voice that was so terrible that they asked that they might not hear it again. They cowered down under it, like poor, frightened children, terrified by the penetrating sound. They could not endure another word; they begged that the voice would be silent. We have come to another voice—the voice of "the sprinkled blood that speaks better than Abel's does" (Heb 12:24). There is a voice from Zion; there is a voice that rolls over the heads of the innumerable company of angels. A voice of the Lord that is full of majesty, and exceedingly comfortable to the "assembly of the firstborn" (Heb 12:23), who know the joyful sound. The blessed Word speaks life, pardon, reconciliation, acceptance, joy, and eternal bliss!

20   **If even an animal touches the mountain, it must be stoned** In the sacred worship of the tabernacle and the temple, the thought of distance must always have been prominent to the devout mind. The mass of the people did not even enter the outer court. Into the inner court none but the priests could ever dare to come; while into the innermost place, or the holy of holies, but once a year one person only ever entered.

The Lord seemed ever to be saying to the whole of His people, with but a few exceptions, "Do not come near here." It was the dispensation of distance, as if the Lord in those early ages would teach man that sin was so utterly loathsome to Him that He must treat men as lepers put without the camp. When He came nearest to them, He still made them feel the width of the separation between a holy God and the impure sinner.

You cannot get nearer to God than that on the footing of works, for Mount Sinai is the symbol of works. Look to the flames that Moses saw, and shrink, and tremble, and despair. You cannot get to God that way. Calvary is *the* mountain.

21 **And the spectacle was so terrifying** The mount of God stood out in terrible sublimity against the sky, holding communion with the stars, but refusing to deal with men. It was sublime, but stern and tempest-beaten. God came upon Sinai with His law, and the dread mount became a type of what the law would be to us. It has given us a grand idea of holiness, but it has not offered us a pathway to it, nor furnished a weary heart with a resting place, nor supplied a hungry soul with spiritual food. It can never be the place where congregated multitudes erect a city for themselves and a temple for the living God. It is not the shrine of fellowship, but the throne of authority and justice.

Moses said, "I am terrified and trembling." You who are under the law, you who are trying to win God's favor by your good works, you who fancy that human merit can bring you salvation, look to the flames that Moses saw, and sink, and tremble, and despair. You who think that you can live as the law requires, and so attain to everlasting life, may well stand shivering and trembling before this almighty though invisible God. His lightnings blaze before your eyes, and His voice of thunder must alarm the stoutest heart. Terrible is the plight of the man who has to depend upon what Sinai can give him.

22 **But you have come to Mount Zion** Every good thing is enhanced in value by its opposite. Light is all the brighter to eyes that have wept in darkness; food is all the sweeter after you have known hunger; and Zion is all the fairer because of

Sinai. The contrast between free grace and law makes grace appear the more precious to minds that have known the rigor of the commandment.

and to the city of the living God You have come to the land of pardon, peace, and promise: You are in the home of life, love, and liberty. You have come to the Lord of adoption, acceptance, and glory. Do not, I ask you, construe the acts and dealings of God with your soul after the mean and slavish manner that unbelief suggests to you, but believe your God in the teeth of all you hear, or see, or feel. The Lord has come to prove you, to put His fear before your face, and to keep you from sin; why look for sweet fruit from the bitter tree of your present grief, and flee not from your God.

to tens of thousands of angels Some of those bright beings are called seraphim, or burning ones, for they come and go like flames of fire. It must have been terrible to look up to Sinai and see it casting forth its flames, but it is with delight that we look toward the angels who excel in strength, and spend that strength in the service of the Lord and His people. These are a wall of fire round about us.

to the festal gathering I suppose he speaks of all the saints after the death and resurrection of our Lord and the descent of the Holy Ghost. He refers to the whole church, in the midst of which the Holy Spirit now dwells. We are come to a more joyous sight than Sinai, and the mountain burning with fire. The Hebrew worshiper, apart from his sacrifices, lived continually beneath the shadow of the darkness of a broken law. He was startled often by the tremendous note of the trumpet—which threatened judgment for that broken law—and thus he lived ever in a condition of bondage.

ILLUSTRATION
The Church around the Holy Mount

When I was visiting one of our sick friends he uttered a sentence that stuck to me. He said, "I have had some education for heaven in attending the Metropolitan Tabernacle." "How is that?" "Because I have been used to worship with a great company of godly people, used to join in the songs of great multitudes, and I shall feel at home among the number that no man can number."

Yes, it is sweet to go up with the multitude who keep holy day. The number adds a charm to the worship, and gives to our hearts a tone of exhilaration that otherwise they might have lacked. Behold, then, the countless bands of the redeemed assembled around the chosen mount!

23 **and assembly of the firstborn** The term "firstborn" often meant, in Scripture, the most excellent, the chief. Jesus Christ, because of the excellence of His character, is said to be "the firstborn among many brothers" (Rom 8:29), "the firstborn over all creation" (Col 1:15), and "the firstborn from the dead, so that in he himself may become first in everything" (Col 1:18). So, although believers are, by nature, the children of wrath, even as others, yet after Christ has renewed them, they become the excellent of the earth in whom should be all our delight.

But the term "firstborn" has a second meaning in Scripture. The firstborn, under the old Mosaic economy, were chosen by God for Himself. When He smote the firstborn of Egypt, He set apart for Himself all the firstborn of Israel. He might have selected the youngest of the family, or the second, if He had chosen to do so, for God does as He wills, and "he will not answer all a person's words" (Job 33:13).

425

ILLUSTRATION
The Firstborn Saved by Jesus' Blood

In the dark and dreadful night, the destroying angel is let loose, with noiseless wings, and with a sharp sword that never misses its mark. He is speeding from house to house throughout all the land of Egypt, and from the firstborn of Pharaoh upon the throne to the firstborn of the slave woman behind the mill, they fall dead, and Egypt's wail goes up to heaven in an exceedingly bitter and piercing cry. But throughout the houses of the Israelites a different scene is being witnessed. The doors are shut; a roasted lamb lies upon the table, and men and women stand around it, girt as for a journey, and with their staffs in their hands, and they eat in haste. There is a firstborn child in his mother's arms, or a firstborn male who is grown up, yet they show no sign of trepidation, though it is well-known that, on that night, the firstborn are to die. Why are they so calm? Had you been present, an hour or two ago, you would have seen that the father, when he slew the lamb, drained the warm life blood into a bowl, and, as his children gathered about him, he said to them, "Come, follow me." And taking with him a bunch of hyssop, he went to the outside of his door, and smote the lintel until it was crimsoned with the blood of the lamb, and then he sprinkled the posts on either side so that the blood was all about the door. "And now," said he, "my children, we are safe. When God sees the blood, He will pass over us, and our firstborn will not be slain. The blood will make them secure."

In like manner, we who are the firstborn of God are saved by the blood of Jesus.

who are enrolled in heaven There is an enrollment about which we should be greatly concerned. There are certain names written in the Lamb's book of life, and it should be to you and to me a matter of solemn interest to inquire if our names are written there. Is your name, is my name, inscribed upon that secret, sacred roll of the elect of God?

24 **and to Jesus, the mediator of a new covenant** The center around which we gather in these days is not Sinai with its thunder and its fire; it is the cross—no, it is heaven. It is the enthroned Savior. It is the great Mediator of a better covenant than that of which Moses came to speak. We gather there, and we make up a part of that vast throng that now surrounds that center. Oh, that we while we hear the sweet voice of the gospel we may lend it a willing ear, and may we not be among the number of those who reject the voice that speaks from heaven to us in the gospel of Jesus Christ.

the sprinkled blood The text does not merely speak of the *shed* blood, but of "the *sprinkled* blood." This is the atonement applied for divine purposes, and specially applied to our own hearts and consciences by faith. For the explanation of this sprinkling we must look to the types of the Old Testament. In the Old Testament, the blood of sprinkling meant a great many things; we meet with it in the book of Exodus, at the time when the Lord smote all the firstborn of Egypt. Then the blood of sprinkling meant *preservation*.

The sprinkled blood very frequently signified the *confirmation* of a covenant. So it is used in Exodus 24: the blood was sprinkled upon the book of the covenant, and also upon the people, to show that the covenant was, as far as it could be, confirmed by the people who promised, "All that the Lord has said we will do."

In many cases the sprinkling of the blood meant *purification*. If a person had been defiled, he could not come into the sanctuary of God without being sprinkled with blood. There were the ashes of a red heifer laid up, and these were mixed with blood and water; and by their being sprinkled on the unclean, his ceremonial defilement was removed.

The sprinkling of the blood meant, also, *sanctification*. Before a man entered upon the priesthood the blood was put upon his right ear, and on the great toe of his right foot, and on the thumb of his right hand, signifying that all his powers were thus consecrated to God. The ordination ceremony included the sprinkling of blood upon the altar all around. Even thus has the Lord Jesus redeemed us unto God by His death, and the sprinkling of His blood has made us kings and priests unto God forever.

One other signification of the blood of the sacrifice was *acceptance and access*. When the high priest went into the most holy place once a year, it was not without blood, which he sprinkled on the ark of the covenant and on the mercy seat, which was on top of it. All approaches to God were made by blood. There was no hope of a man drawing near to God, even in symbol, apart from the sprinkling of the blood. And now today our only way to God is by the precious sacrifice of Christ. The only hope for the success of our prayers, the acceptance of our praises, or the reception of our holy works, is through the ever-abiding merit of the atoning sacrifice of our Lord Jesus Christ. The Holy Ghost bids us enter into the holiest by the blood of Jesus; there is no other way.

that speaks better than Abel's does Abel stands forth before us as the first in a cloud of witnesses, bearing brave testimony, and prepared to seal it with their lives. He died a martyr for the truth—the grandly Godlike truth that God accepts men according to their faith. All honor to the martyr's blood that speaks so effectually for precious truth. Our Lord Jesus Christ, being also a testifier and witness for the faith of God, spoke better things than Abel, because He had more to speak, and spoke from more intimate acquaintance with God. He was a fuller witness of divine truth than Abel could be, for He brought life and immortality to light (2 Tim 1:10), and told His people clearly of the Father.

Abel brought but the type and the figure: the lamb, which was but a picture of the Lamb of God that takes away the sins of the world; but Christ was that Lamb. He was the substance of the shadow—the reality of the type. Abel's sacrifice had no merit in it apart from the faith in the Messiah with which he presented it. But Christ's sacrifice had merit of itself; it was in itself meritorious. What was the blood of Abel's lamb? It was nothing but the blood of a common lamb that might have been shed anywhere. If he had not had faith in Christ, the blood of the lamb would have been as water—a contemptible thing. But the blood of Christ was a sacrifice indeed, far richer than all the blood of beasts that ever were offered.

APPLICATION

Believe and Be Baptized

Let each one of us ask himself or herself, "Shall I be in the assembly?" If anyone says, "I fear that I shall not be there," let him cry mightily unto the Most High to pull him out of the horrible pit, and to set his feet upon the rock, and to make his feet steady (Psa 40:2). Sinner, you will either be there or in that dreadful place where the wailings shall be more terrible than the cry of men in a battle or the shrieks of women in a massacre. You will either be up there in glory or else down there where darkness, death, and long despair sit on their thrones of woe.

Fly, sinner, fly away to Christ! His wounds, like clefts in the rock, are open to the doves that need a shelter. Fly, sinner, fly! The avenger of blood pursues you; I hear the sound of his feet close behind you, and he is about to strike you dead. But the city of refuge is near at hand, standing with open gates ready to welcome you. Fly, sinner, fly! "Believe in the Lord Jesus and you will be saved" (Acts 16:31). "The one who believes and is baptized will be saved" (Mark 16:16). To believe in Jesus is to trust Him; to be baptized is to be immersed in water upon profession of that faith. I dare not alter my Master's commission: "Go into all the world and preach the gospel to all creation. The one who believes and is baptized will be saved, but the one who refuses to believe will be condemned" (Mark 16:15–16). There is no other alternative.

Come to the Sprinkled Blood

Whether Abel's blood sprinkled Cain or not I cannot say, but if it did it must have added to his horror to have had the blood actually upon him. But this adds to the joy in our case, for the blood of Jesus is of little value to us until it is sprinkled upon us. Faith dips the hyssop in the atoning blood and sprinkles it upon the soul, and the soul is clean. The application of the blood of Jesus is the true ground of joy, and the sure source of Christian comfort. The application of the blood of Abel must have been horror, but the application of the blood of Jesus is the root and ground of all delight.

The text says, "You have *come* ... to the sprinkled blood." Now, from the blood of Abel every reasonable man would flee away. He who has murdered his fellow desires to put a wide distance between himself and the accusing corpse. But we come to the blood of Jesus. It is a topic in which we delight as our contemplations bring us nearer and nearer to it. I ask you, Christian friends, to come nearer to it than ever you have been. Think over the great truth of substitution. Portray to yourselves the sufferings of the Savior. Dwell in His sight, sit at the foot of Calvary, abide in the presence of His cross, and never turn away from that great spectacle of mercy and of misery. *Come* to it; be not afraid. Oh, you sinners, who have never trusted Jesus, look here and live!

Listen to the Blood!

Listen to the blood that speaks! It says, "Sinner, I am full of merit: why bring your merits here?" You say, "But I have too much sin." Listen to the blood: as it falls, it cries, "from many trespasses, to justification" (Rom 5:16).

You say, "But I know I am too guilty." Listen to the blood! "Even though your sins are like scarlet, they will be white like snow; even though they are red like crimson, they shall become like wool" (Isa 1:18). You say, "But I have such a poor desire, I have such a little faith." Listen to the blood! "He will not break a broken reed, and he will not extinguish a dim wick" (Isa 42:3).

You say, "But I know He will cast me out if I do come." Listen to the blood! "Everyone whom the Father gives to me will come to me, and the one who comes to me I will never throw out" (John 6:37).

You say, "But I know I have so many sins that I cannot be forgiven." Now, hear the blood once more, and I will be done. "The blood of Jesus his Son cleanses us from all sin" (1 John 1:7). That is the blood's testimony, and its testimony to you. "The Spirit and the water and the blood, and the three are in agreement" (1 John 5:8), and behold the blood's witness is, "The blood of Jesus his Son cleanses us from all sin." Come, poor sinner, cast yourself simply on that truth. Away with your good works and all your trustings! Lie simply flat on that sweet word of Christ. Trust His blood, and if you can put your trust alone in Jesus, in His sprinkled blood, it shall speak in your conscience better things than that of Abel.

HEBREWS
12:25–29

²⁵ Watch out that you do not refuse the one who is speaking! For if those did not escape when they refused the one who warned them on earth, much less will we escape if we reject the one who warns from heaven, ²⁶ whose voice shook the earth at that time. But now he has promised, saying,

> "Yet once more I will shake not only the earth but also heaven."

²⁷ Now the phrase "yet once more" indicates the removal of what is shaken, namely, things that have been created, in order that the things that are not shaken may remain. ²⁸ Therefore, since we are receiving an unshakable kingdom, let us be thankful, by which let us serve God acceptably, with awe and reverence. ²⁹ For indeed our God is a consuming fire.

EXPOSITION

25 **Watch out** That is, "be very circumspect that by no means, accidental or otherwise, you refuse the Christ of God, who now in the gospel speaks to you. Be watchful, be earnest, lest even through inadvertence you should refuse the prophet of the gospel dispensation—Jesus Christ, the Son of God, who speaks in the gospel from heaven to the sons of men." It means, "Give earnest heed and careful attention that by no means and in no way you refuse Him who speaks."

that you do not refuse That which Jesus speaks concerns your soul, concerns your everlasting destiny. It is God's wisdom; God's way of mercy; God's plan by which you may be saved. If this were a secondary matter, you need not be so earnest about receiving it, but of all things under heaven, nothing so concerns you as the gospel. See, then, that you do not refuse this precious Word, more precious than gold or rubies—which alone can save your souls.

ILLUSTRATION
Don't Drink the Poison

If you drank poison and did not know it, I could pity you. If you made all your veins to swell with agony, and caused your death ... But when we stand up and say, "It is poison! See others drop and die; do not touch it!" When we give you something a thousand times better, and ask you to take it, but you will not take it, but *will* have the poison—then if you will, you must.

If, then, you would destroy your soul, it must be so. But we would plead with you: "Watch out that you do not refuse the one who is speaking."

---

the one who is speaking There is not a word of that which He speaks except what is love to your souls. Jesus Christ, the Son of God, did not come armed with terrors to work wrath among the sons of men. All was mercy, all was grace, and to those who listen to Him He has nothing to speak but tenderness and lovingkindness: your sins shall be forgiven; God will wink at the time of your ignorance; your transgressions shall be cast into the depths of the sea; for you there shall be happiness on earth, and glory hereafter. Who would not listen when there is good news to be heard? Who would not listen when the best tidings that God Himself ever sent forth from the excellent glory is proclaimed by the noblest Ambassador who ever spoke to men, namely, God's own Son, Jesus, the once crucified, but now exalted Savior?

those did not escape when they refused the one I believe that the Holy Ghost often, by what we call the common operations that He exercises upon the hearts of men, deals with men's consciences so far as to arouse and warn them, but they quench the Spirit. They, as Stephen says, resist the Spirit as their fathers also did (Acts 7:51). It is a sin that may be committed; and where it is committed often, and long, at last, the Holy Dove departs never to return, and such a soul is given up.

much less will we escape It seems to me that if it be so, that God Himself has taken upon Himself human form, and has come here to effect our redemption from our sin and misery, there cannot be any reason that will stand a moment's looking at for refusing Him who speaks. It must be my duty and my privilege to hear what it is that God has got to say to me. It must be my duty to lend Him all my heart to try and understand what it is that He says, and then to give Him all my will to do, or to be whatever He would have me to do or to be.

26 **I will shake not only the earth** This world is as certainly a mere revolving ball as to human life as it is astronomically; and hopes founded on it will as surely come to nothing as will card houses in a storm. Here we have no abiding city, and it is in vain to attempt to build one. This world is not the rock beneath our feet that it seems to be. It is no better than those green, but treacherous, soft, and bottomless bogs, which swallow up unwary travelers. We talk of *terra firma* as if there could be such a thing as solid earth; never was an adjective more thoroughly misused, for the world and its fashion passes away.

27 **indicates the removal of what is shaken** Material forces are not available in our warfare, for we do not wrestle with flesh and blood. The tyrant may burn our martyrs and cast our confessors into prison, but the pure truth of Jesus is neither consumed by fire nor bound with chains; it has within itself essential immortality and liberty. The doctrine that Christ Jesus came into the world to save sinners is no more

to be wounded by the sword of persecution than is the ocean to be scarred by the keels of navy boats. When winds may be manacled, when waves be fettered, and when clouds may be shut up in dungeons, then—no not even then—may the Word of God be bound.

ILLUSTRATION

God's Church Will Not Be Shaken

I stood this week by the side of a church that once was a considerable distance inland, but now it stands by the ocean. Almost every year a great mass of the clay cliff falls into the sea, and in a year or two this parish church must fall. It stands now in quiet and peace, but on a certain day it will all be swallowed up into the sea, as certainly as the elements still work according to their ordinary laws.

I could not help thinking that the edifice was a type of certain ecclesiastical bodies, which stand upon the clay cliff of statecraft or superstition. The tide of public enlightenment, and above all the ocean tide of God's Spirit, is advancing and wearing away their foundation until at last down the whole fabric must go. What then? Will you hold up your hands and cry, "The church of God is gone"? Stop the foolish utterance; God's church is safe enough. Look, there stands the church of God upon a stormy promontory, where the sea always dashes and perpetually rages on all sides. She fears no undermining, because she is built on no clay cliff, but on a rock against which the waves of hell shall not prevail.

---

the things that are not shaken may remain All that is eternal must, of course, endure forever. The everlasting covenant, "the glorious gospel of the blessed God" (1 Tim 1:11), the purchase of the Savior's blood, the work of the Holy Spirit—all these shall stand fast forever; they can never be shaken. The immutable Word spoken by the mouth of the unchanging God lives and abides forever!

28 **Therefore, since we are receiving an unshakable kingdom** Is it not wonderful that it should be written, "We are receiving a kingdom"? What a gift to receive! This is a divine gift; we have received, not a pauper's pension, but a kingdom that cannot be moved. The old dispensation or kingdom has passed away; its ceremonial laws are abrogated, and its very spirit is superseded by a higher spirit. We have entered upon another kingdom, in which the ruling principle is not law, but love. We are not under the yoke of Moses, but we are the subjects of King Jesus, whose yoke is easy and whose burden is light. The kingdom of Jesus will never end while time shall last, for He is the King Eternal, and immortal; neither will His laws be changed, nor shall His subjects die.

ILLUSTRATION
Our Reward Is to Come

There were two brothers, one of whom had been diligently attentive to his worldly business, to the neglect of true religion. He succeeded in accumulating considerable wealth. The other brother was diligent in the service of the Master, and had learned both to distribute to the poor and for conscience's sake to forego many an opportunity of gain, so that when he lay sick and dying he was in straitened circumstances. His brother somewhat upbraided him, remarking that if it had not been for his religion he would not have been dependent upon others. With great calmness the saintly man replied, "Quiet, quiet! I have a kingdom not begun upon, and an inheritance I have not yet seen."

Speak of laying up for a rainy day: we have infinite goodness laid up for those who fear the Lord, and none can rob us of it.

Other kingdoms go to pieces sooner or later. You and I who are in middle life can remember kingdoms that have been blown down by the wind, or toppled over at the blow of one brave man's sword. Empires that have rivaled Caesar's in apparent strength have been swept down like cobwebs. As houses made of a pack of cards, so have dynasties fallen never to rise again.

let us be thankful We have the kingdom within us: it is not meat and drink, but righteousness and peace, and joy in the Holy Ghost. The Spirit of God within a man is the earnest of heaven, and an earnest is of the same nature as that which it guarantees. We who are born unto God have the firstfruits of the kingdom of God in possessing the indwelling Spirit, and in the firstfruits we see the entire harvest. Rise to this, and under a sense of your immeasurable indebtedness go forth and serve your God with joyful thankfulness. This is the spirit in which to worship the Lord who has given us the kingdom.

serve God acceptably Whatever service we may render to God, we must begin by being receivers. Our first dealing with the most High must not be our bringing anything to Him, but our accepting of everything from Him. We receive; that is our first stage. And I trust it is our last, for if ever we are able to serve the Lord by our gifts, we shall have to confess, "From your hand we have given to you" (1 Chr 29:14). When we are privileged to cast our crowns before Immanuel's throne, they will be crowns that He Himself bestowed upon us of His own sovereign grace.

ILLUSTRATION

Serve as Kings Serve

One of the early Saxon kings was rowed down the river Dee by Kenneth of Scotland, and seven other vassal kings, who each tugged an oar while their lord reclined in state.

The King of kings this day is served by kings. Each man and woman among us is made royal by the very fact of holy service. Let us labor for God not as slaves, but as kings! I confess that sometimes I have not served the Lord as a king. I have put on the ragged robes of my unbelief, and I have come to church mourning and groaning when I ought to have arrayed myself in royal apparel and served my Lord with joy and gladness.

I know sometimes you say, and say truly, "What a poor creature I am, how can I serve God? I do not have this or that gift." Do not attempt to serve Him in the power of gift. Ask for grace, and then worship Him in the power of grace. It is wonderful how grace can make use of very slender gifts and turn them to abundant account. It is great grace that greatly honors God, and great grace is always to be had by the least among us. You may never be an orator, but you may have great grace. You may never be an organizer and take the lead among your fellow Christians, but you may have much grace. You may never attain to ample wealth so as to be able to distribute largely of your substance to the poor, but you may have great grace. Therefore, let us have grace that we may serve God acceptably.

with awe and reverence Let us not think that we are not to be reverent because we gather at the gospel's call. Let us not dream that God, who is a consuming fire on the top of Sinai, is less terrible under the gospel than under the law, for it is not so. The God who gave the law on Sinai has never changed: the God of Abraham, of Isaac, and of Jacob, the God of Moses, who overthrew Pharaoh and his hosts in the Red Sea, and slew Korah, Dathan, and Abiram, and the multitudes of murmurers, idolaters, and fornicators in the wilderness—"this is God our God forever and ever. He Himself will guide us until death" (Psa 48:14).

ILLUSTRATION
The Bride of a Prince

If some poor girl were suddenly called away from the milk pail and lifted from poverty and hard servitude to be the bride of a prince, the very thought of it would bring the crimson to her cheeks. "Can it be!" she would say. I can imagine that when she was brought to court there would be a noticeable bashfulness and shamefacedness about her.

Such holy shame ought to be upon us whenever we stand before the Lord to minister to Him. Is it not said, "You will be ashamed, and you will not open your mouth again" (Ezek 16:63)? Not because of a servile dread of God, but out of an overwhelming sense of His unutterable love we blush to be so highly favored.

---

29 **For indeed our God is a consuming fire** The Lord God who is to be served by us, even as our covenant God, is a "consuming fire." In love He is severely holy, sternly just. We hear people say, "God out of Christ is a consuming fire," but that is an unwarrantable alteration of the text. The text is "Our God"—that is, God in Christ—"is a consuming fire." "Our God" means God in covenant with us; it means our Father God, our God to whom we are reconciled. He, even our God, is still a "consuming fire."

Under the New Testament, God is not an atom less severe than under the old; and under the covenant of grace the Lord is not a particle less righteous than under the law. We are so saved by mercy that no sin goes unpunished: the law is as much honored under the gospel as under the law. The substitution of Jesus as much displays the wrath of God against sin as even the flames of hell would do. While the Lord is merciful, infinitely so, and His name is love, yet still our God is a consuming fire, and sin shall not live in His sight.

APPLICATION

Do Not Turn Away from the One Who Speaks

If they did not escape who refused him that spoke on earth, much more shall we not escape if we turn away from Him who speaks from *heaven*. If Pharaoh did not escape when he refused him who spoke on earth, dreadful shall be that day when the Christ who this day speaks to you, and whom you reject, shall lift up the rods of His anger.

If I speak severely, even for a moment, it is in love. I dare not play with you, sinner; I dare not tell you sin is a trifle. I dare not tell you that the world to come is a matter of no great account. I dare not come and tell you that you need not be in earnest. I shall have to answer for it to my Master. I have these words ringing in my ears, "And as for the watchman, if he sees the sword coming and he does not blow the horn, and the people are not waned, and the sword comes and it takes their lives, he will be taken through his guilt, his blood from the hand of the watchman I will seek" (Ezek 33:6). Refuse what I say as much as you will. Cast anything that is mine to the dogs— have nothing to do with it. But wherein I have spoken to you Christ's Word, and I have told you His gospel—"Believe and live" (John 11:26), "The one who believes in him is not judged" (John 3:18) "The one who believes and is baptized will be saved" (Mark 16:16)—wherein it is Christ's gospel, it is Christ that speaks. I again say to you, for your soul's sake, "Watch out that you do not refuse the one who is speaking" (Heb 12:25). May His Spirit sweetly incline you to listen to Christ's Word.

Invest in the Unshakable Kingdom

If everything should melt away, yet you have "a city that has foundations, whose architect and builder is God" (Heb 11:10). Sometimes foreign princes when they have been afraid of a revolution have invested all their money in the English funds, and then they have said, "Now come what may, my prosperity is safe." Well, it is a blessed thing to invest all your wealth in the heavenly funds; let the earth go to ruin, our treasure is safe. Let the world, like an old waterlogged hulk, go down if she will. It is a wonder that she keeps afloat so long—let her go. I am in the lifeboat that can never sink, and soon shall be on shore where tempests cannot blow. Oh, to rest in assured hope—the hope that does not make ashamed, the hope that shall never be confounded. The hope that when days and years are passed, we shall see the face of Jesus and dwell with Him forever!

There are some of you who have nothing but what may be moved, and you are therefore sure to lose your all. Go away and mourn and lament. Better still, go to the cross, stand under the foot of it, and you cannot be shaken there. Look up to the flowing of the Savior's blood, and trust Him, for nothing can ever shake you then.

As for those of us who possess the things that cannot be shaken, let us stand fast and be of good courage. Whatever may happen during this week, let us play the man. Let us show that we are not such little children as to be cast down by what may happen in this poor fleeting state of time. Our country is Immanuel's land. Our hope is above the sky, and therefore calm as the summer's ocean; we will see the wreck of everything and yet rejoice in the God of our salvation.

Do Not Dread God's Consuming Fire

If God accepts your sacrifice, it will all be consumed by His fire. See, the accepted sacrifice is all gone; it is utterly consumed. When God enables us to serve Him, and takes away from us all self-congratulation, we ought to be very thankful. This proves that it is all burned with fire. If God had not accepted it, then we might have reserved portions of it for ourselves on which to feed our vanity, and that would be to feed ourselves without fear. But if the Lord has taken every morsel from the mouth of self, we have great cause for rejoicing. If the Lord accepts us, His fire will consume us; the zeal of His house will eat us up.

When we go home to the Lord above, we do not dread His presence, though He is a consuming fire. Those whom He has purified and made white are not afraid of the flames of His holiness. Remember that blessed text, "Who of us can live with devouring fire? Who of us can live with everlasting consuming hearths? He who walks in righteousness and speaks uprightness, who rejects the gain of extortion, who refuses a bribe, who stops up his ears from hearing bloodshed and shuts his eyes from seeing evil. That one will live on the heights" (Isa 33:14–16). It shall be the glory of the gracious and the true that God is their element. It shall be their bliss to live in the full splendor of His perfect holiness. They shall be like their Lord, for they shall see Him as He is. Everything that is holy will endure the fire, and as for all within us that is impure, let it be consumed speedily. So let us serve the Lord with fear, but not with terror, and let this service be continued all our days. Let us bring our sacrifices to Him, with repentance for every fault, humbly pleading that of His grace He will accept it, and earnestly desiring that all we have done may resound to His glory through Jesus Christ His Son, to whom be honor, world without end.

HEBREWS 13

HEBREWS
13:1–6

¹ Brotherly love must continue. ² Do not neglect hospitality, because through this some have received angels as guests without knowing it. ³ Remember the prisoners, as though you were fellow-prisoners; remember the mistreated, as though you yourselves also are being mistreated in the body. ⁴ Marriage must be held in honor by all, and the marriage bed undefiled, because God will judge sexually immoral people and adulterers. ⁵ Your lifestyle must be free from the love of money, being content with what you have. For he himself has said, "I will never desert you, and I will never abandon you." ⁶ So then, we can say with confidence,

> "The Lord is my helper, I will not be afraid.
> What will man do to me?"

EXPOSITION

1   **Brotherly love must continue** The word "continue" implies that the "brotherly love" exists. There are many things that might put an end to it; so see to it that, as far as you are concerned, it continues. Under all provocations, and under all disappointments, "brotherly love must continue."

Let each esteem others better than himself; let each seek his brother's good to edification. Let us by no means be divided in heart, for schisms grieve the Holy Spirit, destroy our comfort, weaken our graces, afford occasion for gainsayers, and bring a thousand ills upon us. Whereas in these evil days the Church is so much divided into denominations and sections, follow peace with all those who love the Lord Jesus Christ in sincerity. Hold what you believe with firmness, for you are not to trifle with God's truth; but wherever you see anything of Christ, confess relationship there, and act as a brother toward your brother in Christ.

2　**some have received angels as guests without knowing it** Abraham did so, and Lot did so. They thought they were entertaining ordinary strangers, and they washed their feet, and prepared their food, but it turned out that they had entertained angels. Some people will never entertain angels unawares, for they never entertain anybody. May we be given to hospitality, for that should be part of the character of saints.

3　**Remember the prisoners, as though you were fellow prisoners** What are some churches but semi-religious clubs, mere conventions of people gathered together? They do not have in them that holy soul that is the essence of unity; there is no life to keep them in entirety. Why, the body would soon become disjointed, and a mass of rottenness, if the soul were not in it; and if the Spirit of Christ is absent, the whole fabric of the outward church begins to fall to pieces. For where there is no life, there can be no true union.

ILLUSTRATION

The Church Like a Roman Wall

Some of the old Roman walls are compacted with such excellent cement that it would be almost impossible to separate one stone from another. In fact, the whole mass has become consolidated like a solid rock, so embedded in cement that you cannot distinguish one stone from another.

Happy is the church that is thus built up: where each cares not only for his own prosperity, but for the prosperity of all; where, if there is any joy in one member, all the members rejoice, and if there is sorrow in any one part of the body, all the rest of the body is in sorrow too.

---

also are being mistreated in the body And being likely therefore to take your own turn of suffering, and to need the sympathy of your fellow Christians. Show sympathy to others while they need it, and they will gratefully remember you when you are in bonds or in adversity.

4   **God will judge sexually immoral people and adulterers** And terrible will be their doom when God does judge them. They may think that, because they sin in secret, therefore they shall escape punishment; but it shall not be so. Whether men judge them or not, God will judge them.

ILLUSTRATION

Latimer's Courage in Telling the Truth

Old Hugh Latimer preached before Henry VIII. It was the custom of the court preacher to present the king with something on his birthday, and Latimer presented Henry VIII with a pocket handkerchief with this text in the corner: "God will judge sexually immoral people and adulterers" (Heb 13:4)—a very suitable text for bluff Harry. And then he preached a sermon before his most gracious majesty against sins of lust, and he delivered himself with tremendous force, not forgetting or abridging the personal application. And the king said that next time Latimer preached—the next Sunday—he should apologize, and he would make him so mold his sermon as to eat his own words. Latimer thanked the king for letting him off so easily. When the next Sunday came, he stood up in the pulpit and said: "Hugh Latimer, you are this day to preach before the high and mighty prince Henry, King of Great Britain and France. If you say one single word that displeases his Majesty he will take your head off; therefore, mind what you are doing." But then he said, "Hugh Latimer, you are this day to preach before the Lord God Almighty, who is able to cast both body and soul into hell, and so tell the king the truth outright." And so he did. His performance was equal to his resolution. However, the king did not take off his head; he respected him all the more. The fear of the Lord gave him strong confidence, as it will any who cleave close to their colors.

Drive right straight ahead in the fear of the everlasting God, and whoever comes in your way had better mind what he is doing. It is yours to do what is right, and bear everything they devise that is wrong. God will bless you in it, and therefore you shall praise Him.

---

5   **Your lifestyle must be free from the love of money** Thus covetousness is classed with the very filthiest of vices of the flesh. Let the Christian dread it. God is not selfish; God is love. God does not hoard; He gives liberally (Jas 1:5). He does not refuse the poor; He delights in mercy. He spreads abroad in the midst of His creatures the good things that belong to Him, and He bids them freely gather what He freely gives; even this way He would have us distribute generously and disperse freely without covetousness.

being content with what you have There is a laudable pursuit of gain, without which business would not be properly carried on. But there is a line, scarcely as broad as a razor's edge, between diligence in business and greediness for gain. We can so easily pass from the one into the other that we may hardly be aware of it ourselves. When a man is increasing his investments, when he is extending his agencies, when he is enlarging his warehouse, when he is employing a larger number of persons than before, or even when he is bemoaning the depression of his trade, and his heart is aching because he has to do only half as much business as before, covetousness may insinuate itself into his conversation. It is a snake that can enter at the smallest hole. It lurks in the grass where it is long, but it glides also where the pasture is bare. It may come in either in prosperity or in adversity, and it is needful to whisper in the ear of each believer, whether going up or down in the world, "Your lifestyle—your daily conduct—must be free from the love of money."

ILLUSTRATION
Live by the Well

Ishmael, the son of Hagar, had his water in a bottle, and he might have laughed at Isaac because Isaac had no bottle. Here was the difference between them: Isaac lived by the well.

Now, some of us have little enough in this world; we have no bottle of water, and no stock in hand. But then we live by the well, and that is better still. To depend upon the daily providence of a faithful God is better than to be worth twenty thousand pounds a year.

For he himself has said "He has said" is not only useful to chase away doubts, fears, difficulties, and devils, but it also yields nourishment to all our graces. Here you have nourishment for that which is good and poison for that which is evil. Search, then, the Scriptures, for so shall you grow healthy, strong, and vigorous in the divine life.

But when did God originally say this? Well, you cannot find the exact words in the Scriptures of the Old Testament, but He did say the same in effect to Jacob at Bethel (Gen 28:15), and to Joshua before he went to the invasion of Canaan (Deut 31:8); David said it in the Lord's name to Solomon (1 Chr 28:20), and Isaiah said the same to the whole people of God (Isa 41:10). Whatever God says to one saint He says, virtually, to all saints who have like faith. This renders the Bible such a rich storehouse of comfort to us. No Scripture is of private interpretation, but all Scripture is given for our personal appropriation. No promise is hedged about as the exclusive property of the one man who received it. If the Lord gave a promise to Jacob, it was not meant to be restricted to Jacob, but to belong to all those who, like Jacob, can wrestle in prayer; and if God spoke, as He did, a promise to Joshua, it was not intended to be for Joshua only, but for all who were in similar circumstances to his. All Scripture promises have a message to all believers; and if you believe in Jesus, what God has said to other believers of old He says this day to you.

I will never desert you, and I will never abandon you It would hardly be possible in English to give the full weight of the Greek. We might render it, "He himself has said, I will never, never desert you, and I will never, never, never abandon you." Though that would be not a literal, but rather a free rendering, yet, since there are five negatives in the Greek, we do not know how to give their force in any other way. Two negatives nullify each other in our language. In the Greek, they intensify the meaning following one after another, as I suppose David's five stones out of the brook would have done if the first had not been enough to make the giant reel.

It means that in no one single instance will the Lord leave you, nor in any one particular will He leave you, nor for any reason will He leave you. If you have cast yourself upon His infinite power and grace, He will carry you to the end. Not only will He not desert you altogether, but He will not leave you even for a little while. He may seem for a small moment to hide His face from you, but He will still love you and still supply your needs.

6   **we can say with confidence** This promise of the Lord is fitted to nerve us with courage, as well as to solace us with contentment. Chicken hearts and craven fears ill become the disciples of Christ.

The Lord is my helper, I will not be afraid If God is our helper, why should we shrink or falter? Why should we droop or look dismayed? Why should we hold our peace or speak with bated breath? Are there any of you who are afraid to confess my Lord's name before men, to enlist in His service, to buckle on His armor, to avow yourselves His followers? Do not parley any longer, I ask you, with such ungracious fears.

What will man do to me? Do not let fifty places or five hundred people make you swerve from the course that faith dictates and duty demands. Appeal to God, and He will provide for you. Any temporary loss you may sustain will be much more than made up in the prosperity He awards you, or if not in that way, in the peace He grants you and the honor He confers on you in suffering for Christ's sake.

APPLICATION

Be Content and Not Envious

Let your conversation be without that covetousness that shows itself in envy. If the Lord has given you one talent, use it, but do not waste your time in finding fault with him who has five talents. If your Master makes you a woodcutter, throw your strength into your felling and cleaving. Do not throw the axe at your fellow servant. If He makes you a drawer of water, do not empty your buckets on your neighbor, but do your own service well, and bring what you have done and lay it at your Master's feet. This will be thankworthy; this will be Christlike. You will then be obeying the injunction, "Your lifestyle must be free from the love of money" (Heb 13:5).

And covetousness may show itself in another way, namely, by *perpetually craving and desiring that which we do not have*. The old moralists used to say that the man who wanted to be truly rich would be better off curtailing his appetites than increasing his fortune. Some men seem as if they can never fix their thoughts on what they *have*, but they are always in the other tense and mood, thinking of what they could, would, or should have. Some years ago they told us a little more would content them, and a great deal more has been added to their stores, but still they want a little more now. Let your conversation be without covetousness in that respect, and be content with such things as you have.

In many, this anxiety for acquisition betrays itself in fretful fears about the future, and I must in all honesty grant that this form of the vice sometimes has the appearance of being the most excusable of the whole. "What shall I do," we are apt to say, "in case I should be laid off, and a precarious income should suddenly come to an end? It is not for myself alone. It is for my wife and numerous family that I am chiefly concerned—how could they be provided for?" Many a man lies awake at night desiring to increase his income, not because he is ambitious to be rich, but because he is haunted with the fear of being poor. Gifted, perhaps, for the present with competency, he is still scared with dire forebodings—"What will become of my family if I die?" or "Should such-and-such a source of income be dried up (and it is very precarious), what then will become of my household? What then?" Many are not content with such things as they have because the dread of a distant season of trial is constantly harassing them. They cannot be happy in the present sunshine because perhaps a storm is brewing out of sight. They cannot lie down in peace because they want to lay up against a rainy day. For them, their table is bountifully spread in vain unless they have a store in hand against every contingency that may happen.

Do you notice how precious is that promise that provides for all possible casualties that may befall you? "He himself has said, 'I will never desert you, and I will never abandon you' " (Heb 13:5).

Claim This Promise, and You Have Your Fortune

You have as much as God has been pleased to give you, so be content with such things as you have. "I wish I had a great deal laid by," says one. Do you want more than this: "He has said, I will never desert you, and I will never abandon you"? "I wish I had a large regular income," says another. This looks pretty regular: "I will never desert you, and I will never abandon you." Someone asks, "But does that mean temporal things?" Do you think that God will let your body die of starvation when He promises to take care of your soul? There is an ancient promise for the man who walks righteously and speaks uprightly, "His food will be given; his waters will endure" (Isa 33:16), and it shall still be so. In this matter also, the Lord will not desert you, nor abandon you, if you trust in Him.

It seems to me that the man who can claim this promise has his fortune made for him. If he had made large investments, they might turn out badly; if he possessed large estates, they might have to be sold; if he had wealthy friends, they might all forget him, for memories are not always very strong in the direction in which some people wish they might be. Many a man has fallen from the pinnacle of personal wealth to the pit of personal want, and many others who were waiting for dead men's shoes have had to go barefoot to their own graves. It is poor confidence that trusts in men, but it is blessed confidence that rests in this glorious truth, "He has said, I will never desert you, and I will never abandon you."

God Keeps to the End

If the Lord should forsake us, to say the best of it, our course would be uncertain and before long it would end in nothingness. We know, further, that if God should forsake the best saint alive, that man would immediately fall into sin. He now stands securely on a lofty pinnacle, but his brain would reel and he would fall if secret hands did not uphold him. He now picks his steps carefully; take away grace from him and he would roll in the mire and wallow in it like other men. Let the godly be forsaken by his God and he would go from bad to worse until his conscience, now so tender, would be seared as with a hot iron. Next he would ripen into an atheist or a blasphemer, and he would come to his dying bed foaming at the mouth with rage. He would come before the bar of his Maker with a curse upon his lips, and in eternity, left and forsaken by God, he would sink to hell with the condemned. And among the damned he would have the worst place, lower than the lowest, finding in the lowest depths a lower depth, finding in the wrath of God something more dreadful than the ordinary wrath that falls upon common sinners!

When we thus describe being forsaken by God, is it not satisfactory to the highest degree to remember that we have God's word for it five times over, "I will never, never leave you; I will never, never, never forsake you?" I know those who caricature Calvinism say we teach that, let a man live as he likes, yet if God is with him, he will be safe at the last. We teach no such thing, and our adversaries know better. They know that our doctrines are invulnerable if they will state them correctly, and that the only way in which they can attack us is to slander us and to misrepresent what we teach. No, we do not say so, but we say that where God begins the good work, the man will never live as he likes, or if he does, he will like to live as God would have him live. Where God begins a good work He carries it on; that man is never forsaken by God, nor does he forsake God, but is kept even to the end.

⁷ Remember your leaders, who spoke the word of God to you; considering the outcome of their way of life, imitate their faith. ⁸ Jesus Christ is the same yesterday and today and forever. ⁹ Do not be carried away by various and strange teachings, for it is good for the heart to be strengthened by grace, not by foods, by which those who participate have not benefited. ¹⁰ We have an altar from which those who serve in the tabernacle do not have the right to eat. ¹¹ For the bodies of those animals, whose blood is brought into the sanctuary by the high priest for sins, are burned up outside the camp. ¹² Therefore Jesus also suffered outside the gate, in order that he might sanctify the people by his own blood. ¹³ So we must go out to him outside the camp, bearing his reproach. ¹⁴ For here we do not have a permanent city, but we seek the city that is to come. ¹⁵ Therefore through him let us offer up a sacrifice of praise continually to God, that is, the fruit of lips that confess his name. ¹⁶ And do not neglect doing good and being generous, for God is pleased with such sacrifices.

¹⁷ Obey your leaders and submit to them, for they keep watch over your souls as those who will give an account, so that they can do this with joy and not with groaning, for this would be unprofitable for you.

¹⁸ Pray for us, for we are convinced that we have a good conscience, and want to conduct ourselves commendably in every way. ¹⁹ And I especially urge you to do this, so that I may be restored to you more quickly.

EXPOSITION

7   **Remember** God's people are a thoughtful people. If they are what they ought to be, they do a great deal of remembering

and considering; that is the gist of this verse. If they are to remember and to consider their earthly leaders, much more are they to recollect that great Leader, the Lord Jesus, and all those matchless truths that fell from His blessed lips. I wish, in these days, that professing Christians remembered and considered a great deal more; but we live in such a flurry, and hurry, and worry, that we do not get time for thought.

Our noble forefathers of the Puritan sort were men with backbone, men of solid tread, independent and self-contained men who could hold their own in the day of conflict. The reason was because they took time to meditate, time to keep a diary of their daily experiences, time to commune with God in secret. Take the hint, and try and do a little more thinking.

your leaders, who spoke the word of God to you It is for your own benefit to remember in your prayers those who preach the Word of God to you, for what can they do without divine assistance? and how can you be profited by them unless they are first blessed of God? Therefore, remember them.

considering the outcome of their way of life These holy men ended their lives with Christ; their exit was to go to Jesus, and to reign with him.

imitate their faith There is an itching, nowadays, after originality, striking out a path for yourself. When sheep do that, they are bad sheep. Sheep follow the shepherd, and, in a measure, they follow one another when they are all together following the shepherd. Our Great Master never aimed at originality; He said that He did not even speak His own words, but the words that He had heard from His Father. He was docile and teachable. As the Son of God, and the servant of God, His ear was open to hear the instructions of the Father, and He could say, "I always do the things that are pleasing to him" (John 8:29). Now, that is the true path for a Christian to take: to follow Jesus, and, in consequence, to follow all such true saints as may be worthy of being followed, imitating the godly so far as they imitate Christ.

8   **Jesus Christ is the same yesterday and today and forever**
Jesus Christ is the same now as He was in times gone by. He is
the same today as He was from old eternity. Before all worlds,
He planned our salvation; He entered into covenant with His
Father to undertake it. His delights were with the sons of men
in prospect, and now today He is as steadfast to that covenant
as ever. He will not lose those who were then given to Him,
nor will He fail or be discouraged until every stipulation of
that covenant shall be fulfilled. Whatever was in the heart of
Christ before the stars began to shine, that same infinite love
is there today. Jesus is the same today as He was when He was
here on earth.

I have seen men change. A little frost turns the green forest
to bronze, and every leaf forsakes its hold, and yields to the
winter's blast. So fade our friends, and the most attached ad-
herents drop away from us in the time of trial; but Jesus is to
us what he always was.

ILLUSTRATION

Fight for Jesus to the End

That was an eloquent speech of Henry VI of France, when
on the eve of battle, he said to his soldiers, "Gentlemen,
you are Frenchmen. I am your King. There is the enemy!"

Jesus Christ says, "You are my people. I am your
leader. There is the foe!" How shall we dare to do
anything unworthy of such a Lord as He is, or of such a
citizenship as that which He has bestowed upon us? If we
are indeed His, and He is indeed immutable, let us by
His Holy Spirit's power persevere to the end, that we may
obtain the crown.

---

9   **Do not be carried away by various and strange teachings**
Jesus Christ is the same today as He was yesterday in the
teachings of His Word. They tell us in these times that the
improvements of the age require improvements in theology.
I have heard it said that the way Luther preached would not
suit this age. We are too polite! The style of preaching, they
say, that prevailed in John Bunyan's day is not the style now.
True, they honor these men. They are like the Pharisees; they
build the tombs of the prophets that their fathers killed, and so
confess that they are their fathers' sons, and like their parents
(Luke 11:47). And men who stand up to preach as those men
did, with honest tongues, and do not know how to use pol-
ished courtly phrases, are as much condemned now as those
men were in their time.

They say the world is marching on, and the gospel must march
on too. No, the old gospel is the same. Not one of her stakes
must be removed; not one of her cords must be loosened.
"Hold fast to the pattern of sound words that you heard from
me in the faith and love that are in Christ Jesus" (2 Tim 1:13).
Theology has nothing new in it except that which is false.

The Lord Jesus Christ was the perfect revelation of God.
He was the express image of the Father's person, and the
brightness of his glory. In previous ages, God had spoken to us
by His prophets; but in these last days He has spoken to us by
His Son. Now as to that which was a complete revelation, it is
blasphemous to suppose that there can be any more revealed
than has been made known in the person and work of Jesus
Christ the Son of God. He is God's ultimatum; last of all, He
sends His Son (Mark 12:6).

not by foods Yes, true religion cannot exist without an altar;
but what kind of altar is it? Is it a material altar? Far from it.

10   **We have an altar** We have a sacrifice, which, being once of-
fered, avails forever. We have "one greater than the temple"
(Matt 12:6), and He is to us the mercy seat and the High Priest.
Take it for granted that all the blessings of the law remain

under the gospel. Christ has restored that which He did not take away, but He has not taken away one single possible blessing of the law. On the contrary, He has secured all to His people. I look to the Old Testament, and I see certain blessings appended to the covenant of works, and I say to myself by faith, "Those blessings are mine, for I have kept the covenant of works in the person of my Covenant Head and Surety. Every blessing that is promised to perfect obedience belongs to me, since I present to God a perfect obedience in the person of my great Representative, the Lord Jesus Christ." Every real spiritual boon that Israel had, you have as a Christian.

those who serve in the tabernacle Those who cling to the external and ceremonial observances of religion have no right to the privileges that belong to those who come to the spiritual altar; they cannot share that secret. Those whose religion consists in outward rites and ceremonies can never eat of the spiritual altar at which spiritual men eat, for they do not understand the Scripture and they still serve the Mosaic tabernacle.

11   **burned up outside the camp** The priest was not allowed to burn the bull itself upon the altar, but he was commanded to take up the whole carcass—its skin, flesh, head, and everything—and carry the whole outside the camp. It was a sin offering, and therefore it was loathsome in God's sight, and the priest went right away from the door of the tabernacle, past all the tents of the children of Israel, bearing this ghastly burden upon him. He went until he came to the place where the ashes of the camp were poured out, and there—not upon an altar, but on wood that had been prepared, upon the bare ground—every single particle of the bull was burned with fire.

The distance the bull was carried from camp is said to have been four miles. The teaching of which is just this: when the Lord Jesus Christ took the sin of His people upon Himself, He could not, as a substitute, dwell any longer in the place of the divine favor, but had to be put into the place of separation, and made to cry, *"Eli, Eli, lema sabachthani?"* (Matt 27:46).

12 **Therefore Jesus also suffered outside the gate** Note how remarkably Providence provided for the fulfillment of the type. Had our Lord been killed in a tumult, He would most likely have been slain in the city; unless He had been put to death judicially, He would not have been taken to the usual Mount of Doom. And it is remarkable that the Romans should have chosen a hill on the outside of the city to be the common place for crucifixion and for punishments by death. We might have imagined that they would have selected some mount in the center of the city, and that they would have placed their gibbet in a conspicuous spot, that so it might strike the multitude with the greater awe. But, in the providence of God, it was arranged otherwise. Christ must not be slain in a tumult, and He might not die in the city. When He was delivered into the hands of the Romans, they did not have a place of execution within the city, but one outside the camp, that by dying outside the gate, He might be proved to be the sin offering for His people.

ILLUSTRATION

Unclean Like the Leper

If you had walked through some of the shady glens around the city of Jerusalem, you might have heard in the distance the cry, "Unclean! Unclean! Unclean!"—a bitter wail that sounded like the sighing of despair, as if it came from some poor ghost that had been commanded to walk this earth with restless step forever. Had you come nearer to the unhappy being who had uttered so mournful a sound, you would have seen him cover his upper lip, and again cry, "Unclean! Unclean! Unclean!" to warn you not to come too near him, lest even the wind should blow infection toward you from his leprous skin. If, for a minute, he had moved his hand from his mouth, you would have seen, instead of those scarlet, ruddy lips of health that God had originally put there, a terrible white mark not to be distinguished from his teeth. His lips were unclean, for there the leprosy had discovered itself; and, in a minute, he would have again covered up that lip that had the white mark of disease upon it, and again he would have cried, "Unclean! Unclean! Unclean!"

Of whom was that leper a type? He was a picture of you and me in our natural state; and if the Holy Spirit has made us alive, and made us to know our ruined condition, we shall feel that the leper's cry does well become our unholy lips.

The blessed Son of God was made a curse for us and put to an accursed death by being gibbeted upon the cross, and all because sin anywhere is hateful to God and He must treat it with indignation. The fire of divine justice fell upon our blessed sin offering until He was utterly consumed with anguish, and He said, "It is finished" (John 19:30), and gave up the ghost. Now, this is the only way to put away sin: it is laid upon another, that other is made to suffer as if the sin belonged to Him, and then, since sin cannot be in two places at once, and cannot be laid upon another and rest upon the offerer too, the offerer becomes clear from all sin. He is pardoned and he is accepted because his substitute has been slain outside the camp instead of him.

sanctify the people by his own blood Christian, in your sanctification, look to Jesus. Remember that the Spirit sanctifies you, but that He sanctifies you through Jesus. He does not sanctify you through the works of the law, but through the atonement of Christ. And therefore remember that, the nearer you live to the cross of Jesus, the more sanctification, and growth, and increase in all spiritual blessings His Spirit will give to you.

13   **So we must go out to him outside the camp** It would be a very pleasant thing if we could please men and please God too, if we could really make the best of both worlds, and have the sweets of this and of the next also. But a warning cry arises from the pages of Holy Scripture, for the Word of God talks very differently from this. It talks about a straight and narrow way, and about few that find it. It speaks of persecution, suffering, reproach, and contending even unto blood, striving against sin; it talks about wrestling and fighting, struggling and witnessing. I hear the Savior say, not "I send you forth as sheep into the midst of green pastures," but, "like sheep in the midst of wolves" (Matt 10:16).

ILLUSTRATION

The Church Separate, Like Abraham

The Lord's first word to Abraham is that he should leave his father and his kinsfolk, and the idolatrous house in which he lived, and go to a land that God should show to him. Away he must go. Faith must be his guide, providence his provision, and the living God his only keeper.

The separate life of Abraham, in the midst of the sons of Canaan, is a type of the separated walk of the Church of God.

We must expect, if the Christian soldier is really a soldier, and not a mere pretender to the art of war, that he will have to fight until he joins the triumphant host. If the Church is properly imaged by a ship, we must expect to have storms, and every man on board must look to bear his share.

bearing his reproach That He might sanctify His people, He suffered outside the camp. Christ's separation was in order that His people might be separated. The Head is not of the world, and shall the members be of it? The head is despised and rejected (Isa 53:3)—shall the members be honored? "If anyone loves the world, the love of the Father is not in him" (1 John 2:15). The world rejects Christ—shall the world receive *us*? No, if we are truly one with Him, we must expect to be rejected too. Christ's separation is the type and symbol of the separateness of all the elect.

14   **For here we do not have a permanent city** Then do not look for a continuing city here. Do not build your nest on any one of the trees of earth, for they are all marked for the axe, and they will all have to come down—and your nest too, if you have built upon them.

Our holy faith makes us a separated people, because our Lord in whom we trust was separated and covered with reproach for our sakes. Mere going out from society is nothing; going forth to Him is the great matter. With joy do we follow Him into the place of separation, expecting soon to dwell with Him forever.

but we seek the city that is to come The path of separation may be a path of sorrow, but it is the path of safety. And though it may cost you many pangs, and make your life like a long martyrdom, and every day a battle, yet it is a happy life after all. There is no such life as that which the soldier of Christ leads; for though men frown upon him, Christ so sweetly smiles upon him that he cares for no man. Christ reveals himself as a sweet refreshment to the warrior after the battle, and so blessed is the vision that the warrior feels more calm and peace in the day of strife than in his hours of rest.

If the end of all things is at hand, let them end; but our praises of the living God shall abide world without end. Set free from all the hamper of citizenship here below, we will begin the employment of citizens of heaven. It is not ours to arrange a new Socialism or to set up to be dividers of heritages; we belong to a kingdom that is not of this world—a city of God, "eternal in the heavens" (2 Cor 5:1). It is not ours to pursue the dreams of politicians, but to offer the sacrifices of God-ordained priests. As we are not of this world, it is ours to seek the world to come, and press forward to the place where the saints in Christ shall reign forever and ever.

ILLUSTRATION
Bear Witness to the Truth

Our forefathers died for half a truth, and we will not bear rebuke for a whole one. Two women were tied to the stake at Wigton and drowned in the rising tide—do you know what for? Simply because they would not say, "God save the king." You say, "What does that matter?" Well, it was comparatively a theological trifle. They held a certain theory concerning the bearing of the headship of Christ upon the political position of the king because they thought the thing was wrong. Although I, for my part, would say "God save the king" a thousand times, yet they would not say it once, and died in constancy to their belief. The two women were actually tied to stakes by the seaside. The tide came up, and when the elder woman of the two was drowned, they asked the younger whether she would say it now. But no, she would not. She believed it to be a truth concerning Christ and His kingdom. And though it only touched one of the smallest jewels of His crown, yet she would not do it. Therefore the gurgling waters came up to her chin, and at last rolled over one who had faithfully borne witness to a portion of truth that seems very trifling to us nowadays, but that to her seemed to be worth dying for.

Nowadays, I say, we would not die for the whole Bible, though in other ages saints would have died for the dot of an *i* or the cross of a *t*.

---

15   **Therefore through him let us offer up a sacrifice of praise**
Here we have a description of the believer's position before
God. He has done away with all carnal ordinances, and has no
interest in the ceremonies of the Mosaic law. As believers in
Jesus, who is the substance of all the outward types, we have,
henceforth, nothing to do with altars of gold or of stone: our
worship is spiritual, and our altar spiritual.

What then? Are we to offer no sacrifice? Very far from it.
We are called upon to offer to God a continual sacrifice. Instead
of presenting in the morning and the evening a sacrifice of
lambs, and on certain holy days bringing bullocks and sheep
to be slain, we are to present to God continually the sacrifice
of praise. Having done with the outward, we now give ourselves entirely to the inward and to the spiritual.

continually to God That is to say, without ceasing. Let us
make an analogous precept to that which says, "pray continually" (1 Thess 5:17), and say, "praise continually." Not only in
this place or that place, but in every place, we are to praise
the Lord our God. Not only when we are in a happy frame of
mind, but when we are cast down and troubled. The perfumed
smoke from the altar of incense is to rise toward heaven both
day and night, from the beginning of the year to the year's end.

that is, the fruit of lips that confess his name If you are believers in Christ, you are God's priests, and this is the sacrifice
that you are continually to offer—the fruit of your lips, giving
thanks to God's name.

Bless the Lord at all times. Not alone in your secret chamber,
which is redolent with the perfume of your communion with
God, but yonder in the field and there in the street. In the hurry and noise of the Royal Exchange, offer the sacrifice of praise
to God. You cannot always be speaking His praise, but you can
always be living His praise. The heart once set on praising
God will, like the stream that leaps down the mountain's side,
continue still to flow in its chosen course. A soul saturated
with divine gratitude will continue, almost unconsciously, to

give forth the sacred odor of praise, which will permeate the atmosphere of every place and make itself known to all who have a spiritual nostril with which to discern sweetness.

ILLUSTRATION

An Eloquent, Praiseful Heart

I believe that a life spent in God's praise would in itself be a missionary life. That matronly sister who never delivered a sermon, or even a lecture, in all her days has lived a quiet, happy, useful, loving life, and her family has learned from her to trust the Lord. Even when she shall have passed away, they will feel her influence, for she was the angel of the house. Being dead, she yet will speak.

A praiseful heart is eloquent for God.

---

16   **And do not neglect doing good and generosity** I long to see Christian friends everywhere who will not wait to be asked, but will make the Lord's business their business, and take in hand some branch of work in the church, or among the poor, or for the spread of the gospel. Let your gift be an outburst of a free and gracious spirit, which takes a delight in showing that it does not praise God in word only, but in deed and in truth. In this church let us excel in generous gifts. See that everything is provided in the house of the Lord, and that there is no lack in any quarter. This practical praising of the Lord is the life-office of every true believer.

for God is pleased with such sacrifices. We are to do good to others, to communicate of our own good things to those who need them, and to do this at some sacrifice to ourselves. Christian people should be always doing good. As God is ever doing good, so we can never say we have done all we ought to do, and will do no more.

17   **Obey your leaders and submit to them** There are some people who would be excellent Christians if Christianity consisted in having their own way, and gaining honor for themselves. But as to making themselves the servants of others for Christ's sake, or watching over others for their good, and being content to be made of no reputation in order that other people might be uplifted, they do not go in for that sort of thing. Clearly, they have not learned obedience.

for they keep watch over your souls as those who will give an account The Lord will ever continue to give pastors after His own heart to feed His people, and all attempts made by the flock to dispense with these pastors will lead to leanness and poverty of soul. The outcry against the "one man ministry" does not come from God, but from proud self-conceit, of men who are not content to learn although they have no power to teach. It is the tendency of human nature to exalt itself that has raised up these disturbers of the peace of God's Israel, for they will not endure to submit themselves to the authorities that God has himself appointed.

18   **Pray for us** The movements of God's servants may be controlled by prayer. You cannot tell how much blessing will come to your own souls through the ministry, if you are in the habit of praying about it. The man who comes up to God's house having prayed for God to bless the preacher is not likely to go away unprofited.

19   **so that I may be restored to you more quickly** We may, indeed, even with tears appeal to you who are our brothers in Christ, and entreat you to be earnest in your supplications to God on our behalf. What can we do without your prayers? They link us with the omnipotence of God. Like the lightning rod, they pierce the clouds and bring down the mighty and mysterious power from on high.

APPLICATION

Worship the Unchangeable Christ

If Jesus Christ is immutable, He has an evident claim to our most solemn worship. Immutability can be the attribute of none but God. Whoever is "the same yesterday, and today, and forever" must be divine. Believer, bring your adoration to Jesus; cast down your crown at the feet of Him who was crucified. Give royal and divine honors to Him who stooped to the ignominy of crucifixion.

He claims also of us that we should trust Him. If He is always the same, here is a rock that cannot be moved; build on it. Here is an anchorage, cast your anchor of hope into it and hold fast in time of storm. If Christ were variable, He would not be worthy of your confidence. Since He is evermore unchanged, rest on Him without fear.

And, lastly, if He is always the same, rejoice in Him, and rejoice always. If you ever had cause to rejoice in Christ, you always have cause, for He never alters. If yesterday you could sing of Him, today you may sing of Him. If He changed, your joy might change, but if the stream of your gladness springs solely and only out of this great deep of the immutability of Jesus, then it need never stay its flow. Let us "rejoice in the Lord always; again I say, rejoice" (Phil 4:4). Until the day breaks and the shadows flee away, until the blessed hour arrives when we shall see Him face to face, and be made like Him, let this be our joy, that "he is the same yesterday, and today, and forever."

Are You Becoming More Like Your Master?

Let each of us ask this question: How far has Christ's purpose of sanctifying me been answered in my own case? I know that, in one sense, I am completely sanctified. But, in another sense, I still feel my imperfections and infirmities. How far have I progressed in sanctification during the past year? How much has my faith increased during the year? How many of my corruptions have I overcome? How much nearer am I living to Christ now than on the first Sabbath of last year? How much do I know of the Savior? How much closer do I approach in my likeness to Him? Do I have more power in prayer? Am I more careful in my life? Is my spirit more loving than it used to be? Am I more decisive for that which is right? At the same time, am I more meek in standing up for it?

Am I, in all respects, more like my Master than I was a year ago? Or, on the other hand, have I been going backward? I cannot stand still; I must either go forward in grace or go backward. Which have I been doing during the past year? And I charge you, my heart, whatever answer you have to give to these questions, still to remember that, if you are never so much sanctified, you have not yet attained perfection. I ask you, forget that which is behind, and press forward toward that which is before, looking still unto Jesus, who is both the originator and perfecter of our faith (Heb 12:2). The Lord gives so plenteously of His grace that you may be sanctified wholly—body, soul, and spirit; and I pray that God would preserve you all unto His coming and glory.

Joyfully Bear Christ's Reproach

We turn tail and are frightened because somebody has said a hard thing to us for defending the truth about Jesus and has the salvation of man wrapped in it. May God restore to us more grace, more piety, more love for souls, more care for the kingdom of Christ, a sterner prizing of the truth, and a determination solemnly avowed before the Lord of Hosts, that come what may, we will contend earnestly for the faith once delivered unto the saints. We stand upon the Rock of Ages, confident that God will defend the right, and that right in the end shall come off victorious. God give you grace from this day, more than ever before, to take your place outside the camp, and cheerfully and joyfully to bear Christ's reproach.

Some of you cannot do this; you cannot bear His reproach. You cannot go outside the camp, for you have no vital faith—you have not believed in Jesus. O sinner, you are not to carry Christ's cross first, but look to that cross for salvation. And when He has saved you, as He will if you trust in Him, then take up your cross and carry it, and praise the name of God from this time forth, even forever.

Praise God Continually with a Childlike Faith

To praise God continually will require a childlike faith in Him. You must believe His word, or you will not praise His name. Doubt snaps the harpstrings. Question mars all melody. Trust Him, lean on Him, enjoy Him—you will never praise Him otherwise. Unbelief is the deadly enemy of praise.

Faith must lead you into personal communion with the Lord. It is to Him that the praise is offered, and not to our fellow men. The most beautiful singing in the world, if it is intended for the ears of musical critics, is worth nothing. Praise is only meant for God. I will sing unto the Lord, and unto the Lord alone. You must live in fellowship with God, or you cannot praise Him.

You must also have an overflowing contentment, a real joy in Him. Be sure that you do not lose your joy. If you ever lose the joy of religion, you will lose the power of religion. Do not be satisfied to be a miserable believer. An unhappy believer is a poor creature, but he who is resigned to being so is in a dangerous condition. Depend upon it, greater importance attaches to holy happiness than most people think. As you are happy in the Lord, you will be able to praise His name. Rejoice in the Lord, that you may praise Him.

There must also be a holy earnestness about this. Praise is called a sacrifice because it is a very sacred and solemn thing. People who came to the altar with their victims came there with the hush of reverence, the trembling of awe. We cannot praise God with levity. He is in heaven, and we are upon the earth; He is thrice holy, and we are sinful. We must take off our shoe in lowly reverence and worship with intense adoration or else He cannot be pleased with our sacrifices. When life is real, life is earnest, and it must be both real and earnest when it is spent to the praise of the great and ever-blessed God.

To praise God continually, you need to cultivate perpetual gratitude, and surely it cannot be hard to do that! Remember, every misery averted is a mercy bestowed; every sin forgiven is a favor granted; every duty performed is also a grace received. The people of God have an inexhaustible treasury of good things provided for them by the infinite God, and for all this they should praise Him. I ask you, do not be only a little grateful, but overflow with it. Let your praises be like the waters of fountains that are abundantly supplied. Let the stream leap up to heaven in bursts of enthusiasm; let it fall to earth again in showers of beneficence; let it fill the basin of your daily life, and run over into the lives of others, and from there again in a cataract of glittering joy let it still descend.

In order to have this praise you will need a deep and ardent admiration of the Lord God. Admire the Father—think much of His love; acquaint yourself with His perfections. Admire the Son of God, the altogether lovely One. And as you observe His gentleness, self-denial, love, and grace, allow your heart to be wholly enamored of Him. Admire the patience and condescension of the Holy Ghost, that He should visit you, and dwell in you, and bear with you. It cannot be difficult to the sanctified and instructed heart to be filled with a great admiration of the Lord God. This is the raw material of praise. An intelligent admiration of God, kindled into flame by gratitude and fanned by delight and joy, must ever produce praise. Living in personal converse with God, and trusting Him as a child trusts its father, it cannot be difficult for the soul continually to offer the sacrifice of praise to God through Jesus Christ.

HEBREWS
13:20–25

²⁰ Now may the God of peace, who brought up from the dead our Lord Jesus, the great shepherd of the sheep, by the blood of the eternal covenant, ²¹ equip you with every good thing to do his will, carrying out in us what is pleasing before him through Jesus Christ, to whom be the glory forever. Amen.

²² Now I urge you, brothers, bear with my word of exhortation, for indeed I have written to you briefly. ²³ Know that our brother Timothy has been released, with whom I will see you, if he comes quickly. ²⁴ Greet all your leaders and all the saints. Those from Italy greet you. ²⁵ Grace be with all of you.

EXPOSITION

20 **Now may the God of peace** As if to show that he did not ask of them what he was not himself willing to give, he utters this most wonderful prayer for them. He may confidently say to his congregation "Pray for me," who genuinely from his soul prays for them.

who brought up from the dead our Lord Jesus We believe that Jesus assuredly died, and that He was buried in the tomb of Joseph of Arimathea, but that on the third day He rose again and departed the tomb, no more to die. This we most firmly believe to be a matter of fact; not a fiction, or a piece of poetry, but a matter of fact, like any other reliable history, and we accept it without question.

the great shepherd He is not the great Shepherd when He dies; He is the good Shepherd. He is the great Shepherd when He is brought again from the dead. In resurrection

you perceive His greatness. He lies in the grave slumbering;
He is the good Shepherd then, having laid down His life for
the sheep. Life appears again in Him, the stone is rolled away,
the watchmen are seized with terror, and He comes out the
risen one, no more the dying—now He is the great Shepherd.

In the covenant we are the sheep; the Lord Jesus is the Shepherd.
You cannot make a covenant with sheep—they have not the
ability to covenant. But you can make a covenant with the
Shepherd for them, and so, glory be to God, though we had
gone astray like lost sheep, we belonged to Jesus. He made a
covenant on our behalf, and stood for us before the living God.

It is very beautiful to trace the shepherds through the Old
Testament, and to see Christ as Abel, the witnessing shepherd,
pouring out the blood that cried from the ground; as Abraham,
the separating shepherd, leading out his flock into the strange
country where they dwelt alone; as Isaac, the quiet shepherd,
digging wells for his flock, and feeding them in peace in the
midst of the enemies; as Jacob, the shepherd who is surety
for the sheep, who earns them all by long toils and weariness,
separates them, and walks in the midst of them to Canaan,
preserving them by his own lone midnight prayers. There,
too, we see our Lord as Joseph, the shepherd who is head over
Egypt for the sake of Israel, of whom his dying father said,
"From there is the Shepherd, the Rock of Israel" (Gen 49:24).
Head over all things for His church, the King who governs all
the world for the sake of His elect, the great Shepherd of the
sheep, who for their sakes has all power committed unto His
hands. Then follows Moses, the chosen shepherd, who led his
people through the wilderness up to the promised land, feeding them with manna and giving them drink from the smitten
rock—what a wide theme for reflection here! And then there
is David, the type of Jesus, reigning in the covenanted inheritance over his own people as a glorious king in the midst of
them all. All these together enable us to see the varied glories
of "that great Shepherd of the sheep."

by the blood of the eternal covenant The work He has done has pleased the Father, and therefore He has brought Him back from among the dead. His acceptance is ours: we are accepted in the Beloved (Eph 1:6).

We make with God, after conversion, a covenant of gratitude; we come to Him sensible of what He has done for us, and we devote ourselves to Him. We set our seal to that covenant when in baptism we are united with His church. Day by day, as often as we come around the table of the breaking of bread, we renew the vow of our covenant, and thus we have personal communion with God. I cannot pray to Him except through the covenant of grace, and I know that I am not His child unless I am His: first through the covenant whereby Christ purchased me, and secondly through the covenant by which I have given up myself and dedicated all that I am and all that I have to Him.

ILLUSTRATION
A Binding Oath

You and I are bound by our word. If we took an oath, which I trust we would not, we should certainly feel doubly bound by it. If we had lived in the old times, and blood had been sprinkled on an agreement that we had made, we should regard the solemn sign and never dream of running back from it.

Think for a moment how impossible it is that the Lord should ever break that covenant of grace which He spontaneously made with His own Son, and with us in Him, now that it has been sprinkled with blood from the veins of His own well-beloved Son.

Before God had spoken existence out of nothing, before angel's wing had stirred the unnavigated ether, before a solitary song had disturbed the solemnity of the silence in which God reigned supreme, He had entered into solemn counsel with Himself, with His Son, and with His Spirit, and had in that council decreed, determined, purposed, and predestinated the salvation of His people.

21 **equip you** The expression should be rendered, "Make you fully complete," or "fully fitted" to do His will. We ought to request earnestly that we may be qualified, adapted, and suited to be used of God for the performance of His will.

The original Greek word (though I have not noticed that expositors observe it, yet anyone turning to the lexicon will see it) properly means to reset a bone that is dislocated. The meaning of the text is this: by the fall, all our bones are out of joint for the doing of the Lord's will. The desire of the apostle is that the Lord will set the bones in their places, and thus make us able with every faculty and in every good work to do His will.

with every good thing to do his will God in Christ Jesus, by His almighty grace, must raise us up together with Christ. He who brought again from the dead our Lord Jesus Christ must stoop down to lift us up from the grave of sin, and quicken us into life eternal, or we shall never think His thoughts or follow His ways (Isa 55:8). Into the light where He dwells we can never come except by the operations of His divine Spirit. Jesus says, "No one comes to the Father except through me" (John 14:6) and "No one is able to come to me unless the Father who sent me draws him" (John 6:44). The Holy Ghost must make us alive out of our trespasses and sins, deliver us from the ways in which we walk according to the course of this world, and redeem us from the dominion of the carnal mind, which is enmity against God. By sanctification He must deliver us from our indwelling corruption, and continue the process till He conforms us perfectly to the image of the peerless Son of God. He will work likeness to Jesus in all believers, and it shall be said of us, "They are blameless" (Rev 14:5). Christ

Himself shall say, "They will walk with me in white, because they are worthy" (Rev 3:4).

carrying out in us what is pleasing before him The promise is a double promise when it is confirmed in Jesus. Although we are poor and worthless creatures, yet we can say with David, "Yet not so is my house with God, for he made an everlasting covenant, arranging everything" (2 Sam 23:5).

to whom be the glory forever A rich benediction, fitly closing an epistle, in which the prominent theme is the perseverance of the saints. Lord, fulfill this blessing in us.

22   **bear with my word of exhortation** What the apostle was anxious to receive he was careful to bestow, and therefore he proceeded in the words of our text to plead for his brothers. From this we learn that if we desire others to pray for us we must set the example of praying for them. We cannot expect to be benefited by other men's prayers unless the spirit of supplication dwells in us also. In this matter the Lord will give to us good measure pressed down, shaken, overflowing (Luke 6:38), according as we give unto others. Other hearts shall be stirred up to intercede for us if we ourselves are diligent in intercession. Pray, if you would be prayed for.

23-25   **Greet all your leaders** It seems that there were special persons, who were leaders in the Church of God, who were to be remembered, and thought upon, and considered. They were set apart for this work: "your leaders, who spoke the word of God to you" (Heb 13:7).

APPLICATION

Forgiven So That We Might Be Restored

Just as Jesus is fully restored to the place from which He came, and has lost no dignity or power by having shed His blood, but rather is exalted higher than ever, so God's design is to make us pure and holy as Adam was at first—to add to our characters a force of love that never would have been there if we had not sinned and been forgiven; an energy of intense devotion, an enthusiasm of perfect self-sacrifice, that we never could have learned if it had not been for Him who loved us and gave Himself for us.

God means to make us the princes of the blood royal of the universe, or, if you will, the bodyguards of the Lord of Hosts. He desires to fashion an order of creatures who will come very near to Him and yet will feel the lowliest reverence for Him. He will have them akin to Himself—partakers of the divine nature, and yet the most obedient of servants. Perfectly free agents, and yet bound to Him by bonds that will never let them disobey in thought, or word, or deed. And this is how He is fashioning this central battalion who shall wait upon His eternal marchings forever: He is forgiving us great sins. He is bestowing upon us great blessings; He is making us one with His dear Son. When He has entirely freed us from the shrouds of our spiritual death, He will call us up to where Jesus is and we shall serve Him with an adoration superior to all the rest of His creatures.

Angels cannot love so much as we will, for they have never tasted redeeming grace and dying love. This high devotion is the Lord's aim. He did not bring up the Lord Jesus from the dead that He might live a common life. He lifted him up that He might be head over all things to His Church, and that all things might be under His feet (Eph 1:22). Even so, the destiny of Christians is mysteriously sublime: they are not lifted up from their native death to a mere morality; they are destined to be something more than philanthropists and men esteemed by others. They are to exhibit to angels, and principalities, and powers, the wonderful grace of God, showing in their own persons what God can do with His creatures through the death of His Son.

You Must Go Down To Death

The work described in this text must be wrought in us by the Spirit of God. Jesus is the model to which we are to be conformed. You must go down to death as Jesus did, and be buried with Him, that you may rise with Him. There must be in you the death of all carnal power and strength, or the power of God cannot be revealed in you. You must know the depths as Moses did, even the depths wherein proud self-sufficiency is drowned; you must be baptized in the cloud and in the sea. You must have over you the sentence of condemnation; you must own in your own soul that there dwells in your flesh no good thing, and that you are condemned under the law. Then there must be wrought in you a quickening, a coming to life, a coming up out of the place of condemnation and death.

Happy is he who has come forth from the tomb of his former vain conversation, leaving the graveclothes of worldliness and sin behind, coming up to be clothed with a heavenly mind, and to lead a new life, secret and divine as that of the risen Savior, and like the ascended Lord; for He has "raised us together and seated us together in the heavenly places in Christ Jesus" (Eph 2:6). "For you have died, and your life is hidden with Christ in God" (Col 3:3). Have you realized this? You may have been buried in baptism, but were you at that time a partaker of your Lord's death? You had no right to be buried if you were not dead. Did you really know that death had passed upon you before you were buried with your Savior? And now do you feel the life of God within you, quickening you to newness of life? If so, it will daily lift you to something nobler and better until you shall be ultimately raised to dwell where you shall never again be defiled by sin—where Satan shall be bruised under your feet, and the God of peace shall reign. When you shall dwell in perfect holiness, you shall reign in perfect peace. May He who brought our Lord Jesus from the grave to glory bring you also along the upward way until you are with Him and like Him forever.

Sources

Hebrews 1:1–4
"Depths and Heights (Heb 1:2–3)." *The Metropolitan Tabernacle Pulpit Sermons*, 45:385–93. London: Passmore & Alabaster, 1899.

"Exposition by C. H. Spurgeon: John 10:1–30; Hebrews 1:1–14." *The Metropolitan Tabernacle Pulpit Sermons*, 58:573–76. London: Passmore & Alabaster, 1912.

Hebrews 1:5–14
"Exposition by C. H. Spurgeon: John 10:1–30; Hebrews 1:1–14." *The Metropolitan Tabernacle Pulpit Sermons*, 58:573–76. London: Passmore & Alabaster, 1912.

"Hebrews 1." *The Interpreter: Spurgeon's Devotional Bible,* 733. Grand Rapids: Baker, 1964.

"The Oil of Gladness (Psa 45:7)." *The Metropolitan Tabernacle Pulpit Sermons*, 22:25–36. London: Passmore & Alabaster, 1876.

"Psalm 2: Exposition." *The Treasury of David*. Vol. 1, *Psalms 1–26*, pp. 10–13. London: Marshall Brothers, 1870.

"Psalm 45: Exposition." *The Treasury of David*. Vol. 2, *Psalms 27–57*, pp. 315–22. London: Marshall Brothers, 1870.

"Psalm 97: Exposition." *The Treasury of David*. Vol. 4, *Psalms 88–110*, pp. 194–98. London: Marshall Brothers, 1870.

"Psalm 102: Exposition." *The Treasury of David*. Vol. 4, *Psalms 88–110*, pp. 250–58. London: Marshall Brothers, 1870.

"Psalm 104: Exposition." *The Treasury of David*. Vol. 4, *Psalms 88–110*, pp. 301–12. London: Marshall Brothers, 1870.

"Psalm 110: Exposition." *The Treasury of David*. Vol. 4, *Psalms 88–110*, pp. 460–64. London: Marshall Brothers, 1870.

Hebrews 2:1–9
"The Best of All Sights (Heb 2:9)." *The Metropolitan Tabernacle Pulpit Sermons*, 25:697–701. London: Passmore & Alabaster, 1879.

"Exposition by C. H. Spurgeon: Hebrews 2." *The Metropolitan Tabernacle Pulpit Sermons*, 45:634–36. London: Passmore & Alabaster, 1899.

"Exposition by C. H. Spurgeon: Hebrews 2:1–15." *The Metropolitan Tabernacle Pulpit Sermons*, 45:203–4. London: Passmore & Alabaster, 1899.

"Exposition by C. H. Spurgeon: Hebrews 2; 3." *The Metropolitan Tabernacle
    Pulpit Sermons,* 56:477–80. London: Passmore & Alabaster, 1910.
"Psalm 8: Exposition." *The Treasury of David.* Vol. 1, *Psalms 1–26,* pp. 79–82.
    London: Marshall Brothers, 1870.
"Seeing Jesus (Heb 2:9)." *The Metropolitan Tabernacle Pulpit Sermons,* 13:517–28.
    London: Passmore & Alabaster, 1867.

Hebrews 2:10–18

"'All of One' (Heb 2:11–13)." *The Metropolitan Tabernacle Pulpit Sermons,* 41:289–
    98. London: Passmore & Alabaster, 1895.
"The Captain of Our Salvation (Heb 2:10)." *The Metropolitan Tabernacle Pulpit
    Sermons,* 45:193–202. London: Passmore & Alabaster, 1899.
"Christ—Perfect Through Sufferings (Heb 2:10)." *The Metropolitan Tabernacle
    Pulpit Sermons,* 8:613–24. London: Passmore & Alabaster, 1862.
"Christ's Sympathy with His People (Heb 2:18)." *The Metropolitan Tabernacle
    Pulpit Sermons,* 50:253–63. London: Passmore & Alabaster, 1904.
"The Destroyer Destroyed (Heb 2:14)." *The New Park Street Pulpit Sermons,* 4:9–16.
    London: Passmore & Alabaster, 1858.
"Exposition by C. H. Spurgeon: Hebrews 2." *The Metropolitan Tabernacle Pulpit
    Sermons,* 45:635–36. London: Passmore & Alabaster, 1899.
"Exposition by C. H. Spurgeon: Hebrews 2:1–15." *The Metropolitan Tabernacle
    Pulpit Sermons,* 45:204. London: Passmore & Alabaster, 1899.
"Exposition by C. H. Spurgeon: Hebrews 2; 3." *The Metropolitan Tabernacle
    Pulpit Sermons,* 56:477–80. London: Passmore & Alabaster, 1910.
"The Fear of Death (Heb 2:14–15)." *The Metropolitan Tabernacle Pulpit Sermons,*
    58:37–45. London: Passmore & Alabaster, 1912.
"Fear of Death (Heb 2:15)." *The Metropolitan Tabernacle Pulpit Sermons,* 55:1–12.
    London: Passmore & Alabaster, 1909.
"'I and the Children' (Isa 8:18)." *The Metropolitan Tabernacle Pulpit Sermons,*
    20:529–40. London: Passmore & Alabaster, 1874.
"Men Chosen—Fallen Angels Rejected (Heb 2:16)." *The New Park Street Pulpit
    Sermons,* 2:289–96. London: Passmore & Alabaster, 1856.
"Psalm 22: Exposition." *The Treasury of David.* Vol. 1, *Psalms 1–26,* pp. 324–34.
    London: Marshall Brothers, 1870.
"The Suffering Saviour's Sympathy (Heb 2:18)." *The Metropolitan Tabernacle
    Pulpit Sermons,* 33:409–20. London: Passmore & Alabaster, 1887.

Hebrews 3:1–11

"The Call of 'To-Day'" (Heb 3:7)." *The Metropolitan Tabernacle Pulpit Sermons,*
    55:421–30. London: Passmore & Alabaster, 1909.
"An Earnest Warning against Unbelief (Heb 3:18–19)." *The Metropolitan
    Tabernacle Pulpit Sermons,* 56:469–77. London: Passmore &
    Alabaster, 1910.

"The Entreaty of the Holy Ghost (Heb 3:7)." *The Metropolitan Tabernacle Pulpit Sermons*, 20:121–32. London: Passmore & Alabaster, 1874.
"Exposition by C. H. Spurgeon: Hebrews 2; 3." *The Metropolitan Tabernacle Pulpit Sermons*, 56:477–80. London: Passmore & Alabaster, 1910.
"Exposition by C. H. Spurgeon: Hebrews 3:1–16." *The Metropolitan Tabernacle Pulpit Sermons*, 44:34–36. London: Passmore & Alabaster, 1898.
"Exposition by C. H. Spurgeon: Hebrews 3; 4:1." *The Metropolitan Tabernacle Pulpit Sermons*, 55:430–32. London: Passmore & Alabaster, 1909.
"Exposition by C. H. Spurgeon: Hebrews 3; 4:1–9." *The Metropolitan Tabernacle Pulpit Sermons*, 62:33–36. London: Passmore & Alabaster, 1916.
"Predestination and Calling (Rom 8:30)." *The New Park Street Pulpit Sermons*, 5:129–36. London: Passmore & Alabaster, 1859.

Hebrews 3:12–19

"The Deceitfulness of Sin (Heb 3:13)." *The Metropolitan Tabernacle Pulpit Sermons*, 36:97–108. London: Passmore & Alabaster, 1890.
"An Earnest Warning against Unbelief (Heb 3:18–19)." *The Metropolitan Tabernacle Pulpit Sermons*, 56:469–77. London: Passmore & Alabaster, 1910.
"Exposition by C. H. Spurgeon: Hebrews 2; 3." *The Metropolitan Tabernacle Pulpit Sermons*, 56:477–80. London: Passmore & Alabaster, 1910.
"Exposition by C. H. Spurgeon: Hebrews 3:1–16." *The Metropolitan Tabernacle Pulpit Sermons*, 44:34–36. London: Passmore & Alabaster, 1898.
"Exposition by C. H. Spurgeon: Hebrews 3; 4:1." *The Metropolitan Tabernacle Pulpit Sermons*, 55:430–32. London: Passmore & Alabaster, 1909.
"Exposition by C. H. Spurgeon: Hebrews 3; 4:1–9." *The Metropolitan Tabernacle Pulpit Sermons*, 62:33–36. London: Passmore & Alabaster, 1916.
"A Persuasive to Steadfastness (Heb 3:14)." *The Metropolitan Tabernacle Pulpit Sermons*, 18:169–80. London: Passmore & Alabaster, 1872.
"'Take Heed, Brothers' (Heb 3:12)." *The Metropolitan Tabernacle Pulpit Sermons*, 44:25–34. London: Passmore & Alabaster, 1898.
"To-Day! To-Day! To-Day! (Psa 95:7–8)." *The Metropolitan Tabernacle Pulpit Sermons*, 26:433–44. London: Passmore & Alabaster, 1880.
"A Warning against Hardness of Heart (Heb 3:13)." *The Metropolitan Tabernacle Pulpit Sermons*, 11:157–68. London: Passmore & Alabaster, 1865.

Hebrews 4:1–10

"The Believer's Present Rest (Heb 4:3)." *The Metropolitan Tabernacle Pulpit Sermons*, 55:529–36. London: Passmore & Alabaster, 1909.
"A Delicious Experience (Heb 4:3)." *The Metropolitan Tabernacle Pulpit Sermons*, 35:325–36. London: Passmore & Alabaster, 1889.
"Exposition by C. H. Spurgeon." *The Metropolitan Tabernacle Pulpit Sermons*, 59:121–29. London: Passmore & Alabaster, 1913.

"Exposition by C. H. Spurgeon: Hebrews 3; 4:1." *The Metropolitan Tabernacle Pulpit Sermons*, 55:430-32. London: Passmore & Alabaster, 1909.

"Exposition by C. H. Spurgeon: Hebrews 3; 4:1-9." *The Metropolitan Tabernacle Pulpit Sermons*, 62:33-36. London: Passmore & Alabaster, 1916.

"Exposition by C. H. Spurgeon: Hebrews 4." *The Metropolitan Tabernacle Pulpit Sermons*, 56:83-84. London: Passmore & Alabaster, 1910.

"Fearful of Coming Short (Heb 4:1-2)." *The Metropolitan Tabernacle Pulpit Sermons*, 20:325-36. London: Passmore & Alabaster, 1874.

"The Gospel Cordial." *The Metropolitan Tabernacle Pulpit Sermons*, 57:61-69. London: Passmore & Alabaster, 1911.

"Heavenly Rest (Heb 4:9)." *The New Park Street Pulpit Sermons*, 3:209-16. London: Passmore & Alabaster, 1857.

"In God's Garden of Rest (Heb 4:3)." *Able to the Uttermost: Twenty Gospel Sermons*, 137-45. Bellingham, WA: Logos Bible Software, 2009.

"Profitable Mixture (Heb 4:2)." *The Metropolitan Tabernacle Pulpit Sermons*, 35:313-24. London: Passmore & Alabaster, 1889.

"Rest (Heb 4:3)." *The Metropolitan Tabernacle Pulpit Sermons*, 15:217-28. London: Passmore & Alabaster, 1869.

"September 28." *The Chequebook of the Bank of Faith: Being Precious Promises Arranged for Daily Use with Brief Comments*, 272. New York: American Tract Society, 1893.

Hebrews 4:11-16

"The Believer's Present Rest (Heb 4:3)." *The Metropolitan Tabernacle Pulpit Sermons*, 55:529-37. London: Passmore & Alabaster, 1909.

"Boldness at the Throne (Heb 4:16)." *The Metropolitan Tabernacle Pulpit Sermons*, 56:49-60. London: Passmore & Alabaster, 1910.

"Exposition by C. H. Spurgeon: Hebrews 4:14-16." *The Metropolitan Tabernacle Pulpit Sermons*, 43:109-20. London: Passmore & Alabaster, 1897.

"Hebrews 4:9-16." *The Interpreter: Spurgeon's Devotional Bible*, 735. Grand Rapids: Baker, 1964.

"Sonship Questioned (Matt 4:3)." *The Metropolitan Tabernacle Pulpit Sermons*, 45:121-30. London: Passmore & Alabaster, 1899.

"The Tenderness of Jesus (Heb 4:15)." *The Metropolitan Tabernacle Pulpit Sermons*, 36:313-24. London: Passmore & Alabaster, 1890.

"'The Throne of Grace' (Heb 4:16)." *The Metropolitan Tabernacle Pulpit Sermons*, 17:673-84. London: Passmore & Alabaster, 1871.

"The Word a Sword (Heb 4:12)." *The Metropolitan Tabernacle Pulpit Sermons*, 34:109-20. London: Passmore & Alabaster, 1888.

Hebrews 5:1-10

"Compassion on the Ignorant (Heb 5:2)." *The Metropolitan Tabernacle Pulpit Sermons*, 24:193-204. London: Passmore & Alabaster, 1878.

"Compassion on the Ignorant (Heb 5:2)." *The Metropolitan Tabernacle Pulpit Sermons*, 43:373-82. London: Passmore & Alabaster, 1897.

"The Education of Sons of God (Heb 5:8)." *The Metropolitan Tabernacle Pulpit Sermons*, 47:169-79. London: Passmore & Alabaster, 1901.

"Exposition by C. H. Spurgeon: Hebrews 4:14-16; and 5." *The Metropolitan Tabernacle Pulpit Sermons*, 43:382-84. London: Passmore & Alabaster, 1897.

"Exposition by C. H. Spurgeon: Hebrews 5." *The Metropolitan Tabernacle Pulpit Sermons*, 46:407-8. London: Passmore & Alabaster, 1900.

"Exposition by C. H. Spurgeon: Hebrews 5:1-5." *The Metropolitan Tabernacle Pulpit Sermons*, 47:179-80. London: Passmore & Alabaster, 1901.

"Our Compassionate High Priest (Heb 5:2)." *The Metropolitan Tabernacle Pulpit Sermons*, 38:169-80. London: Passmore & Alabaster, 1892.

"Our Sympathizing High Priest (Heb 5:7-10)." *The Metropolitan Tabernacle Pulpit Sermons*, 32:589-600. London: Passmore & Alabaster, 1886.

"The Savior You Need (Heb 5:9)." *The Metropolitan Tabernacle Pulpit Sermons*, 20:265-76. London: Passmore & Alabaster, 1874.

Hebrews 5:11-14

"The Census of Israel (Num 26:63-65)." *The Metropolitan Tabernacle Pulpit Sermons*, 37:193-204. London: Passmore & Alabaster, 1891.

"Exposition by C. H. Spurgeon: Hebrews 4:14-16; and 5." *The Metropolitan Tabernacle Pulpit Sermons*, 43:382-84. London: Passmore & Alabaster, 1897.

"Exposition by C. H. Spurgeon: Hebrews 5." *The Interpreter: Spurgeon's Devotional Bible*, 736. Grand Rapids: Baker, 1964.

"Strong Meat (Heb 5:14)." *The Metropolitan Tabernacle Pulpit Sermons*, 9:229-40. London: Passmore & Alabaster, 1863.

Hebrews 6:1-12

"Exposition by C. H. Spurgeon: Hebrews 6." *The Metropolitan Tabernacle Pulpit Sermons*, 42:562-64. London: Passmore & Alabaster, 1896.

"Final Perseverance (Heb 6:4-6)." *The New Park Street Pulpit Sermons*, 2:169-76. London: Passmore & Alabaster, 1856.

"Hebrews 6." *The Interpreter: Spurgeon's Devotional Bible*, 737. Grand Rapids: Baker, 1964.

"The Perseverance of the Saints." *The Metropolitan Tabernacle Pulpit Sermons*, 15:289-300. London: Passmore & Alabaster, 1869.

"Things that Accompany Salvation (Heb 6:9)." *The New Park Street Pulpit Sermons*, 3:357-64. London: Passmore & Alabaster, 1857.

Hebrews 6:13-20

"The Anchor (Heb 6:17-20)." *The Metropolitan Tabernacle Pulpit Sermons*, 22:277-88. London: Passmore & Alabaster, 1876.

"'The Blood of the Testament' (Heb 9:19-20)." *The Metropolitan Tabernacle Pulpit Sermons*, 58:121-30. London: Passmore & Alabaster, 1912.

"David's Sublime Consolation (2 Sam 23:5)." *The Metropolitan Tabernacle Pulpit Sermons*, 59:253-64. London: Passmore & Alabaster, 1913.

"Exposition by C. H. Spurgeon: Hebrews 6." *The Metropolitan Tabernacle Pulpit Sermons*, 42:562-64. London: Passmore & Alabaster, 1896.

"'Flee from the Wrath to Come' (Matt 3:7; Heb 6:18)." *The Metropolitan Tabernacle Pulpit Sermons*, 46:577-85. London: Passmore & Alabaster, 1900.

"The Forerunner (Heb 6:20)." *The Metropolitan Tabernacle Pulpit Sermons*, 54:349-57. London: Passmore & Alabaster, 1908.

"The Friend of God (Isa 41:8; Jas 2:23)." *The Metropolitan Tabernacle Pulpit Sermons*, 33:265-76. London: Passmore & Alabaster, 1887.

"'Heirs of God' (Rom 8:17)." *The Metropolitan Tabernacle Pulpit Sermons*, 51:541-52. London: Passmore & Alabaster, 1905.

"Strong Consolation (Heb 6:17-18)." *The Metropolitan Tabernacle Pulpit Sermons*, 15:541-52. London: Passmore & Alabaster, 1869.

"Strong Consolation for the Lord's Refugees (Heb 6:18)." *The Metropolitan Tabernacle Pulpit Sermons*, 23:253-64. London: Passmore & Alabaster, 1877.

Hebrews 7:1-10

"'Accepted in the Beloved' (Eph 1:6)." *The Metropolitan Tabernacle Pulpit Sermons*, 8:529-40. London: Passmore & Alabaster, 1862.

"The Blessing of the High Priest (Num 6:22-27)." *The Metropolitan Tabernacle Pulpit Sermons*, 36:577-88. London: Passmore & Alabaster, 1890.

"Exposition by C.H. Spurgeon: Genesis 14:17-24." *The Metropolitan Tabernacle Pulpit Sermons*, 43:310-12. London: Passmore & Alabaster, 1897.

"Exposition by C. H. Spurgeon: Hebrews 7:1-14." *The Metropolitan Tabernacle Pulpit Sermons*, 61:48. London: Passmore & Alabaster, 1915.

"Hebrews 7:1-25." *The Interpreter: Spurgeon's Devotional Bible*, 22. Grand Rapids: Baker, 1964.

"First King of Righteousness, and after that King of Peace (Heb 7:2)." *The Metropolitan Tabernacle Pulpit Sermons*, 30:121-32. London: Passmore & Alabaster, 1884.

"The Man Christ Jesus (Heb 7:4)." *The Metropolitan Tabernacle Pulpit Sermons*, 31:205-16. London: Passmore & Alabaster, 1885.

"The Priest Ordained by the Oath of God (Heb 7:20-22)." *The Metropolitan Tabernacle Pulpit Sermons*, 27:257-68. London: Passmore & Alabaster, 1881.

Hebrews 7:11-28

"The Ever-Living Priest (Heb 7:23-25)." *The Metropolitan Tabernacle Pulpit Sermons*, 32:445-56. London: Passmore & Alabaster, 1886.

"Expositions by C.H. Spurgeon: Haggai 1–2:9; Hebrews 7:15–28." *The Metropolitan Tabernacle Pulpit Sermons*, 61:36. London: Passmore & Alabaster, 1915.

"Hebrews 7:1–25." *The Interpreter: Spurgeon's Devotional Bible*, 22. Grand Rapids: Baker, 1964.

"Matthew 1:2." *The Gospel of the Kingdom: A Commentary on the Book of Matthew*, 1. London: Passmore and Alabaster, 1893.

"Priest and Victim (Heb 7:27)." *The Metropolitan Tabernacle Pulpit Sermons*, 46:445–54. London: Passmore & Alabaster, 1900.

"The Priest Ordained by the Oath of God (Heb 7:20–22)." *The Metropolitan Tabernacle Pulpit Sermons*, 27:257–68. London: Passmore & Alabaster, 1881.

"Salvation to the Uttermost (Heb 7:25)." *The New Park Street Pulpit Sermons*, 2:241–49. London: Passmore & Alabaster, 1856.

Hebrews 8:1–13

"Christ a Sanctuary (Isa 8:14)." *The Metropolitan Tabernacle Pulpit Sermons*, 62:349–57. London: Passmore & Alabaster, 1916.

"Christ the Maker of All Things New (2 Cor 5:17)." *The Metropolitan Tabernacle Pulpit Sermons*, 22:685–96. London: Passmore & Alabaster, 1876.

"The Covenant Pleaded (Psa 74:20)." *The Metropolitan Tabernacle Pulpit Sermons*, 25:5–12. London: Passmore & Alabaster, 1879.

"Exposition by C. H. Spurgeon: Hebrews 8:7–13." *The Metropolitan Tabernacle Pulpit Sermons*, 48:36. London: Passmore & Alabaster, 1902.

"Exposition by C. H. Spurgeon: Jeremiah 31:27–37." *The Metropolitan Tabernacle Pulpit Sermons*, 43:108. London: Passmore & Alabaster, 1897.

"Exposition by C. H. Spurgeon: Jeremiah 31:29–37." *The Metropolitan Tabernacle Pulpit Sermons*, 58:324. London: Passmore & Alabaster, 1912.

"The Final Perseverance of the Saints (Job 17:9)." *The Metropolitan Tabernacle Pulpit Sermons*, 23:361–72. London: Passmore & Alabaster, 1877.

"God's Law in Man's Heart (Heb 8:10)." *The Metropolitan Tabernacle Pulpit Sermons*, 43:97–107. London: Passmore & Alabaster, 1897.

"Jeremiah 31:31–37." *The Interpreter: Spurgeon's Devotional Bible*, 440. Grand Rapids: Baker, 1964.

"A Lesson from the Great Panic (Heb 12:27)." *The Metropolitan Tabernacle Pulpit Sermons*, 12:265–76. London: Passmore & Alabaster, 1866.

"Our Glorious Transforming (Eph 2:13)." *The Metropolitan Tabernacle Pulpit Sermons*, 62:37–45. London: Passmore & Alabaster, 1916.

"Priest and Victim (Heb 7:27)." *The Metropolitan Tabernacle Pulpit Sermons*, 46:445–54. London: Passmore & Alabaster, 1900.

"The Putting Away of Sin (Heb 9:26)." *The Metropolitan Tabernacle Pulpit Sermons*, 16:37–48. London: Passmore & Alabaster, 1870.

"The Sparrow and the Swallow (Psa 84:3)." *The Metropolitan Tabernacle Pulpit Sermons*, 53:253–64. London: Passmore & Alabaster, 1907.

"The Wondrous Covenant (Heb 8:10)." *The Metropolitan Tabernacle Pulpit Sermons*, 58:517–26. London: Passmore & Alabaster, 1912.

Hebrews 9:1–14

"The Annual Atonement (Lev 16:30)." *The Metropolitan Tabernacle Pulpit Sermons*, 32:541–52. London: Passmore & Alabaster, 1886.

"The Blood of the Testament (Heb 9:20)." *The Metropolitan Tabernacle Pulpit Sermons*, 26:625–36. London: Passmore & Alabaster, 1880.

"Christ a Sanctuary (Isa 8:4)." *The Metropolitan Tabernacle Pulpit Sermons*, 62:349–57. London: Passmore & Alabaster, 1916.

"Exposition by C. H. Spurgeon: Hebrews 9." *The Metropolitan Tabernacle Pulpit Sermons*, 41:406–8. London: Passmore & Alabaster, 1895.

"Expositions by C. H. Spurgeon: Hebrews 9 and Exodus 24:1–10." *The Metropolitan Tabernacle Pulpit Sermons*, 58:130–32. London: Passmore & Alabaster, 1912.

"Expositions by C. H. Spurgeon: Leviticus 16:1–31 and Hebrews 9:1–22." *The Metropolitan Tabernacle Pulpit Sermons*, 40:333–36. London: Passmore & Alabaster, 1894.

"Hebrews 9:1–14." *The Interpreter: Spurgeon's Devotional Bible*, 95. Grand Rapids: Baker, 1964.

"One Greater than the Temple (Matt 12:6)." *The Metropolitan Tabernacle Pulpit Sermons*, 22:49–60. London: Passmore & Alabaster, 1876.

"Our Lord's Entrance Within the Veil (Heb 9:12)." *The Metropolitan Tabernacle Pulpit Sermons*, 35:145–56. London: Passmore & Alabaster, 1889.

"Perfection in Faith (Heb 10:14)." *The New Park Street Pulpit Sermons*, 5:59–64. London: Passmore & Alabaster, 1859.

"The Purging of the Conscience (Heb 9:13–14)." *The Metropolitan Tabernacle Pulpit Sermons*, 31:337–48. London: Passmore & Alabaster, 1885.

"The Red Heifer (Heb 9:13–14)." *The Metropolitan Tabernacle Pulpit Sermons*, 25:361–73. London: Passmore & Alabaster, 1879.

Hebrews 9:15–22

"The Blood of Christ's Covenant (Zech 9:11)." *The Metropolitan Tabernacle Pulpit Sermons*, 57:109–16. London: Passmore & Alabaster, 1911.

"The Blood of the Testament (Heb 9:20)." *The Metropolitan Tabernacle Pulpit Sermons*, 26:625–36. London: Passmore & Alabaster, 1880.

"'The Blood of the Testament' (Heb 9:19–20)." *The Metropolitan Tabernacle Pulpit Sermons*, 58:121–30. London: Passmore & Alabaster, 1912.

"The Blood-Shedding (Heb 9:22)." *The New Park Street Pulpit Sermons*, 3:89–96. London: Passmore & Alabaster, 1857.

"Hebrews 9:15–28." *The Interpreter: Spurgeon's Devotional Bible*, 738. Grand Rapids: Baker, 1964.

"Exposition by C. H. Spurgeon: Hebrews 9." *The Metropolitan Tabernacle Pulpit Sermons*, 41:406–8. London: Passmore & Alabaster, 1895.

"Exposition by C. H. Spurgeon: Hebrews 9:18–28." *The Metropolitan Tabernacle Pulpit Sermons*, 51:430–31. London: Passmore & Alabaster, 1905.

"Exposition by C. H. Spurgeon: Hebrews 9 and Exodus 24:1–10." *The Metropolitan Tabernacle Pulpit Sermons*, 58:130–32. London: Passmore & Alabaster, 1912.

"Expositions by C. H. Spurgeon: Leviticus 16:1–31 and Hebrews 9:1–22." *The Metropolitan Tabernacle Pulpit Sermons*, 40:333–36. London: Passmore & Alabaster, 1894.

"The Savior's Precious Blood (1 Pet 1:19)." *The Metropolitan Tabernacle Pulpit Sermons*, 60:97–106. London: Passmore & Alabaster, 1914.

"An Unalterable Law (Heb 9:22)." *The Metropolitan Tabernacle Pulpit Sermons*, 60:373–82. London: Passmore & Alabaster, 1914.

"With or Without Blood-Shedding (Heb 9:22)." *The Metropolitan Tabernacle Pulpit Sermons*, 51:421–30. London: Passmore & Alabaster, 1905.

Hebrews 9:23–28

"Between the Two Appearings (Heb 9:26–28)." *The Metropolitan Tabernacle Pulpit Sermons*, 37:145–56. London: Passmore & Alabaster, 1891.

"Christ's One Sacrifice for Sin (Heb 9:26)." *The Metropolitan Tabernacle Pulpit Sermons*, 38:553–62. London: Passmore & Alabaster, 1892.

"Exposition by C. H. Spurgeon: Hebrews 9." *The Metropolitan Tabernacle Pulpit Sermons*, 41:406–8. London: Passmore & Alabaster, 1895.

"Exposition by C. H. Spurgeon: Hebrews 9:18–28 and 10:1–25." *The Metropolitan Tabernacle Pulpit Sermons*, 51:430–32. London: Passmore & Alabaster, 1905.

"Facts and Inferences (Psa 37:35–37)." *The Metropolitan Tabernacle Pulpit Sermons*, 57:13–21. London: Passmore & Alabaster, 1911.

"Hebrews 9:15–28." *The Interpreter: Spurgeon's Devotional Bible*, 738. Grand Rapids: Baker, 1964.

"Jesus Putting Away Sin (Heb 9:26)." *The Metropolitan Tabernacle Pulpit Sermons*, 13:373–84. London: Passmore & Alabaster, 1867.

"Our Hiding-Place (Isa 32:2)." *The Metropolitan Tabernacle Pulpit Sermons*, 49:529–40. London: Passmore & Alabaster, 1903.

"Our Lord's Entrance Within the Veil (Heb 9:12)." *The Metropolitan Tabernacle Pulpit Sermons*, 35:145–56. London: Passmore & Alabaster, 1889.

"Perfection in Faith (Heb 10:14)." *The New Park Street Pulpit Sermons*, 5:59–64. London: Passmore & Alabaster, 1859.

"A Personal Application (Heb 9:26)." *The Metropolitan Tabernacle Pulpit Sermons*, 16:649–60. London: Passmore & Alabaster, 1870.

"The Putting Away of Sin (Heb 9:26)." *The Metropolitan Tabernacle Pulpit Sermons*, 16:37–48. London: Passmore & Alabaster, 1870.

"The Two Advents of Christ (Heb 9:27–28)." *The Metropolitan Tabernacle Pulpit Sermons*, 8:37–48. London: Passmore & Alabaster, 1862.

Hebrews 10:1–18

"All Fulness in Christ (Col 1:19)." *The Metropolitan Tabernacle Pulpit Sermons*, 17:121–32. London: Passmore & Alabaster, 1871.

"Believers Sent by Christ, as Christ Is Sent by the Father (John 17:18)." *The Metropolitan Tabernacle Pulpit Sermons*, 36:265–76. London: Passmore & Alabaster, 1890.

"Death and Its Sentence Abolished (Col 2:13–14)." *The Metropolitan Tabernacle Pulpit Sermons*, 45:25–35. London: Passmore & Alabaster, 1899.

"Exposition by C. H. Spurgeon: Hebrews 9:18–28 and 10:1–25." *The Metropolitan Tabernacle Pulpit Sermons*, 51:430–32. London: Passmore & Alabaster, 1905.

"Exposition by C. H. Spurgeon: Hebrews 9:24–28 and 10." *The Metropolitan Tabernacle Pulpit Sermons*, 54:357–60. London: Passmore & Alabaster, 1908.

"Exposition by C. H. Spurgeon: Hebrews 10:1–22." *The Metropolitan Tabernacle Pulpit Sermons*, 46:455–56. London: Passmore & Alabaster, 1900.

"The First and the Second (Heb 10:9)." *The Metropolitan Tabernacle Pulpit Sermons*, 46:505–16. London: Passmore & Alabaster, 1900.

"Hebrews 10:1–31." *The Interpreter: Spurgeon's Devotional Bible*, 739. Grand Rapids: Baker, 1964.

"'Lo, I Come': Exposition (Heb 10:5–7)." *The Metropolitan Tabernacle Pulpit Sermons*, 37:241–52. London: Passmore & Alabaster, 1891.

"The Only Atoning Priest (Heb 10:11–14)." *The Metropolitan Tabernacle Pulpit Sermons*, 18:73–84. London: Passmore & Alabaster, 1872.

"Perfect Sanctification (Heb 10:10)." *The Metropolitan Tabernacle Pulpit Sermons*, 26:157–68. London: Passmore & Alabaster, 1880.

"Perfection in Faith (Heb 10:14)." *The New Park Street Pulpit Sermons*, 5:59–64. London: Passmore & Alabaster, 1859.

"A Saviour Such as You Need (Heb 10:15–18)." *The Metropolitan Tabernacle Pulpit Sermons*, 12:553–64. London: Passmore & Alabaster, 1866.

Hebrews 10:19–25

"Exposition by C. H. Spurgeon: Hebrews 9:24–28 and 10." *The Metropolitan Tabernacle Pulpit Sermons*, 54:357–60. London: Passmore & Alabaster, 1908.

"Exposition by C. H. Spurgeon: Hebrews 10:19–39." *The Metropolitan Tabernacle Pulpit Sermons*, 48:609–12. London: Passmore & Alabaster, 1902.

"Holding Fast Our Profession (Heb 10:23)." *The Metropolitan Tabernacle Pulpit Sermons*, 32:229–40. London: Passmore & Alabaster, 1886.

"Perfection in Faith (Heb 10:14)." *The New Park Street Pulpit Sermons*, 5:59–64. London: Passmore & Alabaster, 1859.

"The Plague of the Heart (1 Kgs 8:38–40)." *The Metropolitan Tabernacle Pulpit Sermons*, 25:457–68. London: Passmore & Alabaster, 1879.

"The Red Heifer (Heb 9:13–14)." *The Metropolitan Tabernacle Pulpit Sermons*, 25:361–72. London: Passmore & Alabaster, 1879.

"The Rent Veil (Heb 10:19–20)." *The Metropolitan Tabernacle Pulpit Sermons*, 34:169–80. London: Passmore & Alabaster, 1888.

Hebrews 10:26–39

"Alto and Bass (Luke 1:53)." *The Metropolitan Tabernacle Pulpit Sermons*, 44:373–80. London: Passmore & Alabaster, 1898.

"A Command and a Promise (Jas 4:8)." *The Metropolitan Tabernacle Pulpit Sermons*, 56:409–18. London: Passmore & Alabaster, 1910.

"Exposition by C. H. Spurgeon: Hebrews 9:24–28 and 10." *The Metropolitan Tabernacle Pulpit Sermons*, 54:357–60. London: Passmore & Alabaster, 1908.

"Exposition by C. H. Spurgeon: Hebrews 10:19–39." *The Metropolitan Tabernacle Pulpit Sermons*, 48:609–12. London: Passmore & Alabaster, 1902.

"Future Punishment a Fearful Thing (Heb 10:31)." *The Metropolitan Tabernacle Pulpit Sermons*, 12:169–80. London: Passmore & Alabaster, 1866.

"Hold Fast Your Shield (Heb 10:35)." *The Metropolitan Tabernacle Pulpit Sermons*, 21:625–36. London: Passmore & Alabaster, 1875.

"Human Responsibility (John 15:22)." *The New Park Street Pulpit Sermons*, 4:223–40. London: Passmore & Alabaster, 1858.

"'Lay Hold on Eternal Life' (1 Tim 6:12)." *The Metropolitan Tabernacle Pulpit Sermons*, 37:529–40. London: Passmore & Alabaster, 1891.

"The Living Care of the Dying Christ (John 18:8–9)." *The Metropolitan Tabernacle Pulpit Sermons*, 40:313–21. London: Passmore & Alabaster, 1894.

"The Only Atoning Priest (Heb 10:11–14)." *The Metropolitan Tabernacle Pulpit Sermons*, 18:73–84. London: Passmore & Alabaster, 1872.

"Tender Words of Terrible Apprehension! (Psa 9:17)." *The New Park Street Pulpit Sermons*, 6:461–68. London: Passmore & Alabaster, 1860.

"Unbelievers Stumbling; Believers Rejoicing (Rom 9:33)." *The Metropolitan Tabernacle Pulpit Sermons*, 10:289–300. London: Passmore & Alabaster, 1864.

"A Visit to the Harvest Field (Jas 5:7–8)." *The Metropolitan Tabernacle Pulpit Sermons*, 17:685–96. London: Passmore & Alabaster, 1871.

"The Vital Force (Heb 10:38)." *The Metropolitan Tabernacle Pulpit Sermons*, 15:517–28. London: Passmore & Alabaster, 1869.

Hebrews 11:1–7

"Enoch (Gen 5:21–24; Heb 11:5–6; Jude 14–15)." *The Metropolitan Tabernacle Pulpit Sermons*, 22:433–44. London: Passmore & Alabaster, 1876.

"Exposition by C. H. Spurgeon: Hebrews 11." *The Metropolitan Tabernacle Pulpit Sermons*, 45:381–84. London: Passmore & Alabaster, 1899.

"Exposition by C. H. Spurgeon: Hebrews 11." *The Metropolitan Tabernacle Pulpit Sermons*, 57:345–48. London: Passmore & Alabaster, 1911.

"Exposition by C. H. Spurgeon: Hebrews 11." *The Metropolitan Tabernacle Pulpit Sermons*, 59:166–68. London: Passmore & Alabaster, 1913.

"Exposition by C. H. Spurgeon: Hebrews 11:1–13; and 32–40." *The Metropolitan Tabernacle Pulpit Sermons*, 50:322–24. London: Passmore & Alabaster, 1904.

"Exposition by C. H. Spurgeon: Hebrews 11:1–21." *The Metropolitan Tabernacle Pulpit Sermons*, 39:46–48. London: Passmore & Alabaster, 1893.

"Exposition by C. H. Spurgeon: Hebrews 11:1–21." *The Metropolitan Tabernacle Pulpit Sermons*, 54:574–76. London: Passmore & Alabaster, 1908.

"Exposition by C. H. Spurgeon: Hebrews 11:1–26." *The Metropolitan Tabernacle Pulpit Sermons*, 61:466–68. London: Passmore & Alabaster, 1915.

"Faith (Heb 11:6)." *The New Park Street Pulpit Sermons*, 3:1–8. London: Passmore & Alabaster, 1857.

"Faith Essential to Pleasing God (Heb 11:6)." *The Metropolitan Tabernacle Pulpit Sermons*, 35:445–56. London: Passmore & Alabaster, 1889.

"Noah's Faith, Fear, Obedience, and Salvation (Heb 11:7)." *The Metropolitan Tabernacle Pulpit Sermons*, 36:301–12. London: Passmore & Alabaster, 1890.

"What Is Essential in Coming to God? (Heb 11:6)." *The Metropolitan Tabernacle Pulpit Sermons*, 47:385–93. London: Passmore & Alabaster, 1901.

Hebrews 11:8–22

"Abraham, a Pattern to Believers (Heb 11:9–10)." *The Metropolitan Tabernacle Pulpit Sermons*, 39:37–45. London: Passmore & Alabaster, 1893.

"Abraham's Prompt Obedience to the Call of God (Heb 11:8)." *The Metropolitan Tabernacle Pulpit Sermons*, 21:373–84. London: Passmore & Alabaster, 1875.

"Abraham's Trial: A Lesson for Believers (Gen 22:1)." *The Metropolitan Tabernacle Pulpit Sermons*, 37:493–504. London: Passmore & Alabaster, 1891.

"An Inscription for the Mausoleum of the Saints (Heb 11:13–14)." *The Metropolitan Tabernacle Pulpit Sermons*, 31:105–12. London: Passmore & Alabaster, 1885.

"The Call of Abraham (Heb 11:8)." *The New Park Street Pulpit Sermons*, 5:289–96. London: Passmore & Alabaster, 1859.

"Exposition by C. H. Spurgeon: Hebrews 11." *The Metropolitan Tabernacle Pulpit Sermons*, 45:381–84. London: Passmore & Alabaster, 1899.

"Exposition by C. H. Spurgeon: Hebrews 11." *The Metropolitan Tabernacle Pulpit Sermons*, 47:394–96. London: Passmore & Alabaster, 1901.

"Exposition by C. H. Spurgeon: Hebrews 11." *The Metropolitan Tabernacle Pulpit Sermons*, 59:166–68. London: Passmore & Alabaster, 1913.

"Exposition by C. H. Spurgeon: Hebrews 11:1–13; and 32–40." *The Metropolitan Tabernacle Pulpit Sermons*, 50:322–24. London: Passmore & Alabaster, 1904.

"Exposition by C. H. Spurgeon: Hebrews 11:1–21." *The Metropolitan Tabernacle Pulpit Sermons*, 39:46–48. London: Passmore & Alabaster, 1893.

"Exposition by C. H. Spurgeon: Hebrews 11:1–26." *The Metropolitan Tabernacle Pulpit Sermons*, 61:466–68. London: Passmore & Alabaster, 1915.

"Go Back? Never! (Hebrews 11:15–16)." *The Metropolitan Tabernacle Pulpit Sermons*, 61:457–65. London: Passmore & Alabaster, 1915.

"Jacob Worshipping on His Staff (Heb 11:21)." *The Metropolitan Tabernacle Pulpit Sermons*, 24:121–32. London: Passmore & Alabaster, 1878.

"Joseph's Bones (Heb 11:22)." *The Metropolitan Tabernacle Pulpit Sermons*, 16:697–708. London: Passmore & Alabaster, 1870.

"The Obedience of Faith (Heb 11:8)." *The Metropolitan Tabernacle Pulpit Sermons*, 37:157–68. London: Passmore & Alabaster, 1891.

"Patience, Comfort, and Hope from the Scriptures (Rom 15:4)." *The Metropolitan Tabernacle Pulpit Sermons*, 47:541–51. London: Passmore & Alabaster, 1901.

"The Two Pivots (Exod 3:6; Heb 11:16)." *The Metropolitan Tabernacle Pulpit Sermons*, 45:361–72. London: Passmore & Alabaster, 1899.

Hebrews 11:23–31

"Driving Away the Vultures from the Sacrifice (Gen 15:11)." *The Metropolitan Tabernacle Pulpit Sermons*, 33:637–48. London: Passmore & Alabaster, 1887.

"Exposition by C. H. Spurgeon: Hebrews 11." *The Metropolitan Tabernacle Pulpit Sermons*, 45:381–84. London: Passmore & Alabaster, 1899.

"Exposition by C. H. Spurgeon: Hebrews 11." *The Metropolitan Tabernacle Pulpit Sermons*, 57:345–48. London: Passmore & Alabaster, 1911.

"Exposition by C. H. Spurgeon: Hebrews 11." *The Metropolitan Tabernacle Pulpit Sermons*, 59:166–68. London: Passmore & Alabaster, 1913.

"Exposition by C. H. Spurgeon: Hebrews 11:1–26." *The Metropolitan Tabernacle Pulpit Sermons*, 61:466–68. London: Passmore & Alabaster, 1915.

"The Hiding of Moses by Faith (Heb 11:23)." *The Metropolitan Tabernacle Pulpit Sermons*, 24:361–72. London: Passmore & Alabaster, 1878.

"Jericho Captured (Josh 6:2–3)." *The Metropolitan Tabernacle Pulpit Sermons*, 11:265–76. London: Passmore & Alabaster, 1865.

"Moses: His Faith and Decision (Heb 11:24–26)." *The Metropolitan Tabernacle Pulpit Sermons*, 34:349–60. London: Passmore & Alabaster, 1888.

"Rahab (Heb 11:31; Jas 2:25)." *The Metropolitan Tabernacle Pulpit Sermons*, 18:397–408. London: Passmore & Alabaster, 1872.

"Rahab's Faith (Heb 11:31)." *The New Park Street Pulpit Sermons*, 3:97–104. London: Passmore & Alabaster, 1857.

"The Way to Honour (Prov 27:18)." *The Metropolitan Tabernacle Pulpit Sermons*, 19:349–60. London: Passmore & Alabaster, 1873.

Hebrews 11:32-40

"Exposition by C. H. Spurgeon: Hebrews 11." *The Metropolitan Tabernacle Pulpit Sermons*, 45:381-84. London: Passmore & Alabaster, 1899.

"Exposition by C. H. Spurgeon: Hebrews 11." *The Metropolitan Tabernacle Pulpit Sermons*, 47:394-96. London: Passmore & Alabaster, 1901.

"Exposition by C. H. Spurgeon: Hebrews 11." *The Metropolitan Tabernacle Pulpit Sermons*, 57:345-48. London: Passmore & Alabaster, 1911.

"Exposition by C. H. Spurgeon: Hebrews 11." *The Metropolitan Tabernacle Pulpit Sermons*, 59:166-68. London: Passmore & Alabaster, 1913.

"Expositions by C. H. Spurgeon: Hebrews 11:1-13; and 32-40." *The Metropolitan Tabernacle Pulpit Sermons*, 50:322-24. London: Passmore & Alabaster, 1904.

"Faith (Heb 11:6)." *The New Park Street Pulpit Sermons*, 3:1-8. London: Passmore & Alabaster, 1857.

"God's Cure for Man's Weakness (Heb 11:34)." *The Metropolitan Tabernacle Pulpit Sermons*, 12:349-60. London: Passmore & Alabaster, 1866.

"Obtaining Promises (Heb 11:33)." *The Metropolitan Tabernacle Pulpit Sermons*, 8:97-108. London: Passmore & Alabaster, 1862.

"The Seven Sneezes (2 Kgs 4:34)." *The Metropolitan Tabernacle Pulpit Sermons*, 25:121-24. London: Passmore & Alabaster, 1879.

"Something Worth Seeking (Matt 6:33)." *The Metropolitan Tabernacle Pulpit Sermons*, 53:205-12. London: Passmore & Alabaster, 1897.

"'They Were Tempted' (Heb 11:37)." *The Metropolitan Tabernacle Pulpit Sermons*, 26:169-80. London: Passmore & Alabaster, 1880.

Hebrews 12:1-4

"Exposition by C. H. Spurgeon: Hebrews 12." *The Metropolitan Tabernacle Pulpit Sermons*, 54:466-68. London: Passmore & Alabaster, 1908.

"Exposition by C. H. Spurgeon: Hebrews 12." *The Metropolitan Tabernacle Pulpit Sermons*, 61:622-24. London: Passmore & Alabaster, 1915.

"Exposition by C. H. Spurgeon: Hebrews 12:1-17." *The Metropolitan Tabernacle Pulpit Sermons*, 57:357-60. London: Passmore & Alabaster, 1911.

"Exposition by C. H. Spurgeon: Hebrews 12:1-17." *The Metropolitan Tabernacle Pulpit Sermons*, 58:539-40. London: Passmore & Alabaster, 1912.

"A Honeycomb (Heb 12:3)." *The Metropolitan Tabernacle Pulpit Sermons*, 18:541-52. London: Passmore & Alabaster, 1872.

"Our Lord's Heroic Endurance (Heb 12:3)." *The Metropolitan Tabernacle Pulpit Sermons*, 58:529-39. London: Passmore & Alabaster, 1912.

"The Rule of the Race (Heb 12:1-2)." *The Metropolitan Tabernacle Pulpit Sermons*, 34:433-44. London: Passmore & Alabaster, 1888.

"The Shameful Sufferer (Heb 12:2)." *The New Park Street Pulpit Sermons*, 5:89-96. London: Passmore & Alabaster, 1859.

Hebrews 12:5-11

"The Cause and Cure of a Wounded Spirit (Prov 18:14)." *The Metropolitan Tabernacle Pulpit Sermons*, 42:577-87. London: Passmore & Alabaster, 1896.

"Chastisement (Heb 12:5)." *The New Park Street Pulpit Sermons*, 1:363-70. London: Passmore & Alabaster, 1855.

"Exposition by C. H. Spurgeon: Hebrews 12." *The Metropolitan Tabernacle Pulpit Sermons*, 56:345-48. London: Passmore & Alabaster, 1910.

"Exposition by C. H. Spurgeon: Hebrews 12." *The Metropolitan Tabernacle Pulpit Sermons*, 61:622-24. London: Passmore & Alabaster, 1915.

"Exposition by C. H. Spurgeon: Hebrews 12:1-17." *The Metropolitan Tabernacle Pulpit Sermons*, 57:357-60. London: Passmore & Alabaster, 1911.

"Exposition by C. H. Spurgeon: Hebrews 12:1-17." *The Metropolitan Tabernacle Pulpit Sermons*, 58:539-40. London: Passmore & Alabaster, 1912.

"Expositions by C. H. Spurgeon: Isaiah 35; Hebrews 12:1-6; Isaiah 35." *The Metropolitan Tabernacle Pulpit Sermons*, 63:10-212. London: Passmore & Alabaster, 1917.

"God Incarnate, the End of Fear (Luke 2:10)." *The Metropolitan Tabernacle Pulpit Sermons*, 12:709-20. London: Passmore & Alabaster, 1866.

"God's Hand at Eventide (Ezek 33:22)." *The Metropolitan Tabernacle Pulpit Sermons*, 58:85-94. London: Passmore & Alabaster, 1912.

"Hebrews 12:1-14." *The Interpreter: Spurgeon's Devotional Bible*, 740. Grand Rapids: Baker, 1964.

"The Spirit of Bondage and of Adoption (Rom 8:15)." *The Metropolitan Tabernacle Pulpit Sermons*, 30:15-24. London: Passmore & Alabaster, 1884.

Hebrews 12:12-17

"Exposition by C. H. Spurgeon: Hebrews 12." *The Metropolitan Tabernacle Pulpit Sermons*, 56:345-48. London: Passmore & Alabaster, 1910.

"Exposition by C. H. Spurgeon: Hebrews 12:1-17." *The Metropolitan Tabernacle Pulpit Sermons*, 57:357-60. London: Passmore & Alabaster, 1911.

"Exposition by C. H. Spurgeon: Hebrews 12:1-17." *The Metropolitan Tabernacle Pulpit Sermons*, 58:539-40. London: Passmore & Alabaster, 1912.

"Holiness Demanded (Heb 12:14)." *The Metropolitan Tabernacle Pulpit Sermons*, 50:457-67. London: Passmore & Alabaster, 1904.

"Household Sin and Sorrow (Gen 27:35)." *The Metropolitan Tabernacle Pulpit Sermons*, 61:397-407. London: Passmore & Alabaster, 1915.

"The Winnowing Fan (Heb 12:14-15)." *The Metropolitan Tabernacle Pulpit Sermons*, 16:385-96. London: Passmore & Alabaster, 1870.

Hebrews 12:18-24

"The Blood of Abel and the Blood of Jesus (Heb 12:24)." *The Metropolitan Tabernacle Pulpit Sermons*, 12:481-92. London: Passmore & Alabaster, 1866.

"The Blood of Sprinkling (Heb 12:24-25)." *The Metropolitan Tabernacle Pulpit Sermons*, 32:121-32. London: Passmore & Alabaster, 1886.
"'The Church of the Firstborn' (Heb 12:23)." *The Metropolitan Tabernacle Pulpit Sermons*, 56:337-45. London: Passmore & Alabaster, 1910.
"Exposition by C. H. Spurgeon: Hebrews 12." *The Metropolitan Tabernacle Pulpit Sermons*, 56:345-48. London: Passmore & Alabaster, 1910.
"Exposition by C. H. Spurgeon: Hebrews 12." *The Metropolitan Tabernacle Pulpit Sermons*, 61:622-24. London: Passmore & Alabaster, 1915.
"The General Convocation around Mount Zion (Heb 12:22-24)." *The Metropolitan Tabernacle Pulpit Sermons*, 28:625-36. London: Passmore & Alabaster, 1882.
"The Mediator—The Interpreter (Exod 20:18-20)." *The Metropolitan Tabernacle Pulpit Sermons*, 35:409-20. London: Passmore & Alabaster, 1889.
"The Only Road (John 14:6)." *The Metropolitan Tabernacle Pulpit Sermons*, 62:613-24. London: Passmore & Alabaster, 1916.
"Open House for All Comers (Luke 15:2)." *The Metropolitan Tabernacle Pulpit Sermons*, 11:697-708. London: Passmore & Alabaster, 1865.
"The Voice of the Blood of Christ (Heb 12:24)." *The New Park Street Pulpit Sermons*, 4:269-76. London: Passmore & Alabaster, 1858.

Hebrews 12:25-29

"Acceptable Service (Heb 12:28-29)." *The Metropolitan Tabernacle Pulpit Sermons*, 28:25-36. London: Passmore & Alabaster, 1882.
"Exposition by C. H. Spurgeon: Hebrews 12." *The Metropolitan Tabernacle Pulpit Sermons*, 54:466-68. London: Passmore & Alabaster, 1908.
"Exposition by C. H. Spurgeon: Hebrews 12." *The Metropolitan Tabernacle Pulpit Sermons*, 61:622-24. London: Passmore & Alabaster, 1915.
"God's Word Not to Be Refused (Heb 12:25)." *The Metropolitan Tabernacle Pulpit Sermons*, 61:613-22. London: Passmore & Alabaster, 1915.
"Kicking Against the Pricks (Acts 9:5)." *The Metropolitan Tabernacle Pulpit Sermons*, 12:493-504. London: Passmore & Alabaster, 1866.
"A Lesson from the Great Panic (Heb 12:27)." *The Metropolitan Tabernacle Pulpit Sermons*, 12:265-76. London: Passmore & Alabaster, 1866.

Hebrews 13:1-6

"Exposition by C. H. Spurgeon: Hebrews 13." *The Metropolitan Tabernacle Pulpit Sermons*, 40:203-4. London: Passmore & Alabaster, 1894.
"Exposition by C. H. Spurgeon: Hebrews 13:1-21." *The Metropolitan Tabernacle Pulpit Sermons*, 55:311-12. London: Passmore & Alabaster, 1909.
"Godly Fear and Its Goodly Consequence (Prov 14:26)." *The Metropolitan Tabernacle Pulpit Sermons*, 22:229-40. London: Passmore & Alabaster, 1876.

"God's Glory in the Building up of Zion (Psa 102:16)." *The Metropolitan Tabernacle Pulpit Sermons*, 55:265–74. London: Passmore & Alabaster, 1909.

"A Lesson and Fortune for Christian Men of Business (Heb 13:5)." *The Metropolitan Tabernacle Pulpit Sermons*, 32:37–48. London: Passmore & Alabaster, 1886.

"Never! Never! Never! Never! Never! (Heb 13:5)." *The Metropolitan Tabernacle Pulpit Sermons*, 8:601–12. London: Passmore & Alabaster, 1862.

"'Never, No Never, No Never.' (Heb 13:5–6)." *The Metropolitan Tabernacle Pulpit Sermons*, 55:301–10. London: Passmore & Alabaster, 1909.

"A Vile Weed and a Fair Flower (Heb 13:5–6)." *The Metropolitan Tabernacle Pulpit Sermons*, 24:697–708. London: Passmore & Alabaster, 1878.

"The Winnowing Fan (Heb 12:14–15)." *The Metropolitan Tabernacle Pulpit Sermons*, 16:385–96. London: Passmore & Alabaster, 1870.

Hebrews 13:7–19

"The Education of Sons of God (Heb 5:8)." *The Metropolitan Tabernacle Pulpit Sermons*, 47:169–79. London: Passmore & Alabaster, 1901.

"Exposition by C. H. Spurgeon: Hebrews 13." *The Metropolitan Tabernacle Pulpit Sermons*, 40:203–4. London: Passmore & Alabaster, 1894.

"Exposition by C. H. Spurgeon: Hebrews 13:1–21." *The Metropolitan Tabernacle Pulpit Sermons*, 55:311–12. London: Passmore & Alabaster, 1909.

"The God of Peace and Our Sanctification (Heb 13:20–21)." *The Metropolitan Tabernacle Pulpit Sermons*, 23:445–56. London: Passmore & Alabaster, 1877.

"Hebrews 13:10–14." *The Interpreter: Spurgeon's Devotional Bible*, 105. Grand Rapids: Baker, 1964.

"The Immutability of Christ (Heb 13:8)." *The New Park Street Pulpit Sermons*, 4:41–48. London: Passmore & Alabaster, 1858.

"Jesus Christ the Immutable (Heb 13:8)." *The Metropolitan Tabernacle Pulpit Sermons*, 15:1–12. London: Passmore & Alabaster, 1869.

"'Let Us Go Forth' (Heb 13:13)." *The Metropolitan Tabernacle Pulpit Sermons*, 10:365–76. London: Passmore & Alabaster, 1864.

"A Life-Long Occupation (Heb 13:15)." *The Metropolitan Tabernacle Pulpit Sermons*, 34:565–76. London: Passmore & Alabaster, 1888.

"The Sin-Offering for the Common People (Lev 4:27–31)." *The Metropolitan Tabernacle Pulpit Sermons*, 18:241–52. London: Passmore & Alabaster, 1872.

"Suffering without the Camp (Heb 13:12)." *The Metropolitan Tabernacle Pulpit Sermons*, 46:49–56. London: Passmore & Alabaster, 1900.

"The Tenderness of Jesus (Heb 4:15)." *The Metropolitan Tabernacle Pulpit Sermons*, 36:313–24. London: Passmore & Alabaster, 1890.

"The Two Draughts of Fishes (Luke 5:4; John 21:6)." *The Metropolitan Tabernacle Pulpit Sermons*, 8:193–204. London: Passmore & Alabaster, 1862.

"The Unchangeable Christ (Heb 13:8)." *The Metropolitan Tabernacle Pulpit Sermons*, 40:193-202. London: Passmore & Alabaster, 1894.

Hebrews 13:20-25

"The Blood of the Covenant (Heb 13:20-21)." *The Metropolitan Tabernacle Pulpit Sermons*, 20:433-44. London: Passmore & Alabaster, 1874.

"The Blood of the Everlasting Covenant (Heb 13:20)." *The New Park Street Pulpit Sermons*, 5:417-24. London: Passmore & Alabaster, 1859.

"Exposition by C. H. Spurgeon: Hebrews 13." *The Metropolitan Tabernacle Pulpit Sermons*, 40:203-4. London: Passmore & Alabaster, 1894.

"The God of Peace and Our Sanctification (Heb 13:20-21)." *The Metropolitan Tabernacle Pulpit Sermons*, 23:445-56. London: Passmore & Alabaster, 1877.

"God's Thoughts and Ways Far above Ours (Isa 55:8-9)." *The Metropolitan Tabernacle Pulpit Sermons*, 23:673-84. London: Passmore & Alabaster, 1877.

"Jesus Affirmed to Be Alive (Acts 25:18-19)." *The Metropolitan Tabernacle Pulpit Sermons*, 34:181-92. London: Passmore & Alabaster, 1888.

"Jesus—The Shepherd (Isa 40:11)." *The Metropolitan Tabernacle Pulpit Sermons*, 11:541-52. London: Passmore & Alabaster, 1865.

"'Thou art Now the Blessed of the Lord' (Gen 26:29)." *The Metropolitan Tabernacle Pulpit Sermons*, 38:13-24. London: Passmore & Alabaster, 1892.

"The Two Pillars of Salvation (Rom 4:24-25)." *The Metropolitan Tabernacle Pulpit Sermons*, 40:181-89. London: Passmore & Alabaster, 1894.

Scripture Index

Old Testament

Genesis

1:3 111
3:15 281
4:9 70
5:24 327
6:9 328
14:18–20 173
18:19 157
19:17 356
24:27 380
27:33 416
28:15 448
32:10 353
32:31 353
49:24 472
50:24 357

Exodus

5:2 283
7:1 368
13:13 76
14:11 36
19:18 .... 207, 421
20 209
20:15 210
24 427
33:15 65

Leviticus

5:11 244
16:2 296

17:14 231
18:4–5 206
18:5 208

Numbers

6:24–25 297

Deuteronomy

4:31 156
5:17 210
5:18 210
27:26 208
31:6 305
31:8 448
32:8 76
32:10 93

Judges

5:12 371

1 Samuel

15:22 270
15:33 103
26:21 373

2 Samuel

7:14 16
23:5 .... 157, 206, 475

1 Kings

17:4 374
17:9 374

1 Chronicles

28:20 448
29:14 437

Ezra

1:9 135

Job

4:7 418
4:18 110
13:15 .... 312, 369
15:15 110
23:13 274
33:13 425
38:11 212

Psalms

2 .... 16, 122
2:8 41
16:10 124
18:13 421
22 133
22:22 39
32:8 393
32:10 393
33:9 274
37:17 147
39:12 345
40:2 429
40:8 259
45:6 186
45:6–7 17

45:15......................... 21
48:14......................... 439
50:13.........................271
50:16.........................275
51:1-2.........................313
51:11.........................312
51:12.........................92
73:26 305
90:16 357
95 .... 61, 93
97 16
98:1 128
100:2 21
102:25-27................. 19
102:26......................... 19
103:12 13
104:4 17
110...................180, 187
110:1.........................122
110:4 .... 173, 177, 180, 187
121:1.........................335
139:8.........................310

Proverbs

1:24.........................337
1:24-27 416
9:10 402
13:24.........................398
17:17...................50, 349
18:14 132
19:2......................... 65
20:30 404
22:6 359
22:15 398
24:16.........................147

Matthew

3:15......................... 169
3:17.........................7, 122

Song of Solomon

1:12 138

Isaiah

1:18 ....63, 430
1:19 95
8:18 42
26:20 183
30:21.........................212
33:14-16 442
33:16 451
40:5 357
41:10 448
42:1.........................94
42:3.........................430
44:21 156
45:7......................... 397
46:10......................... 274
53:3................. 168, 462
53:6 ....119, 121
53:11......................... 157
53:12 .... 226, 281
54:13 ....65, 125
55:2...................95, 286
55:8 474
55:9 113
63:9 395

Jeremiah

2:2 156
3:22 212
6:14.........................182
8:11 182
8:22 51
9:1 29
31:3.........................280

New Testament

4:3 107
4:9 108
5:28 210

31:33 205
31:34 281
50:20 13

Ezekiel

16:63......................... 439
18:20 208
33:6 440
34:4 418

Daniel

3:17-18.....................369
3:27 108
4:35......................... 274
9:24 281

Hosea

14:8......................... 393

Joel

2:32 327

Micah

5:5 94
6:6-7 273
6:7 271
6:8......................... 270

Habakkuk

2:4.........................328

Zechariah

7:11 338
14:20.........................214
14:21 276

Malachi

3:3 323
3:17......................... 217

6:28 379
6:33 376
7:13.........................312

8:20......................260
10:16..............355, 461
10:25....................390
10:34....................368
10:37.................... 367
11:28 ....63, 289, 301, 422
11:29......................94
12:6................105, 457
15:27 313
17:5..........................7
22:14....................337
25:23....................306
26:30 40
26:39 124
26:41.................... 106
26:63 392
26:74 148
27:25.................... 242
27:42...................... 33
27:46 459
28:19...................... 55
28:20 33

Mark

1:11........................122
9:7............................7
9:23 330
12:6....................457
12:7 345
14:26......................40
15:31...................... 33
16:15–16 430
16:16 ....55, 429, 440

Luke

3:6........................357
4:3 107
4:9–10....................107
6:38 475
10:28 209
11:47 457

12:24...................... 379
12:49...................... 368
13:7 330
14:27 368
14:33 367
18:13......................308
22:27......................28
22:42 272
23:34......................391
23:43 322
24:39......................123

John

1:3..........................60
1:5..........................337
1:11........................ 345
1:14 94
1:19 278
2:10 6
3:18......................440
3:36 235
5:17 96
6:37 431
6:44 474
7:37 297
8:29 455
8:56 344
10:26 14
10:27...................... 14
10:28–29 152
11:25...................... 313
11:25–26 32
11:26 440
11:35...................... 168
13:10 301
14:6..................193, 474
14:8 7
14:9......................40
14:11 7
14:19 252
14:22 76

15:8......................406
16:33 389
17............................42
17:11........................42
17:23....................204
17:24......................42
19:30..165, 276, 394, 460
20:13.................... 102
20:17......................40
20:28 283

Acts

4:36 56
7:20 359
7:51 434
9:4........................ 395
10:38....................418
16:31 ....81, 302, 429
17:28 394
17:31......................122
20:28......................232

Romans

1:22........................118
3:14........................ 166
3:20 ....85, 145
5:16...................... 430
6:14...................... 385
8:3 270
8:15......................403
8:29 425
9:8........................158
9:15.................... 66, 158
9:16 158
10:10........................68
10:17..................95, 286
11:29 153
12:1 236

1 Corinthians

2:9.......................... 226
3:7 307

3:9 307
3:15 345
10:12 .... 415, 419
10:13 108
15:19 406
15:25 357
15:55 320
15:56 ....44, 45

2 Corinthians
4:6 271
4:17 407
5:1...........................462
5:19..........................182
6:17..........................155
8:9........................... 53
12:9.................125, 401

Galatians
1:8 35
3:26 43
4:9 225
6:7 181

Ephesians
1:4 413
1:6 ....273, 473
1:11........................ 274
1:22........................ 476
2:6 477
2:9 85
3:8 ....21, 273
3:20 113
5:25........................12, 232
5:32........................... 73
6:10 409

Philippians
1:6 310
1:21 .... 33, 394
2:7 59
2:12..........................153
4:4 467

Colossians
1:15 425
1:17 10
1:18 425
1:19 ....8, 272
2:9 ....196, 272
3:3 477
3:4 293

1 Thessalonians
4:7...........................412
4:16.......... 260, 344, 357
4:18 47
5:17........................464

1 Timothy
1:11.......................... 435
1:15 95
2:5 196

2 Timothy
1:10........................ 428
1:13 457
4:2 xi
4:7 422

Hebrews
1:7...........................149
1:9 21
2:8 7
2:10 127
2:11 349
2:14....................... 38, 168
2:16......................... 117
2:17..........................49
2:18..........................50
3:12............................68
3:15 .... 87, 296
4:3 94
4:7 .... 61, 87
4:14.........................122
5:2 37
6:17..........................156

6:19 ....154, 293
7:4 182
7:8 173
7:16..........................179
7:26 226
8:10 212
9:12........................ 228
9:13......................... 229
9:14......................... 228
9:15 228
9:22 ....224, 231, 242
9:27 343
10:9 206
10:10.......................253
10:12 285
10:13 41
10:14 .... 109, 292
10:22.......................290
10:26 .... 11, 301
11:1.......................... 331
11:6 v
11:10..........................441
11:16.........................355
11:17 359
12:2.......22, 169, 392, 468
12:3............168, 391, 394
12:4......................... 168
12:8.........................400
12:11 407
12:12 395
12:14 181
12:21 208
12:23 ....421, 422
12:24.................. 186, 422
12:25 440
13:5 ....450, 451
13:7......................... 475
13:8........................ 19
13:10 .... 105, 290

James

1:5.............................447
1:22.........................338
3:18..........................412

1 Peter

1:5............................108
2:24 ....50, 232
4:5 264
5:8 44

2 Peter

2:19...........................337

1 John

1:5............................421
1:7..............287, 380, 431
2:1 237
2:15.........................462
3:2 30
3:15.........................210
4:18........................289
5:8 431
5:10..........................197

Jude

3 253

Revelation

1:7...........................260
1:10.........................380
3:4 475
4:11 322
6:16 312
12:1 264
14:4..........................169
14:5.........................474
15:3 368
19:6 8
21:27 385
22:12........................357

Index of Illustrations by Theme

Adoption, 159, 401, 426

Adultery, 446

Apostasy, 69, 75, 148, 149, 151, 347

Assurance, 36, 43, 85, 344, 348, 354

Atonement, 180, 227, 241, 246, 251, 253,
254, 257, 284, 426

Baptism, 292

Blasphemy, 148

Character, 326

Church
fellowship, 295, 413, 415, 425, 445
and nature, 435, 445, 461

Comfort, 127, 400

Commitment, 88, 305, 463

Contentment, 91, 227, 448

Courage, 43, 372, 403, 446

Covenant, 180, 190

Creation Renewal, 341

Death, 46, 47, 246, 309, 433, 436

Debt, 180

Disability, 401

Discipleship, 136

Discipline, 397, 399, 400, 401, 402,
403, 405, 417

Doubt, 160

Education, 118, 126, 139

Encouragement, 52

Eschatology, 261, 341

Eternity, 303, 425, 436

Evangelism, 120, 465

Faith, 28, 30, 85, 88, 130, 227, 309, 317,
319, 322, 324, 326, 327, 328, 338, 344,
354, 360, 365, 372, 374, 376, 377, 397

Family, 110, 136

Fear, 43, 46, 47, 149, 164, 322, 402

Foolishness, 47, 119

Forgiveness, 160, 246, 258

Freedom, 360

Giving, 52

Glory, 403

God's
Faithfulness, 151, 162, 473
Grace, 274
Love, 280, 327, 399, 439
Mercy, 274, 280, 284, 300
Presence, 209, 234, 327
Providence, 397, 448
Power, 8
Presence, 68
Providence, 36
Sovereignty, 91

Good Works, 324, 328

Gospel, 101

Guidance, 36, 127, 211

Guilt, 160, 402

Healing, 8, 51, 70, 376

Heaven, 253, 377, 425

Hell, 303

Holiness, 214, 251, 282, 291, 405, 459,
461

Honesty, 92

Hope, 164, 344

Humility, 100, 439

Jesus 128, 178, 386, 456

Jesus'

    Birth, 258

    Death, 101, 276

    Divinity, 178

    Humanity, 126, 127, 178, 192

    Passion, 388

    Resurrection, 164

Jesus, Salvation, 8

Joy, 92, 275

Judgment, 303

Kingdom of God, 436, 438

Law, 190, 209, 211, 360

Laziness, 26, 63

Love, 120

Lust, 446

Mercy, 120

Mission, 465

Music, 377

Obedience, 63, 126, 130, 291, 300, 338, 446

Parables, 118

Patience, 118, 307, 410, 417

Peace, 411

Persecution, 305, 322, 377, 390, 463

Perseverance, 293, 309, 322, 386, 390, 392, 417, 456

Poverty, 52

Power, 376

Prayer, 110, 194

Pride, 64, 100

Promises, 189, 344, 374

Purity, 459

Reconciliation, 411

Redemption, 246, 258, 276

Repentance, 300

Reverence, 149, 402

Sabbath, 90, 91, 92

Sacrifice, 241

Salvation, 128, 159, 214, 227, 246, 254, 258, 282, 317, 347, 348, 433, 459

Scripture, 102, 104

Service, 52, 234, 275, 436, 438, 439

Sexual Immorality, 446

Sickness, 68, 401

Sin, 64, 72, 75, 211, 246, 257, 258, 276, 402

Spiritual Warfare, 403

Substitution, 276

Suffering, 51, 52, 139, 390, 392, 399, 401, 405

Temptation, 52, 72, 162

Thankfulness, 151, 194

Truth, 70, 446

Victory, 164

Watchfulness, 261, 413, 415

Weakness, 401

Wealth, 436

Wisdom, 104, 118, 139, 209

Work, 436

Worship, 425, 465